# THE CHATHAM ADMINISTRATION

# THE CHATHAM ADMINISTRATION 1766–1768

BY

## JOHN BROOKE

LONDON

MACMILLAN & CO LTD

NEW YORK · ST MARTIN'S PRESS

1956

MACMILLAN AND COMPANY LIMITED
*London Bombay Calcutta Madras Melbourne*

THE MACMILLAN COMPANY OF CANADA LIMITED
*Toronto*

ST MARTIN'S PRESS INC
*New York*

PRINTED IN GREAT BRITAIN

# FOREWORD

THE title *England in the Age of the American Revolution* was given by me twenty-five years ago to a book meant as the first volume of a larger work. But feeling uncertain even then whether circumstances would allow me to complete my scheme, I hinted by one asterisk on the cover and the title-page at volumes that were to follow without clearly announcing their coming : a lame compromise which enabled critics to denounce the title as a misnomer. When after a lapse of some twenty years I resumed the work, I could no longer expect to complete it unaided ; and I am therefore happy to have found collaborators among younger historians with whom I now hope to carry through the scheme. *England in the Age of the American Revolution* will be the title of the series of which Mr. John Brooke's volume on *The Chatham Administration* forms part. My original volume, when rewritten and reprinted, will fall into its place within that series, and will be called *Newcastle and Bute*, while its previous title will appear at the top, as in this present volume. Nor will it now form the first volume of the series : this will be enlarged to cover the thirty years 1754–1784.

My collaborators in the series are also members of the team working with me on the same period of the *History of Parliament* ; and the two ventures draw to some extent on the same materials. Yet they differ widely in character. The *History of Parliament*, an analytical survey of the House of Commons based on the biographies of Members, is not meant to supply a chronological narrative of political events or constitutional developments, which is the task of *England in the Age of the American Revolution*. And while the *History of Parliament* is a co-operative undertaking in which the individuality of the collaborators merges into that of the team, every volume of *England in the Age of the American Revolution*

v

will be individual work, the author's garden plot on which he labours.

I concluded my volume on Newcastle and Bute with the sentence, 'My next book, if ever written, will be on "The Rise of Party"'. Here was a promise, which has now been redeemed in this volume on *The Chatham Administration* by my closest collaborator, Mr. John Brooke.

L. B. NAMIER

*August 29, 1955*

# PREFACE

I WISH to thank those without whose help this book could not have been written.

First, I wish to thank the following who have kindly allowed me to quote from manuscripts in their possession : the Marquess Camden ; the William L. Clements Library, University of Michigan ; Mr. Humphrey FitzRoy Newdegate ; the Earl Fitzwilliam and the Trustees of the Wentworth Woodhouse Estates ; the Duke of Grafton ; Mr. David Holland ; the Henry E. Huntington Library, San Marino, California ; the Marquis of Lansdowne; Sir John Murray, K.C.V.O., D.S.O.; and the Earl of Powis. I acknowledge with gratitude the kindness of the late Duke of Bedford who allowed me to quote from the Woburn MSS.

I have built upon the foundation laid by Sir Lewis Namier, and the careful reader will notice to what an extent this book is a development and expansion of his ideas. I have closely co-operated with him during the last four years, and have learnt much from our association. In addition, he read my manuscript and made many valuable suggestions for its improvement.

Lastly, without the sympathy and co-operation of my wife I could not have written a line. But what I owe to her cannot well be acknowledged here.

J. BROOKE

*August* 15, 1955

# CONTENTS

# INTRODUCTION

THE main theme of British domestic politics from 1760 to 1770 is the search for a stable Administration which would command the confidence of both Crown and Parliament. When in July 1766 George III commissioned William Pitt to form an Administration, this problem seemed on the way to being solved. Since Pitt's resignation in 1761 he had been an incalculable and disrupting force : too considerable to be neglected, too unco-operative to be assimilated. He opposed the Grenville Ministry, but would not work with the opposition ; he supported the Rockinghams over the repeal of the Stamp Act, but turned against them when that measure was passed. It was clear that nothing but full powers would satisfy him, that he would be the auxiliary of no one ; and in July 1766 George III gave him plenary authority to form a Ministry, and, in the months to follow, a degree of confidence enjoyed by neither Grenville nor Rockingham. It seemed that stability was at last returning.

Yet twelve months later the King's Administration was in the melting-pot — for the sixth time in seven years — and stability seemed as far away as ever. The first two chapters of this book tell how Pitt (now Earl of Chatham) with every advantage on his side — full support from the King, the goodwill of Parliament, and the memories of success and glory associated with his name and genius — threw them all away, and caused chaos to come again. It is a story without parallel in British political history, and not to be explained simply in terms of politics. Chatham set out to break all parties, to achieve that unanimity and harmony for which all politicians claimed to strive ; yet within six months he had aligned in opposition against him the three party groups then in Parliament.

One of the first acts of his Administration was to propose an inquiry into the East India Company, which it was understood would be followed by a measure compelling them to yield part of their revenue to the State. Chatham never explained the details of his plan to his colleagues in the Cabinet, and the inquiry was opposed there by two men on whom its success largely depended — the Minister in the House of Commons, Henry Seymour Conway, and the Chancellor of the Exchequer, Charles Townshend. In December 1766 Chatham went to Bath : he did not return to London until March 1767, and during his absence his two recalcitrant colleagues had largely succeeded in frustrating his intentions. Soon he withdrew completely from the political scene, and for over two years did not attend either at Court or in Parliament. Although he retained his office of Lord Privy Seal until October 1768, the task of leading the Administration he had created devolved on the Duke of Grafton, a weak, indolent, and incapable man, unwilling to take decisions without Chatham's authority.

The tale of Chatham's Administration is curious and melancholy : never was so much expected from a statesman and so little fulfilled. The great war Minister, who rallied the nation round his measures and brought them to triumphant success, failed miserably where men of less ability would have succeeded. It will be clear as the story develops that he was suffering from some mental disturbance which paralysed his will and action. The biographer of Chatham must account for this and relate it to his previous history. I have not attempted to do so in this book : it would involve a technique which I do not command. It has become fashionable for the historian to present his characters in terms drawn from psycho-analysis : he had better not do so unless he is quite sure of his ground, and can stand challenge by an expert.

Chatham's withdrawal encouraged the opposition groups to combine against his pusillanimous deputy. Their union was neither sincere nor lasting, and their attempt to defeat the Administration in the House of Lords failed. Yet it was sufficient to dishearten the Duke of Grafton and force him to try to reconstruct the Ministry by taking in part of the opposition. He failed to do this before Parliament rose in July 1767 : a weak and divided Ministry was not well placed for bargaining with an opposition even but temporarily united and expecting the resignation or overthrow of their opponents. The session ended with the Ministry on the verge of breaking up : Conway was about to resign, Townshend's attitude was equivocal, while Chatham was unable or unwilling to reassume command.

The negotiations of July 1767 were the most complicated and significant of all the negotiations for a new Ministry during the first ten years of George III's reign. The Court wished to take in only part of the opposition — Conway preferred the Rockinghams and Grafton the Bedfords — but Rockingham, with whom the negotiations were conducted, insisted on trying to form a 'comprehensive Administration' including all parties. His jealousy and distrust of Grenville prevented this : he was forced to admit to the King that his plan was not feasible nor, when pressed by Conway, would he agree to come in with his own followers only. The Court gained no new strength from these negotiations, but they split the opposition and made it possible to detach one party.

Chapters VI and VII attempt to analyse and illustrate the nature of party at this time. I have used the word 'party' as the least unsuitable : 'faction' has an invidious sense which was not always present, and 'connection', though an apter word, is not sufficiently comprehensive. But 'party' in the eighteenth century had few of the implications it has today : I have tried to show why, and what it did imply. I have analysed the composition and outlined the history of the four groups who followed a prominent politician : Chatham, the Duke of Bedford, George Grenville, and Lord Rockingham.

Rockingham having refused to come in alone, it could have been predicted that a similar offer would not be refused by the Bedfords. When Parliament met in December 1767 Grenville was disinclined to opposition, Rockingham had found fresh occasion to dissent from him, and the Bedfords were ripe for the plucking. They sounded the Court and soon entered the Administration, which at last achieved some sort of stability.

Parliament was dissolved in March 1768. The new Parliament had to decide what to do with John Wilkes, who, expelled the House in 1763, was now back in England and returned to Parliament by Middlesex. The controversy over Wilkes's case raised fierce party conflict and gave new life to what had seemed a dying opposition. This Parliament was also responsible for the measures which turned discontent in the American colonies into open war. I have discussed the General Election from the point of view of the parties, and have studied the men who then entered Parliament for the first time to learn what effect they had on the party composition of the House.

In the last chapter I deal with the events leading to the resignation of Chatham in October 1768. Although Chatham had taken no part in politics since March 1767, Grafton still considered himself as only *locum tenens* until his recovery. But the entry of the Bedfords and the replacement of Conway as Minister in the House of Commons by Lord North, Townshend's successor at the Exchequer, had altered the balance in the Cabinet. Grafton and the King, by their intention to dismiss Lord Shelburne, who was closely connected with Chatham but obnoxious to them both, brought about Chatham's resignation. This left Grafton in complete command, but armed with an authority he was unsuited to exercise. Long the *de facto* head of the Administration, he now became its head *de jure*.

During the years 1766 to 1768 the parties hardened into the forms they assumed during the American Revolution. All other questions — the American problem, relations with the East India Company, or foreign affairs — were subordinate to party conflict. This volume is a study of the origin of parties, and deals mainly with the men who led and composed them. In another volume I hope to carry the story to the point where the American problem threatened to develop into civil war.

# CHAPTER I

# THE FORMATION OF THE CHATHAM ADMINISTRATION

On July 6, 1766, Lord Rockingham wrote to the Duke of Newcastle :

> An event has just now happened which is highly neces-
> sary that your Grace should be early apprized of — and
> which in my opinion must end well.
>
> I mean by *well* that we shall either have done with being
> Administration — or we shall be so — better and more firm
> and strong than we have been.[1]

This event was Lord Northington's announcement to the King
of his wish to resign the Great Seal on the ground that the
Administration was too weak to continue. The Rockingham
Ministry was breaking up.

Ever since the end of April, when the Duke of Grafton
had decided to resign, the Administration had been in decline.
Grafton's resignation was a symptom, not a cause, of this : the
causes were weakness in Parliament ; disunion in the Cabinet ;
the failure to secure the support of Pitt, the most powerful
debater in the House of Commons ; and the refusal to admit
the friends of Lord Bute to a share of power proportionate to
their abilities. Since the repeal of the Stamp Act the Administration had drifted, without plan or purpose, until Grafton's
resignation brought them face to face with harsh reality.

The King's first reaction had been fear lest Grafton's
retirement should cause the Ministry to fall to pieces, and he
should be forced to take back the Grenvilles. Next, he urged
the Rockinghams to continue at least until the end of the
parliamentary session, hoping that they would either attempt
a *modus vivendi* with Bute's friends, or else give him time to

[1] Add. MS. 32976, ff. 19-21.

form a new Administration. With this end in view he reluctantly accepted the Duke of Richmond as Secretary of State,
and the Administration, thus patched up, hobbled on.

Grafton's resignation was a warning which the Rockinghams
preferred to ignore. Grafton professed to have entered the
Ministry in order to keep the door open for Pitt, and when
Pitt demanded the reconstruction of the Cabinet and the
withdrawal of both Rockingham and Newcastle, Grafton
thought this not too high a price to pay for the master's
presence. Rockingham not unnaturally did not agree, and
was prepared to carry on without Pitt. But to do so effectively
he would have had to come to terms with Bute's friends, and
this he would not do.

George III had appealed to Pitt three times since his
resignation in 1761, and each time had failed to induce him to
return to office. Pride alone would have made him hesitate
to repeat this experience. But it was not pride only : it was
the fear of finding himself in a similar situation as the year
before, when the negotiation with Pitt had failed and he had
been compelled to take back the Grenvilles on their own
terms. Since then the reconciliation between Pitt and Temple
on the one hand and Grenville on the other had made the King
fear that the return of Pitt would also mean the return of
Grenville. So the Rockinghams must be induced to carry on
as best they could, else, the King wrote to Lord Egmont on
May 1, 'the absurdity of men will force me into accepting *the
family* than which there is nothing I would not rather submit
to'.[1]

The King, in his letter of May 3, laid the situation
before Bute, and asked if a new Administration could be
formed from Bute's friends.[2] The anxiety and distress of
mind under which he laboured is obvious throughout, and in
one passage towards the end he writes: 'Indeed, if I am to
continue the life of agitation I have these three years, the
next year there will be a Council [of] Regency to assist in

---

[1] *The Correspondence of King George III*, ed. by the Hon. Sir John
Fortescue, I, no. 301.

[2] *Letters from George III to Lord Bute, 1756–1766*, ed. by Romney
Sedgwick, pp. 246-50.

that undertaking'. Bute's reply has not survived, but the essence of his advice is clear from the King's letter of July 12.[1] It was that only Pitt or Grenville could hope to form a stable Ministry, and to one or the other must the King turn. The King was thus forced to send for Pitt again. The problem now was how to arrange matters so that the King should know for certain that Pitt would take office before he broke with the Rockinghams. Had this negotiation failed, Rockingham might have driven as hard a bargain for his remaining in office as Grenville had done the year before.

The King's first thought, so he wrote, had been to ask Bute to sound Pitt, but 'the promises extorted of me when this Ministry was formed not to consult you whilst it subsisted made that impossible'. He turned to the Lord Chancellor Northington, unconnected with the Rockinghams and professing political allegiance to the King alone. Northington was solicitous for his own position, and did not wish to be buried under the ruins of the Rockingham Ministry. He saw that under the circumstances Pitt was the only man the King would entrust with the formation of a new Ministry, and his attachment to the Crown and enlightened self-interest prompted him to act as negotiator. Some time in May he learnt from Lord Camden that Pitt was willing 'to try to form an Administration of the best of all party's and an exclusion to no descriptions', which gave the King 'great comfort'.[2] The task now facing him was to find some convenient ground on which to part with the Rockinghams, without the possibility of recrimination on their part.

Such an opportunity seemed to occur at the end of May when Rockingham contrived to offend the King on a personal matter concerning his family. Although Rockingham was insistent in demanding that placemen who voted against Administration should be dismissed, he refused to oblige the King by bringing before Parliament a proposal to divide the late Duke of Cumberland's allowance between the King's three brothers. He first agreed to do so, but then Conway, Minister in the House of Commons, who had been ill in the country, developed conscientious scruples 'arising from the lateness in the session and the thinness of Parlt. at this juncture'.[1] This behaviour drew from Horace Walpole the comment that Conway and his friends were not fit to be Ministers.[2] The King was extremely annoyed : 'Because a few weak boys are unwilling this session to pass the provision for my brothers', he wrote to Egmont on May 28, 'my word is to be set at naught'.[3] Northington, aware of what was in the wind and resenting Rockingham's proposal that he should resign the Great Seal and become Lord President of the Council, told the King he would request permission to cease attending the Cabinet's discussions on strengthening the Ministry.[4] But the affair blew over, and the King was unable to make use of it as an excuse for opening negotiations with Pitt.

Rockingham, however, was incurable. On June 3, Jeremiah Dyson, a Lord of Trade but considered by Rockingham to be one of Bute's friends, moved a motion against the Ministry, and the Cabinet decided to ask the King to dismiss him. The King consulted Northington, who advised him not to agree to this request if he intended to change the Administration ; but if not he must do so, for then the Ministers would require all the support they could get.[5] Dyson was not dismissed. The fall of the Rockinghams was at hand.

The session ended on June 6 and Northington asked permission to decline attending Cabinet meetings.[6] The King was now prepared to negotiate with Pitt, and decided to use Northington's secession as a pretext for dismissing the Administration. On July 4 the plan was formed. On July 6 the Ministers saw the King, and Northington asked permission to resign as he could no longer attend the Cabinet. That evening the King drafted his letter to Pitt,[7] which Northington forwarded the next day.[8]

[1] Rockingham to the King, May 27, 1766 ; Fortescue, I, no. 317.
[2] Horace Walpole, *Memoirs of the Reign of King George the Third*, ed. by G. F. Russell Barker, ii. 234.          [3] Fortescue, I, no. 319.
[4] Northington to the King, May 29, 1766 ; *ibid.* no. 320.
[5] Northington to the King, June 5, 1766 ; *ibid.* no. 335.
[6] Sedgwick, p. 252.                              [7] Fortescue, I, no. 343.
[8] *Chatham Correspondence*, ii. 434-5.

(ii)

William Pitt was fifty-seven when he was summoned by George III to give his thoughts 'how an able and dignify'd Ministry may be form'd'.[1] He had been in Parliament since 1735 and had spent a large part of this period in opposition. From 1757 to 1761 he had borne the major share of responsibility for the war against France, and it had been largely due to his drive and initiative that the war, begun so unpromisingly for Britain, had been brought to a successful conclusion. This had been accomplished in spite of the timidities and hesitations of less daring colleagues, and when Pitt resigned in 1761 their relief was only tempered by fear of what he might do in opposition.

Pitt's conduct between 1761 and 1766 had been equivocal, a source of embarrassment to his friends and of uneasiness to his enemies. His attendance in Parliament had been irregular, due partly to gout but more to his aloof temper. As a result he had not been the formidable figure which his opponents had feared. Moreover, foreign policy, in which Pitt's interest chiefly lay and in which his reputation had been achieved, ceased to be an important issue in parliamentary politics after 1762. He exerted himself only on important occasions, such as the debate on the preliminaries of peace in December 1762, or the motion on General Warrants in February 1764. On these occasions the effects of his oratory could be neutralized by a thorough whipping-up of the Ministry's supporters. He had never cultivated a party in the House of Commons, indeed he discouraged potential followers. Consequently his weight in the House depended on the impression produced by his speeches, rather than on the votes of his followers. Nor did he fit easily into a plan of opposition. He would declare himself unconnected or unconsulted or unaware of the issues involved, or pronounce opposition to be factious anyhow. When asked to take the lead he would say he was unworthy of such prominence, and when not consulted he would show his resentment by disconcerting moves, damaging to his would-be

[1] The King to Pitt, July 7, 1766 ; Fortescue, I, no. 343.

allies. Yet he liked to be sought after, and there was always a steady stream of pilgrims to his house at Hayes to ask the advice of the oracle. That advice was often phrased in the manner of an oracle, and the pilgrim would come back no wiser than when he went but a great deal more mystified.

The King found it equally difficult to enlist Pitt's support. In August 1763 on the death of Lord Egremont he had sent for Pitt, but the only result had been to strengthen the Grenville Administration by the acquisition of Bedford, and to confirm Grenville's suspicions of Bute who had advised the move. In 1765 Pitt gave Temple's refusal to take the Treasury as the reason for his own inability to come into office. Indeed, his refusal was the *raison d'être* of the Rockingham Administration, a mere substitute for the one Pitt refused to form. He had supported Rockingham on the repeal of the Stamp Act, but once that measure was through had no further use for the Ministry, and during the last weeks of the session openly turned against it. When invited to co-operate, he had taken refuge behind the slogan 'measures not men', but it was the men who composed that Administration he distrusted, not their measures. He would not again allow Newcastle's jealousy and timidity to clog his policy, he would not again waste time and energy in overcoming the fears or obtuseness of colleagues less bold or far-sighted. He would be master in the Cabinet, and his colleagues would be admittedly his instruments rather than his equals. It followed from this that he would not come into office again unless he had a clear call from the King, and unless he felt himself supported by the full confidence and weight of the Closet. When that call came he would step forward, as he had done in 1757, the saviour of his country ; this time from internal faction not from foreign danger, and this time with full power and with colleagues of his own choosing.

(iii)

Pitt's first audience was on July 12, and must have relieved the King of many of his doubts and misgivings.[1] For Pitt

---

[1] The King's memorandum on the formation of Chatham's Ministry ; Fortescue, I, no. 143.

was not a man to haggle about trifles once he was sure of the royal confidence.  He declared his wish 'to dissolve all factions and to see the best of all partys in employment', but that he intended to take the existing Administration as the basis of his own.  He wished the offer of the Treasury to be made to Temple, but removed the King's misgivings by declaring that he would still accept office if Temple declined.  The other point about which the King was most concerned was the position of Bute and his friends, and here Pitt showed good manners and good sense.  As to Bute's political influence, the King wrote : 'Mr. Pitt said my declarations of last year that Ld. Bute should not interfere in political matters made him quite easy on that head'.  Bute could continue as the King's private friend : Pitt 'hop'd the Crown would ever see those they like and not allow Ministers to presume to meddle with their private acquaintances of their conduct'.  With respect to Bute's friends Pitt was a little more guarded, but far from unaccommodating.  He did not object in principle to restoring James Stuart Mackenzie (Bute's brother, dismissed by Grenville), and promised to consider others as places became available.  In short, whatever doubts or fears the King might have had on the wisdom of sending for Pitt had been almost removed after this audience, and his willingness to comply with the King's wishes must have been a welcome change after the jealous suspicions of the Rockinghams.

On July 15 the King saw Temple, but this audience was less pleasing.  The King was convinced before it took place that Temple did not mean to accept : [1] the conversation did not extend to particulars as did that with Pitt, but Temple did not hide his dislike of the Rockinghams.  The next day Temple saw Pitt, and on July 17 told the King he would not take office.

Did Pitt seriously believe Temple would accept, and, if not, why did he press Temple upon the King ?  There can be little doubt after the experience of the previous year that Pitt had not built his plans on Temple's taking the Treasury.  In Pitt's scheme Temple was to be responsible for the patronage

---

[1] The King to Northington, July 15, 1766 ; *ibid.* no. 352.

and financial work of government, which Pitt himself neither cared for nor understood. But he was not likely to allow Temple to interfere seriously in matters of policy, or in appointments to offices where policy was determined. He had, however, seriously misjudged his brother-in-law : pompous and pretentious, Temple would no longer take second place even to Pitt, and he had recently been in fundamental disagreement with Pitt over the repeal of the Stamp Act. He told the King 'that he must be at *least* equal to any man' in the King's service,[1] and proposed Lord Gower for Secretary of State as a test of Pitt's willingness to allow him an equal share of power. When that was refused he made his speech, as the King had said he would, and returned to Stowe, to assume a more congenial rôle in a senseless and mischievous opposition.

For the place which Temple had refused Pitt substituted one who, though far more compliant and deferential, was an equally unfortunate choice. Augustus Henry Fitzroy, third Duke of Grafton, had, through rank and favour with Pitt, obtained the seals of Secretary of State at the age of twenty-nine. He had few other qualifications. Indolent and bored by business, he preferred the turf to the Cabinet ; he had a justified diffidence in his own abilities, and no standards by which to measure those of others. Proud yet sensitive, the duty he owed to his rank and name alone brought him into politics. He told Pitt :

> I should be ready to undertake . . . any office in which Mr. Pitt should wish to place me ; but that the situation of the First Lord of the Treasury, or that of Lieutenant of Ireland, were accompanied with circumstances so very disagreeable to me, that no consideration should induce me to embark in either.[2]

But his objections were brushed aside. Now Pitt was to feel the disadvantages of the habits of non-co-operation he had practised for so many years : Grafton knew himself to be unfit for the Treasury, yet Pitt had no one else to whom he

---

[1] The King to Northington, July 17, 1766 ; Fortescue, I, no. 356.
[2] *Autobiography and Political Correspondence of Augustus Henry, 3rd Duke of Grafton*, ed. by Sir William Anson, p. 89.

could turn to fill the most important office in the King's service. Grenville or Rockingham, with none of Pitt's ability or vision, could command the services of more reliable colleagues than he, the greatest statesman of the age. He who walks alone in politics is lost.

As Chancellor of the Exchequer Grafton wished to take Charles Townshend, then Paymaster-General. It was another unfortunate choice. 'That splendid shuttlecock', as Rigby once described him, was the most brilliant and unstable politician of his day. Highly gifted with all the qualities which made for easy and superficial success, he used his talents to flatter and please his audience of the moment and, intoxicated with their applause, piled absurdity on absurdity. He had no political judgment and no insight into character : his gifts were all on show, he carried no ballast. His wit and his spirits had captivated Grafton, unable to dig below the surface of a character. Pitt, the only man Townshend feared, was not so easily deceived and tried to dissuade Grafton from his choice. But, writes Grafton, 'the credit I gave Mr. Townshend made me very unwisely persist in my first wishes ; and Mr. Pitt at last gave way, though much against his inclination. . . .'[1] But, when the post was offered, Townshend did not take it without displaying his wayward temperament, first accepting, then refusing, finally accepting again. He told the King 'that what he held was more honourable and worth £7000 whilst the other was but £2500, that if he accepted he hoped he should have some indemnification'.[2] If he accepted, he must be able to say it was by the King's 'express commands' and not by choice ; and he told William Dowdeswell that he was 'commanded by the King to accept the office . . . an office of the greatest labour and difficulty. . . .'[3] But Pitt would not give him a seat in the Cabinet, and without this he was not in the first rank of Ministers, merely second at the Treasury Board. Charles Townshend was a disappointed man when he went to the Exchequer : Pitt's collapse gave him the oppor-

[1] Ibid. p. 92.
[2] The King to Pitt, July 25, 1766 ; Fortescue, I, no. 363
[3] Townshend to Dowdeswell, July 29, 1766 ; Dowdeswell Papers, in the William L. Clements Library, Ann Arbor, U.S.A.

tunity to play a part he would never otherwise have dared, and Grafton was soon to regret the sole appointment he was allowed to make.

## (iv)

Pitt intended to take no office of business, but to become Lord Privy Seal and direct his Administration from a seat in the Lords.  His decision to take a peerage was apparently unknown to Northington and Camden until it was too late to dissuade him, and both they and Grafton lamented it.  Grafton writes : 'Our conception of the strength of the Administration had been, till that moment, derived from the great advantage he would have given to it by remaining with the Commons'.[1] Yet it was unavoidable : Pitt's health would not allow him to attend regularly in the Commons.  But once again he suffered by being a lone wolf in politics : he had no follower of sufficient stature for the vital post of Minister in that House, and had to take over Conway from the Rockinghams.

The Minister in the House of Commons was largely responsible for good relations between them and the King, an essential condition for the smooth working of government. Much depended on his debating skill and knowledge of parliamentary tactics, his sense of the moods of the House and of the ambitions and connections of individual members.  A long apprenticeship to parliamentary business was an essential qualification.  It was also his duty to represent the mood of the Commons to the King and the other Ministers.  Since the government desired the support of independent members, not obliged to it for their seats, the Minister must ensure that as much as possible was conceded to their opinion, the Ministry's case presented in the most favourable light, and support sought in the lobbies as well as on the floor of the House. Even highly unpopular measures could be got through if sufficient determination and energy were shown, as was illustrated by the passage of Grenville's resolutions on General Warrants in February 1764.

When the First Lord of the Treasury was a commoner he

[1] Grafton, *Autobiography*, p. 97.

was also Minister in the House of Commons, and the course of business was much simplified. For the larger share of government patronage was distributed from the Treasury. But when the First Lord was a peer the system nearly always ran into difficulties. A considerable share of Treasury patronage had to be delegated to the Minister in the House of Commons if the machine was to run smoothly, with some loss of the influence and prestige which the First Lord usually enjoyed. The danger was that if the First Lord delegated too much of his patronage, the Minister would take over too much of his authority ; if too little, the Minister would find his influence in the Commons insufficient. The most stable Administrations in the eighteenth century were those of commoners : Sir Robert Walpole, Henry Pelham, Lord North, and the younger Pitt. With the growth of organized parties in the nineteenth century this problem disappeared. Party allegiance, not patronage, held the government majority together, and both First Lord of the Treasury and Leader of the House of Commons owed allegiance to a common body — the party. But when there was no common allegiance and each Minister held tenure individually to the Crown, each tried to obtain for himself as large a segment of the Crown's patronage as he could — which did not make for stability or harmony.

Henry Seymour Conway was a soldier rather than a politician, devoted to his profession but not of outstanding ability in it. Dismissed from his regiment in 1764 because of his vote on General Warrants, he had acquired a martyr's reputation with the opposition. In 1765 he had become Secretary of State and Minister in the House of Commons, due probably to his connection with the Duke of Cumberland and to Charles Townshend's refusal to join the Rockinghams. As Secretary of State he was industrious and conscientious, though lacking imagination ; as Minister in the House of Commons he was a total failure. He did not enjoy his position, but longed for the day when he could return to the Army. Proud, reserved, and sensitive, with an over-scrupulous conscience and too nice a sense of honour, 'always preferring his own character to the service of his friends',[1] he 'could not be induced to traffic with Members',[2] and 'paid too much deference to what men would say of him'.[3] Thus wrote Horace Walpole, Conway's intimate friend and the man who probably knew him best.

The two most important offices in the Administration, from the point of view of the House of Commons, were filled by men with little aptitude for them because Pitt had no one better on whom he could rely. In many ways the choice of Conway was a more serious matter than that of Grafton. Pitt's decision to go into the Lords was, in Walpole's words, 'quitting the field to Grenville and every rising genius'.[4] Townshend on the side of the Ministry, and Grenville on that of opposition, were able to secure the attention of the House to an extent impossible had Pitt remained a commoner.

Although Conway had never been a follower of Pitt he had hoped for Pitt's inclusion in the Rockingham Ministry, and had considered resigning with Grafton over that issue. Conway and Grafton were allied by marriage,[5] Conway sat in the House for Grafton's borough of Thetford, and their friendship was to be the salvation of the Ministry in the difficult year ahead. Yet Conway was undecided whether to remain in office, and Pitt, knowing how important it was to retain him, early offered him the lead in the Commons. At their conversation on July 13 Pitt was conciliatory and persuasive.[6] The Administration was to be formed as far as possible 'of the best, and ablest men, without any regard to parties, distinctions, or *connections*', but the Rockinghams were to be the basis on which Pitt would build. Changes were to be as few as possible, though changes he feared there must be. He was frank about these : the Duke of Richmond must surrender the Seals,[7] and some provision must be made for Bute's friends. Conway confessed

---

[1] Walpole, *Memoirs*, ii. 230.    [2] *Ibid*. pp. 297-8.
[3] *Ibid*. iii. 56.    [4] *Ibid*. ii. 248.
[5] Conway's brother, Lord Hertford, had married Lady Isabella Fitzroy, Grafton's aunt.
[6] Newcastle to John White, July 20, 1766 ; Add. MS. 32976, f. 76. Conway informed Newcastle of this conversation.
[7] Richmond had married the daughter of Conway's wife by her first husband, Charles, third Earl of Ailesbury.

his dilemma to Newcastle,[1] but Rockingham did not encourage his followers to resign, and Conway's acceptance involved him in no breach with his former colleagues.

## (v)

One man resigned from the Administration because he disliked Pitt and opposed his policy — Lord Egmont, First Lord of the Admiralty, classed by Rockingham as one of Bute's friends. Lord Hardwicke, whose brother John Yorke — a junior Lord of the Admiralty — resigned with his chief, described Egmont's reasons as

the incompatibility of his system of foreign affairs with Lord Chatham's ; that he could submit to be overruled by a majority in Council, and hoped he was open to conviction, but could not bear to be *dictated* to.[2]

It is an interesting comment on the practice of the eighteenth century Cabinet and a revealing one on the men who accepted office under Pitt, and was considered by Hardwicke as 'a handsome declaration' and 'a rational distinction'.

Chatham tried to use the opportunity given by Egmont's resignation to split the potential opposition. Temple had proposed Lord Gower, the Duke of Bedford's brother-in-law, as Secretary of State, in order 'to make a merit with [the] Bedfords'.[3] Pitt's veto had been Temple's pretext for refusing to come in. Pitt did not object to Gower personally or politically, but he would not allow Temple an equal right to nominate to the Cabinet. When Egmont resigned, Pitt commissioned Grafton to offer the Admiralty to Gower, a man who had never displayed any sign of administrative ability. It was believed

[1] Newcastle to White, July 20, 1766 ; Add. MS. 32976, f. 79.

[2] Hardwicke to Rockingham, August 24, 1766 ; Rockingham Papers, R1-423. Part printed in Lord Albemarle, *Memoirs of the Marquis of Rockingham and his Contemporaries*, ii. 10-11. Egmont disliked Pitt's proposed alliance with Prussia and Russia ; Yorke's resignation was connected with his brother Charles's. The Yorke family disliked Pitt and thought him no friend to their pretensions.

[3] Fortescue, I, no. 143.

that the Bedfords were anxious for office, and that Gower was one of those most eager to return to Court.[1]

Grafton embarked on the negotiation 'with more desire . . . than expectation of success'.[2] On August 15 he saw Lord Tavistock, and requested him to inform the Duke of the offer to Gower. To Tavistock's question, was this to be the only opening made to the Bedford group, Grafton replied that for the present it was,

> but that Lord Chatham's idea was, a great and conciliating plan, but not to turn out those, who should be willing to act with the present Administration, but that time was requisite to bring this about.[3]

However, he threw out hints that other openings might follow. Bedford forwarded the offer to Gower and wrote to Grafton (August 17) : 'I hope your Grace will excuse me from making myself the middle man betwixt the Administration and Lord Gower. . . .'[4] On August 22 Gower declined.[5]

It is difficult to believe that Pitt seriously expected Gower to accept. Yet in his letter to the King of August 23 he described Gower's reasons for refusing as 'couch'd with obscurity, and to me not quite intelligible'.[6] There was nothing obscure about them. 'Tho' I am acquainted with the commanders in chief of the Administration', wrote Gower to Grafton on August 22,

> and I do assure your Grace that I have not the least personal objection to any one, yet your Grace must know how un-

---

[1] There are many references in contemporary correspondence to the Bedfords' eagerness for office, particularly by the followers of Grenville. See William Gerard Hamilton to Temple, August 3, 1766 (*Grenville Papers*, iii. 289-92) ; and Temple to Grenville, August 21, 1766 (*ibid.* pp. 305-7). Walpole gives an account of an approach by the Bedfords to Administration (*Memoirs*, ii. 252).

[2] Grafton, *Autobiography*, p. 99.

[3] Bedford to Gower, August 17, 1766 ; *Bedford Correspondence*, iii. 342-3.

[4] *Ibid.* pp. 343-4. Bedford's letter was opened by a clerk in the Post Office named Saxby, who was dismissed from his place, said to be worth £1200 a year. (Charles Lloyd to Grenville, September 2, 1766 ; Grenville MSS., in the possession of Sir John Murray.)

[5] Grafton, *Autobiography*, pp. 100-1.

[6] Fortescue, I, no. 380.

pleasant it is to be in a *responsible* office . . . unconnected
with the individuals who compose that Administration. . . .[1]

Gower would not desert the Bedford group, with which he had
been connected all his political life : he would come in with
the group, but not singly.  Nor would it have been good sense
for him to do so ; his stature as a member of a 'political pack'
was far greater than as an unconnected individual.

No eighteenth-century Minister exalted the position of the
Crown higher than did Pitt.  Grafton describes his 'determination to stand in the gap to defend the Closet against every
contending party'.[2]  No eighteenth-century Minister wrote to
George III in such terms as Pitt did : even in an age when
ceremonious language, especially to the monarch, was a sign
of good breeding, Pitt's expressions seem exaggerated and even
at times insincere.  He was for ever throwing himself at the
King's feet, protesting his duty and submission, and thanking
him for his 'boundless condescension' and 'infinite goodness'.
The belief that to support the measures of the Crown was the
duty of a good subject was often on his lips, yet he spent the
greater part of his political life in opposition ; and, achieving
a distinction rare among his contemporaries, contrived to
offend both George II and George III.  Still, this contradiction is not so paradoxical as it seems.  Pitt's aggressive
temperament thirsted for power, and, when in office, to exalt
the power of the Crown and assert its right to choose its
Ministers freely was ultimately to exalt his own, as the choice
of the Crown.  Out of office, he used the subterfuge common
to all opposition groups — that the King was ill advised by his
Ministers, who alone must be saddled with the consequences
of policy.  This may have been so, but it did not prevent
George II and George III from taking offence.

## (vi)

The other Cabinet offices were filled with men less unsuited
to their departments.  Sir Charles Saunders, described by
Walpole as one of Pitt's 'favourite and most successful admirals

---

[1] Grafton, *Autobiography*, p. 101.          [2] *Ibid.* p. 90.

in the last war',[1] was nominated to the Admiralty. He was closely connected with the Keppel family, and of little weight in politics. Lord Camden was the expected choice for the Great Seal, Northington taking the less onerous office of Lord President of the Council. Pitt had selected Lord Shelburne as Secretary of State for the Southern Department, a man of high intellectual calibre but arrogant and unpopular, who was soon on bad terms with both the King and his colleagues. Lord Granby was made Commander-in-Chief,[2] and the patronage of the Army was transferred to him.[3]

Pitt's Cabinet included three men who had served with Rockingham : Conway, Grafton, and Northington. Outside the Cabinet only three men were dismissed : Lord Breadalbane, father-in-law of the second Earl of Hardwicke, removed from the office of Privy Seal of Scotland to make way for James Stuart Mackenzie ; [4] and Lord George Sackville, Pitt's *bête noire*, who owed his office of joint Vice-Treasurer of Ireland to 'the penury of trained forces' the Rockinghams had at their command. The third to be dismissed was Lord Grantham, joint Postmaster-General, who was compensated by his son being appointed to the Board of Trade. Grantham was an old friend of Newcastle (as Sir Thomas Robinson he had been Secretary of State and Minister in the House of Commons when the Duke first took the Treasury in 1754), and Newcastle 'complained extremely' to Conway 'that it was very cruel usage' and considered himself 'most extremely ill-used by it'.[5] But Grantham did not complain : he was seventy-one, and probably accepted his retirement as a fair exchange for the office given to his son.

---

[1] *Memoirs*, ii. 256.

[2] Not without a protest from Lord Ligonier (aged eighty-five), who thought himself 'able to execute any commands relative to the duty of Commander-in-Chief which he may receive from his Majesty'. (Ligonier to Lord Barrington, August 7, 1766 ; Fortescue, I, no. 377.) Ligonier was compensated with an earldom and the reversion of part of his pension to his nephew.

[3] Barrington to Charles Yorke, August 15, 1766 ; Add. MS. 35638, f. 15.

[4] Copy of a letter from Chatham to Breadalbane, August 19, 1766 ; Add. MS. 35424, f. 14.

[5] Newcastle to Rockingham, September 18, 1766 ; Add. MS. 32977, ff. 95-9.

There were six resignations outside the Cabinet.  Charles Yorke had been disappointed when Rockingham could not secure the Great Seal for him, and had grudgingly accepted his old post of Attorney-General.  The King seemed to be willing to make him Lord Chief Justice of the Common Pleas (vacant by Camden's promotion), but Yorke would not consider it without a peerage.[1]  Pitt, according to Lord Hardwicke, tried to prevent Yorke from resigning, 'with smooth and flattering conversation . . . urging the services he could do and the weight he carried in the House of Commons'.[2]  But Yorke's eyes were never off the Woolsack ;  George Onslow, watching the Lord Chancellor's procession at the opening of the legal term, described how Yorke's 'countenance did indeed shew to the observation of every body, the feelings of his mind'.[3] He remained with the Rockinghams, hoping that with them he would achieve his ambition ;  and his brothers, Lord Hardwicke and John Yorke, reluctantly followed him.

Lord Dartmouth, an earnest, conscientious man, with little understanding of party, would have remained if made Secretary of State for the Colonies, but refused to carry on with the limited powers of First Lord of Trade.  His successor, Lord Hillsborough, far from wanting more power desired less. He accepted 'provided the Board should be altered from a Board of representation to a Board of report upon reference only . . . that every executive business that has by degrees crept into the Board should revert to the proper offices . . .', and that he should not be of the Cabinet.[4]  The colonies continued to be the concern of two departments until Grafton

[1] Yorke to Rockingham, July 30, 1766 ; Rockingham Papers, R1-417. See also Lord Hardwicke's 'Memorial of Family Occurrences from 1760 to 1770' ; Add. MS. 35428, f. 11.  Yorke replied to the King's hint that the Common Pleas was vacant : 'Surely, Sir, your Majesty will not wish me to take it in a manner different from that in which Lord Campden has enjoyed it'.  Camden became Chief Justice of the Common Pleas in 1761 ; he was made a peer by Rockingham in 1765, not in right of his seat on the bench, but to please Pitt.  The Chief Justice of the Common Pleas was not normally a peer, though Wedderburn claimed it in 1780.

[2] *Ibid.*

[3] Onslow to Newcastle, November 7, 1766 ; Rockingham Papers, R1-439.  Presumably sent by Newcastle to Rockingham and never returned.

[4] Hillsborough to Grenville, August 6, 1766 ; *Grenville Papers*, iii. 294-6.

set up the Secretaryship of State for the Colonies in January 1768.

William Dowdeswell, Rockingham's Chancellor of the Exchequer, a country gentleman turned politician, was offered his choice of the Board of Trade (apparently without the Cabinet) or joint Paymaster-General, but refused and eventually became the leader of the Rockingham opposition in the Commons.[1] He told the King,

> that in what his Majesty might intend for me he considered the high station to which he had already raised me, and the manner in which I had discharged my office to his satisfaction and I persuaded myself with no small degree of public approbation.    I said, that it might be the misfortune some times to have been raised too high.    Men could not after being much exalted stoop to certain offices which they might have at first accepted.[2]

Lastly, Lord John Cavendish resigned his seat at the Treasury Board.    On July 26 he wrote to Newcastle :

> My reason for what I have done is that as I have always thought Mr. Pitt's style too high for my temper and I have been a long time tired of the confinement of my employment, it appeared to me I could not have a better opportunity of getting out, than in company with those, with whom I have been so long intimately connected, both in publick and private life.[3]

His 'violent warmth' was not approved by either Rockingham or Newcastle.[4]

More significant than the small number of resignations was the return to Court of men who had served under Grenville but opposed the Rockinghams.    Lord Hillsborough, Charles

---

[1] Dowdeswell to Chatham, July 31, 1766 ; *Chatham Correspondence*, iii. 22-3.   Charles Lloyd, Grenville's private secretary, told him that Dowdeswell refused because 'of his great uncertainty as to his re-election'. (August 5, 1766 ; *Grenville Papers*, iii. 292-4.)   This is unlikely : Dowdeswell was very popular in Worcestershire, and never had to face a contested election there.

[2] Dowdeswell to his wife, July 30, 1766 ; Dowdeswell Papers.

[3] Add. MS. 32976, f. 269.

[4] Rockingham to Newcastle, July 26, 1766, and Newcastle's reply of the same date ; *ibid.* ff. 253-6.

Jenkinson, Lord le Despenser, Robert Nugent, and Hans Stanley were some of those who accepted office during the first six months of Pitt's Administration. The Court was their party, office their goal, and opposition foreign and uncongenial. The Rockingham Ministry had been an unnatural interlude in the smooth normality of their lives. Pitt's return to power was the signal for the birds to come back to their nests.

On July 29 the King signed the warrant creating Pitt Earl of Chatham, and on the following day Chatham kissed hands for the Privy Seal.[1]

[1] The King to Pitt, July 29, 1766; Fortescue, I, no. 372.

C

# CHAPTER II

## THE GROWTH OF OPPOSITION

WHAT was the attitude of the Rockinghams, and especially of those who had lost their places, to the new Administration?

It was taken for granted by Chatham's friends that his Administration would be formed on the basis of the previous one, and Temple's refusal seemed to facilitate this. On July 24 Lord Camden wrote to Thomas Walpole :

Ld. T.'s wild conduct, tho Mr. P. is grievously wounded by it, may, for aught I know, turn out to be a favourable circumstance, to reconcile him more to the present Ministry, out of which corps he must form, as he always intended, this our Administration.[1]

On July 12, the day Chatham had his first audience of the King, Newcastle wrote to Rockingham on the conduct their friends should hold :

I will hazard to your Lordship my present opinion that, as many of our friends, as they shall permit to stay in their employments, should do it. . . . For, if that is done, they can have no pretence to carry removals to the cruel extent, that my Ld. Bute and Mr. Grenville did. . . . In all events, I think an idea of a formal opposition would be most impolitick, and unjustifiable. . . . I should hope, there would always be a firm friendship, concert, and communication, between all those . . . who agree in principle, and who have acted together during the last opposition and since the establishment of the present Administration.[2]

Nor was this Newcastle's opinion only. On July 20 he reported Rockingham as having said,

[1] Grafton, *Autobiography*, pp. 94-5. The name of Camden's correspondent is omitted.
[2] Add. MS. 32976, ff. 111-12.

that our utmost endevours should be used to engage the Duke of Grafton, and Mr. Pitt, to consent that the Duke of Grafton should be at the head of the Treasury. . . . If Lord Temple was to come there . . . my Ld. Rockingham thinks . . . that neither Mr. Conway nor any of our principal friends should remain in the Administration. . . .[1]

When Grenville was dismissed in 1765 his friends and those of the Duke of Bedford resigned in a body, and immediately set about concerting plans for opposition. But the Rockinghams not only remained behind to serve under Chatham, but Rockingham himself discouraged resignations. 'I was much surprized', he wrote when Lord John Cavendish resigned, 'as I did think that our friends would have waited and been more temperate.'[2] 'I thought it was a settled point', wrote Burke to Rockingham on August 21, 'that none should go out without the concurrence of the party.'[3]

Of course a call for resignations in July 1766 would not have met with even the partial response of 1762. Newcastle's friends in particular had no wish to wander once more in the wilderness. Their attitude was correctly expressed by Horace Walpole : 'Newcastle's people are weary of following him in and out, and see what everybody else sees but himself, that seventy-three and ambition are ridiculous comrades'.[4] The mass resignation of the Grenville and Bedford groups in 1765 was not in accordance with contemporary practice, but was an anticipation of what would happen in an age of disciplined and coherent political parties. The Rockinghams in 1766 were not a united group, and they had little sense of party or political tactics.

Although most of Rockingham's followers who remained in office were henceforth lost to him, this was not the result he had intended. Chatham had never cultivated a party, and when he returned to power had only a few personal friends to be accommodated. Consequently, Rockingham hoped that Chatham would be compelled to rely on the members of the

---

[1] Newcastle to White, July 20, 1766 ; *ibid.* f. 79.
[2] Rockingham to Newcastle, July 26, 1766 ; *ibid.* ff. 253-4.
[3] *Burke Correspondence*, i. 105-9. But Burke always exaggerated the unity and discipline of the Rockingham group.
[4] Walpole to Sir Horace Mann, August 1, 1766.

last Administration, who would act as a Rockingham garrison within its citadel. Protected by Grafton and Conway they would enjoy all the advantages of office, and yet maintain their allegiance to Rockingham. 'We think ourselves perfectly safe in your hands and the Duke of Grafton's', wrote Newcastle to Conway on July 29.[1] Temple's refusal pleased Rockingham because, he wrote to Newcastle on July 18, 'I now think the Corps will be kept together'.[2] Newcastle was jubilant : 'Pitt must fling himself into us' — Conway and Grafton now had him in their hands.[3] Even as late as August 29 Rockingham's object was 'to keep up a good humoured correspondence with those parts of the present system who were parts of ours . . .',[4] and although by now he was convinced that Chatham and Bute were allies, yet thought that Chatham must 'condescend to try to be very much reconciled with us as otherwise I can not see on what support he can rely'.

It was a grave error of judgment to cast Chatham for the rôle of Minister *fainéant* to Rockingham. It was also a grave misunderstanding of the reality of politics. It does not seem to have occurred to Rockingham that his followers who remained in Administration would insensibly, if they wished to keep their places or hoped for better ones, come to acknowledge Chatham as their leader, whatever their previous connections with Rockingham. Those who remained in office would come under the influence of the strongest force in eighteenth-century politics, the obligation every man of goodwill had to serve the Crown to the best of his ability, and self-interest would walk hand in hand with duty. At times of acute political conflict this idea could exert a greater strength than that of party, and Conway was only the most prominent, but not the only man, who found in the moment of trial that his allegiance to King George was more binding than his allegiance to King Rockingham.

---

[1] Add. MS. 32976, f. 315.
[2] *Ibid*. ff. 161-2. Dated by Rockingham, 'Past 12 o'clock. July the 17th 1766.' Rockingham wrote most of his letters to Newcastle in the early hours of the morning, usually without changing the date.
[3] Newcastle to Rockingham, July 18, 1766 ; *ibid*. f. 173.
[4] Rockingham to Newcastle, August 29, 1766 ; *ibid*. ff. 488-9.

The Duke of Richmond, of far keener insight than Rockingham but whose influence was small, realized what would happen. On July 8 he wrote to Rockingham :

> I confess I suspect my information [that the King had sent for Pitt] to be true, but think you had better not communicate it to any one but Mr. Conway, for if it is known and that Mr. Conway's sentiments gett among our friends, it will be a race among them who shall go first to Mr. Pitt.[1]

Even Lord Hardwicke, not an acute politician but not lacking sense, in his disillusionment at seeing his brother as far off the Great Seal as ever, 'animadverted' to Newcastle 'on the shabby policy of throwing over their followers to Lord Chatham'.[2]

But before the new Ministers had kissed hands Rockingham was beginning to doubt whether Chatham would play the compliant rôle which had been assigned to him. On July 18, when Temple's refusal was known, he was in an optimistic mood, although, he told Newcastle, 'I don't yet feel that we are free from various unpleasing circumstances. . . .'[3] During the next few days, however, he became irritated at Chatham's failure to consult him. On July 21 he wrote : 'I saw Genl. Conway again this morning, who knows nothing more than we all did yesterday'.[4] And on July 23 : 'I have neither seen Genl. Conway nor heard from him — and know of *nothing*'.[5] On July 26 he complained of the 'total silence of Mr. Pitt', who had not consulted 'our friends' and that, 'neither directly nor indirectly thro' either Conway or the D. of Grafton any mark of attention or civility, of even desiring or wishing for their concurrence has as yet been made'.[6]

It was not only to Newcastle that he complained. Conway, one of his representatives in the Cabinet, was made to feel that his friends outside were aggrieved at Chatham's behaviour. Conway had a very sensitive conscience, which anticipated the

---

[1] Rockingham Papers, R1-386.
[2] Hardwicke to Charles Yorke, August 29, 1766 ; Add. MS. 35362, ff. 29-30.
[3] Add. MS. 32976, ff. 161-2.
[4] Rockingham to Newcastle, July 21, 1766 ; *ibid.* ff. 199-200.
[5] Rockingham to Newcastle, July 23, 1766 ; *ibid.* f. 219.
[6] Rockingham to Newcastle, July 26, 1766 ; *ibid.* ff. 253-4.

reproaches he was later to receive from his former colleagues. Pressed by John Cavendish,[1] he persuaded Chatham to pay Rockingham a courtesy call, but when Chatham went 'his Lordship was not at home'.[2]  The day before this visit took place Rockingham had told Conway,

> after his total want of attention or civility to many considerable friends of ours and of positive assurances of his good intentions towards our friends in general . . . I really think that I should be wanting to myself and others to have any personal communication with Mr. Pitt.[3]

He concluded with warning Conway 'that Mr. Pitt's intentions and conduct are and will be the most hostile to our friends'.

It was a ridiculous affair, but no important consequences followed.  Chatham showed no resentment at such behaviour from a man whom Walpole describes as 'more childish in his deportment than in his age'.[4]

Charles Watson-Wentworth, second Marquess of Rockingham, was born in 1730 and inherited at the age of twenty the vast estates of his father in Yorkshire, Northamptonshire, and Ireland.  He also inherited his father's political tradition — support of the Administrations of Sir Robert Walpole and Henry Pelham — which had raised him to the rank of Marquess. The son naturally transferred his support to Pelham's brother and successor, the Duke of Newcastle, with whom he formed an intimate political friendship.  But Rockingham was much more than a follower of Newcastle : he was politically important in his own right.  His influence in Yorkshire was greater than that of any other landowner, and his friendship with Sir George Savile, eighth Baronet, gave him a position in that county which even his father had not enjoyed.  He had his own little following in the House of Commons, and his prestige and his wealth exerted some influence upon the country gentlemen who sat for many of Yorkshire's pocket boroughs.

---

[1] Walpole, *Memoirs*, ii. 252-3.
[2] George Onslow to Newcastle, July 28, 1766 ; Add. MS. 32976, f. 309. 'He himself [Rockingham] is very happy with what he has done', added Onslow.
[3] Rockingham to Conway, July 26, 1766 ; Albemarle, ii. 5-6.
[4] Walpole, *Memoirs*, ii. 139.

A man of such standing, raised in the Walpole-Pelham tradition, a force in politics but without the energy or ambition to play for the highest stakes, naturally gravitated towards Court office. Rockingham was made a Lord of the Bedchamber in 1751, and was high in favour with George II. He shared the fortunes of Newcastle and Devonshire in the early years of George III, and in the first negotiations for a new Ministry in 1765 was still considered only for Court office. Selected by the Duke of Cumberland for his First Lord of the Treasury, he grew to like a post at which he had not aimed and became loath to give it up. During his year at the head of Administration, he acquired three things which lasted all his life : a group of followers which, with a few exceptions, remained faithful through sixteen years of hopeless and largely profitless opposition ; a liking for the first place, and a preference for it in opposition to a lesser rank in Administration ; and a deep and thoroughly justified distrust of Chatham as a political ally.

Without great abilities, with little application, diffident and ineffective as an orator, Rockingham has shone in history with the reflected light of other men : the friend of Savile, the patron of Burke, the ally of Fox. 'A weak, childish and ignorant man, by no means fit for the head of Administration', is Walpole's severe, but not unjust stricture.[1] Rockingham was ambitious, but without energy or boldness : he preferred to work with a few men whom he could trust — to be the leader of a clique rather than of a party. To co-operate with others who did not acknowledge his supremacy would invite comparisons which he feared, and involve adjustments which he could not make. He aimed high, not to satisfy ambition but to overcome self-distrust ; yet caution, timidity, and irresolution held him back. His political sympathies were restricted : questions affecting property interested him most (the Nullum Tempus bill, the Irish absentee land tax), and he had no understanding of ideas which challenged the basis of his influence. He was no reformer, but looked back to an imaginary Golden Age when 'Revolution families' and 'Whig principles' had ruled the land, and attributed all evil to the

[1] *Ibid.* iii. 222.

overriding influence of the Crown. He raised his prejudices to the dignity of principles : dislike of Bute, distrust of Chatham, jealousy of Grenville inspired and justified his politics. Defeat in America, not Rockingham's leadership, brought his party back into power in 1782, for Rockingham triumphed only when other men failed.

## (ii)

What of the two other political groups in Parliament — the followers of George Grenville and the Duke of Bedford — uneasy allies both in Administration and opposition ?

In 1761, when Grenville succeeded Pitt as Minister in the House of Commons, he had neither a political following nor the necessary self-confidence to be a party leader. By 1765, when it required the assistance of a Royal Duke to turn him out, Grenville had acquired both. His Administration was by far the strongest of the first ten years of George III's reign : he began in politics as junior partner in the firm of Pitt and Temple : he ended as a leader in his own right, with a following far larger than Pitt's and a reputation far greater than Temple's.

Grenville has received harsh and summary treatment from historians. 'The worst Administration which has governed England since the Revolution', was Lord Macaulay's verdict. The author and lifelong defender of the ill-omened Stamp Act, he has been regarded as the begetter of the misfortunes of the following years, and loaded with much of the responsibility for the loss of the American colonies. Grenville never forgot the Stamp Act, never forgave those who repealed it, and never ceased to urge the policy he had initiated upon a divided Cabinet and an attentive House of Commons. Yet he only initiated this policy : it was left to others to carry it through, with consequences they did not expect. It was in the years from 1766 to 1770 that the alienation of the colonies from Great Britain increased with alarming rapidity ; and it was the irresponsibility of Charles Townshend, the narrow, short-sighted views of Hillsborough, the refusal of Chatham to direct the Administration he had formed, the struggles of the Rockinghams to force themselves back into power, and the timidity of Grafton and Camden, the friends of America, which brought about a situation almost beyond the powers of statesmanship to handle. Shelburne alone emerges with credit from these years, but Shelburne was distrusted and disliked by his Cabinet colleagues, and in January 1768 gave up the responsibility for American affairs.

The opinion entertained of Grenville by two of his contemporaries is well known, and has unduly influenced historians. George III is reputed to have said that he would rather see the Devil in his Closet than George Grenville.[1] Less well known, less picturesque, but far more revealing of Grenville's character, is the King's remark that 'that gentleman's opinions are seldom formed from any other motives than such as may be expected to originate in the mind of a clerk in a counting house. . . .'[2] Or consider Walpole's summary :

His ingratitude to his benefactor, Lord Bute, and his reproaching Mr. Pitt with the profusion of a war which he had sometimes actively supported, and always tacitly approved, while holding a beneficial place, were but too often paralleled by the crimes of other men ; but scarce any man ever wore in his face such outward and visible marks of the hollow, cruel, and rotten heart within.[3]

Once again it is picturesque, but so obviously inspired by hatred as to be grotesquely untrue. Walpole's second thoughts are better :

Mr. Grenville was, confessedly, the ablest man of business in the House of Commons, and, though not popular, of great authority there from his spirit, knowledge, and gravity of character.[4]

What was it about the man that could inspire the dislike revealed in the King's remarks and in the first passage from Walpole ? In part these comments are subjective, the result of unpleasant personal experiences ; but if they have no

---

[1] Walpole, *Memoirs*, iii. 50.
[2] The King to Conway, February 18, 1767 ; Fortescue, I, no. 468, corrected by Sir Lewis Namier, *Additions and Corrections*, pp. 69-70.
[3] Walpole, *Memoirs*, i. 215.                    [4] *Ibid.* iv. 125.

objective truth, they do indicate the dislike he could arouse in two men of dissimilar minds but both well acquainted with men and affairs. Yet to the end of his life Grenville was heard with respect in the House of Commons ; and his political following, though not as numerous, was as devoted as Rockingham's and far abler.

To understand Grenville it is essential to remember his rapid rise to political eminence, first a humble dependant of Pitt and Temple, next obliged to Bute for his seat in the Cabinet and for his place at the head of the Treasury. 'Too much memory is a deadly danger in politics' both for men and nations ; Grenville never forgot that he had risen through the help of other men, and never forgave them for it. Yet in many ways his virtues were of great value in politics and government. An indefatigable worker, thoroughly conversant with finance and trade (the subject of most debates in Parliament), politically and personally honest, and acting upon sound if narrow principles of government, he brings a professional touch into politics — a refreshing contrast to the dilettantism of Grafton or Rockingham. His speeches in the Commons may have bored the wits, but the country gentlemen, who felt the burden of the land tax, listened to him keenly and took careful note of what he said. But with all these virtues there was a narrow, cramped outlook. The larger view escaped him, there was no vision, no grasp of the wider problems of Empire. Grenville's ideal was a carefully kept balance sheet, with every penny wisely spent and duly accounted, but with little attention paid to assets that could not be reduced to pounds, shillings, and pence. More than most politicians of his day he held the legalistic view of the problems of government common to them all : it is significant that he was Lord Mansfield's favourite politician. His was the mind to cope with the financial problems which followed the Seven Years' War, but not to pave the way for a new and more generous relationship between Great Britain and her colonies.

Grenville brought no fresh capital to his group when, in 1766, he linked his fortunes with those of his brother, Lord

Temple. For Temple had neither a following nor an appeal. His vanity and pomposity repelled, and as he seemed to desire to be in permanent opposition no politically ambitious man would follow him. It was clear that the brothers would enter into a vocal opposition against Chatham, but one which need not be feared and which would reduce itself to a hard core of irreconcilables, as Administration attracted more and more of their followers over to its side. Already former members of Grenville's Administration who had gone with him into opposition against the Rockinghams had joined Chatham, and more were to follow. The chaos in the Administration during 1767 helped to maintain the numbers of the Grenville group, but after Administration settled down in 1768 there were further desertions, and finally, after Grenville's death, most of the group went over to Lord North, leaving Temple to indulge in solitude his 'most sovereign contempt for the Royal closet' and his boast 'that he was the only man the King had never duped'.[1]

### (iii)

The third political group forming part of a potential opposition to the Chatham Ministry was that centred round the Duke of Bedford.

The Bedford group had been an element in politics since the days of Henry Pelham. It had retained an individuality and a consciousness of its own, sometimes working with the Pelhams, sometimes against them, but never merging itself into any Administration. During the early years of George III, the Bedfords had served with both Newcastle and Bute, and Bedford had been the ambassador sent to negotiate the Treaty of Paris. They had joined Grenville's Administration, and the Duke had distinguished himself by the violence of his opposition to the influence of Bute. Dismissed in 1765, they had continued their alliance with Grenville in opposition to the Rockinghams, and yet had managed to retain their separate identity and their separate will.

[1] See the character of Temple by Shelburne in Lord Fitzmaurice, *The Life of Lord Shelburne* (1912 edition), ii. 25-8.

It was always difficult to say where, at any one instance, the dominant political influence in the Bedford group lay. The Duke himself, when he was moved to exert it, had a mind and will of his own which he used with energy in the pursuit of any political object in which he happened to be interested. Proud of his name and of his family's services in English history, he was not an easy man to browbeat when roused. 'The Duke of Bedford, whom the rest [of the Newcastle-Pitt Cabinet] always summoned when they wanted to combat Pitt and did not dare', is Walpole's significant remark.[1] Superficially Bedford had nothing to gain from Pitt's return to office, since their opinions differed at every point : Bedford loved peace and disliked Pitt's forward foreign policy, was concerned at the effects of war on the nation's finances, and advocated a 'firm' policy towards the colonies. Moreover, by 1766 his active political life was nearing its end : he was suffering from a disease of the eyes which threatened him with blindness, and he himself had no wish for office. But contemporaries often credited one or the other of Bedford's followers as being responsible for the decisions taken in his name.

The Duke's second wife, Gertrude, daughter of John, first Earl Gower, was a strong-minded woman, by no means uninterested in politics. Her influence on the Duke cannot be estimated, since it was not exerted in any obvious manner. But William Gerard Hamilton thought it worth while to report to Temple on August 3, 1766, that 'the Duchess of Bedford does not scruple to declare her very sanguine wishes for a junction with Mr. Pitt'.[2] The correspondence of the period is full of references to the Duchess's moods and wishes, and their probable effects on the behaviour of the Bedford group, while there is hardly a similar reference to the wife of any other prominent politician. The Duchess and her brother, Lord Gower, were eager to return to Court, and considered they had nothing further to gain from the alliance with Grenville. They only waited for a favourable opening from Chatham to urge their wishes on the Duke.

The third member of the trio at the centre of the Bedford

---

[1] *Memoirs*, i. 54.　　　　[2] *Grenville Papers*, iii. 289-92.

group was Richard Rigby, the Duke's political man of business. Rigby was the type of politician whom post-Reform Bill historians selected as an example of all that was worst in eighteenth-century politics.[1] Energetic, with a coarse, jovial vulgarity, convivial and hospitable (especially to peers and people of importance),[2] Rigby's ambition was limited and easily attainable. He coveted a comfortable place with a good income and no responsibility for policy, above all the Pay Office.[3] His income from his paternal estate in Essex was not large for one who wished to rank as an equal with men of fashion and wealth. He had been the intimate friend of Henry Fox, and no doubt appreciated how profitable Fox's long tenure of the Pay Office had been. Rigby's part in the events of 1766 and 1767 is important and at times decisive. For Rigby, Bedford's most outstanding follower in the Commons, was the main link with the Grenvilles, and it was on him that Grenville based his hope of retaining Bedford's alliance. It was a slender hope indeed, for Rigby had already shown that he had no use for friendship in politics once it had ceased to be of profit to him. Grenville was to learn, as Henry Fox had done before him, that Rigby could desert an ally without shame or apology. But in the summer of 1766 Rigby was not yet prepared to go over to Chatham : he saw no prospect of obtaining the Pay Office from a man whom he disliked and who treated him with contempt, and preferred to go into opposition until the opportunity came of making a better bargain. But Rigby's influence was not sufficient to counteract the desire of the Duchess and Lord Gower to return to Court : if, however, a situation developed in which the Duke felt his importance slighted, Rigby knew how to use the opportunity, and his influence might become decisive.

[1] See, *e.g.*, the article on him in the *D.N.B.*, which in addition is grossly inaccurate.

[2] An anonymous eulogist says of him : 'In the prime of life Mr. Rigby sacrificed pretty freely to conviviality'. *Authentic Memoirs and a Sketch of the Real Character of the late Right Hon. Richard Rigby* (published in 1788), p. 19.

[3] When he got the Pay Office in 1768 he described it as 'the best office in the King's service'. Rigby to Bedford, June 10, 1768 ; Woburn MS., lvii, f. 78, part printed in *Bedford Correspondence*, iii. 401.

John Montagu, fourth Earl of Sandwich, was the aristocratic counterpart to Rigby — more ambitious, but less
influential. He had been connected with Bedford since the
1740's, and was important in his own right and because of
the followers he brought with him. Sandwich was the perfect
type of eighteenth-century politician, accepting uncritically,
exploiting skilfully, and enjoying whole-heartedly the con-
ventions of his age. No opportunity to extend his influence
ever escaped him : whether it was an election for a member of
Parliament or a Fellow of Eton, an East India director or an
Elder Brother of Trinity House, Sandwich was busy marshalling
his supporters, soliciting all who might be able to influence
voters, and using to the full all the apparatus of interest and
connection to secure his end.[1] In an executive capacity he
was very efficient, and his restless mind longed for business.
His ancestor Edward, the first Earl, was a distinguished naval
officer and led the fleet over to Charles II in 1660 ; *post tot
naufragia portum* was the family motto ; and the Admiralty had
long been, as Sandwich wrote to Bedford on November 5,
1747, 'the single object of my views'.[2] Like Rigby, he saw
opposition only as a method of forcing open the door of office,
and he was prepared to accept a post not of Cabinet rank
rather than none at all.[3]

Rumours of the Bedfords' inclination to take office were
prevalent ; Grenville happened to be at Woburn when Tavistock arrived with the offer of the Admiralty to Gower, and
was shown the letters which Bedford wrote to Grafton and
Gower.[4] Grenville describes his reception as kind and friendly ;
Bedford, annoyed at Chatham's clumsy attempt to split his
group,

> declared very strongly to Mr. Grenville that he continued
> firm in his former opinions, made many declarations of his

[1] Edward Leeds (Sheriff of Huntingdonshire) wrote to Charles Yorke
on October 30, 1768 : 'The great master of electioneering politicks in
Huntingdonshire [Sandwich] has taught me that no attempt is to be omitted
where there is a bare possibility of making a vote'. Add. MS. 35638, f. 382.
[2] Woburn MS., xviii, f. 63.
[3] See his letter to Bedford of November 28, 1766, quoted on p. 63.
[4] Grenville to Temple, August 20, 1766 ; *Grenville Papers*, iii. 302-5.

strongest and most friendly dispositions towards him, and that he would nor could have nothing to do with Lord Chatham, the *totality* of whose measures he disapproved.[1]

For the time being events had favoured Rigby rather than the Duchess and Gower, and the alliance with Grenville was reaffirmed. All now depended on Chatham's next move.

(iv)

Meanwhile Administration was having its troubles, arising both from its policy and personnel — from the scruples of the discontented General Conway and the ambitions of the restless Charles Townshend.

Townshend had two immediate objects in view : a seat in the Cabinet, and a peerage for his wife. Still, he addressed his importunities not to Chatham but to Grafton, whose eyes had not yet been opened to Townshend's true nature : Grafton used his influence with Chatham, and in October Townshend was called to the Cabinet. He had attained his first objective.

The peerage was not so easily obtained. John, second Duke of Argyll, father of Caroline, widow of Francis, Earl of Dalkeith, and wife of Charles Townshend, had been created Duke of Greenwich in the peerage of Great Britain. He died in 1743 without male issue, when the dukedom of Greenwich became extinct while the dukedom of Argyll devolved on his brother. Townshend claimed that the King had promised him 'that the title of Greenwich should be settled on Lady Dalkeith and her male issue' by her second marriage, and considered this was 'a natural and favorable opportunity' of renewing his 'very earnest and anxious application'.[2] His brother, Lord Townshend, had solicited to be made a Marquess. 'I must press it at this juncture', wrote Charles to Grafton on October 10, 'least any mark of kindness shown to Lord Townshend should be construed to preclude me. . . .'[3]

[1] Grenville's Diary, August 16, 1766 ; *ibid.* p. 377.
[2] Townshend to Grafton, October 9, 1766 ; Grafton MS. 436.
[3] Grafton MS. 438.

George III, however, thought the peerage was already too large ; on Chatham's recommendation he created two British dukedoms and one Irish that autumn, but was not disposed to yield to further requests which brought no additional strength to Administration. At the end of the year Townshend was still disappointed, and Grafton continued to hear 'his daily train of grievances'.[1]

Conway, too, had personal grievances. He had accepted office in 1765 with regret at having to leave the Army, and in the hope that one day he would be able to return. The promotion of Lord Granby to be Commander-in-Chief reminded him that he was losing ground in his profession. Like Townshend, he addressed his complaints to Grafton, and so worried did Grafton become and so convinced that Conway's dissatisfaction might weaken the Ministry, that on October 9 he wrote to Chatham :

> I cannot be silent on another point, which I see, day after day more hangs on General Conway's mind. He is in a situation which really nothing but his good wishes for the public could make him go through ; so much does it differ from his natural turn, particularly as he sees himself secluded from his real profession, which no inducement will ever make him lose sight of. Unless he has some prospect of appearing in it on a proper footing, I am confident that he will remain an unhappy and a hurt man. I have so studied him on this point, that I assure you my opinion is truly, that business suffers from the ascendant which this disappointment works on his mind, and I beg to submit it seriously to your Lordship's consideration.[2]

Chatham's reply (October 11) was devoid of understanding or sympathy :

> The last paragraph of his Grace's letter, affords a very melancholy perspective, and if the purpose hinted at, be not at a very considerable distance, no eligible, or solid plan, for carrying on the King's business upon the true grounds, can be imagined.[3]

---

[1] Grafton, *Autobiography*, p. 105.
[2] *Chatham Correspondence*, iii. 100-2.
[3] Grafton MS. 590.

Grafton hastened to correct what he believed was a mis-understanding. Conway was not likely to resign his present post, but 'if he is honoured with some military one, enough to show that he has not quitted that line, his mind will be easy, and he will go on with his civil business with alacrity' (October 14).[1] Chatham's reply put an end to this attempt to set Conway's mind at rest (October 15) :

> What his Grace hints at the end of his letter is a matter fit for conversation alone. In the mean time, there being no example of such a union of functions, at one and the same time, the idea suggested must be subject to the utmost difficulties.[2]

This was Chatham at his worst, in his most unaccommodating mood, completely disregarding the feelings of those he hoped to work with, unable to lead men except by driving them. He made no attempt to weld together the collection of individuals who composed his Cabinet. They were heads of executive departments, not makers of a common policy. His Administration was already straining and creaking before it had existed six weeks, and before the great question of the forthcoming session, the East India inquiry, had yet been discussed.

The appointment of an Ambassador to Madrid to succeed Lord Rochford illustrates how difficult it was to work with Chatham. The post fell within Shelburne's department, but the appointment to an embassy of such importance could obviously not be made without Chatham's approval. Apparently Sir Joseph Yorke, Minister at The Hague and Lord Hardwicke's brother, was the first choice, and on October 6 Shelburne wrote to Chatham, then at Bath : 'Sir Joseph Yorke still declining Spain . . . I have sent to Lord Buckingham to return to town. . . .'[3] Buckinghamshire had been Ambassador at St. Petersburg and was connected with Grenville ; on October 7 he saw Shelburne and refused the Madrid embassy.

He did not mention all his reasons [wrote Shelburne to Chatham on October 8] but spoke of his connection with

---

[1] *Chatham Correspondence*, iii. 107-9.          [2] Grafton MS. 589.
[3] *Chatham Correspondence*, iii. 90-5. Misdated October 5.

Mr. Grenville, and that his connections in the House of Commons required his presence, they having suffered much while he was in Russia. . . .[1]

Shelburne continued :

The Spanish Ambassador of late has inquired almost daily about it. The Duke of Grafton, General Conway, and myself have, by the King's commands, consulted upon it . . . but without being able to hit upon any very proper person who is likely to accept it. Lord Hyde, Lord Grantham, and Sir James Gray were the only names that occurred. It is unnecessary to mention Lord Huntingdon or Lord Hillsborough, as they have offices here, which I should suppose they would prefer to it.

Chatham replied the following day suggesting Lord Huntingdon, Groom of the Stole, as 'extremely proper, every way, for an embassy of such importance'.[2] But Huntingdon declined, 'on account of his health not agreeing with that climate'.[3] At this Chatham, without much enthusiasm, recommended Sir James Gray. 'Nor, indeed,' he wrote to Shelburne on October 12, 'can this important matter admit of further delay.'[4]

At this point, after a fortnight's day-to-day discussions had failed to provide a suitable person, the unfortunate Conway took a hand. On October 18 Shelburne wrote to Chatham :

It had come round to the King, that if a nobleman was not sent to Spain, Prince Masserano would be recalled, in order to send a man of inferior rank. This, as well as other considerations, has made the King very desirous some nobleman should be found, and made General Conway think of Lord Hillsborough. I cannot say it met my idea . . . but as the King put it upon my saying, that his affairs might suffer by a delay of ten days . . . I did not think the objection of weight enough to urge it further. This matter therefore waits till Lord Hillsborough comes.[5]

[1] Shelburne to Chatham, October 8, 1766 ; *Chatham Correspondence*, ii. pp. 96-8. See also Buckinghamshire to Grenville, October 9, 1766 ; *Grenville Papers*, iii. 327-8.
[2] *Chatham Correspondence*, iii. 98-100.
[3] Shelburne to Chatham, October 11, 1766 ; *ibid.* pp. 104-5.
[4] *Ibid.* pp. 105-7.          [5] *Ibid.* pp. 113-15.

Conway's suggestion provoked from Chatham the following reply (October 19) :

> The idea of a change in the Board of Trade, by proposing the embassy to Spain to Lord Hillsborough was, I confess, the thing in the world the least expected by me. What are the motives to this desultory step, unfixing the most critical office in the kingdom, so happily fixed, through and by my channel, I cannot imagine. The favour I have to beg of your Lordship is, that when this offer is made to Lord Hillsborough his Lordship may be expressly told, that the proposal *does not come with my advice or suggestion.*

Then followed the portentous comment :

> I own this incident has made no small impression upon my mind, and gives abundant room to think that I am not likely to be of much use.[1]

What was it Chatham resented ?  Was it Conway's interference — or was it the King's ?  At any rate, his petulance reduced all to the required degree of compliance.  Shelburne wrote on October 28 :

> General Conway made not the least hesitation to give up all thoughts of the offer to Lord Hillsborough, the moment I told him your Lordship's opinion : the King likewise. . . .[2]

The end of the story is told by Walpole : 'Sir James Gray goes to Madrid.  The embassy has been sadly hawked about ; not a peer that would take it.'[3]

Two months later Chatham himself 'unfixed the most critical office in the kingdom' when he transferred Hillsborough from the Board of Trade to the Post Office.

## (v)

At the beginning of October Chatham set out for Bath, where he was soon joined by Northington and Camden.  The 'junior'

---

[1] *Ibid.* pp. 115-17.                    [2] *Ibid.* pp. 121-3.
[3] Walpole to Mann, October 26, 1766.  There was at least one peer who would have taken it.  Shelburne, in his letter to Chatham of October 28, says that Augustus Hervey told him 'in very great confidence' that Sandwich 'might be brought to take it', which 'might accelerate further arrangements'. But the offer had been already made to Gray.  See also p. 271.

Ministers remained in London to transact routine business, but both Grafton and Shelburne kept in close touch with Chatham. Shelburne informed him that Grafton was 'very diligent at the Treasury',[1] but Grafton's activities lay also in other fields. To him fell the delicate business of negotiating dukedoms for Lord Northumberland and Lord Cardigan, the one in lieu of a place, the other the result of an old promise.[2] The main business for the forthcoming session was to be the inquiry into the affairs of the East India Company, which Chatham intended as preliminary to a financial settlement between the Company and the Crown. Grafton, as head of the Treasury, handled the early negotiations with the directors of the Company,[3] but this matter did not start in earnest until Chatham returned to London, for no one knew what sort of settlement he wished to make.[4] It was not his way to confide in his colleagues ; nor does he appear ever to have determined what kind of a settlement he wanted.

Before Parliament met an attempt was made to strengthen Administration by taking in the Bedfords. Grafton knew that the Court lacked spokesmen in the Commons, and that the political groups, if only they acted together, would prove a formidable opposition. With Chatham in the Lords, his Administration was even weaker in debating talent in the Commons than the Rockinghams had been. On October 17 Grafton wrote :

> On thinking over the House of Commons, it appears that the ability among the leaders will be at least divided, if not

[1] Shelburne to Chatham, October 18, 1766 ; *Chatham Correspondence*, iii. 113-15.

[2] This is a good example of the influence Chatham had with the King at this time. George III created only three dukedoms (apart from Royal dukedoms) — those of Northumberland, Montagu, and Leinster (an Irish one) — all in the autumn of 1766.

[3] At the first meeting with the directors on August 28, Grafton, Conway, Shelburne, and Camden were present and, at Grafton's invitation, Townshend, although he was not yet of the Cabinet. His presence suggests that Grafton felt the need of someone more acquainted with 'business' than himself. See Grafton to Chatham, August 27, 1766 ; *Chatham Correspondence*, iii. 57-60.

[4] 'Lord Chatham never did open to us, what was his real and fixed plan.' Grafton, *Autobiography*, p. 110.

drawn up against the well-wishers to Administration ; though the numbers of the voters will be clear. . . . If the discontented are not in some measure broke into, I do see a strong phalanx of able personages, who will give full employment, by the business they will raise up.[1]

Chatham replied in a confident tone (October 19) : 'As to the phalanx your Grace mentions, I either am full of false spirits infused by Bath waters, or there is no such thing existing'.[2]

Chatham's confidence arose partly from disdain, partly from belief that the negotiation with the Bedfords, just now beginning, would provide extra strength for the Ministry, and rob the potential opposition of much of its sting. This negotiation was begun unknown to Grafton and apparently also to the King, though it must be presumed that Chatham had secured his approval before leaving for Bath. It was opened by Northington, who saw Bedford on October 19 and found him not unfavourable towards entering the Administration. Bedford declared he had 'no factious views', 'did not desire opposition, nor to weaken the hands of government', but 'would not derogate from those measures we had approved whilst in power'.[3] So far as it went this was a promising beginning, and when Bedford saw Lord Weymouth two days later Weymouth concurred in what had been said.

On October 24 Chatham saw Bedford and outlined the policy he intended to follow, paying the most tender regard to the Duke's susceptibilities :

He declared his wish to continue the present pacific situation of affairs in Europe ; that he would not advise the King to pay for or even court foreign alliances ; but that there was *a great cloud of power in the north*, which should not be

[1] *Chatham Correspondence*, iii. 110-12.
[2] Grafton, *Autobiography*, pp. 108-9. Camden was equally elated. On October 23 he wrote to Thomas Walpole : 'I am so dissipated by the diversions and so high spirited with the waters of this place that I cannot relish, as I ought, the gravity of business'. (Lullings MSS., in the possession of Mr. David Holland.) But Camden always tried to keep in step with Chatham.
[3] Bedford's Journal ; *Sir Henry Cavendish's Debates*, ed. by John Wright, i. 591-2. The MS. of this journal appears to be lost : it is not among the Woburn MSS.

neglected ; that he was for economical measures as much as anyone, but that the fleet must not be neglected ; that measures for the proper subordination of America must be taken ; that the militia must be sustained . . . that he had been sent for by no other intervention than that of Lord Northington.[1]

Every one of these points was designed to counter a possible objection or appeal to a known prejudice of the Duke's, and to put him in a receptive frame of mind for the concrete proposals which would follow. For it was on these concrete proposals, not on general policy, that the negotiation would succeed or fail, and on these Bedford might be influenced by the dissatisfaction of an important follower to reject the offer. There was less chance of this if he were sweetened beforehand.

No further step was taken during the next week, during which Bedford visited Weymouth at Longleat. Gower and Rigby were due to come, and when they arrived Bedford discussed the offer with them over dinner. It was decided to invite definite offers from Chatham, and on October 31 Bedford saw him again to elicit something more specific.[2] Chatham confirmed the statement of his policy made the week before, adding that he 'hoped it was not understood to intend any violent measure towards the Americans at this time, unless absolutely necessary', a qualification Bedford did not disapprove. When it came to discussing places and peerages, however, the negotiation stuck. Bedford's demands were high : 'employments of magnitude' for Weymouth, Gower, and Rigby, 'the rest who had suffered upon our accounts should be, as occasions offered, provided for', the Garter for Bedford's son-in-law the Duke of Marlborough, a peerage for Thomas Brand, and a hint of 'other applications' which would have to be considered. In short, Bedford was demanding that his group be restored to the privileged position they had held under Grenville.

Such a position could be attained only at the expense of the Rockinghams who had remained in Administration. Had Chatham been prepared to pay this price he could have won

---

[1] *Cavendish's Debates*, i. 592.        [2] *Ibid.* pp. 592-3.

the Bedfords, but in so doing he would lose as much as he
would gain.  There was, however, one great difference between
these two groups : the Bedfords asked to be admitted as equal
partners, the Rockinghams wished to be dominant.  But this
advantage was never considered by Chatham : faced with
pressure from a political group his reaction was, as a rule, to
dig in his toes, refuse all concessions, and retire to the vantage
ground of the King's unfettered right to choose his servants
and the duty of all men of goodwill to support his Administration.  But though disposed to admit the Bedfords, his offer was
not encouraging.

> Lord Chatham replied, with lamenting that there were hardly
> any vacancies, and that, the King having determined on a
> conciliating plan, those who would continue to act with them
> should not be removed. . . .

He offered to make Gower Master of the Horse if Portland
should resign,[1] Weymouth could be joint Postmaster-General
immediately, and something should be done to make Rigby
'easy'.[2]  Nothing was said about Marlborough's Garter,
Brand's peerage, or the claims of Bedford's other followers.
Chatham ended with the pious hope that the arrangement
might be concluded before the meeting of Parliament.

These terms stood no chance of being accepted.  Bedford
left his followers to make their own decision and they agreed
unanimously to reject them, but wished the rejection to be
made 'in such a way . . . as not to shew their dislike of re-
entering into the King's service, but that they must wait till the
bottom should be enlarged'.[3]  Chatham seemed genuinely
disappointed when Bedford told him on November 1 that his
group could not come in at present.  He warned the Duke
'that by not accepting at present, the bottom would be more
narrowed', and went out of his way to assure him that no 'secret

---

[1] Portland was Lord Chamberlain.  It had been decided that if he
should resign Lord Hertford, Master of the Horse, should have his staff.

[2] On October 31 Grafton told Portland that Chatham had offered to
call Gower to the Cabinet, to make Weymouth Postmaster-General and
Rigby Secretary at War.  (Portland to Newcastle, November 7, 1766 ;
Add. MS. 32977, ff. 336-9.)  This suggests that Grafton was ill-informed
of the proposed arrangements.        [3] *Cavendish's Debates*, i. 593.

influence' was exerted at Court and that if it was he would resist it. Bedford in turn warned Chatham against 'two particular connections', Bute's and Newcastle's, and they parted 'on exceeding good terms'.

There can be little doubt but that Chatham genuinely desired to win over the Bedfords. Why then did he try to do so on the cheap and thus run the risk of driving them back into the arms of Grenville ? *Plus royaliste que le roi*, he preferred to ignore the reality of party and to pretend that office was given by favour of the Crown, uninfluenced by considerations of party. He identified himself with the King and surveyed the political groups from the Throne. He fought faction as he had fought the French, but tried to overcome it by pretending it did not exist.

### (vi)

The thoughts of politicians were now turning towards the meeting of Parliament. That Grenville would oppose was never doubted by anybody : the only doubt was how many would follow him. Thomas Whately, formerly Grenville's Secretary to the Treasury and one of his staunchest supporters, wrote to him on October 20 about the prospects for opposition.[1] Much would depend on finding a popular topic but the outlook was not unfavourable : although both the friends of Rockingham and Bute held a moderate language, it would probably not be long before they drifted into opposition. 'Angry men cannot be long lukewarm ; parties cannot subsist in a state of indifference ; and the Session will probably furnish fair occasions enough for them to show their resentment.' There were hopes even of those in Administration : Lord North was conscious of 'the uneasiness of his situation', Charles Townshend's language was 'very discontented', opinions were divided on the part Sir Gilbert Elliot would take. But there was not a word about the Bedfords. However, Horace Walpole, a supporter of Administration, wrote on October 26 :

George Grenville will be very tiresome, and as teasing as tiresomeness can make him ; but I should think would not

[1] *Grenville Papers*, iii. 331-6.

be much supported. His friends the Bedfords rather look from him, and the dismissed part of the last Administration are inclined to lie still.[1]

In the eighteenth century politicians going into opposition, like kings going to war, had to produce some excuse, however specious, for their behaviour ; more than this, they had to convince themselves they were acting from principle in order to stimulate a righteous zeal. The Bedfords obviously could not go to Parliament on November 11 to oppose an Administration with whose principles they professed no quarrel and which they were hoping to join ten days before. Besides, they hoped and expected that Chatham would make another offer soon, and were prepared to fish for it if necessary.[2] So when Lord Lorne asked if Bedford wished him to be at the meeting of Parliament, the Duke replied there was no necessity for him to come.

I think we must be guided by events and by the measures the Administration shall adopt, as likewise by their inclination to be well or ill with us. I judge by what I have observed since I have been here [at Bath], that there is no disinclination towards us, nor any design to pursue measures derogatory to our way of thinking.[3]

When Rigby returned to London he called on Grenville. As no arrangement had yet been reached with Chatham it was too early to break with Grenville. Moreover, his help might be useful : should Chatham be tardy in making new and more favourable proposals a little spirited opposition at the commencement of the session might quicken him. So Rigby saw Grenville on November 6, and did all he could to minimize the importance of the recent negotiation and to renew the links between the two groups. 'He spoke slightingly of Lord Chatham', 'declared firmly and roundly that he would support

[1] To Sir Horace Mann.
[2] Rigby told Bedford on November 2 that he intended to see the Lord Chancellor, 'and discourse [with] him . . . without committing myself to him'. (Woburn MS., liv. f. 96.) Probably Rigby meant Northington, and forgot that he was no longer Lord Chancellor.
[3] Lorne to Bedford, October 23, 1766 ; Bedford to Lorne, October 31, 1766. *Ibid.* f. 88.

and maintain all his former opinions', told Grenville that Bedford 'was ready to oppose if he saw any ground held out to him to act upon' (probably true enough, but hardly a fair summary of Bedford's intentions), and that Bedford 'preferred Mr. Grenville to any man in England' (again probably true, but it had not stopped Bedford from negotiating with Chatham).[1] Nothing is reported by Grenville of the details of the conversations at Bath, or of Rigby's intention to sound Northington, and it seems probable that Rigby avoided discussing these matters, preferring to emphasize his group's solidarity with Grenville.

It is doubtful whether Grenville was deceived. If so, his conversation next day with Gower, who spoke 'with stronger symptoms of the Duke of Bedford and his party taking no active part', could have left him in little doubt that the Bedfords did not intend to go forthwith into opposition.[2] And in their conversation of November 9 Bedford cleared up all possibility of doubt. He informed Grenville of his talks with Chatham but did not go into details, and then spoke of the attitude he would take when Parliament met :

He thought the melancholy and disordered state of the kingdom such as required all the assistance it could receive ; that therefore he doubted whether he and his friends should disturb the government . . . that he himself should always adhere to and continue in the principles and opinions he had professed last year, but that as to the rest, the disturbing government might in the present exigence be a remedy worse than the disease.[3]

After this it was small comfort for Grenville to be told that 'it was his earnest wish to see him again at the head of Government'. The conversation ended :

When Mr. Grenville said that the Court laboured industriously to divide his Grace and his friends from him (Mr. Grenville), the Duke said how could it be otherwise, where their opinions differed.

[1] Grenville's Diary ; *Grenville Papers*, iii. 379-80.
[2] Grenville's Diary ; *ibid.* pp. 380-1.
[3] *Ibid.* p. 381. See also Bedford's account of this conversation in *Cavendish's Debates*, i. 593.

But the refusal of the Bedfords to go with Grenville did not make him give up his intention to oppose, especially since he had found a point on which he could rally some opinion to his side. It had been a poor harvest, and shortage of grain had led to riots in the southern and eastern counties. A Committee of the Privy Council, to which all members in the neighbourhood of London were summoned, decided to impose an embargo on the export of corn. The Duke of Newcastle had attended this meeting and had given his opinion emphatically in favour of the embargo. It was Grenville's contention, fortified by the advice of Lord Mansfield,[1] that this embargo was illegal, and that if it was necessary Parliament should have been summoned to consider the situation.

What forces had he to carry on this opposition ? Without the Bedfords he had to depend on former members of his Administration not yet satisfied by Chatham. Thus Sir Fletcher Norton professed to wish to act with Grenville, but although Norton's language was 'great anger and disgust at the ill-treatment he had met with', he 'did not seem inclined to take any active part'. Grenville found that those who had expectations from the Court were not inclined to support him : Jenkinson 'could not divide himself' from his patron Sir James Lowther who supported Administration, 'knowing no other person who would give him a seat'.[2]  In December Chatham appointed Jenkinson to the Admiralty Board, and he resumed his official career, interrupted by the Rockinghams in 1765 and to be interrupted by them again in 1782. Robert Nugent's language was 'so different' and 'seeming in opinions so contrary to Mr. Grenville's' that Grenville had to cross him off the list of his supporters.[3] Still, there was a fair band of stalwarts left and Grenville was to prove in the debates on the Indemnity Bill that he was, now that Pitt had taken a peerage, by far the most effective debater in the House of Commons.

The Rockinghams attended the Administration's eve of session meetings in full force, but not the Bedfords nor, of course, the Grenvilles. Rumours of fresh negotiations with

---

[1] Mansfield to Grenville, November 10, 1766 ; *Grenville Papers*, iii. 337-9.          [2] *Ibid.* p. 381.          [3] *Ibid.* p. 382.

the Bedfords were in the air, and it was the general opinion that they would soon enter the Administration. When the Address to the King's Speech was debated on November 11 Grenville proposed two amendments, condemning the embargo on the export of corn as illegal and regretting that Parliament had not been summoned earlier, but, meeting with no support except from his own group, did not press them to a division. Though his followers were few they were vocal : seven of them spoke in the debate, a larger number of speakers than Rockingham could have mustered.[1] It seemed that Walpole's forecast rather than Whately's was to prove true. Yet before Parliament rose for the Christmas recess Grenville had regained the initiative, the Administration had suffered a substantial loss of prestige in the Commons, and all three groups — Grenvilles, Bedfords, and Rockinghams — were in opposition. Whately was the better prophet after all.

### (vii)

Rockingham set out for Yorkshire in August,[2] highly discontented with Chatham, deeply suspicious of his intentions, yet not prepared for opposition. What reasons had he for discontent and how far were his suspicions genuine ?

Had Chatham treated Rockingham's followers as a privileged group, had he excluded from office all whom Rockingham and Newcastle had proscribed in 1765, and had he allowed Grafton and Conway a substantial share in the allotment of places — in short, had he smiled on those whom Rockingham favoured and frowned on those whom Rockingham disliked, Rockingham might have been satisfied. But probably not for long. Instead, Chatham showed a most disturbing tendency to go his own way, and refused to treat Rockingham's friends as a privileged group.

---

[1] The seven were : Simon Luttrell, Whately, James Harris, Thomas Pitt (Chatham's nephew), Henry Seymour (half-brother to Lord Sandwich), Lord Catherlough, and Wedderburn. But Luttrell soon left Grenville.

[2] There to receive addresses from the manufacturing towns of Yorkshire and Lancashire thanking him for his services to the manufacturing and trading community, addresses 'soon forgot by their makers', as Burke wrote on his copy (now among the Burke MSS. in the Northamptonshire Record Office).

Former followers of Bute were reinstated — Mackenzie to his old post of Keeper of the Privy Seal of Scotland (though without the disposal of Scottish patronage), Lord le Despenser to the Post Office ; or were highly favoured — Lord Northumberland was honoured with a dukedom. Hopes of office were held out to others as places became vacant. The friends of Bute, expelled by the Rockinghams the year before, were gradually returning.

It was this which caused the discontent, and it was the fear that this trend would accelerate which caused the suspicion. Rockingham was haunted by the belief that Bute was still a potent factor in government — 'the Minister behind the curtain' — able to influence policy and yet bearing no responsibility. It is true that Grenville and Bedford too had entertained such a suspicion, and still did so at times — witness Chatham's anxiety to reassure Bedford on this point during their negotiations at Bath. But with Grenville and Bedford the suspicion was dying, though it was to linger on for a little while yet : with Rockingham it increased until its patent absurdity convinced even him that it was not true.

What weakened suspicion of Bute's influence with Grenville and Bedford was their knowledge that had it been a reality Chatham was the last man to have tolerated it. But with Rockingham it was a deep, psychological necessity, necessary to explain the failures and enhance the triumphs of his own Administration. The repeal of the Stamp Act was a far more glorious victory if it could be represented as having been won against the opposition of an irresponsible yet almost omnipotent favourite. The failure of the Rockinghams to win the lasting confidence of the Commons was far less discreditable if it could be explained by the influence of Bute, acting through a small group of personal followers within the ranks of Administration, and with the connivance of the King himself. And when the Rockinghams went into an opposition originating in no conflict of principle it was far easier to justify it as directed against a pernicious violation of the constitution : an 'inner Cabinet' of 'King's friends' wielding the real power. The defection of Rockingham's followers to Chatham and Grafton might be

explained by their seduction by Bute ; the fidelity of those
who remained was enhanced as having withstood the tempta-
tions held out by Bute. Bute's influence explained everything :
as late as 1768 he was held responsible for the dismissal of
Sir Jeffery Amherst, and the Portland-Lowther struggle in
Cumberland was seen as a fight against Bute. Whenever
anyone wished to curry favour with Rockingham he talked of
'secret influence' behind the Throne. Thus Wedderburn in
1769,[1] Grenville in 1770,[2] and finally even Chatham [3] spoke in
Parliament of the 'secret influence' of Bute or the Princess
Dowager. Opposition to 'secret influence', springing originally
from Bute's friendship with the King, was the *raison d'être* of
the Rockingham party right up to 1782.

Grenville and Bedford had some justification for their
suspicion of Bute, for in 1763 his influence was a reality.
Between 1763 and 1765 it waned slowly. When the Rockinghams came to power the King gave a promise that he would
not permit Bute to interfere, a promise which he kept. By the
autumn of 1766 Bute's influence was at an end and all correspondence between him and the King had ceased. The
group known as 'Bute's friends', bereft of his leadership, ceased
to exist as an independent force. Some joined Chatham and
returned to the Court party, their natural home ; others, not
provided for, joined Grenville as the most congenial of the
party groups.

The Rockinghams believed themselves to be the one
group who could be relied upon to oppose Bute's influence,
and not to favour them was to favour Bute. The appointment
of Sir Charles Saunders, a friend of Lord Albemarle, was
tepidly commended by Rockingham as 'rather reconciliatory
towards us'.[4] But already — and this was only August 29 —
Rockingham was convinced that Chatham had surrendered to
Bute :

> I still continue anxious [he wrote to Newcastle] that we and
> our friends should be quiet — and that our only object should
> be to keep up a good humoured correspondence with those

[1] Walpole, *Memoirs*, iii. 231.      [2] *Ibid*. iv. 66-7.
[3] *Ibid*. pp. 62-3.      [4] Add. MS. 32976, ff. 488-9.

parts of the present system who were parts of ours. . . . I see nothing in a contrary conduct but confusion and in fact I believe we should answer Ld. Chatham's and Ld. Bute's views very effectually if we grow angry and disunite.

During the autumn, as Chatham showed no inclination to favour the Rockinghams, every action of his was represented in the most untoward manner, and trifles light as air became of the most serious import. Lord Monson, Chief Justice in Eyre North of Trent, was offered promotion in the peerage in exchange for his office.[1] He refused, and forwarded copies of the letters which had passed between him and Grafton to Rockingham and Newcastle. Rockingham commented, 'It both surprized and concerned me much', and off he went to complain to Conway.[2] But when Chatham offered to make Lord Scarbrough joint Postmaster-General, the debit he had incurred with respect to Monson was not compensated by a similar credit with respect to Scarbrough, though Scarbrough was the brother-in-law of Sir George Savile, and more closely connected with the party than Monson. Promotions of Rockingham's friends were taken for granted as proper ; dismissals or neglect of them were 'fresh instances of the sacrifice of our best friends'.[3]

On matters of policy Rockingham was silent : he had no criticisms to offer, policy did not interest him. One of Chatham's plans on coming to office was the creation of a

[1] But not, of course, in such direct terms : that was not Chatham's way. 'I hope I have not gone too far in my letter to Lord Monson', wrote Grafton to Chatham on October 9. 'I understood that to him there was not to be an offer of exchange from the place to an Earldom, but that I was to acquaint him that for the King's Service it was necessary that his place should be opened, that to prove it arose from no disregard *I had reason to think* a rise in the Peerage would be granted if desired by his Lordship.' (Part of this letter, but not the above sentences, is printed in *Chatham Correspondence*, iii. 100-2.) A copy of Grafton's letter to Monson is in Add. MS. 32977, f. 198. Cf. the manner in which a pension was offered to Newcastle on his retirement : 'the idea was only to *convey* your Majesty's generous *dispositions* to *make* an offer in case the Duke of Newcastle shou'd be willing to accept'. (Pitt to the King, July 29, 1766 ; Fortescue, I, no. 371.)

[2] Rockingham to Newcastle, October 8, 1766 ; Add. MS. 32977, ff. 213-14. Dated 'Tuesday noon : 3 o'clock. Oct. the 8th 1766.' Tuesday should be Wednesday.

[3] Newcastle to Rockingham, October 7, 1766 ; *ibid.* f. 201.

triple alliance between Great Britain, Prussia, and Russia, to counterbalance the Family Compact of France and Spain. It is significant that the King, although he disliked Frederick of Prussia and abhorred the thought of an alliance with him, consented to Chatham's plan. Hans Stanley was named Ambassador to Russia, but, before he set out, preliminary inquiries were made at Berlin to test Frederick's disposition. The plan was soon abandoned : Frederick, with Poland almost ripe for partition, desired a good understanding with Russia, while Russia would conclude no treaty with Britain which did not make a Turkish war a *casus foederis*. It was a legitimate criticism of Chatham's policy that by attempting the alliance with Prussia and Russia he had neglected the possibility of a *rapprochement* with Austria, a criticism voiced by Egmont and Conway. Shortly before the King sent for Chatham Conway had assured the Austrian Ambassador that no negotiations with Prussia were contemplated ; now he begged Chatham (in vain) to wait 'some few days . . . to digest this matter'.[1] But Rockingham had no comment to make on this sudden change in foreign policy, nor on the way it was to be effected : the subject is never mentioned in his letters. Newcastle alone of his correspondents was sufficiently interested or informed to discuss foreign affairs :[2] 'men not measures' was Rockingham's concern.

(viii)

It was not surprising, therefore, that, when the break came between Chatham and Rockingham, it should be over a personality rather than a policy.

During the last years of Newcastle's life, when his power had gone and nearly all his former friends and dependants had left him, there was no one whose loss he deplored more than that of his nephew and heir, Lord Lincoln, or whose desertion roused so much bitterness and anger than that of John Shelley, M.P. for East Retford, also a nephew of Newcastle. Both

[1] Conway to Chatham, July 29, 1766 ; *Chatham Correspondence*, iii. 15-19.
[2] See his letter to Rockingham, September 17, 1766 ; Add. MS. 32977, ff. 91-5.

Lincoln and Shelley were typical of many who had passed their political lives under Newcastle's wing, and for whom the words Pelham and Administration were synonymous. When Newcastle resigned in 1762 they, like many others, had to find their way on the sea of politics without their familiar helmsman. Opposition was a game they had never played and could not learn : support of Administration was the only political principle they knew. Newcastle's ineptitude in opposition, the smallness of his following, their lack of unity, and the realization that the future lay with other men, caused many of his former followers to try to find their way back to Court on their own, and along devious and uncharted paths. Lincoln and Shelley had joined Pitt, judging that his return to power was more probable than that of their uncle.

Such conduct was not unnaturally resented by Newcastle as base treachery. There was much to be said for his point of view. No eighteenth-century politician was more reproached for his perfidy and broken promises, yet he was kind and even generous, slow to take lasting offence and quick to forgive insults and injuries, of which he had to endure many. But he promised too much to too many people, which was almost as bad as promising too little. Moreover, his followers soon learnt that bullying and threatening, even from the humblest, were surer ways to favour than reminders of past services and promises of future loyalty. To those connected with the Pelham family or seated in the county of Sussex Newcastle was generous indeed, but with a generosity which his age did not reproach. He had given lucrative sinecures to both his nephews : Lincoln was joint Comptroller of the Customs of London and Auditor of the Exchequer ('the amplest sinecure in England, except the Archbishoprick of Canterbury', wrote Walpole [1]) ; Shelley was Clerk of the Pipe and Keeper of the Records in the Tower of London. Newcastle had obtained from George II a second dukedom (the only one that monarch ever gave [2]), with a special remainder to Lincoln, and to him the Duke had leased the manor of Newark and, in effect, his

---

[1] *Memoirs*, i. 188.
[2] Apart from those to the royal family.

E

electoral interest in the borough.[1]  In short, both nephews had been particularly favoured by Newcastle, and his bitterness at their desertion is very human and understandable. There is also much to be said for the nephews. Newcastle was a nuisance and a bore to his friends and relatives. His jealousies, his fears, his childish suspicions, his craving for company at Claremont, his resentment on suspecting that anything was being hidden (a suspicion from which not even his most devoted followers and most faithful friends were exempt), were trying and contemptible, and were even worse in opposition than in office. He would have been wiser to have recognized, as did his ablest adviser, Lord Hardwicke, that his age and the advent of a new King made his retirement from politics desirable. But Newcastle had no children : he could not, like Hardwicke, stand aside and be content to see his children make their way in the new reign. At seventy-three he found no peace except in the bustle of politics, and he remained an active politician until the last year of his life. His former followers gradually found their way back to Court, and the old Duke ended his days a lonely and pathetic figure, with men who had never shared his greatness and neither understood nor cared for him.

Still, it was both unrealistic and hardly fair to friends with many years of active political life before them to expect them to follow him into an opposition based on no political principle and with little hope of a return to Court. Those who did so welcomed 1765 as the restoration of the years of plenty ; and in 1766 Newcastle's disavowal of opposition to the new Ministry gave them an opportunity to remain in office without an unpleasant breach with their former chief and benefactor. That it was possible to serve under Chatham and yet remain on good terms with Newcastle is shown by the examples of George Onslow (his nephew by marriage) and Thomas Pelham (the heir to Newcastle's barony of Pelham of Stanmer and to his estates in Sussex), who retained their places in 1766 and the Duke's friendship to the day of his death. But neither Lincoln nor Shelley would take the trouble to humour Newcastle

[1] Abstract of the lease of the manor of Newark ; Add. MS. 33060, f. 196.

or to make allowance for his oddities, which would have been
only a decent recompense for his generosity.

Chatham had promised to make Shelley Treasurer of the
Household, a post which in 1765 had been given to Lord
Edgcumbe. Newcastle knew of this as early as August 14,
but his concern was not for Edgcumbe but for Thomas
Pelham, who held the inferior place of Comptroller of the
Household.[1] Conway too knew of Chatham's intention and
felt himself involved, since Edgcumbe had been a friend of
Conway's late patron, the Duke of Devonshire. He did not
object to the change, provided Edgcumbe were suitably
compensated. Grafton attempted to persuade Chatham to
make Shelley's promotion less unaccommodating to the
Rockinghams, but he pleaded feebly and with subserviency
(September 26) :

> I was told at Court (and really mention it only to give
> information, quite easy on the determination), that the
> Treasurer's staff vacant was never offered to another before
> the Comptroller had had the compliment of it ; provided
> they both sat in the same house of Parliament. Perhaps the
> pure offer of it would be esteemed greatly, when in fact they
> are so near in value and in dignity, that either would be
> indifferent to a new person.[2]

Chatham's reply (a PS. to his letter of September 27) ended
this attempt at moderation : 'The Treasurer of the Household's staff, having been so long fixed, and communicated to
the party, a change in it would not be proper or practicable'.[3]

Chatham offered to make Edgcumbe a Lord of the Bedchamber as compensation for the loss of his staff : the difference
in salaries was small, but the loss of standing involved in such
a change was great. Only Chatham would have made such a
proposal, and only he would have resented its refusal as an
affront to the King. Edgcumbe received the notice of his
dismissal on November 17, and Conway was informed by

[1] Newcastle to Rockingham, August 14, 1766 ; Add. MS. 32976, ff.
413-14.
[2] Grafton to Chatham, September 26, 1766 ; *Chatham Correspondence*,
iii. 79-82.                                        [3] Grafton MS. 592.

Chatham the same day.[1] Conway immediately protested :
the Bedchamber was not the equivalent for which he had
stipulated, declared himself 'much distressed and hurt',
hinted at resignation, and represented 'the offence that will
. . . be given to a set of gentlemen of great weight in this
country' whom he had expected 'that far from being the objects
of particular neglect or resentment . . . would rather . . .
meet the favour and protection of government'.[2]  This last
argument, far from dissuading Chatham, was more likely to
confirm him in the course he had taken.  Sure of the King's
support, he could afford to be haughty towards the politicians.

That same evening Conway saw Rockingham, and dis-
culpated himself of all responsibility for Chatham's action.[3]
Rockingham reviewed the cases of Lord Monson and Lord
Scarbrough : they were 'strong overt acts' which 'justified
our warmth'.[4]  Conway agreed, declared he felt himself ill-
treated, 'wished himself out, but doubted whether he could
be justified in throwing the King's affairs into *confusion*' by
his resignation.  That was precisely what Rockingham hoped
would happen, but he knew Conway too well even to hint at
his desire.  Rather it was his task to play on Conway's unconcealed dissatisfaction and uneasiness, to suggest his obligations
to his friends, and to make him overlook those to the Crown.
It was a delicate game to play with so nice a man, and
Rockingham was far too heavy-handed.  He failed : at the

---

[1] Both Walpole (*Memoirs*, ii. 267) and Rockingham (Albemarle, ii. 19)
represent Conway as having heard accidentally of Edgcumbe's dismissal,
though their accounts differ.

[2] Conway's letter to Chatham is in *Chatham Correspondence*, iii. 126-9,
under the date of November 22.  This is the editor's dating and is incorrect : it should be November 17.  The postscript, which enables the
letter to be correctly dated, is omitted.

[3] Rockingham's account of his conversation with Conway is given in his
letter to Scarbrough of November 21, 1766 (misdated by Rockingham
November 20), Rockingham Papers, R1-441.  Part of it is incorrectly
printed in Albemarle, ii. 19-24.  Rockingham writes that Conway asked
to see him ; Walpole (*Memoirs*, ii. 267) implies that Rockingham sought
this conversation.  But Walpole did not wish to represent Conway as under
any obligations to Rockingham.

[4] It is not clear how Rockingham convinced himself that the transfer
of Scarbrough from an office worth £500 per annum to one worth £2000
plus perquisites would have been a 'strong overt act'.

critical moment loyalty to the Crown rather than to party prevailed.

On November 19 a grand council of the Rockingham party was held in Grosvenor Square.[1] It was there decided :

That something must be done to shew spirit, to keep our friends together, and to encourage Mr. Conway to persist in the good disposition he was in at present ; that if nothing was done the party and all the friends of the late Administration would be weeded out by degrees, our friends angry and discouraged, and everything left to the arbitrary dispositions of my Lord Chatham. . . .

Rockingham, Richmond, John Cavendish, White, and Burke were for resignations as 'necessary to show Mr. Conway the support he would have'.[2] Newcastle (apparently with the approval of Portland and Bessborough) doubted if they would achieve much good.[3] But Rockingham's 'rashness and warmth'

[1] Present 'at some part of the day' : Richmond, Newcastle, Portland, Rockingham, Albemarle, Dartmouth, Bessborough, Grantham, John Cavendish, White, Dowdeswell, and Edmund Burke. Of these Dartmouth and Grantham soon ceased to play any part in the affairs of the opposition. For Newcastle's account of this meeting, see Add. MS. 32978, ff. 1-5. Rockingham's account is given in his letter to Scarbrough of November 21. Rockingham says little of Newcastle's opposition to the resignations ; Newcastle much. Rockingham also says that the meeting took place at George Onslow's house in Curzon Street ; Newcastle, that it took place at Rockingham's house in Grosvenor Square. When Newcastle came to London he used Onslow's house as his 'dressing place', and in his letter of November 18 (Add. MS. 32977, ff. 417-18) had asked Rockingham to send John Cavendish or 'any other friend' to meet him there and inform him what arrangements had been made for the 'grand council'. So some preliminary conversation may have taken place at Onslow's. But it would be the last touch of absurdity if the meeting at which the Rockinghams decided to go into opposition had been held at the house of one of the Lords of the Treasury. Newcastle, moreover, is more reliable than Rockingham in these matters.

[2] For Richmond and Burke, see Walpole, *Memoirs*, ii. 269-70 ; for Cavendish, see Newcastle to Bessborough, November 22, 1767 (Add. MS. 32978, ff. 35-6) ; for White, see Bessborough to Newcastle, November 24, 1766 (*ibid.* f. 59). Newcastle joins Dowdeswell with Burke as having too much influence over Rockingham. But Dowdeswell, while apparently approving of the resignations, thought that as a 'plan concerted by the party' they would be 'ineffectual' and be 'disavowed', nor was his influence with Rockingham yet decisive. See his letter to Rockingham of November 20, 1766 ; Rockingham Papers, R1-450.

[3] Newcastle believed Portland had 'his doubts upon the measure' ; Bessborough's moderation is apparent from his later behaviour.

(as he himself expressed it) carried the day, and it was decided that Portland, Scarbrough, Bessborough, and Monson, as 'persons of the first quality and consideration', should resign; 'farther resignations in the House of Commons might follow afterwards'.[1] Thus 'spirit' would be shown, Conway would be supported, and Chatham must 'either treat our friends better or retire'. If Conway resigned, Chatham, with no reliable Minister in the House of Commons, would be unable to carry on; if Conway secured Edgcumbe's reinstatement, Rockingham would become in effect the 'disposer' of employments.

Newcastle opposed resignations on two grounds : he did not believe the example set by the peers would be followed by the commoners, and in any case thought that Conway would disapprove of them and would 'think himself in honor the more obliged to stand by and act with my Lord Chatham's Administration' ; nor did he believe that Chatham would give up if Rockingham's friends resigned, but would try to take in fresh allies — the Bedfords or even the Grenvilles.[2] Rockingham, however, 'did not quite assent to the supposition that *if* Mr. Conway staid all our friends would', and believed that if Conway went 'no one thought that a single friend of our's would remain'. Yet on November 24 Newcastle was told by Onslow that neither Onslow himself, nor Thomas Townshend junior, nor 'Spanish' Charles Townshend would resign, and that even Sir William Meredith was doubtful what part to take.[3] And on the following day, Newcastle wrote that

[1] On November 18 Rockingham had suggested to Newcastle that he should refuse to re-elect Shelley at East Retford (Add. MS. 32977, ff. 415-16). Newcastle seemed disposed to agree (see the draft of his letter to Shelley, November 18, *ibid*. f. 413), consulted Portland and White (*ibid*. f. 419), and finally got Onslow to write to Shelley that 'the Duke of Newcastle does not intend to oppose Mr. Shelley's re-election' (*ibid*. f. 437). It seems clear that Portland and White, more cognizant of affairs in Nottinghamshire than Newcastle, did not encourage him to take violent measures.

[2] 'I am afraid our good friend the Marquess is too much set upon *resignations*, and flatters himself with such immediate success as I own I can have no notion of. He supposes Lord Chatham will resign in *two days* ; he does not know my Lord Chatham. . . .' Newcastle to Bessborough, November 22, 1766 ; Add. MS. 32978, ff. 35-6.

[3] Newcastle to Portland, November 24, 1766 ; *ibid*. f. 52.

Sir Henry Bridgeman (M.P. for Ludlow) 'talked to me very strongly against resignations'.[1] Rockingham later admitted that his 'old friends' had disappointed him, and that their conduct had been 'provocative'.[2] In the end only three commoners resigned — Sir Charles Saunders, Admiral Keppel, and Meredith — all members of the Admiralty Board.

On the morning of November 21 Portland saw Conway to announce the intended resignations.[3] Portland began by complaining of Chatham's treatment of 'the party' as 'one continued plan of ingratitude and oppression of which I instanced many examples' (presumably Monson and Scarbrough). He recited the virtues of the Rockinghams which entitled them to a very different treatment : 'our patience and forbearance'; 'unasked and unsolicited we had from principle supported government'; 'the rank, the character and influence of the persons who composed this party'. Conway 'could not deny any one of the assertions . . . allowed the provocation and objected to nothing but our precipitancy . . . and beg'd the execution of our determination might be suspended'. On this Portland agreed to defer the resignations till Monday (November 24), provided that suitable terms were agreed to by Chatham. These terms were :

that the satisfaction to Lord Edgcumbe must be *immediate*, that assurances must be given to the party of regard, respect and countenance, that they must stand as forward to be provided for as any other persons whatever, and that he [Conway] must be admitted to that confidence and those communications which could alone give us security for any promises that might be made in the present exigency. . . .

Conway promised to do his best, Grafton was willing to co-operate, and there was reason to think 'that an accommodation might be affected [*sic*]'.

No Minister could have agreed to such an ultimatum, least of all one so imperious as Chatham and possessing to such a

---

[1] Newcastle to Rockingham, November 25, 1766; *ibid.* f. 62.
[2] Rockingham to Dowdeswell, September 9, 1767; Rockingham Papers, R1-551.
[3] Portland to Newcastle, November 21, 1766; Add. MS. 32978, ff. 11-12.

degree the King's confidence. To have done so would have meant yielding his place to Rockingham and admitting the Rockinghams to be the dominant group within the Administration. Rockingham would have determined what amount of 'regard, respect and countenance' his followers were to receive, and it would have been Rockingham who would have been admitted to 'that confidence and those communications'. Out of place, he would yet have been the real power in the Administration : a 'Minister behind the curtain' with an 'inner Cabinet'. Chatham was to be reduced to the part of a nominal Minister, the King's right to choose his servants was to be set aside, and Conway was to be deprived of all power of independent action and confined to the rôle of Rockingham's lieutenant.

But on the day when Rockingham's ultimatum was presented its success was jeopardized by one of his own followers, and had Chatham been able to seize the unexpected opportunity he might have scored an undeserved triumph. Lord Bessborough, joint Postmaster-General, one of the more intelligent and moderate of Rockingham's followers, hit upon a way out of the difficulty which would at the same time satisfy Edgcumbe and enable Chatham to save his face. On the morning of November 21 Bessborough went to Rockingham and offered to resign his own place to Edgcumbe and take the Bedchamber instead. Rockingham dismissed the idea — 'it would not answer any one purpose' — but apparently did not take Bessborough seriously.[1] Bessborough went to Edgcumbe with his proposal and Edgcumbe, ambitious of obtaining the Post Office,[2] conveyed the suggestion to Conway. Conway welcomed this opportunity of settling the affair and eagerly told Chatham of Bessborough's 'very handsome' and 'accommodating offer'.[3] But before the day was over Conway learnt that such moderation would satisfy neither of his masters. Rockingham repudiated the suggestion 'that such a plaister

---

[1] Rockingham to Newcastle, November 22, 1766; Add. MS. 32978, ff. 23-5.

[2] Newcastle to Portland, November 24, 1766; *ibid.* f. 53.

[3] Conway to Chatham, November 21, 1766 ; *Chatham Correspondence,* iii. 130. Misdated November 25.

would cure the wounds of the affronts we had received', and demanded 'more concessions' and 'ample security to our friends'.[1] But Rockingham need not have worried : Chatham was also eager that moderation should fail. In the phrase attributed to him by Walpole, 'he would not suffer connections to force the King',[2] or in Townshend's more moderate words, 'a motive of accommodation seems to have been construed into a plan of authority, and what was designed to express good humor and prevent connexion has been disliked as stipulation and presumption'.[3] Far from being the peace-maker, the unhappy Conway was compelled to tell Rockingham that Monson also was to be removed.

On November 27 the Rockinghams resigned, Keppel being also dismissed from his post as Groom of the Bedchamber. Chatham commented characteristically to Saunders 'that it was of little consequence . . . who carried a white staff, but that was not the case of those who were employed in such important stations as the head of the Admiralty'.[4] But then why did Chatham insist on a white staff for Shelley ?

Seven resignations were not sufficient to bring Chatham down : more were required, and from men of 'business', if that was to be done. Yet Rockingham had secured the retirement of all he could influence : those still in office were Newcastle's friends rather than his, and were not easily persuaded to sacrifice themselves. Some friction occurred between Newcastle and Rockingham over this question. Rockingham was disappointed because there were so few resignations and was annoyed that Newcastle had been proved right and he wrong. 'Your Grace well knows', he wrote to Newcastle on December 4, 'how many of your friends divide their affection and let Lord Chatham in for part'.[5] It was true,

---

[1] Add. MS. 32978, ff. 23-5.   [2] *Memoirs*, ii. 270.
[3] Townshend to Grafton, November 21, 1766 ; *Autobiography*, pp. 103-104. Apparently even the King 'expressed his concern that his [Bessborough's] generous offer . . . had not been received'. See Newcastle's memorandum of the meeting of November 27 ; Add. MS. 32978, ff. 131-3.
[4] *Ibid.* f. 133. Newcastle described this as 'a most impertinent and silly reflection'.
[5] *Ibid.* ff. 168-9.

but Newcastle could do little about it. No doubt he would have been flattered had his friends and relations resigned, but he had learnt something from the experience of 1762 and would not put pressure on them. Nor, had he done so, would he have succeeded.[1]

The dispute was fought out over Thomas Pelham, whose 'honour' was held to be compromised by the appointment of Shelley over his head, and who therefore became a test case. On December 2 he saw Rockingham and told him :

> That were I a single man it wou'd signify but little to me the keeping my place, and that I shou'd readily resign to follow those to whom and to whose principles I shou'd ever profess myself attached, but that as a father of seven children I thought I was not at liberty to put myself out of all power of providing for them. That it was impossible I shou'd be happy which ever part I took, either to resign or remain in office, for that the Court was greatly altered to me as the part I valued the most in my office, that of waiting on his Majesty in private, was taken from me, and the Duke of Portland, whom I allways looked upon as a protection to me, had resigned. . . . His Lordship said he cou'd not pretend to advise, not being certain whether my remaining in was the sure way of providing for my children, that Mr. Dowdeswell had twelve children and had refused a place of £3,000 per annum, and that he thought it very likely I and many other of our friends who remained in might be turned out. I told him . . . that unless I cou'd be assured that his Lordship and the Duke of Portland were convinced that tho' I remained in office I was in no one article changed from what I had ever been, and that I had not in the least forfited their good opinion I wou'd not remain a moment, for that I knew my own feelings so well, were I ever to hear myself by chance accused of ingratitude towards them I cou'd never after hold up my head. His Lordship said he shou'd certainly never think that of me.[2]

---

[1] Newcastle believed he could persuade Lord Gage to resign, 'but he would say afterwards the Duke of Newcastle had made him do a *damned silly* thing'. (Newcastle to Rockingham, December 5, 1766 ; *ibid*. ff. 185-6.) Newcastle's belief was not well-founded : Gage wanted a British peerage, and the way to get one was not by following Rockingham.

[2] Pelham to Newcastle, December 4, 1766 ; *ibid*. ff. 172-3.

As Pelham plaintively put it to Newcastle, 'since I cou'd not drown my seven children I was obliged to take care of them'.[1] Newcastle thought the same, and so did Portland ; [2] Rockingham, therefore, with bad grace, gave up the attempt. 'But', he wrote to Newcastle on December 4, 'I hope that because I did *not advise him* to resign it is not constru'd or represented as *advising* him *not* to resign.'[3] Pelham continued to hold office until 1782.

On November 25, 1766, on the motion for a committee to inquire into the state of the East India Company, the Rockinghams voted for the first time against Chatham's Administration, and thus began a period of opposition which ended only with the fall of Lord North in 1782. United with the followers of Bedford and Grenville, they seemed almost strong enough in 1767 to bring down the faint-hearted Grafton, but after the defection of the Bedfords in December 1767, the excitement of the Wilkes affair in 1768, and the failure of the petitioning movement in 1769, their enthusiasm gradually evaporated until on the eve of the American war even the stoutest and most irreconcilable began to despair. The disasters of the American war brought to their side true converts, camp followers, and fellow-travellers, until in March 1782 they were strong enough to be the only alternative to North. The American war not only swelled their numbers, it gave them a policy and a cause, which brought them posthumous renown in the nineteenth century. Yet the Rockinghams did not go into opposition to resist the alleged unconstitutional power of George III or for more liberal treatment for the American colonies. When they began their opposition the King had surrendered his political power into the hands of a Minister who had been their ally in the repeal of the Stamp Act, and had even denied to Great Britain the right to tax her colonies. The Rockinghams went into opposition because that Minister, rash and arrogant, had

---

[1] *Ibid.*

[2] Newcastle to Rockingham, December 4, 1766 ; *ibid.* f. 166.

[3] *Ibid.* ff. 168-9. In fact Pelham had narrowly escaped the loss of his place. One of the terms Chatham proposed to Bedford had been to restore Lord Charles Spencer to his former office, now held by Pelham. See below, p. 63.

dismissed one of their number from office : they broke with
him on no grounds of principle or policy, and they were ready
to coalesce against him with the men who had opposed their
American policy only the year before.  But during this period
of opposition they devised principles and the logic of events
forced a policy upon them, neither of which influenced their
behaviour in November 1766.

(ix)

On November 20, Lord Hardwicke, conveying the latest
rumours of negotiations with the Bedfords, wrote to Rockingham :

> At first *sight* it does not seem probable that Lord *Chatham*
> would *brusque* the Duke of Newcastle's and your Lordship's
> friends in the manner he does, without having a resource
> from another quarter.[1]

Hardwicke did not realize the full extent of Chatham's *hauteur* :
in the space of a fortnight he contrived to 'brusque' both
Rockingham and Bedford and made possible their coalition
against him.

Since the breakdown of the negotiations at Bath at the
beginning of November the Bedfords had held aloof from
Administration, waiting to see what turn events would take
when Parliament met.  Hoping for another offer from Chatham,
they refused to join Grenville in opposition at the beginning
of the session.  But there was one among them who did not
care for this policy of waiting on events and sought to hasten
Chatham's offer by making mischief in the Commons.  Unlike
Gower, who was friendly with Grafton, Rigby had no links
with Administration but strong ones with Grenville.  He had
already indicated to Grenville his wish for opposition,[2] and
confirmed it by voting against the Court on November 25.  He
was quite as eager as Gower or the Duchess of Bedford to
return to Court, and had no scruples about forsaking Grenville
when the time was ripe, but, judging that Chatham's terms

---

[1] Rockingham Papers, R1-449.
[2] Grenville's Diary, November 11, 1766 ; *Grenville Papers*, iii. 382-4.

would not be sufficiently high, preferred the game of political blackmail, using Grenville as a cat's-paw. But Rigby's policy was temporarily out of favour with the Duke : it needed another eccentricity from Chatham to bring it back again. This was soon supplied.

The keen nose of Lord Sandwich had already begun to sniff what was in the air. On November 28 he wrote to Bedford from Hinchingbrooke, reminding the Duke of his 'political attachments' :

> Nothing has since happened to make me alter my opinion of men and things, and I flatter myself your Grace will consider me among the number of your friends, whither [sic] attack or defence is the plan you mean to pursue.
> I will only add one word more, which is that I find that views of ambition are not so violent after a man is past 48 as before that period, and that therefore I shall not be so burthensome to you as I should have been while the blood in my veins flowed with greater warmth.[1]

Sandwich's information was good : Chatham saw Gower on the evening of November 27,[2] who set out for Woburn the following day, whither Rigby had preceded him. Chatham's terms were almost the same as those he had offered in October : Gower was to be Master of the Horse (in place of Hertford, who had succeeded Portland as Lord Chamberlain), Weymouth joint Postmaster-General, and Rigby 'should likewise be provided for' to Bedford's satisfaction. Apart from a proposal to restore Lord Charles Spencer to his place of Comptroller of the Household, no definite offer was made to any other of the Bedfords, who had to be satisfied with the intention 'to deal the favors of the Crown with an equal hand to those who should have abilities and power to serve it'.[3]

Bedford and Gower thought this 'the properest opening we are likely to have', but others of their connection could not be expected to take such a favourable view. Although

---

[1] Woburn MS., liv. f. 112.
[2] Chatham to the King, November 27, 1766 ; Fortescue, I, no. 424.
[3] Bedford to Marlborough, November 29, 1766 ; *Bedford Correspondence*, iii. 355-6.

Sandwich's 'views of ambition' were 'not so violent' they would hardly have been satisfied with the vague promise of possible future favour. Marlborough was disappointed at only receiving a distant assurance of the Garter, thought little of the offer of a stick at Court for his brother,[1] and wanted to know what was to be done for Mr. Keck.[2] Nothing was promised to the peerage hunters, Lord Lorne, Lord Garlies, and Thomas Brand. But most important of all, the offer to Rigby was so contemptuously phrased and so tinged with threats that it sharpened his distrust of Chatham and increased his partiality for Grenville.[3] Rigby was now at Woburn and able to influence the Duke ; but his arguments were of no avail against those of the Duchess and her brother,[4] and he had gloomily to admit to Grenville that the Duke was coming to town to conclude a treaty which 'disgraced and dishonoured' the Bedfords 'for ever'.[5]

Chatham had seven places vacant with which to win over the Bedfords. It is true that he had already given one of the plums to Hertford, but there was a Cabinet office vacant (the head of the Admiralty), two further seats at that Board, and

[1] Marlborough to Bedford, November 30, 1766 ; *ibid.* pp. 356-8. Spencer refused the offer because the expenses of re-election and the fees payable on entering office would amount to a year's income, 'so that I should be out of pocket by it which I could by no means afford if I were not to keep it that time'. But he emphasized that these disadvantages only applied to '*this* place'. See his letter to Bedford, November 30, 1766 ; Woburn MS., liv. f. 120.

[2] Anthony Tracy Keck, M.P. for Woodstock. He was given a secret service pension of £600 per annum in 1760, but lost it in 1765. See L. B. Namier, *The Structure of Politics at the Accession of George III*, pp. 559-60.

[3] Chatham wrote to Grafton on November 26 : 'I doubt much whether Mr. Rigby is even, after yesterday's vote, admissible : if he is, it is as much as can be said, and that only on condition of another conduct'. Grafton MS. 586.

[4] Walpole told Grafton (and he was probably correct) that Lord Tavistock and Lord Upper Ossory favoured accepting Chatham's terms. His letter, dated 'Monday morning' [December 1, 1766], is *ibid.* 779.

[5] Grenville's Diary, December 1, 1766 ; *Grenville Papers*, iii. 391-2. At this time, when Rigby saw little prospect of getting what he wanted from Administration, he naturally drew closer to Grenville and emphasized their solidarity. He told Grenville that he had begged to be excused from taking office till the end of the session, but that Bedford had said 'he would not hear of that'. Rigby was such a convincing dissembler that it is difficult to gauge the truth of this.

the offices of Master of the Horse, Cofferer, joint Postmaster-General, and Chief Justice in Eyre. These, together with the promise of the Garter for Marlborough, peerages whenever any were made (there was no general creation of peerages until 1776), and one or two pensions, would have brought in the Bedford group, added a substantial voting strength to Administration, and checked the plans for a united opposition which were already forming in some minds. Rigby's dissatisfaction need not be taken too seriously.

> If a place is given to him [Walpole wrote to Grafton on December 1] the Duke of Bedford will make him of course vote for whatever his Grace and Lord Gower shall vote, and I shou'd think the Duke wou'd take it kind to have no mention made of past transactions ; and any altercations may produce difficulties, which considering the Duke's present amicable disposition, are not likely otherwise to arise. Mr. Rigby will be as good a courtier as any body when once in place.[1]

But Chatham seems to have decided that the Admiralty was no longer to be merely one of the prizes of the political game : no mention was made of the seats vacant there in his conversation with Gower on November 27 and the First Lord's place, for which Gower was deemed so suitable in August, was now given to Sir Edward Hawke. It was to Chatham's credit that he should wish to see the Board of Admiralty composed of seamen and 'men of business' ; but it was folly to dispose of the one available Cabinet office without informing Bedford. Only three of the Bedfords were to be provided for, the rest were dependent on Chatham's favour. Instead of attempting to win their confidence, to soften present disappointments with the hope of future benefits, Chatham treated the negotiation as an act of grace and favour on the part of the Crown, the consequences of which were immaterial.

> Unions, with whomsoever it be [he wrote to Grafton on November 26], give me no terrors : I know my ground : and I leave them to indulge their own dreams. If they can

[1] Grafton MS. 779.

conquer, I am ready to fall . . . *faction will not shake the Closet, nor gain the publick.*[1]

'Unions' may have had no terrors for Chatham, but Grafton, a prey to timidity and irresolution, was almost jostled out of his seat by faction before six months were past.

Bedford reached London at five o'clock in the afternoon of December 1, and discussed the position with some of his friends.[2] Did he resent Chatham's refusal to confide in him ? Letters from two of the peerage hunters, both earnestly pressing their claims, brought home the realization that in accepting such terms he ran the risk of losing some of his followers.[3] Chatham's attitude towards the Admiralty posts did not offer a promising future for those not included in the present bargain. At the most he offered the Bedfords the position of a tolerated minority, and if they accepted there would be a clear line of demarcation between the privileged and the non-privileged, with the danger of friction between them.

The interview between Chatham and Bedford took place at seven o'clock the same evening.[4] On Bedford's part it was not so much an interview for ratifying a treaty as an attempt to rally together his divided followers. In addition to those for whom provision was adumbrated he named Henry Thynne, Brand, Lord Lorne, Lord Essex, Keck, Vernon, Neville, Lord Tavistock, Lord Sandwich, and Lord Scarsdale. The list was made comprehensive in order that none could complain of being left out or not being cared for. These demands stood no

---

[1] Grafton, *Autobiography*, p. 107.

[2] See the entry in his diary for December 1 ; *Cavendish's Debates*, i. 596. The friends who assisted at this discussion were Gower, Upper Ossory, Rigby, and Vernon. Vernon, not included in the arrangements, almost certainly opposed them. See his remark to Lord George Cavendish, reported by Portland to Newcastle on December 2 ; Add. MS. 32978, f. 135.

[3] Garlies's letter to Bedford (he also reminded Gower and Marlborough of his pretensions), dated December 1, 1766, is in Woburn MS., liv. f. 140. Brand's letter, also of December 1, is *ibid.* f. 136.

[4] Chatham's account of this interview is given in his letter to the King, 9.30 P.M. [December 1, 1766], Fortescue, I, no. 429. Bedford's is in Woburn MS., liv. f. 132. According to Rigby, the interview was marked by some acrimony, Bedford resenting Chatham's phrase that 'the Cabinet was not afraid'. Grenville's Diary, December 2, 1766 ; *Grenville Papers*, iii. 392-3.

chance of being accepted. At 10.30 P.M. Rigby wrote to Grenville, marking his letter 'Very private' :

> I can't refrain, from the satisfaction which I feel, from informing you, that I think it infinitely most probable (not absolutely certain) that I shall not differ from you on any publick measures.[1]

Chatham referred Bedford's demands to the King, who rejected them with his usual 'firmness',[2] and the next day called on Bedford to convey the King's decision. No attempt was made by either side to leave the door open for future negotiations.

It only remained for Bedford to rally his followers before leaving for Woburn. But this time he did not make any personal explanation to Grenville : he left that to Rigby, who did his best to excuse what Grenville described as 'this absurd negotiation, in which the poor Duke of Bedford is so much disgraced'.[3] No clearer demonstration could have been given of the lack of concert between the two leaders, or of the importance of Rigby as the link between them.

The first phase of the Ministry 'founded on a great and conciliating plan' was over ; far from conciliating, Chatham had failed to unite his Cabinet and had prepared the ground for a combined opposition. He now ran away, and left the work of conciliation to his henchmen Grafton and Conway.

---

[1] Add. MS. 42084, f. 217.

[2] The King to Chatham, past 11 P.M., December 1, 1766 ; Fortescue, I, no. 430. Although the King declared, 'I cannot exceed the bounds you acquainted Lord Gower were the utmost that would be granted', Chatham persuaded him to allow Tavistock to be called to the Lords. See Chatham to the King, 50 minutes past 4 P.M., December 2, 1766 ; *ibid.* no. 433. Bedford does not mention this in his diary.

[3] *Grenville Papers*, iii. 393.

F

# CHAPTER III

# THE ABDICATION OF CHATHAM

THE outlook for Administration at the beginning of 1767 was bleak and unpromising when contrasted with the confident hopes of only six months before. Chatham had failed in almost every task he had set himself. The attempt to root out faction had only increased it : the party groups had rallied and concentrated their strength, and though their disagreements with each other were profound and their personal jealousies prevented a lasting union, they were all fixed in opposition. The great northern alliance to counterbalance the Bourbon powers had never matured : there was no enthusiasm for it outside the mind of its originator, neither in the British government nor amongst its presumptive allies. The settlement with the East India Company — 'this transcendent object' as Chatham described it — was opposed in the Cabinet almost as soon as it was considered, and needed tact and diplomacy for its accomplishment — qualities which he notoriously lacked. Only in his relations with the King had there been no disappointment : George III never doubted that 'firmness' would eventually overcome all obstacles and his support for his Minister never faltered.

During the next twelve months — the period that was to see the collapse of Chatham and the feeble and unwilling efforts of Grafton to assume his master's rôle — the stability and success of the Administration depended upon Conway. As Minister in the House of Commons he held the decisive post, since there was no one able or willing to take his place. Chatham might retire into seclusion but the Administration he had formed could still carry on, weak and divided though it was. But Conway's resignation would have been the end. Had he been ambitious and unscrupulous, he could have supplanted Chatham and made himself the effective first Minister ; lacking these qualities, but conscientious and unduly sensitive to the charge of ambition or presumption — 'a mammon of righteousness' — he became the sport of the contending party groups instead of their master. The theme of the year 1767 is the struggle for the soul of Conway.

The aims of the contending forces were thus focused and sharpened : Grafton and the King had but one aim — to keep Conway in, Rockingham to get him out. Bedford sat upon the fence and waited to see which side would outbid the other for his support ; while Grenville, barred by the dislike of the King and the jealousy of Rockingham from becoming an effective ally of either, grew indifferent to the struggle for power. In the last years of his life Grenville attained something approaching the eminence and detachment of an elder states- man. Respected in the Commons, aloof from party squabbles, he was able to give his attention to the real problems of govern- ment, which the King was too harassed to do, Grafton too indolent, and Rockingham too ignorant. Because of his unpopularity and his isolation Grenville rose superior to all in his concern for the peace and welfare of the nation, albeit upon his own narrow principles.

On December 2 Lord Hardwicke wrote to Charles Yorke : 'Mr. Conway has declared to his friends that he will not remain in office much *longer*. Lord Rockingham will endeavour to *accelerate* this resolution.' [1] The Edgcumbe affair was the climax of Conway's mounting discontent, and from it he plunged into a state of uncertainty and indecision which both Rockingham and Grafton tried to exploit. To resign or not to resign was his problem, and whatever he did there was torment for his sensitive conscience ; he could never decide whether the reproaches of Grafton and Horace Walpole or of Rockingham and the Cavendishes would be the more galling. Relying on Conway's disgust at Edgcumbe's dismissal and on his disagreement with Chatham's East India policy, Rockingham had at first been optimistic. On December 4 he wrote to Newcastle : 'I have some reasons to hope that

[1] Add. MS. 35362, ff. 53-4.

General Conway will not long be the prop of this Administration. I shall be heartily rejoiced when that event happens.' [1]
But on December 7 he wrote in a more cautious mood : 'I
don't rely at present so much on a flattering expectation which
I had that General Conway will soon quit. At the same time
various circumstances may bring it on.' [2] To get Conway to
make up his mind was more difficult than Rockingham at first
had supposed.

Horace Walpole has described in his *Memoirs* the battle he
waged with Rockingham to keep Conway in office, and no
doubt at times he exaggerates the importance of his efforts :
Conway did not stay in merely to please Walpole. But
Walpole's counsel was nevertheless a real factor and Grafton
acknowledges that assistance in his *Autobiography*.[3] On
November 25, the night of the first division on the East India
inquiry, Walpole wrote to Grafton :

> Your Grace has heard of today's debate and division, and
> of the very obliging behaviour of Lord John Cavendish
> and that party to Mr. Conway, tho' varnished over with
> many compliments. May I take the liberty of begging your
> Grace to urge this home to him, and to show him how little
> they deserve the struggle he is making for them. Surely it
> dispenses him from trying it farther. I have just told him
> so, and that when they abandon him, he is free from all
> engagements with them. They have left him for George
> Grenville, whom they had so much disclaimed ; and the
> very cautious Mr. Yorke has stepped forth into strong
> opposition. I am sure that the more your Grace shall paint
> this to him as *factious* behaviour, the more impression it will
> make on him. If Lord Chatham would throw in a friendly
> word or two to him, it will make him feel their ill-treatment
> more strongly. I beg pardon for using so much freedom,
> but shou'd be so hurt at seeing any separation between your
> Grace and Mr. Conway, whose integrity was so made for
> each other, that I cannot resist any occasion of doing all in
> my power to preserve that connection, and of both with
> Lord Chatham.[4]

---

[1] Add. MS. 32978, ff. 168-9.          [2] *Ibid.* ff. 206-7.
[3] Pp. 140-1.                          [4] Grafton MS. 777.

Walpole was seconded in these endeavours by Lord Hertford, whose mind and temper did not relish opposition,[1] and who now, with the Chamberlain's staff firmly fixed in his hand, tried to settle his unsteady brother.   On December 4 he wrote to Grafton :

I had a good deal of conversation last night with my brother upon the state of parties in this country and his own situation ; he sees with calmness and good wishes the difficulties that may attend Administration and will I flatter myself go as farr as his own delicate feelings will allow him to act in conjunction with those who form the present sistem. He does not mean to quitt Administration immediately, tho' he seems upon the whole to think that he cannot act long in the post he now holds. I need not repeat the different reasons which concur towards forming that opinion. Your Grace knows them ; I wish there was a cordial confidence established between Lord Chatham and himself, I beleive both wish it though the different manners of the men must in some measure have thrown obstacles in the way. He is sensible of the regard shewn to him in thinking of some military command for him. I heartily wish some arrangement of that sort was now practicable, that I must submit to better judgment. Your Grace knows of my feelings and wishes upon this occasion both publick and private and will I am sure excuse me for giving you this trouble if I can contribute by anything I can offer to the service of Administration or the satisfaction of a brother's mind.[2]

---

[1] In 1782, when expecting to be dismissed by the Rockinghams, Hertford wrote to the King : 'I have served your Majesty more than twenty years and chief part of that time in very high emploiments, nor can I in a single instance charge my mind with having failed to your Majesty in the least degree during so long a period'. (Fortescue, I, no. 21 ; the editor misread the date as 1762.)  But in 1767 Lord Bristol described him as 'an excellent sollicitor, has a constant appetite for all preferments for himself and family, with the quickest digestion and the shortest memory of past favours of any of the present noblemen of this moderate and reasonable age' (Bristol to Chatham, January 24, 1767.  The above is omitted from the letter as printed in *Chatham Correspondence*, iii. 171-2).  Bristol's own appetite for preferments was by no means moderate, and in addition he pocketed the salary and equipage money of Lord-Lieutenant of Ireland without setting foot in the country, though the post had been given him on the understanding that he would reside.

[2] Grafton MS. 802.

These three, Grafton, Walpole, and Hertford, united by ties of interest and relationship,[1] fought the battle with Rockingham for the soul of Conway.

## (ii)

The directors of the East India Company were warned on August 28 that their affairs were to be the subject of a parliamentary inquiry, and it soon became clear that this was to be the main business of the session. Before Parliament had met conflicting opinions had arisen among the directors, the stockholders, and in the Cabinet itself.

Chatham's motives in instituting this inquiry were financial rather than political, and governed by expediency rather than principle. He did not intend any fundamental change in the structure of the Company or in its relations with the State. As a result of the Seven Years' War the Company had acquired territorial responsibilities and financial advantages in Bengal, which had been strengthened by Clive's assumption on its behalf of the *diwani*, the news of which reached England in the late spring of 1766. A company of merchants, with an annually elected directorate responsible only to the shareholders, was ill equipped to undertake territorial responsibilities in a country separated from England by a six months' voyage. But it was not this aspect of the situation which impressed contemporaries. They were dazzled by the financial gain the Company had acquired through Clive's action, which he himself had estimated at over £2,000,000 a year. The immediate effect in England had been increased speculation in East India stock and a rise in dividend from 6 per cent to 10 per cent, which reminded timid observers of the excesses of the South Sea Company, and gave the impression that the Company was a great deal wealthier than in fact it was.[2]

---

[1] Hertford and Walpole were first cousins ; Lady Hertford was Grafton's aunt.

[2] This book is concerned only with the impact of the East India inquiry on parliamentary politics. For a comprehensive study of the inquiry, see Lucy S. Sutherland, *The East India Company in Eighteenth Century Politics*, chapter vi.

Chatham saw in the Company a source of financial gain for the nation. In this he was following an established custom, for the State had long sought financial advantages in return for the grant of the Company's privileges. Recent events had sharpened the State's appetite and rendered its demands more specious. It could be argued that the Company had become rich through the help of the State, and that now the State was in need it had the right to call on the Company for assistance. The military forces of the Crown had helped to win Bengal ; some part of the wealth of Bengal, now flowing into private hands, should be diverted to the Crown. Chatham, like most of his contemporaries, grossly over-estimated this new source of wealth and the amount it could contribute to the nation's needs. But his plan was viewed sympathetically by the country gentlemen, who welcomed anything which promised relief from the land tax. The recent increase in speculation gave an ethical edge to Chatham's policy : to make money through buying and selling stock was looked at askance by the more conservative and complacent elements in eighteenth-century society, while fortunes acquired in India were assumed (not always incorrectly) to be the fruits of plunder and extortion.

Chatham's plan was that Parliament should determine that the Company had no right to its territories in India, that these territories were vested in the Crown which was entitled to enjoy the revenues therefrom, but that part of those revenues should be returned to the Company in exchange for the Company undertaking the administration of the territories. The determination of the right was the essence of his scheme and the only part of it which he fully explained or showed any concern for : he gave no details of what kind of financial settlement he desired but insisted that it would follow logically from the determination of the right. This was not only because the question of right suited Chatham's rhetoric better than that of finance — 'the multiplication table did not admit of being treated in epic' [1] — but also because it was on the question of right that he was challenged and defied in the Cabinet. None of his colleagues questioned the equity of the

[1] Walpole, *Memoirs*, ii. 307.

State's drawing a revenue from the Company, but Conway and Townshend, whose agreement was a *sine qua non* for the success of Chatham's plan, believed the Company should retain the title-deeds of its Indian territories. They wished to negotiate on that basis rather than challenge it at the outset, and held that the method of the conference table would give the Crown a better bargain in a shorter time than that of the big stick. Chatham ignored these objections and never considered which method was likely to bring the more satisfactory result. The determination of the right was to him the first object of the inquiry, and no terms could be discussed until that had been settled. He preferred a battle *à outrance* to an advantageous compromise : was it the battle which appealed to him rather than the plunder ?

Chatham entrusted the introduction of this delicate business in the House of Commons to his chief liaison officer in the City, Alderman Beckford, M.P. for London, in preference to Conway, the spokesman of the Cabinet, or Townshend, the representative of the Treasury. If a settlement was intended which was to satisfy both Crown and Company, this was a regrettable and irresponsible choice, but for an all-out attack on the Company the choice of Beckford was an unmistakable sign of Chatham's intentions. As the self-appointed advocate of the smaller merchants against the monopolistic Company Beckford was more concerned to do harm to the Company than good to the State. He was a frequent and voluble speaker in the House and affected the lofty sentiments and sonorous phrases of his master, but too often drew laughter rather than applause. He did not convince the Company of the fair intentions of Administration, and he inspired no confidence in either the politicians or the independent members of the House.[1]

On November 25 Beckford made his motion for a com-

---

[1] John Scott (M.P. for Wick Burghs), who supported Administration, wrote to Shelburne on November 29, 1766 : 'I think we that are considerable East India proprietors have . . . reason to complain of the measure of allowing such a hurlo-thrumbo as Beckford and a declared enemy to the Company to make the motion in so hostile a manner. If it had come in a decent manner from the Treasury Bench I for one shou'd have supported instead of opposing it.' (Lansdowne MSS.)

mittee 'to inquire into the state and condition of the East
India Company', the further phrase 'together with the conduct
of all or any persons concerned in the direction or administration of the said Company' being deleted on an amendment
proposed by Conway.  Beckford's motion was carried by 129
to 76, the followers of Grenville and Rockingham being in
the minority.  Thurlow and Rigby of the Bedfords both
spoke against the motion.  This was the first of the great
debates on East Indian questions which were to occupy
so much of the time of the House during the next twenty
years.

Rockingham, unlike Grenville, who numbered Clive's
group among his followers, had no strong links with the
Company, although certain of his friends, such as the two
Burkes and George Dempster, were in process of acquiring
them.  On the day of the inquiry Newcastle had written to
Rockingham : 'What does your Lordship and our friends
think about Beckford's motions upon the East Indian affairs ?
Or what do our friends intend to do upon it in the House
of Commons ?' ¹  Newcastle was not always consulted by
Rockingham on what line their group was to take in the House
of Commons : he no longer had any followers of sufficient
stature there to take a leading part in the debates.  Still, the
Rockinghams had gone to the Cockpit meeting barely a week
before as supporters of the Administration, and must have
known then that the motion for an inquiry was to be moved
soon in the session.  Their opposition to it was not upon the
merits of the question : it was their reply to Chatham's
rejection of their ultimatum on Lord Edgcumbe.  Lord John
Cavendish spoke against Administration rather than against
the inquiry, and there had been no discussion among the
Rockinghams on what part to take in the debate.  In his reply
to Newcastle, dated 'past 11 o'clock' on the same evening,
Rockingham wrote :

The House of Commons is still setting [sic] and I have just
heard that Beckford's motions have been very cavalierly

¹ Add. MS. 32978, f. 62.

treated — that Charles Townshend has spoke *rather* on Beckford's side but *languid*. The House in much confusion and nobody seeming to know what was to be done.[1]

At this time Rockingham was more concerned with Conway's reply to Portland's threat of resignation than with East Indian affairs. But he soon realized that the division in the Cabinet might profit his followers.

Rockingham's remark on Townshend's speech is echoed by Grenville in his diary.[2] Townshend was plainly discontented at the way Chatham's plan was shaping. Did he also resent having to play second fiddle to Beckford on this business ?

The next stage was a motion for papers to be laid before the House, but before that came on the minority in the Cabinet went into open defiance of Chatham and raised the possibility of a split. Conway's discontent was so unconcealed and his position so critical for Administration that the King (probably prompted by Grafton) wrote to him on December 6 :

I am so sanguine with regard to the East India affair that I trust Tuesday will convince the world that whilst Administration has no object but the pursuing what may be of solid advantage to my people that it is not in the power of any men to prevent it ; indeed my great reliance on its success in the House of Commons is on your abilitys and character, and I am certain I can rely on your zeal at all times to carry on my affairs as I have no one desire but what tends to make the happiness of my people.[3]

Clearly Conway was still undecided what part to take.

Tuesday, December 9, was the day on which Beckford was to move for papers to be laid before the House, and on December 6 a meeting was held to discuss the business of that day.[4] At this meeting the opposition of Conway and Town-

---

[1] Add. MS. 32980, ff. 74-5.          [2] *Grenville Papers*, iii. 389.
[3] Fortescue, I, no. 436.
[4] I assume this was not a Cabinet meeting since Chatham was not present while Dyson apparently was. It was probably a meeting of Ministers and 'men of business' in the House of Commons. Such meetings were sometimes held to discuss business which concerned the Commons only. In this case the purpose of the meeting may have been to consider what papers Beckford should move for in the House. It is not clear whether Beckford was present or not.

shend threatened disastrous consequences for Administration :
it seemed for a moment that they could not remain long in the
Cabinet. Chatham, when told that they objected to the state
of the Company's revenue in India being laid before the
House, wrote a most extraordinary letter to Grafton (December 7) :

> I grieve most heartily at the report of the meeting last
> night. If the enquiry is to be contracted within the ideas
> of Mr. Chancellor of the Exchequer, and of Mr. Dyson, the
> whole becomes a *farce*, and the *Ministry a ridiculous phantom.*
> Mr. Beckford will move his questions, (waving for the present the bonds and transfers), and upon the issue of Tuesday
> must turn the decision of the present system, whether to
> stand or make way for another scene of political revolution.
> Mr. Dyson's behaviour cannot be acquiesced in. Mr. C.
> Townshend's fluctuations and incurable weaknesses cannot
> comport with his remaining in that critical office. Your
> Grace will not, I trust, wonder at the pain I feel for the
> King's service and personal ease, as well as for the *redemption* of a nation, within reach of being saved at once by
> a kind of gift from heaven ; and all marred, and thrown
> away by fatal weaknesses, cooperating with the most glaring
> factions. What possible objection, fit to listen to, can be
> made to the bringing the revenues in India before the House ?
> I hope Mr. Beckford will walk out of the House, and leave
> the name of an enquiry, to amuse the credulous, in other
> hands, in case this question be not fully supported and
> carried. For my own part, I shall wash my hands of the
> whole business, after that event.[1]

Chatham made no attempt to win over the dissidents, to
suppress Townshend's deviation, or soothe Conway's discomfort, though the one was amenable to firm treatment and the
other to gentle encouragement. When his supremacy was
questioned he seemed to have neither the will nor the energy
to reassert it, so that his friends looked helplessly for direction
which never came and his enemies profited through the resulting confusion.

Grafton and the King did their best to bring Conway and

[1] Grafton, *Autobiography*, pp. 110-11.

Townshend into line with the rest of the Cabinet. The danger was that the two rebels would openly dissociate themselves from Beckford's motion or even directly oppose it. The day before the debate Grafton was despondent, but he saw Townshend that evening and reported to the King that there was a hope 'that Mr. Townshend will at least sit quiet, if he does not support the measure'.[1] To spur on the unwilling Conway, Grafton asked his brother, Charles Fitzroy, to second the motion, and thus closely identified himself with its success. He was able to tell the King that Conway would support it 'tho' it had been opposed in any quarter whatever'.[2] The danger of the Cabinet parading its disunion on the floor of the House was averted, but without Chatham's intercession the King and Grafton could merely postpone it to another day.

To what extent was the opposition aware of this difference of opinion ? Rockingham was a close friend of Conway and on good terms with Townshend. Did Chatham mean the phrase 'fatal weaknesses cooperating with the most glaring factions' to be taken literally ? It seems unlikely. Rockingham discussed the approaching debate with Dowdeswell and Charles Yorke,[3] but showed no sign of being aware how critical it was for the Court, and by then he had given up hope of Conway's immediate resignation. He did not attend the Commons, his usual practice when an important debate was held, and appeared more interested in the debate on the Indemnity Bill in the Lords. His correspondence shows him as yet unaware of the issues involved in the East India inquiry and of its potentialities as a weapon against Administration.

Parliament was too near the adjournment to give any hope of success or even of a substantial minority against Administration. Many opposition members, with nothing to keep them in London, had gone into the country, while those who held places of business in Administration had necessarily to remain. Charles Yorke's motion to adjourn the debate for three months was rejected by 140 to 56. The papers asked for could safely

[1] Grafton to the King, December 9, 1766 ; Fortescue, I, no. 438.
[2] Ibid.
[3] Rockingham to Newcastle, December 8, 1766 ; Add. MS. 32978, ff. 221-3.

be laid before the House without involving the Company in any difficulty. Three Members connected with the Company spoke for the motion (Henry Crabb Boulton, Peregrine Cust, and Laurence Sulivan), to one against (George Dempster), and Dempster, closely connected with Rockingham, was by no means as prominent in the Company's affairs as the others. Most of those who spoke against Beckford's motion were connected with Grenville, not with Rockingham. The debate raised little heat but was marked by two interesting speeches. Burke taunted Chatham as 'an invisible deity' (not yet true but soon to be so) in a speech which seems, from the very imperfect reports which are available, to have been in his best manner—satirical but not abusive. Townshend gave no indication of his disagreement with Chatham, but Conway did not conceal his uneasiness and described himself as a passenger in Administration.

It was not a good start to a parliamentary inquiry of such importance, but it was a better one than had at first seemed possible. The inquiry was adjourned until January 22 ; Chatham returned to Bath, and Townshend remained in London to try for a settlement behind his master's back. Meanwhile the first tentative approaches were made for a union of the opposition.

### (iii)

The idea of a union between Rockingham and Bedford had been suggested by Newcastle as long ago as November 22, when it was hoped that Conway's resignation would precipitately dissolve the Ministry. 'If that should be the case', Newcastle wrote to Rockingham, 'I should think something should be attempted with the Bedfords, who I hear are in a better disposition to receive it than they have been.'[1] The idea had also occurred to Rockingham but he did not wish to move too soon. 'Every report and every circumstance', he replied on the same day, 'continues to shew that the Bedfords are *loose* and yet in honour at present we can not make any overtures towards them.'[2]

---

[1] *Ibid.* f. 27.    [2] *Ibid.* ff. 23-5.

There were three essentials for a successful opposition : a
popular question ; a knot of good debaters, secure of the
respect and attention of the House ; and a following sufficiently
large to harass Administration, sufficiently determined to keep
up the pressure, and sufficiently united to resist attempts to
buy off sections of it.  The popular question was at hand in
the East India inquiry :  it was not an ideal subject for
opposition polemics, it had not the genuine appeal of General
Warrants, but presented as a violation of charter rights and an
attack on private property it could be turned to good account
by skilful hands.  Grenville had shown what could be made
out of such unpromising material as the Indemnity Bill :  what
would he not be able to do with a question that was bound to
drag on for several months ;  that aroused fierce opposition
from those who were hoping for an increased dividend or were
'bulling' East India stock ;  and that caused such deep divisions
in the Cabinet itself ?  Good debaters were to be found only
in the Grenville group :  neither in numbers nor quality was
the vocal section of Rockingham's followers equal to Grenville's.  Support could only come through a firm union with
Grenville and Bedford, and through a vigorous, well-conducted
opposition, designed to attract the independent section of the
House.

It was nonsense for Rockingham to withdraw his forces
from Administration, to oppose with insufficient numbers, and
to refuse to coalesce with other opposition groups — pre-
destined to lose followers not to gain them.  The luxury of
opposition *per se* could be afforded only by those who were
indifferent to office, and was not conducive to the maintenance
of a strong party group.  The Rockingham group at all times
contained a number of men who did not want office, and who
preferred the unanimity of a small clique to the diversity of a
larger following.  Their views were combated by Bessborough.

I am sure nothing can be done [he wrote to Newcastle on
November 24] without enlarging our bottom.  I am not of
Mr. White's opinion, that it does not signify how small the
bottom is, provided the world have a good opinion of the
men.  Your Grace knows well that that won't carry a ques-

tion in the House of Commons. . . . The opposition upon the small bottom which we have must make us ridiculous in the eyes of the world, and ruin all our poor friends by being turned out of their places, and this will happen if we have not strength.[1]

If Rockingham and the Cavendishes hoped that the antagonism aroused by Chatham's conduct and policy would do their work for them, without any exertion or sacrifice on their part, the divisions in the House of Commons would soon undeceive them.

Lord Rockingham seems to hope [wrote Newcastle to Albemarle on December 6] that my Lord Chatham's behaviour will exasperate some of our *half-friends*, or friends in conjunction with my Lord Chatham . . . and particularly his open declaration in favour of my Lord Bute's friends will induce many to resign now ; I heartily wish it may do so but the appearances in the House of Commons are not like it, 48 to 166.[2]

So long as the Bedfords considered they were on the threshold of office an approach to them would have been futile. But though there were certain sections of the Rockingham group who were not averse to Grenville, Rockingham himself would not consider the idea of a coalition with him, and indeed at one time appeared to entertain the delusion that Grenville was about to join the Administration and take the lead in the House of Commons.[3] On the eve of Chatham's last negotiation with the Bedfords Lord Lyttelton approached Lord Hardwicke on the subject of a coalition, and a few days later sounded Rockingham himself.[4] The Yorkes were the least averse of Rockingham's followers to such a junction :

[1] Add. MS. 32978, f. 59.

[2] *Ibid.* f. 194. The figures refer to a motion to adjourn on the report stage of the Indemnity Bill (December 5). The figure of 164 for the majority given by Conway in his report to the King (Fortescue, I, no. 435) is incorrect. Newcastle on this occasion, as so often, was out of touch with events in the Commons. The Rockinghams voted with the Court on this division.

[3] Newcastle to White, October 16, 1766 ; Add. MS. 32977, f. 250.

[4] Hardwicke to Charles Yorke, November 28, 1766 ; Add. MS. 35362, ff. 48-9. Rockingham to Dowdeswell, January 8, 1767 ; Rockingham Papers, R1-477, part printed in *Cavendish's Debates*, i. 581-2, and in Albemarle, ii. 31-4.

both Charles and John Yorke had served under Grenville and had only resigned after repeated complaints from Newcastle to their father. Neither Hardwicke nor Charles Yorke differed fundamentally from Grenville on the attitude to be adopted towards the colonies ; and neither had anything to gain from Chatham, who, so long as he remained in office, would retain Camden on the Woolsack. But Lyttelton's proposal, almost certainly made without Grenville's knowledge, stipulated the Treasury for either Temple or Grenville, and Rockingham, though according to Hardwicke he had no idea what to do if Chatham were unable to go on, could not bear to see a Grenville at the Treasury.

But when Chatham's negotiation with the Bedfords broke down, coalition with them became a practical proposition and Bessborough once more pressed it on Newcastle (December 11) :

> But my Lord your Grace has reason to be uneasy on account of the small minority [on the East India division of December 9], that is serious indeed. Your Grace may remember I foretold it at Lord Rockingham's but I was not believed by Lord John or Mr. White, and I will now venture to say that it will continue so, if the alliance is not cultivated and formed that I then recommended. How can it be otherwise ? Is there any plan ? Do you know your friends ? No one knows what he is to do, or which side to take. I do assure your Grace this is exactly the case. The persons I mean I am sure are ready to join you and form a plan with you whenever you please, but as it now is we are only laughed at, and indeed I think with good reason.[1]

Newcastle agreed, and added words of very good sense (December 12) :

> A probable plan of success is the only way to get our *friends*, *good friends*, back ; they all more or less look after power, and whatever carries a face of probability with it is the only way to get numbers, *even* of those we thought *the very best men*.[2]

Finding some support for his idea, Bessborough now came out into the open. As an advocate for coalition he had some

---

[1] Add. MS. 32978, ff. 273-4.    [2] *Ibid.* f. 285.

weight, for he was one of those who had resigned over Edgcumbe's dismissal.  On the same day he replied :

> I don't like the doctrine that I have heard from some of our
> young friends, give him rope enough and he will do the
> business for us.  Perhaps that may happen but it may like-
> wise happen that it may be a very long rope, and difficult to
> find an end to it.  There is in my opinion but one true step
> to be taken, and which I have mentioned before.  Strengthen
> your bottom by joining with the Duke of Bedford and his
> friends.  I don't know that Mr. G——c is the *sine qua non*
> your Grace mentions.  Try what can be done, and don't
> wait at this critical time to see if they will advance to you
> first ; I know some of our young friends are for waiting for
> that event, which possibly may never happen, for I know
> some of them are as proud as any of us.  My Lord, it be-
> hooves you to do something *in regard* to some very honourable
> personages who have resigned through friendship to you
> and attention to the Whig cause.  If you let it sleep, you
> may lose all your opportunity, and be laughed at.[1]

Union with the Bedfords was not an objectionable proposition to Rockingham.  The Bedfords had no candidate for the
Treasury and no dominant personality in the Commons : they
were more fitted for the rôle of junior partners than the
Grenvilles.  If the Grenvilles entered into partnership with
the Rockinghams, they would contribute the larger share of
capital to the joint concern, and would demand the larger
share of control over patronage and policy.  Even if Grenville
could be headed off from the Treasury, he would still be
supreme in the Commons : no arrangement of offices could
take that from him.  Grenville had tasted power and would
never again be the junior partner to any other, least of all to a
peer whose voice was never heard in the Lords.[2]  The great
obstacle to a coalition with Bedford was the belief that he
would demand the return of Grenville to the Treasury.  It
was true that he had made no such demand of Chatham, but
with Chatham he was negotiating to join an Administration *in*

---

[1] *Ibid.* f. 282.

[2] During the whole of the period covered by this book, Rockingham
never once spoke in the House of Lords.

G

*esse* and with the approval of the Crown ; with Rockingham he
would negotiate to join an Administration *in posse*, which
would have to be forced on the King, and his terms would
be correspondingly higher. Chatham could remain Minister
without Bedford's support ; Rockingham needed it to become
Minister. It did no harm to insist on Grenville for the Treasury
when the negotiations were unofficial and there seemed no
likelihood of his getting it. But when the King commissioned
Grafton to sound Rockingham in July 1767 and negotiations
for a new Administration became a reality, Bedford dropped
his claim for Grenville. However, so long as opposition was
the game it was good policy to maintain the connection with
Grenville, already badly strained by the events of the autumn.

But if Rockingham's jealousy of Grenville blinded him as
to his value as an ally, others were not under the same disability. Charles Yorke thought Grenville 'the most usefull
person we could have in the House of Commons upon money
matters'.[1] Albemarle wrote of him : 'He is well heard and
respected in the House of Commons, and by many out of it,
by more than we imagine'.[2] Dowdeswell came to value
Grenville's co-operation in the House and so did Burke, in
spite of his veneration for Rockingham's opinions and prejudices. In 1769 Burke worked in close contact with Whately,
Grenville's man of business, and it was one of Burke's complaints against Richmond in August 1767 — one month after
Rockingham had flounced out of the conference room at
Newcastle House in a passion of rage and jealousy against
Grenville — that he had 'a leaning to Conway' and 'a dislike
of the Grenvilles'.[3]

On December 17 Newcastle and Bessborough met Rockingham at Claremont, to consider whether or not to sound the
Bedfords.[4] Rockingham and Newcastle still disclaimed

---

[1] Bessborough to Newcastle, December 13, 1766 ; Add. MS. 32978,
f. 299. Rockingham told Newcastle and Bessborough on December 17
that Yorke favoured a coalition with Grenville.
[2] Albemarle to Newcastle, December 6, 1766 ; *ibid.* f. 192.
[3] Burke to Rockingham, August 18, 1767 ; *Burke Correspondence*, i.
138-44.
[4] Newcastle's account of this meeting is Add. MS. 32978, ff. 404-7.

'general opposition'; they would oppose 'upon such points *only*, as were wrong in themselves, and not inconsistent with our former behaviour in the last opposition'. Rockingham gave an account of his conversation with Lyttelton, and of Lyttelton's condition that either Temple or Grenville should take the Treasury.

My Lord Rockingham [wrote Newcastle] told my Lord Lyttelton very plainly that that was what we could not consent to . . . that our whole conduct had been to show the impropriety of Mr. Grenville's measures, and that the last Administration had acted upon a direct contrary principle, and had endeavour'd to overturn all that he had done, and had succeeded in it, and by that had given great satisfaction and obtained the approbation of the nation.

That after that it was not consistent with their honor and consciences to be bringing Mr. Grenville again into that office where he had conducted himself, and in a manner that had been so much blamed by them, and had produced the very contrary behaviour in the last Treasury.

Newcastle 'extremely approved this conversation'; Bessborough's opinion is not stated. There was something in what Rockingham said, but it would have been more convincing had he applied the same arguments to the Bedfords.

Next, it was decided 'that a proper agreement with the Duke of Bedford was much to be wished', on the understanding that neither Grenville nor Temple were to be admitted 'as Ministers'.[1] Bessborough was to sound Gower 'as to the Duke of Bedford's disposition to unite with us', and Rockingham gave assurances to Newcastle against 'the danger of our being drawn in by the Duke of Bedford to oppose some points upon which we had differ'd with his Grace during the opposition'. Dowdeswell was to conduct the Rockingham orchestra in the Commons and to try to get them to play in unison (or to get them to play at all), and with him Newcastle coupled Sir George Savile, a choice which Rockingham approved but which Savile certainly would not. Rockingham was to go to Welbeck and talk the matter over with Portland.

---

[1] *I.e.* as members of the Effective Cabinet.

But these first limited decisions were blasted by the frosty wind that blew from Welbeck. On December 17 Portland wrote to Newcastle :

I can not for various reasons think it at all necessary to make the first advances, I had almost said it would be imprudent so to do. If you seek their connection and desire their assistance *in general*, will it not shew an anxiety of acquiring power at any rate ? Will it not make them rise in their demands ? Will it not authorize them to prescribe the terms ? And in case of failure will it not give your enemies a pretence, and the impartial world some ground to suppose that that uprightness and disinterestedness to which you owe your great credit had been warped by an eagerness after power and emoluments ? [1]

When this opinion was reinforced by White and Albemarle, Newcastle suffered a minor fit of 'the jitters' and began to wonder if he had not been too hasty. On December 19 he beseeched Rockingham to suspend the negotiation :

I would submit it to your Lordship whether if my Lord Bessborough has not already said any thing to my Lord Gower, in consequence of our advice and request to his Lordship, in which I myself was as forward as any body, the whole may not be suspended till your Lordship returns to Town from Welbeck and Yorkshire. [2]

In vain did Bessborough warn him (December 19) :

I believe in a short time you will find they will not treat with us, but will take some care of themselves, and I believe it has been said amongst them that they never would consent (if they did join us) to put Lord R——m at the head of the Treasury. [3]

But Newcastle's fears (unwarranted as usual) had totally reversed his inclinations. On December 20 he wrote to Rockingham : 'I am so overjoyed that my own forwardness in

---

[1] Add. MS. 32978, f. 378. Sixteen years of opposition lessened the Duke's dislike for coalitions and whetted his appetite for 'power and emoluments'. Portland was First Lord of the Treasury in the Fox-North coalition.
[2] *Ibid.* ff. 414-16.   [3] *Ibid.* f. 429.

beginning a negotiation with the Bedfords, tho' with very proper restrictions, has been stopp'd in time'.[1]

How much reality was there behind this first move towards a coalition ? Newcastle certainly took it seriously and so did Bessborough. But did Rockingham ? On January 8 he gave Dowdeswell a full account of his conversation with Lyttelton, but said nothing about his meeting with Bessborough and Newcastle. On the Bedfords he had but two short paragraphs :

I don't find the Bedfords are determined as to their conduct. Many of them lean to George Grenville, some of them still *hanker* after making up with Lord Chatham and others of them want they should come to us.

As this is their state it would not be adviseable for us to make approaches as it might furnish them with either an opportunity of some merit with G. G. in returning to him, or perhaps enable them to make a better bargain with Lord Chatham, indeed *at best* a bargain *now* with Lord Chatham must be upon very humiliating terms to them.[2]

Did Rockingham regard the whole episode as merely a whim of Newcastle which must be humoured ? Did he find greater satisfaction in indulging his aversion to Grenville than in forwarding the union with Bedford ? At any rate, by the time Rockingham returned to London on January 7, both he and Newcastle seem to have forgotten all about it, and for the next three months hardly mention it in their correspondence.

(iv)

On December 31, 1766, the directors of the East India Company were empowered by the General Court to open negotiations with the Ministry, Townshend having informed them that the Cabinet would not refuse to consider their proposals ; [3] and on January 6, 1767, they formulated their terms. Grafton, when forwarding them to Chatham, then at Bath, remarked (January 8) : 'I have every reason to desire whenever the negotiation is to be opened, that it may be in your Lordship's

<hr />

[1] *Ibid.* ff. 438-9.        [2] Rockingham Papers, R1-477.
[3] Townshend to Grafton, January 1, 1767 ; Grafton MS. 447.

presence : it is of the utmost consequence it should ; I mean even in the first overtures'.[1]

But Chatham did not intend to negotiate until the question of right had first been decided. He described the proposals as 'captious' and 'preposterous', and summarily rejected them (January 10) :

> The points on which the committee are of opinion it is requisite and necessary to treat entirely pass by the great objects of parliamentary enquiry and national justice. . . . On this self-evident state of the thing, I am forced to declare I have no hopes from the transaction ; my only hope centres in the justice of Parliament, where the question of right can alone be decided ; and which cannot (upon any colourable pretence) be in the Company. . . . I hope soon to be at your Grace's orders in town, though I see not the least use I can be of in this matter ; possibly rather in the way of others, from whom I have the misfortune to differ *toto coelo* upon these matters.[2]

The last sentence was of course a hit at Townshend, who was popularly supposed to have inspired this proposal. Newcastle had written to Rockingham on January 9 :

> You will hear that my Lord Chatham's friends are very uppish upon what has passed in the East India Company ; that they shall get a million etc. What it is it is all owing as I hear to Charles Townshend, and by some accounts it looks as if the great man was a little jealous about it, and says, there are still great difficulties, they should not *hollow* [*sic*] *too soon*.[3]

Parliament was to meet on January 16 and the East India inquiry was fixed for January 22. On the 11th Chatham set out for London, but an attack of gout forced him to return to Bath and to take to his bed. The unhappy Grafton, who had pinned all his hopes of peace of mind and political stability on Chatham's presence in London, and who was confronted with a Cabinet in which fresh divisions were appearing, wrote on January 21 :

[1] *Chatham Correspondence*, iii. 163-6.
[2] Grafton, *Autobiography*, pp. 111-12.    [3] Add. MS. 32979, f. 145.

I will not attempt to express to your Lordship the real concern I felt on receiving the note from you, that brought the news of your being confined at the Bath with a severe fit of the gout.  Indeed, my Lord, the distress it brings on all concerned in the affairs of the public is the greatest ; and nothing but your absence can again give hopes to desponding factions, that an opening is made for any possibility of their success. . . . Your Lordship must have observed a *peevish* cast in some of our late councils, the bad effects of which your presence can alone prevent ; little as I wish to engage you to take one disagreeable step, yet must I profess that it is my opinion that without you we shall see great confusion arise here.  What I can do in the mean time I will heartily exert, provided I have your advice to proceed upon.[1]

He did not get that advice, but instead another lecture on the iniquity of factions who were betraying 'this transcendent object', the East India inquiry.

Allow me, my dear Lord [Chatham wrote on January 23], to say, that it is not my absence which affects this business, but an unfortunate original difference of opinions among the King's servants, which, totally contrary to my notions, by enervating at the outset the principle of the parliamentary enquiry, shook the whole foundation of this great transaction, and has, in my opinion, thrown it into confusion inextricable ; *for* the consideration of the Company's right to the enormous revenues is the hinge upon which must turn the very essence of the question, namely, *whether the Company is to receive,* on this head, *indulgence and benefit from Parliament, or whether the Company is to make a grant to the public.*  This right must, of necessity, be admitted or decided one way or other, before a just rule can be laid down whereby to judge if the proposal, when made, be adequate.  The aim of the Company seems to be . . . to reduce the King's servants to make demands upon the Company . . . instead of receiving from them applications to supply a want of title. . . . If this be the project, as I believe, of this notable negociation, I know one of the King's servants who will beg to be excused running his head into such a snare ; in this case Parliament alone

---

[1] *Chatham Correspondence*, iii. 168-9.

can decide, and fix the public lot. . . . If this transcendent
object fails, it will not be by the force of factions from without, but from a certain infelicity, (I think incurable), which
ferments and sours, (as your Grace has observed), the
councils of his Majesty's servants.[1]

Although Chatham's ill humour seemed to be directed
against the Company, it was Townshend who was the real
target. Townshend had realized that the best way to check
Chatham's plan for a parliamentary inquiry was to induce the
Company to offer proposals so favourable that it would be
difficult for Administration to reject them.[2] While he protested
his loyalty to the Administration and disclaimed any intention
to negotiate apart from the other Ministers, he professed to
believe that Chatham's plan involved 'substituting the public
in the place of the Company in the collecting, investing,
conducting and remitting the revenue', and made it quite
clear that he wanted the matter to be determined 'upon the
ground of reciprocal advantage' without 'the necessity of a
parliamentary decision'.

Chatham took no steps either to explain the exact nature
of his plan (probably because he had not yet thought it out
himself), or to check his undisciplined lieutenant. His refusal
to accept responsibility, his professed intention of leaving the
decision to Parliament, seems incredible conduct in a statesman
charged with affairs of such importance. Contemporaries
could not account for his absence at this time by illness alone.
Walpole supposed that his gout might be pretended,[3] and
Rockingham reported that 'at Bath this fit of the gout is
understood to be political'.[4] The King, as distressed as
Grafton at Chatham's absence, wrote to Northington on
February 2 :

I was agreably surprized this day with hearing that you
arrived last night in Town ; I owne the accounts I had

[1] Grafton, *Autobiography*, pp. 113-14. The draft for this letter is in
*Chatham Correspondence*, iii. 199-201, incorrectly dated February 9.
[2] Townshend to Grafton, docketed 'December 1766'; Grafton MS.
446.                                              [3] *Memoirs*, ii. 293.
[4] Rockingham to Newcastle, January 24, 1767 ; Add. MS. 32979, f. 311.

received did not give me any room to expect it ; but your resolution is superior to that of others afflicted with the gout.[1]

On January 20 the papers for which Beckford had moved on December 9 were presented to the House, and he proposed that they should be printed. But Beckford's brief hour of triumph had passed, the initiative was now in other hands ; and he was never again to know the bliss of denouncing the Company, with the full support of Chatham at hand and a majority in the House of Commons behind him. Townshend, free of bit and rider, requested Beckford to 'defer that motion for a few days, as he hoped to settle all matters with the East India Company to the satisfaction of the public, and, consequently, there might be no occasion for exposing these papers'.[2] There was nothing for Beckford to do but to withdraw his motion, and two days later the inquiry was further postponed until February 6, Townshend declaring 'that he thought the East India Company had a right to their territorial revenues', and Conway 'that he was unwilling to have the right determined by a vote of Parliament'. In desperation Beckford begged for Chatham's advice and 'directions what steps to take and what motion to make'.

He asked in vain. While the captain lay afflicted in his cabin, his mutinous lieutenant had seized the helm and was changing course as fast as he could. Townshend, quick to seize the advantage Chatham's absence gave him, was intent on making a great name for himself. Newcastle wrote to Rockingham on January 23 :

> Onslow told me yesterday morning that Charles Townshend told him the day before, that all was done and in a better way than could have been expected ; that they (the Treasury) should make a great figure, equal to my brother's time, at the conclusion of the Peace of Aix-la-Chapelle, when the whole National Debt was reduced to 4 per cent.[3]

That this was not entirely bragging, but had a more solid foundation, is shown by Conway's letter to Chatham of

[1] Fortescue, I, no. 462.
[2] Beckford to Chatham, January 27, 1767 ; *Chatham Correspondence*, iii. 176-8. [3] Add. MS. 32980, f. 159.

January 24 : 'Mr. Townshend from his late conversations with the directors is very sanguine. They are preparing immediately to come to Administration with even very advantageous proposals.' [1]  Conway tried to soften Chatham's wrath at this attempt to side-track the question of right by telling him Grenville's opinion, that if the directors petitioned the Crown for the renewal of their charter the right to their territories should be decided in Westminster Hall. But this was no balm. There was nothing Chatham could do if he was unable or unwilling to come to London to discipline his rebellious crew. Grafton was quite incapable of stopping Townshend ; Conway sided with him ; Shelburne, the one man who might have checked Townshend, had no authority and would have found no ally ; and the King, though anxious that 'the East India affair be not whittled to a mere nothing',[2] would not interfere. Chatham had to admit that the inquiry must be postponed 'pending the duration of the transaction with the Company', though he added that he expected their proposal to be 'very inadequate', and looked forward to the question of the right being decided.[3]  This was an acknowledgment of defeat and inspired Townshend to fresh presumptions.

## (v)

It was not only the East India inquiry which suffered through Chatham's absence ;  on other questions the conduct of Administration attested the need of his leadership. The Cabinet had not been designed to take decisions independent of him ; when called upon to do so its inadequacy as a policy-making body was clearly revealed. Composed for the most part of men either unfitted to exercise political authority or who, in their excessive adulation of Chatham, had subordinated their wills to his, it was at sixes and sevens without his direction and each man tended to take the part his nature determined him. Conway, to avoid wider responsibilities which would provoke

---

[1] *Chatham Correspondence*, iii. 172-5.
[2] The King to Grafton, January 17, 1767 ; Fortescue, I, no. 459.
[3] Chatham to Shelburne, January 31, 1767 ; *Chatham Correspondence*, iii. 181-2.

a conflict of loyalties, buried himself in the work of his department, and his example was followed by the service chiefs Granby and Hawke, executive heads rather than advisers on policy. Grafton, supported by Northington, tried to keep to the line laid down by Chatham, but without authority to command compliance. George Grenville, whose tidy mind would never have tolerated such a state of affairs, wrote to Lord Buckinghamshire on January 27 with a touch of wit rare in his correspondence :

> The Earl of Chatham is still at Bath, and consequently the King's Administration has got the gout and hobbles terribly. Mr. C. Townshend indeed seems to wish to move a little more nimbly and to try to walk a little without crutches.[1]

Townshend, a political adventurer delighting in chaos and confusion, drove the Cabinet along a path they never intended to take, since he was the only man prepared to offer an alternative policy to that of Chatham. He not only succeeded in frustrating Chatham's plan for the East India inquiry, but in an affair ultimately of far greater consequence accomplished far worse mischief.

On January 26, in the Committee of Supply on the Army estimates, Grenville moved an amendment that the expense of the troops stationed in America should be met by the colonies themselves, the newly acquired territories excepted. This was easily defeated by 106 votes to 35, Grenville finding no support outside his own group. The debate was rendered memorable for both Britain and America by a speech from Townshend which, in the words of Sir Roger Newdigate,[2] 'adopted the principle against the motion'. In answer to Grenville he said he agreed with the idea behind the Stamp Act but considered this was not a suitable time to reintroduce it, ridiculed Chatham's favourite principle of a distinction between internal and external taxation, and 'pledged himself that something should be done this sessions towards creating a revenue to bear the burden'.[3] Lord George Sackville endeavoured to

---

[1] H.M.C., Lothian MSS., pp. 274-5.
[2] Newdigate MS. B2548.          [3] Ibid.

pin him down to a definite pledge to tax the colonies, and Townshend explained that he did not necessarily mean a revenue sufficient to cover all the expense of the troops, although he hoped in time that would come too.

Grafton in his *Autobiography* gives an account of this incident,[1] and though he wrote forty years after the event there is no reason to doubt his general accuracy.[2] Conway sat astonished at this 'unauthorized proceeding', for the matter had never been raised in the Cabinet. At the Cabinet meeting the next night Townshend defended himself : he had responded to the mood of the House, 'bent on obtaining a revenue of some sort from the colonies'. Conway could only agree that this was so, as indeed it was. Grafton ends :

> No one of the Ministry had authority sufficient to advise the dismission of Mr. Charles Townshend, and nothing less could have stopped the measure, Lord Chatham's absence being in this instance, as well as others, much to be lamented.

From this pledge resulted the Townshend duties of June 1767.

When Grafton wrote his *Autobiography* in 1806 this incident had assumed a significance which it did not possess in 1767. In 1806 the United States had been independent for over twenty years and no one then defended those who had insisted on Britain's right to tax her colonies. But in 1767 few politicians were prepared to deny that right, and the incident created little stir. Grafton does not mention it in his correspondence with Chatham. Conway, in his report of the debate to the King, says nothing about it.[3] Walpole, though he gives a short account of the debate in his *Memoirs*,[4] does not notice it. Grenville, who might have been expected to regard it as a triumph for his policy, seemed not to realize its significance. There is nothing about this debate in the correspondence of Rockingham and Newcastle, the men who had repealed the Stamp Act. But Sir Roger Newdigate, M.P. for

[1] Pp. 126-7.
[2] Grafton is incorrect in one particular : it was Lord George Sackville, not Grenville, who obtained a definite pledge from Townshend. But this lapse of memory does not invalidate Grafton's account as a whole.
[3] Conway to the King, January 26, 1767 ; Fortescue, I, no. 469.
[4] II, p. 293.

Oxford University, a Warwickshire country gentleman representative of his class in his dislike of the land tax and his wish to see the burden of American defence shared by those for whom it was undertaken, took notes of the debate and recorded Townshend's pledge. Only Shelburne, who had charge of American affairs, considered the incident to be of sufficient importance to merit discussion with his chief.

On February 1 he wrote a long letter to Chatham on East Indian and American affairs,[1] in which he gave a full account of Townshend's pledge and of the rumour that the Chancellor of the Exchequer intended to establish a Board of Customs in America. He concluded his account : 'I believe your Lordship will think the speech I have just mentioned to you is not the way to make anything go down well in North America'.

Chatham in his reply (February 3)[2] denounced the Assembly of New York for failing to comply with the Mutiny Act — 'A spirit of infatuation has taken possession of New York'. On America he was still sensible, though gloomy and listless ; appreciative of the temper of opinion in Parliament where 'disobedience to the Mutiny Act will *justly* create a great ferment . . . open a fair field to the arraigners of America, and leave no room to any to say a word in their defence' ; but unaware of what the colonies were thinking and feeling. He said not a word in reply to Shelburne's account of the Townshend pledge. And when he talked of seeing Shelburne shortly in London he gave no encouragement that anything would be done to check the reckless course Townshend was now taking.

Whether these clouds will pass away or not is to me very problematical. The appearances are not favourable : one thing is still always clear ; that in pursuing steadily one's duty one cannot lose one's way.

Chatham, in common with Beckford, Shelburne, and his other followers, did not see that the real issue in America was not taxation, but sovereignty. They did not comprehend that the colonists objected not to Parliament's right to tax them,

---

[1] *Chatham Correspondence*, iii. 182-8.       [2] *Ibid.* pp. 188-90.

but to Parliament's right to govern them. Consequently, they were bewildered by events in America and unable to suggest any remedy. 'What demon of discord blows the coals in that devoted province [New York],' asked Chatham ; [1] Shelburne described the colonists as 'these infatuated people' ; [2] while Beckford wrote, 'The devil has possessed the minds of the North Americans'.[3] Nor, had Chatham understood what was involved, would he have been sympathetic towards colonial aspirations ; a separate sovereignty in America would have seemed to him a source of weakness not of strength — a perpetual invitation to French aggression. But the demand for sovereignty by the colonists received support as a result of British provocation, and Chatham would never have taken the course pursued wilfully and recklessly by Townshend, unwittingly and timidly by Grafton.

The Rockinghams were silent on January 26. Dowdeswell was in the House and Burke was within handy distance,[4] but neither spoke against a policy which threatened to undo all the good achieved by the repeal of the Stamp Act. In truth, the pro-Americanism of the Rockinghams was rather accidental than conscious, a shibboleth in British party politics rather than a serious factor in imperial affairs. The Rockinghams prided themselves on their consistency ; the word occurs over and over again in Rockingham's correspondence — 'we who were determined to act consistently' ; [5] 'that all our strength depends upon . . . our having *and meaning to persist in acting* a consistent part' ; [6] 'the weight we have only arises from the firmness of our conduct and our consistency' ; [7] etc., etc. In a letter to Dowdeswell, written on September 9, 1767, at a time when Rockingham felt obliged to defend the line he

[1] Chatham to Shelburne, February 3, 1767 ; *Chatham Correspondence*, iii. 188-90.

[2] Shelburne to Chatham, February 16, 1767 ; *ibid*. pp. 206-11.

[3] Beckford to Chatham, February 12, 1767 ; *ibid*. pp. 201-3.

[4] In the Burke Papers now in the Northamptonshire Record Office there is a note from Dowdeswell to Burke, written from the House during the debate of January 26. He gives the substance of Grenville's amendment, but says there is no appearance of a division.

[5] Rockingham to Dowdeswell, January 8, 1767 ; Albemarle, ii. 31-4.

[6] Rockingham to Newcastle, March 15, 1767 ; Add. MS. 32980, ff. 296-8.

[7] Rockingham to Newcastle, March 26, 1767 ; *ibid*. ff. 384-5.

had taken during the negotiations of July, he thus explained what he meant by 'consistency' :

> I desire to establish the two fundamental principles on which we set out. . . .
> Our first principle was, that *Lord Bute's power* was dangerous and therefore to be resisted.
> Our second arose from Mr. G. Greenvile's conduct as a Minister, whose measures and opinions we opposed and afterwards corrected, and therefore consistency requires that we never should aid to throw Government into his hands.[1] . . .

Reduced to simple terms, then, Rockingham meant by 'consistency' opposition to Bute and opposition to Grenville.

It did not take Rockingham long to equate Chatham with Bute. As early as August 29, 1766, he had written to Newcastle : 'I understand that the Administration profers being *totally* unconnected with Lord Bute. I believe it of many of them — but not at all of Lord Chatham.'[2]  Still his distrust of Chatham dates at least from January 1766 when Chatham refused to join Rockingham's Administration, and in its origins was not unjustified. This alone would have prevented close collaboration on American matters ; but besides repealing the Stamp Act with Chatham's support, Rockingham had enacted the Declaratory Act against Chatham's judgment. And if 'consistency' required that the repeal of the Stamp Act should be defended against Grenville, it also meant that the Declaratory Act should be defended against Chatham. The clearest statement of this view is contained in a letter from Rockingham to Hardwicke, written on July 26, 1767. After describing how, at the conference of July 20, Rigby had conveyed a demand from Grenville 'for a declaration of our creed on the subject of North America', Rockingham wrote :

> that I did not think it was either decent or proper to call upon us for a declaration, that if the words meant only to maintain and support the rights of Great Britain over its colonies, nothing in our conduct could give ground for a suspicion that we did not, and had not always meant that

[1] Rockingham Papers, R1-551.     [2] Add. MS. 32976, ff. 488-9.

this country should maintain its sovereignty ; that a question like this might have been proper if it had been a treaty between Lord Temple and Mr. George Grenville and Lord Chatham ; but to us it carried a reflection which I thought we ought to feel.[1] . . .

The other aspect of Rockingham's American policy was determined by his jealousy of Grenville. 'Consistency' took the form less of opposing the taxation of America than of opposing it when suggested by Grenville. For in January 1767 Rockingham was as much in opposition to Grenville as he was to Chatham. His followers were always on the alert to counter Grenville's American policy ; less ready to do so when a similar policy was advocated by Bedford or Townshend. Bedford had taken a leading part in opposing the repeal of the Stamp Act and had felt very strongly on that measure.[2] Rockingham, however, was perfectly prepared to assume office with Bedford — but then Bedford had no candidate for the Treasury or the lead in the House of Commons. And up to the day of Townshend's death the Rockinghams expected him — the begetter of the second attempt to tax America — to hold high office in any Administration of which they should be a part. But the Rockinghams were 'consistent' — when they returned to office in 1782 they took care to have the resolution of the House of Commons which had expelled Wilkes thirteen years earlier declared illegal — and having once opposed the taxation of America they continued to do so for ever after, and when that policy proved disastrous they acquired a reputation for statesmanship and foresight. The Rockinghams had 'greatness thrust upon them'.

Grenville, alone among the party leaders, held a completely logical policy towards America. He had none of the refinements of Chatham or Rockingham, and had correspondingly

---

[1] Rockingham Papers, R1-539 ; part printed in Albemarle, ii. 50-4.

[2] In Woburn MS., liii. ff. 16 and 20, there are two papers drawn up by Bedford in January 1766, giving his reasons for opposing the repeal. In one of them he writes : 'I would in the course of every debate that shall happen during the discussion of this whole affair consider the submission of the Americans to the Stamp Act as the palladium which, if suffered to be removed, puts a final period to the British Empire in America'.

much greater influence because his policy was simple and could be clearly understood. He held that America could be taxed and ought to be taxed, and he repeated it over and over again *ad nauseam*. Indeed, one might almost say that from 1766 onwards Grenville's politics consisted of little else but a defence of the wisdom and justice of the Stamp Act. His reputation for sound finance was so high, his stature in the House of Commons was so commanding, and there was so much truth and popular appeal in what he had to say, that no Administration could afford to ignore his arguments and their influence on the House. The American policy of Grafton and North was framed, or rather stumbled upon, with one eye on Grenville, and represented a compromise between his views and those of the pro-American section of the Cabinet. Bedford never changed his opinion that the repeal of the Stamp Act was a wrong measure, but he did not keep repeating it day in and day out, and this was another reason why Rockingham found him a much more acceptable partner than Grenville. But granted the supposition held by most politicians on the eve of the American revolution — that Great Britain held full sovereignty in America — there was much to be said for Grenville's views, little for Rockingham's, and nothing at all for the miserable compromise Grafton and North put into effect.

(vi)

The East India inquiry, due to open on February 6, was postponed for a further fortnight in order to allow the Company to prepare new proposals. These were received by the Treasury on February 6 and were dutifully transmitted by Grafton to Bath, the Duke taking care not to venture an opinion on their value as a basis for negotiation. Once again he made an earnest plea for Chatham's return :

> There is no interpretation that the ill-wishers to the present system do not endeavor to give to your absence, and, I am sorry to say, they succeed so far as to make every one feel the languor under which every branch of the Administration labours from it. My Lord Chancellor, the Lord President,

H

and myself . . . are . . . most thoroughly convinced that your presence is absolutely necessary to give dignity to the Administration, and to carry thro' this affair (the most important of all) of the East India Company, in which they all think that there is no stirring without your assistance and concurrence ; and on my part I am ready and desirous to declare that whatever shall appear to you to be the most eligible mode to terminate it, that same shall I most thoroughly join in. . . .[1]

Chatham's reply was even more extraordinary than his answer to the proposals of January 6.[2] He inveighed against the minority in the Cabinet as vigorously as before.

In the mean time reports about my absence seem quite immaterial : those of my not being satisfy'd with certain notions, and with a conduct consequential to them, from the beginning of the East India enquiry to this hour, I should be sorry to remove : on the contrary I would have this clearly understood. . . .

There was a testiness and petulance in his manner, like that of a very young child or a very old man : the subject seemed to be getting on his nerves. He showed no sympathy for Grafton's unfortunate situation and gave no hope of an early return to London : 'As soon as I can recover strength enough, I will set out ; but I cannot imagine the least utility in my lying short by the way, or being confined to my bed the moment I reach London'. The prospect of a negotiation had overtaken his demand for a decision on the right, and he refused to comment on the Company's proposals.

Parliament is *the only place* where I will declare my final judgement upon the whole matter, if ever I have an opportunity to do it. As a servant of the Crown I have no right or authority to do more than simply to advise that the *demands* and the *offers* of the Company should be laid before Parliament, referring the whole determination to the wisdom of that place.

[1] February 8, 1767 ; *Chatham Correspondence*, iii. 194-8, with a copy of the Company's proposals.
[2] February 9, 1767 ; Grafton, *Autobiography*, pp. 116-17.

His followers, bewildered and frustrated, pressed for his return,[1] but to no purpose.

Beckford described the proposals of February 6 as 'unreasonable' and 'insolent', and asked what he should do when the inquiry came on. They were discussed by the Cabinet on February 14,[2] and it was agreed to refer them back to the directors for further explanation. The Cabinet had only maintained the appearance of unity by postponing a decision. Grafton ends his account of the Cabinet meeting : 'I will only add that the whole passed last night with a cordiality which *Cabinets* of late have not shewn, and owing greatly, as I think, to the presence of my Lord President, whose manly conduct and experience have been of the greatest service'.

On February 16 Chatham at last set out for London, but he was taken ill at Marlborough and had to put up at an inn there. Once again Grafton's hopes were disappointed, Townshend received yet another reprieve, and the inquiry was further postponed to March 6. On February 21 Grafton received from the directors their replies to the Cabinet's questions of the 14th. The issue of a negotiation for a settlement or an inquiry into the right could be delayed no longer. It must be faced, even if Chatham were not present, and even if it resulted in a fundamental and final split in the Cabinet.

Grafton found the replies of the directors unsatisfactory and even unintelligible. 'I profess', he wrote to Chatham on February 22, 'that I thought I could *guess* better at the meaning of their propositions before than *now* I can after their explanations.'[3] His simple loyalty to Chatham dictated to him the next steps : to brief the speakers and draft the resolutions for the committee of inquiry. But he knew he could not carry Townshend and Conway in this policy without the pressure of Chatham behind him. If Chatham would only interpose his authority, his original plan could still be carried through. And if Chatham could not come to London, Grafton was willing to go to Marlborough 'to talk this whole matter over

---

[1] Shelburne to Chatham, February 6, 1767 ; *Chatham Correspondence*, iii. 191-3. Beckford to Chatham, February 12, 1767 ; *ibid*. pp. 201-3.
[2] Grafton to Chatham, February 15, 1767 ; *ibid*. 204-6.
[3] *Ibid*. pp. 216-18, with a copy of the directors' replies.

with your Lordship, and to receive and communicate your wishes upon it'.

It was probably Chatham's last opportunity to settle the East Indian question according to his original ideas. Late though it was, it was not too late to impose agreement on the Cabinet. Administration was not pledged to negotiate with the Company; the extremer elements in the Company were not yet out of hand; Townshend might yet be stopped; and Shelburne, now alive to the harm Townshend was doing, still stood by Chatham's policy. Opposition was dormant and had advanced no further towards a union. The King stood firmly by Chatham; he could carry the Cabinet; Conway might yet be mollified into acquiescence or even acceptance; and if Townshend had gone he would have been neither a loss to the Ministry nor a gain to opposition. Yet Chatham refused to receive Grafton until he was well enough to attend to business, or to give his opinion on the directors' replies or his advice on the preparations for the inquiry. 'He desires further to add', he wrote to Grafton on February 23, 'that with regard to East India regulations his fix'd purpose has always been and is, not to be a proposer of plans, but, as far as a seat in one House enables, an unbiass'd judge of them.' [1]

There could be no reasoning with him in that state of mind. Grafton had to console himself with the hope that Chatham might yet be well enough to attend Parliament on March 6, by which time the Cabinet must take a decision on the directors' replies to their questions. It was in the Cabinet, not in Parliament, that the fate of Chatham's policy would be decided. But before that decision was taken there was an unpleasant experience for the Court in the House of Commons.

(vii)

Since Parliament reassembled in January opposition had been languid. The East India inquiry had been postponed so many times that some doubted if it would ever be held. Still, if a settlement were reached with the Company it would have

[1] Grafton, *Autobiography*, pp. 120-1.

to come before Parliament, and until that was ready there were few topics on which opposition could be raised. Grenville, riding his favourite hobby horses of reduction of expense and taxation of America, had attempted two divisions, but these had been rather demonstrations than assaults and had not been supported by other opposition groups. Attendances in the Commons had been low and not much was heard about a union of opposition.

The Rockinghams, like everyone else, had eagerly listened to coffee-house gossip about divisions in the Cabinet, but without very strong hopes of a sensational outcome. Eighteenth-century cabinets were frequently at odds within themselves but outside pressure was needed to bring about disintegration. Newcastle 'beg'd the Archbishop [of York] to inform himself of the true state of this affair of the East India Company',[1] and devoured the scraps of information or rumour tossed him by George Onslow, but even he could work up little enthusiasm about parliamentary business. Lord Mansfield was invited to Claremont, but that discreet man found 'private and public business' to keep him away.[2] The East India inquiry seemed to be sufficiently embarrassing to Administration without requiring the interference of the opposition. In default of any other topic Newcastle and Rockingham began to prepare for the day when Parliament should be asked to pay the debts on the Civil List or to provide extra allowances for the King's brothers.[3]

It was the Grenvilles who were the most active in searching for topics of opposition out of the poor materials available. Whately tried to stir up the Rockinghams and Bedfords, but found it discouraging work. On February 5 he wrote to Grenville :

I have been talking to Wood on the subject of Rigby's absence. I took care to explain to him that all I said was from myself. He agreed with me intirely on the folly of not

[1] Newcastle to Rockingham, January 9, 1767 ; Add. MS. 32979, f. 145.
[2] Newcastle to the Archbishop of York and the Archbishop's reply, both January 10, 1767 ; *ibid.* ff. 164 and 167.
[3] Newcastle to Rockingham, February 14, 1767 ; Add. MS. 32980, f. 82. Rockingham to Newcastle, March 1, 1767 ; *ibid.* ff. 194-6.

being more alert, and said he would do all in his power to
bring up Rigby next week, assuring me at the same time that
the whole party were very earnest to engage, that Lord
Tavistock would come down any day you desired, and that
Lord Gower would take a zealous part if he had an opportunity. . . . I have set Wedderburn's inventive genius to
work to consider of good questions for a division. He delays
his own about the excise till he finds whether the Rockinghams will support it, but he will not delay it long, and if any
other occurs will let you or me know.[1]

But were the Bedfords anxious for opposition ? Had they,
even now, abandoned hope of taking office ? Were they so
keen on co-operating with Grenville as Whately would have
had him believe ? Horace Walpole, self-appointed political
spy and gossip columnist to the Duke of Grafton, 'so zealous
for the Administration of your Grace and Lord Chatham that
I attend to the smallest particulars', did not think so. On
January 17 he wrote to Grafton :

After the permission your Grace has given me of telling
you any thing particular that I hear, it becomes my duty to
do so. Lord Gower told me last night, I thought with
design, that he heard my Lord President was at the point
of death. I shoud not have taken so much notice of this, if
I did not know from the best authority that the Duchess of
Bedford and Lord Gower are still most desirous of connecting with Lord Chatham, and have fixed the Duke of
Bedford to that point. I was myself on Thursday with the
Duchess : George Grenville was with the Duke : she sent
twice to know if he was gone, and three or four times repeated
these words, *When once he gets into the house there is no
getting him out.* This wanted no key and yet she added, *I
heard he was locked up by the snow, but I knew he woud force
his way to town.* In short, my Lord, they are so convinced
of their error in having persuaded the Duke of Bedford to
swell his terms last time, that I beleive they may be had very
cheap at present. Above a fortnight ago their language was,
that if my Lord President shoud retire and be succeeded by
Lord Talbot, the Steward's stick for Lord Gower and a

very few trifles woud make every thing else easy. My Lord Gower himself, I am persuaded, woud open himself to your Grace : my taking the liberty to say I wish this accession is because I am aware that if we cannot persuade Mr. Conway to stay, the Bedfords (if they are not previously secured) will be more difficult afterwards.[1]

Yet in the middle of February opposition shook off its apathy and inflicted a *coup de main* which, though it did no lasting damage, yet helped to revive the idea of a united opposition. The reduction of the land tax as a suitable topic on which all groups could join in a combined assault against Administration was suggested by Whately as long ago as October 20. In confiding to Grenville his hopes for the next session he wrote : 'I should be glad if any popular topic could be thought of, to make a stand upon it. A reduction of the land tax to [*sic*] one shilling in the pound is to a degree, though not entirely, of that nature . . . but perhaps better subjects will occur to you.'[2]

In February the Rockinghams took up this 'popular proposition' of taking a shilling off the land tax, which had been at four shillings in the pound ever since the war. It was an ideal subject, for it could cause no differences between the three opposition groups and it would command the support of the country gentlemen. The suggestion seems to have been made by Dowdeswell, but Rockingham took it up eagerly. On February 11 a small group of his followers met to discuss the matter. In addition to Rockingham and Dowdeswell, there were Burke, White, and Sir William Baker. Charles Yorke refused to attend.[3] He wrote to Lord Hardwicke (February 11) :

I *confess myself* (to your Lordship *in private*) a little cold ; not only because the dimunition of the tax will give false hopes now, and lay false odium hereafter on those who revive it, but because I think that the people are too much in the secret of parliamentary craft, will owe and feel no thanks, will not be influenced in the approaching elections by it.[4]

[1] Grafton MS. 786.    [2] *Grenville Papers*, iii. 331-6.
[3] Hardwicke to Yorke, February 11, 1767 ; Add. MS. 35362, ff. 61-2.
[4] *Ibid*. ff. 63-4.

Hardwicke went, however, and reported to his brother the same evening :

> You conjectured rightly that our meeting was upon a proposition of Dowdeswell's to take off a shilling in the land tax. He made out a tolerable Budget without it and endeavoured to show that a million of debt might be paid. Besides he had heard that Grenville would move it, and that the country gentlemen in general would come into it.[1]

Edmund Burke also doubted the wisdom and utility of this measure, 'gave no opinion and went away early'. He did not vote in the division.

On February 21 the Rockinghams held another meeting where it was decided that Dowdeswell should try for the lead, 'in order to intercept the possible *popularity* falling into G. Greenvile'.[2]  But they were not by any means unanimous : in addition to Yorke and Burke Lord Albemarle was 'much against the thing', while his brother, Admiral Keppel, told Newcastle that 'if Mr. Dowdeswell moved it he believed he should be for it, but if Mr. Grenville moved it he should certainly be against it'.[3]  On this Newcastle remarked to Rockingham, with unconscious irony, 'The jealousy of Mr. Grenville is very great every where'.  Sir George Savile, the most sensible and disinterested of Rockingham's followers, gave him a well-balanced review of the arguments for and against reducing the land tax, and concluded that it should not be moved merely as a point of opposition.

> Now as to the question of expediency I am still more at a loss for I am no counter of noses.  This sort of expediency is not to be neglected, it ought often to hinder one's trying everything that is proper, but I hope it is never to make one do anything improper.  I mean that the best thing in the world had better often be left unattempted, if prudence tells one that one has not numbers to support it.  But never let us drive a wrong or a dubious point because we have numbers,

---

[1] Add. MS. 35362, ff. 65-6.
[2] Rockingham to Newcastle, February 21, 1767 ;  Add. MS. 32980, ff. 138-9.
[3] Newcastle to Rockingham, February 22, 1767 ;  *ibid.* ff. 144-6.

and it will be a *strong point, a devilish stroke,* a fine topic of opposition, popular, etc.[1]

On February 22 Newcastle sent out his whips.[2] To Thomas Pelham, M.P. for Sussex, he stressed the importance of pleasing his constituents — 'a knight of the shire cannot be expected to do otherwise'. This was the excuse George Cooke, M.P. for Middlesex, gave to Chatham to explain his vote against Administration.

My particular situation as Member for Middlesex, and being chose by the unanimous and affectionate voice of my constituents, rendered it impossible for me not to vote for the three shillings, as I am certain had I done otherwise I should at once have forfeited their good opinion — it being a point wherein they are so deeply interested, and in general taxed to the height. . . . Under these circumstances I hope your Lordship will not take it amiss.[3]

When the House went into the Committee of Ways and Means on February 27 Townshend proposed the land tax of four shillings in the pound, but began on the defensive by appealing to the good sense and patriotism of the country gentlemen. He was followed by Dowdeswell, who proposed the reduction to three shillings, which was seconded by Sir Edmund Isham, M.P. for Northants, and supported by Sir Roger Newdigate. All three were country gentlemen ; two were members for counties ; two were independent in politics ; and Dowdeswell was only a recent recruit to the political arena. Five other county members spoke in the debate : four for Dowdeswell's amendment — Thomas de Grey (Norfolk), Robert Henley Ongley (Bedfordshire), John Ward (Worcestershire), and John Hewitt (Nottinghamshire), to one against — Lord Granby (Cambridgeshire).[4] When the division was

---

[1] Albemarle, ii. 34-7.      [2] Add. MS. 32980, ff. 147-53.
[3] *Chatham Correspondence*, iii. 222-4.
[4] Of the eighty English Knights of the Shire fifty voted for the 3s. land tax, nine against. The nine were : Lord Granby (Cambridgeshire), George Pitt (Dorset), Humphry Sturt (Dorset), Robert Shafto (co. Durham), Frederick Vane (co. Durham), Sir William Maynard (Essex), Lord Strange (Lancashire), Lord Brownlow Bertie (Lincolnshire), and George Onslow (Surrey).

taken at near 11 P.M. 206 voted for Dowdeswell's amendment and 188 against.

In Grenville's Diary is a description of the scene in the House after the division : 'The joy in the House of Commons was very great, all the country gentlemen coming round Mr. Grenville, shaking him by the hand, and testifying the greatest satisfaction'.[1] Rockingham, though delighted with the result, did not flatter himself that it would have any serious political effects. On March 1 he wrote to Newcastle : 'For tho' in truth it is not quite a serious defeat yet it is a very unpleasant event'.[2] Newcastle called it a 'great and surprizing success', and added, 'I wish we may keep up to our numbers in the East India affair, but I much doubt it'.[3] Savile did not know whether to be glad or sorry, and added a warning which Rockingham ignored : 'This triumph or victory or whatever it may be seems rather to call for extreme caution and reserve than for hot pursuit'.[4]

Nobody thought that Chatham should resign as a result of this defeat. His normal majority was not affected : many members voted with the opposition on February 27 who would never do so again. The King, in his letter to Conway of February 27, fairly summed up the motives of those who had counselled and aided this vote :

> Those who have voted for it can have been guided only by the incitements that too frequently direct the conduct of politicians, the shadow of popularity (for the reality must consist alone in what is of advantage to the country) and a desire of giving trouble . . . tho the fate of this day on that account is disagreable, I doubt not on all other occasions a great majority will appear in their favour.[5]

The Administration could have fought the matter out afresh on the report, but to do so would have risked a further defeat and would have involved the charge of not accepting the verdict of the House. Rockingham thought that his followers should

---

[1] *Grenville Papers*, iv. 211-12. Misdated, Thursday, February 26.
[2] Add. MS. 32980, ff. 194-6.
[3] Newcastle to Rockingham, February 28, 1767 ; *ibid.* ff. 187-8.
[4] Albemarle. ii. 40-2.                           [5] Fortescue, I, no. 474.

be prepared for such an attempt, but none came, and the land tax remained at three shillings until December 1770.

Grafton in his *Autobiography*[1] says that Chatham blamed Townshend for this defeat. But it was Conway, the Minister in the House of Commons, and Grafton, First Lord of the Treasury, who were really responsible. Ever since the estrangement with Chatham in December Conway had tried to conceal his discomfort by immersing himself in the details of his departmental work and neglecting the business of the House of Commons, where, as the spokesman of the Cabinet, he might clash with the Rockinghams. In this way he tried to reconcile the contradictions in his position : to do his duty to the King, and yet to give no cause of complaint to his former allies. And Grafton was not the man to attend to Conway's business if Conway did not do so himself. The inactivity of the opposition in January and February had spread a feeling of false security, which Grafton and Conway enjoyed too eagerly and too carelessly. But for several days before the division there had been rumours of what was to be attempted ; it could not be kept secret ; and yet no precautions appear to have been taken. Was any attempt made to marshal the troops of Administration, to check the would-be deserters, to encourage the faint-hearted, to seduce the enemy — in short, to use the engines of interest and connection which the Ministry had at its command ? Rockingham was a sluggish and dilatory man but he could be roused into intense, though short-lived, activity if his interest was awakened, and on this occasion he took considerable pains to achieve his end. There is among his papers a list of M.P.s, drawn up a fortnight before the division.[2] It is arranged in three columns. In the first column, under the heading 'Apprized', are forty-three names; the second is headed 'Not apprized' and contains thirty-two names ; while the third is headed 'By whom should be apprized'. Rockingham himself and sixteen of his followers shared this duty. There is no trace of any such activity in

----

[1] P. 122.

[2] R81-189. The list is dated 'Saturday night February the 13, 1767' and should presumably be dated February 14, which was a Saturday.

the Grafton Papers, and it would be foreign to Conway's character. The papers of George Grenville show the energy and care he took to secure a majority on General Warrants in 1764, and had he been in office in 1767 it is difficult to imagine his being defeated. Against a popular question an Administration had to earn its majority, and could not expect it to come automatically. Conway and Grafton were defeated on the land tax division because they did not take the trouble to prepare for victory.

### (viii)

On Monday March 2, Chatham arrived in London where he was so anxiously awaited by his First Lord of the Treasury. He was not a moment too soon. Some reply had to be given to the last paper from the East India Company, which had been awaiting consideration since February 21, and the Committee of Inquiry was due to begin its work on March 6. He found his colleagues smarting from their defeat on the land tax and utterly unprepared for the Committee. Grafton and Shelburne looked to Chatham for a lead, and hoped that now he had at last arrived the confusion resulting from his absence would soon be over. Grafton had retained his faith in Chatham's ability, almost at the last moment, to prevent the Cabinet from splitting in two, but his hopes were pinned on a very sick man, drained of all energy and will, whose powers, even in their greatest days, could hardly have remedied the consequences of three months' neglect. For some weeks it had been common talk in political circles that Townshend was secretly negotiating with the Company, and it was rumoured that a settlement was near completion which would be very favourable to Administration.[1] The Committee of Inquiry could be postponed no longer : either the Company's proposals must be accepted as a basis for negotiation, or a decision against the Company must be sought in the House.

This issue was fought out in the Cabinet on March 3.[2]

---

[1] Rockingham to Charles Yorke, February 10, 1767 ; Add. MS. 35430, ff. 65-6.
[2] The date of this Cabinet meeting is open to some doubt : apparently three were held in one week. Northington, in his letter to the King of

Chatham was not present, but Granby and Hawke, the two service chiefs, were.[1] It was decided that the inquiry should continue, but only after strong opposition from Conway and Townshend who both refused to have anything to do with it in the House.[2] Conway presented a memorandum to the King containing his reasons for wishing to accept the Company's proposals as a basis for negotiations, but the King supported the majority of the Cabinet.[3] Nevertheless, with the two leading men in the Commons in complete disagreement with the rest of the Cabinet on House of Commons business, what prospect was there of the Ministry long surviving? Had Conway and Townshend resigned at this point, could Chatham have gone on?

It was now that Chatham made a final effort to restore his authority, an effort which failed and which was but the prelude to almost three years' inactivity in politics. On the evening of March 4, two days before the inquiry was due in the Commons, Lord North was offered Townshend's office but refused.[4] The King, disappointed but still hopeful that Townshend could be replaced, authorized Grafton to consult

March 1 (Fortescue, I, no. 479), says he has appointed the Cabinet to meet the next day. Conway and Townshend opposed Camden's proposal to take a decision on the question of the right, no agreement was reached, and on March 3 Grafton reported to Chatham. Lord George Sackville in a letter to General Irwin of March 2 and 3 (*H.M.C.*, *Stopford-Sackville MSS.*, i. 120) speaks also of a Cabinet meeting on East India business to be held on March 3. Lastly, there is a letter from Chatham to Grafton, dated 'Bond Street, Wednesday', printed in Grafton, *Autobiography*, p. 124, in which Grafton is asked to call a Cabinet apparently on East India business, for the next day. This letter must have been written on March 4 or March 11. March 4 seems preferable for two reasons : at the Cabinet of March 12 American affairs only seem to have been discussed (see the letters from Grafton and Shelburne to Chatham, both obviously written on March 13, printed in *Chatham Correspondence*, iii. 231-6) ; secondly, by March 12 a decision had been taken on the East India inquiry and there was no need for the Cabinet to discuss it at that date. This gives March 3 or March 5 as the date of the Cabinet at which Conway and Townshend refused to conduct the inquiry in the Commons. But Conway's memorandum on his reasons for wishing to accept the Company's proposals was presented to the King on March 4 (Fortescue, I, nos. 482 and 483), and North was offered Townshend's place on the evening of March 4 (*ibid.* no. 484). Both these events must have happened after the Cabinet meeting.      [1] Walpole, *Memoirs*, ii. 305.

[2] *Ibid.* pp. 302-5.                      [3] Fortescue, I, nos. 482 and 483.

[4] North to Grafton, [March 4, 1767] ; Grafton, *Autobiography*, p. 123. Grafton to the King, March 5, 1767 ; Fortescue, I, no. 484.

Chatham again.[1]    No other offer seems to have been made.
The trumpet had sounded but the walls still stood ; Chatham,
like a man on a death-bed, lapsed back into inertia, and this
point virtually marks the end of his Administration.  There
was no suggestion that Conway should be dismissed ; if
Chatham could not replace Townshend he could not hope to
replace Conway.

Meanwhile opposition was preparing for the inquiry.
Rockingham was singularly well-informed, from 'such indis-
putable authority as leaves it beyond doubt' — was it
Townshend himself ?  On the night on March 5 he wrote to
Newcastle :

> Your Grace may rely on this — that Charles Townshend and
> Mr. Conway are of one opinion — the rest of the Cabinet
> of another.  I hope and believe it will appear *openly* tomorrow
> as neither of them will take the conduct of the East India
> affair in the House of Commons tomorrow, and I hope Sir
> William Meredith and Dowdeswell will draw it out and shew
> that Townshend and Conway do not agree with the other
> Ministers.  It is even not impossible that Charles Townshend
> may not be Chancellor of the Exchequer by the House of
> Commons hour.  I hear Lord North has been desired to
> conduct the affair.  Some think he will but I rather collect
> that he will not venture the attempt.[2]

He felt sure that the Administration could not last many days,
and speculated a little on the prospect of forming a new one
with Conway and Townshend.  He wrote to Charles Yorke
the same night asking to see him before the debate [3] — it was
always an indication that something important was in the wind
when Rockingham consulted Yorke.  Yet the debate proved
a damp squib.  Beckford moved that all proposals made to the

---

[1] The King to Grafton, March 5, 1767 ; *ibid.* no. 485.
[2] Add. MS. 32980, ff. 207-8.  The offer of the Exchequer to North
was intended to be kept secret, but according to Shelburne was revealed by
North himself to Townshend.  See North to Grafton [March 4, 1767],
*Autobiography*, p. 124 ; and Shelburne to Chatham [March 13, 1767],
*Chatham Correspondence*, iii. 232-6.  But the well-informed Walpole does
not mention the offer to North in his *Memoirs*, which suggests that Conway
did not know of it.
[3] Add. MS. 35430, f. 67.

Crown by the Company during the last six months should be laid before the House, and that the East India papers already presented should now be printed. There was no division and little enthusiasm for one. Conway and Townshend did not touch on their disagreement with the rest of the Cabinet until Sir Edward Hawke blurted out that the latest proposal had been rejected by the majority of the Ministers. Even so the King had good reason to congratulate Grafton, and to hope that Conway 'may be persuaded to take a more active part on this occasion than there was any reason to imagine'.[1] Even Chatham did not take too gloomy of view of the event. He wrote to the King on March 7 in a more florid style than even he was accustomed to use :

> The appearance of returning reason and sobriety in the House of Commons is solely owing to his Majesty's well-known magnanimity and wisdom in the present great crisis. The preposterous unions of clashing factions will not, till things change their nature, outweigh and finally overbear the honest sense of the nation, dutifully attach'd to a most benignant Sovereign, pursuing nothing but the welfare and happiness of his people.[2]

Undoubtedly the Rockinghams missed a great opportunity on March 6, the opportunity of a far bigger triumph than the one they secured on the land tax. Had they divided on Beckford's motion they would have forced Conway and Townshend to have declared themselves. Indeed Townshend admitted as much after the event, according to the garrulous George Onslow, who occasionally threw tit-bits of this sort to Newcastle when they were too late to be of any use.[3] How came Rockingham, who had such good knowledge of the division in the Cabinet, to fail to take advantage of it ? Were his tactics really so feeble ? Or was it that he was too well-informed, and believed that the building was so shaky that it did not even need a push to bring it down ? Grenville and

---

[1] Fortescue, I, no. 488.
[2] *Ibid.* no. 491. In the passage as printed Chatham uses thirty-six capital letters.
[3] Newcastle to Rockingham, March 8, 1767 ; Add. MS. 32980, f. 228.

Rigby, who had no such contacts in the Cabinet, did not realize their opportunity. It would be characteristic of Townshend to lull Rockingham into the belief that the Administration was so near breaking up that a parliamentary attack was unnecessary, and then to laugh at him for failing to launch it.

At all events opposition soon woke up. On March 7 Rigby wrote to Grenville regretting that they had failed to make a stand against printing the papers, and suggesting that a petition from the Company might be presented to the House 'praying that the state of their affairs might not be exposed to all foreign powers etc. etc.' [1] Rockingham soon came round to the view that printing the papers was 'as wrong and as dangerous a measure as can be', and that opposition to it would be 'a matter conscientiously right'.[2] Sir Laurence Dundas acted as contact man with the Grenvilles and Bedfords, and the combined opposition prepared to bring their batteries into action. Rockingham warned Newcastle 'not to give the alarm to Administration', and the Duke, by now convinced that it was 'the most absurd and the most dangerous measure that ever was proposed', included among the recipients of his whip poor Thomas Pelham, who would have risked seeing his seven children starve had he voted against the Court,[3] and Bartholomew Burton, Director of the Bank of England, 'whose secrecy I can depend upon', but who voted with Administration.[4] It was to be a great secret; James West was asked 'to muster his troops without letting them know the occasion'. But since they were all friends together, why not let Conway and Townshend into the secret too?

> It must be left to your Lordship's judgment [wrote Newcastle to Rockingham on March 8] who know more of them, whether you should communicate this motion to Charles Townshend and Conway; if they do not agree to it they are determined to purchase my Lord Chatham's *protection* at any rate.

[1] *Grenville Papers*, iv. 6-7.
[2] Rockingham to Newcastle, March 8, 1767; Add. MS. 32980, ff. 220-1.
[3] Newcastle to Rockingham, March 8, 1767; *ibid.* ff. 226-7.
[4] *Ibid.*

On Monday, March 9, Robert Jones, M.P. for Huntingdon, a Director of the East India Company and an intimate friend of Lord Sandwich, presented a petition from the Company against printing their papers, and Dowdeswell moved that the order for printing should be discharged. He was well supported by all sections of the opposition : Meredith, Yorke, and the two Burkes for the Rockinghams ; Rigby and Thurlow for the Bedfords ; and George Grenville. Townshend was not in the House, and Conway, the main speaker for Administration, was backed by a good speech from Sir Gilbert Elliot and a rousing attack on the Company from Barré.[1] Conway spoke well : he complained that he had received no warning of the petition, and moved to adjourn the debate until Wednesday to give time to the directors to decide which papers they did not wish printed. His motion for adjournment was carried by 180 to 147[2] — a fright for the Court but a disappointment to the opposition. Had he opposed Dowdeswell's motion outright he would probably have been defeated.

To be so near victory was a tantalizing experience for the opposition, and those who dissented from Rockingham's tactics felt it more than if they had been beaten by a large majority. John Yorke concluded his account of the debate which he sent to Lord Hardwicke :

I ought to have said that Conway spoke with more spirit than usual, but not like one who meant to resign. I am sick of the intrigue between our friends and that division in the Ministry. Each aims to dupe the other, and in the mean time it makes any approach towards George Grenville impracticable and I am sure the Marquis will make nothing of them.[3]

Rockingham, however, seemed well pleased. 'I don't think', he wrote to Newcastle on March 10, 'a majority of 33 on a question of adjournment a mighty matter of exultation for Administration.'[4] After consulting Rigby and Lord Temple

---

[1] This seems to have been the first speech by Barré on the East India question.    [2] Not 140 as given in the *Journals of the House of Commons*.
[3] Add. MS. 35608, ff. 8-9.
[4] Add. MS. 32980, ff. 250-1. See also Rockingham to Charles Yorke, March 10, 1767 ; Add. MS. 35430, ff. 69-70.

I

he agreed to renew the battle on Wednesday. 'I think with some pains we may *add* a few more and I think the Bedfords and Greenvillites may also *add* and I hope for *some* out of the 180.' [1] But how simple it would all be if only Conway would come over! 'It was *unlucky* that Conway did so well today,' Rockingham wrote to Charles Yorke in the early hours of March 10, 'I wish he had been setting with Charles Townshend.' [2]

But the troops mustered on March 11 to no purpose. After examining the Chairman and Deputy Chairman of the Company, Townshend and Conway both declared against printing the correspondence and accounts, and the order of the House was amended without a division. 'Much talk, no division, and no diner [*sic*]', wrote White to Newcastle that evening.[3] Beckford and Barré had reason to look 'wonderfully dejected',[4] for March 11 marks the failure of Chatham's policy. The Committee of Inquiry, postponed to March 20, could safely begin ; there was no one now who would press for a decision on the right. But Townshend did not profit by his triumph : the initiative in East India matters now passes to Shelburne in the Cabinet and to Sulivan in the Company. And for the opposition, it marks the end of Rockingham's policy of relying on Conway and Townshend to do his work for him, and a return to the idea of a united opposition.

[1] Add. MS. 32980, ff. 250-1.    [2] Add. MS. 35430, ff. 69-70.
[3] Add. MS. 32980, f. 276.
[4] West to Newcastle, March 11, 1767 ; *ibid*. f. 262.

# CHAPTER IV

# THE UNION OF OPPOSITION

AFTER the excitement of the early days of March there came a period of calm, during which the opposition made no serious attack in either House. Yet underneath the surface strange movements were going on : the party leaders alternately sparred and negotiated with each other ; there was much whispering in corners ; and the air was thick with rumours and uncertainty. Most of the time of the House of Commons was taken up with the East India inquiry : the examination of witnesses began on March 20 and the Committee held fourteen sittings until the House adjourned for the Easter recess on April 16. The evidence produced had little effect on the determination of policy but it gave the House some insight into what had been happening in India.[1] Meanwhile the Cabinet had begun negotiations with the Company. On March 19 proposals drawn up by Laurence Sulivan were rejected by the General Court, but after the election of directors on April 9 new proposals were accepted by the Cabinet as a basis for negotiations. The opening of negotiations patched up the quarrel within the Cabinet, though this was soon to break out again, and fresh divisions were to appear both on East India and American affairs.[2]

Chatham took no part in these events. He remained in London, but did not attend either the Cabinet or the Closet. Nor was he kept informed of what was happening. The King and Grafton were prepared to wait patiently until he was sufficiently recovered to take part in business, and did not wish

[1] Reports of the evidence given before the Committee are in Newdigate MS. B26U.

[2] For an account of these negotiations, see L. S. Sutherland, *The East India Company in Eighteenth Century Politics*, pp. 162-70.

to intrude upon him for fear of postponing that recovery.[1]
Apart from some gossip and surmises of Walpole's,[2] we know
little of him at this time, and even his absence does not become
politically important until later.

The defeat of Administration on the land tax and its
narrow majority on the East India division of March 9 had
convinced Rockingham that there was some advantage to be
gained from co-operating with the Bedfords and Grenvilles
and propelled him into discussions of a possible alternative
Ministry.  He advanced by slow and reluctant steps towards
the idea of a united opposition, but did not abandon his hope
that Conway and Townshend would soon resign and that
Chatham would consequently be unable to carry on.  If that
happened, whom would the King send for but Rockingham ?
Indeed, he became more convinced than ever that Townshend
at least, if not Conway, would soon quit, and this naturally
delayed his progress towards the united opposition.  At this
time Conway and Townshend were frequent guests at his
supper table ;  what was discussed there is not known, but
Rockingham's hopes are evident from his correspondence with
his wife and with Newcastle.

On March 17 he went to a ball given by Townshend, and
reported to Newcastle the next day :  'Charles was in high
spirits and his conversation both in *publick* and *private* last
night very agreable.  Nothing quite decisive but not far from
it.'[3]  But Conway was not so obliging — nor so decoying ?
On March 19 Rockingham wrote :  'I had a moment's conversation with Charles Townshend — all well.  I wish it was
as well in the other quarter.'[4]  However, after entertaining
the two 'rebels' to supper on March 24, he wrote in the early
hours of the following morning :

My two supper visitors are gone.  We must still have three
or fours days patience — or rather suspense.  I am still of
opinion that good may ensue — whether in *both* or in one
I cannot quite ascertain, but I continue to like the appear-

---

[1] See the King's letter to Chatham, April 30, 1767 ;  Fortescue, I,
no. 504.                                                [2] *Memoirs*, ii. 319-20.
[3] Add. MS. 32980, ff. 333-4.                          [4] *Ibid*. ff. 343-4.

ances.  Whatever is the event it is right to give a full trial and above all things to keep this matter strictly *secret*.[1]

They were again in Grosvenor Square for supper on March 27, but Newcastle was in London until the following day and Rockingham told him orally what had passed.[2]  On March 29 he wrote : 'I saw Charles Townshend last night.  No actual decision, much talk of probability of its soon happening, but upon the whole not ground sufficient for our sanguine expectations.'[3]

Newcastle had good reason to fear that Rockingham would not be able 'to bring Charles Townshend to a decision'.[4] 'Hope deferred maketh the heart sick', and the Rockinghams were getting impatient.  'I most sincerely wish', wrote Hardwicke on March 27, 'you could bring your supper friends to some decision.  I think the *whole* depends upon it and that their postponing it can end in nothing but mischief.  If only *one* of them could be induced to *determine* the other would either follow soon, or make a very indifferent figure in.'[5]  But there is in the Grafton MSS. a letter from Townshend, docketed March 29, in which he explains to Grafton his plans for the forthcoming Budget and loan.[6]  It does not read like the letter of a man contemplating resignation.  And on March 30 Rockingham wrote to his wife : 'I have seen again and again *the two* who we wished to take a decisive step — at present neither the one or the other do'.[7]

From the end of March Conway and Townshend drop out of Rockingham's correspondence.  But here is the entry in Grenville's Diary for April 1 :

Mr. Charles Townshend comes every day in the House to talk with Mr. Grenville, and to abuse Lord Chatham and laugh at the Administration ; and speaking in relation to what would be proper to be done in America, he said Mr. Conway was upon that subject below low-water mark.[8]

[1] *Ibid*. f. 372.        [2] *Ibid*. ff. 384-5.        [3] *Ibid*. ff. 418-19.
[4] To Rockingham, March 29, 1767 ; *ibid*. f. 420.
[5] Rockingham Papers, R1-488.                [6] Grafton MS. 451.
[7] Rockingham Papers, R156-8.
[8] *Grenville Papers*, iv. 222.  See also the entry for March 26, pp. 218-20.

Townshend may have been 'outrageous' at the way East India affairs were shaping, as Newcastle claimed he was,[1] but he seemed to be having his own way on American affairs. Grafton told Chatham how, at the Cabinet of March 12 when the American extraordinaries were discussed, Townshend had

> declared that if the reduction of them was not determined before the closing of the Committee of Supply, by drawing the troops nearer the great towns, laying the Indian charges upon the provinces, and by laying a tax on the American ports, he would not remain Chancellor of the Exchequer.[2]

'His behaviour', concluded Grafton, 'on the whole was such as no Cabinet will, I am confident, ever submit to.'

Shelburne described his conduct as 'excessive on every occasion', and then went on to say : 'It appears to me quite impossible that Mr. Townshend can mean to go on in the King's service'.[3]   But the Cabinet did submit, and Townshend did continue in the King's service.   He defied the other Ministers ; he tantalized Rockingham with hints of resignation ; he titillated Grenville with gibes at Chatham and Conway. By the death of the dowager Duchess of Argyll [4] on April 16 his wife succeeded to a fortune estimated at £4000 per annum.[5] He told Grafton on April 24 that his family was now 'in great affluence and ample station' [6] and that

> the relish for this is heightened in me by the recollection of former incertainties, the neglect of my family, and the delay of every favor I have ever had reason to expect from the Crown.   I am now out of the reach of fortune, and can act without anxiety.

---

[1] Newcastle to Rockingham, March 15, 1767 ; Add. MS. 32980, ff. 300-1.
[2] Grafton to Chatham, March [13], 1767 ; *Chatham Correspondence*, iii. 231-2.
[3] Shelburne to Chatham, [March 13], 1767 ; *ibid*. pp. 232-6.
[4] Jane, second wife of John Campbell, second Duke of Argyll, and mother of Caroline, who married first, Francis Scott, Earl of Dalkeith, and secondly, Charles Townshend.
[5] Rockingham to Lady Rockingham, April 16, 1767 ; Rockingham Papers, R156-14.
[6] Grafton MS. 452.   The letter is dated 'Friday evening', and docketed 'Ap. 23d 1767.   Rx 24th.'   It was probably written on April 24, which was a Friday.

His political prospects were fair, for if Conway should ultimately resign who could succeed him but Townshend ? But he had not yet obtained a peerage for his wife, and was not completely satisfied with his state. In any case, satisfied or not, he was a disturbing and incalculable figure, and neither Grafton nor Rockingham could take his measure.

## (ii)

The party groups, in consequence of their collaboration during the East India debates, began to distrust each other a little less. The men who had to do the work in the Commons — Dowdeswell and Burke, Rigby and Whately — shared a companionship which predisposed them towards co-operation. Facing the same problems and making war on the same enemy, they saw how much more serviceable it was to work together than to work against each other. Perhaps they even came to share a common attitude of impatience with their chiefs, whose jealousies kept their official relations cold. For while there could only be one First Lord of the Treasury or two Secretaries of State, and the Cabinet could not be extended to include all whose rank or service to the party made them eligible, there were a number of congenial and profitable employments open to those who fought the battle in the Commons but who were not eligible for Cabinet rank.

Contact between Rockingham and the Bedfords was made tentatively and informally, and was at first confined to expressions of regard and hopes of collaboration.[1] Rockingham at this time was dallying with Conway and Townshend, and was not the man to venture courageously where the ground was uncertain. Newcastle urged him on and would have liked him to go much faster.[2] When Newcastle observed 'cudling [sic] and whispering' in the House of Lords between Grafton, Camden, and Sandwich, he began to get alarmed at the 'hurt these appearances must do just at this time' ;[3] and his alarm increased when Albemarle reported the rumour that Sir

---

[1] Rockingham to Newcastle, March 15, 1767 ; Add. MS. 32980, ff. 296-8.
[2] Newcastle to Rockingham, March 16, 1767 ; *ibid.* ff. 312-13.
[3] Newcastle to Rockingham, March 21, 1767 ; *ibid.* ff. 358-9.

Fletcher Norton was going over to the Court.[1] He was obviously tiring of his self-appointed rôle as Rockingham's adviser, and impatient to play a more active part.

He pressed Rockingham to see Rigby. 'He is not only the best intentioned of any of them', he wrote on March 16, 'but the most able to do service.'[2] And again on March 21 : 'Rigby has more sense and I believe is better disposed than any of them'.[3] Finally, unable to contain himself any longer, he asked Albemarle to 'fling out in discourse to Rigby that when he is in the neighbourhood he might just call at Newcastle House' (March 25).[4] Rockingham, when informed of this, urged caution (March 26) : 'Nothing but too much eagerness on our side *can hurt* us. The weight we have only arises from the firmness of our conduct and our consistency, and it much behoves us in this matter to act with the utmost propriety.'[5] But Newcastle merely took offence ; he complained to Albemarle on March 27 that Rockingham's letter was 'reserved, full of caution, *and advice*, and plainly shewing a dislike to my interfering in the great affair now depending'.[6] On March 28 he had his conversation with Rigby.[7] But it proved disappointing, for he only learnt what he might have known already from Albemarle, that 'it was in vain to think of an union with the Duke of Bedford and his friends if Mr. Grenville was not satisfied',[8] and that Grenville would be satisfied with nothing less than an equal share of power with Rockingham.

Meanwhile, Grenville in his turn was being urged towards the united opposition ; with a very gentle pressure perhaps, for he was not an easy man to guide and was not inclined to act on considerations of party expediency. On March 24 he criticized in the Commons the proposed grant to the King's brothers, a measure the Rockinghams could not oppose since they had intended to introduce it themselves the year before.

---

[1] Newcastle to Rockingham, March 26, 1767 ; Add. MS. 32980, f. 386.
[2] *Ibid.* ff. 312-13.      [3] *Ibid.* ff. 358-9.      [4] *Ibid.* f. 374.
[5] *Ibid.* ff. 384-5.      [6] *Ibid.* f. 396.      [7] *Ibid.* ff. 410-12.
[8] Rigby told Grenville that he had convinced Newcastle 'of the unreasonableness of Lord Rockingham's idea' and that 'the Duke himself was more moderate'. Grenville's Diary, March 28, 1767 ; *Grenville Papers*, iv. 220-1.

Grenville would not barter for Rockingham's friendship one jot of his financial purity, the source of so much of his strength in the House. Still, he had to consider his followers, and on the East India question at least the two parties were in agreement. 'I heard yesterday from several friends', wrote Lord Hyde on March 13, 'that the present opposition should be kept together : heterogeneous as it is some general terms of agrement should be settled.'[1] And on March 23 Lyttelton submitted a paper Cabinet 'to be formed if Lord Chatham should go out', so 'heterogeneous' that it would not have survived the first session.[2]

Neither Grenville nor Rockingham would communicate with each other directly and had to do so through Rigby : hardly a wise proceeding if serious negotiations were intended, since Rigby had his own game to play, if necessary at the expense of both. On March 26 he informed Grenville that he had already had several conversations with Rockingham, but had told him 'that he [Rigby] could say nothing . . . without previously speaking to Mr. Grenville with whom he meant to act'.[3] Rigby claimed 'that the Duke of Bedford was stronger than ever in those ideas', and 'thought nobody fit to be at the head of Government but Mr. Grenville'. Grenville had heard all this before — in November 1766 shortly after Bedford's first negotiation with Chatham had failed. Was he taken in by it now? At any rate, it appears in his diary without comment.

Rigby then asked 'what sort of language he should hold to Lord Rockingham and Lord Albemarle'. Grenville said he wanted to see

an extensive plan free from exclusions . . . but if the Rockingham party meant only to unite for the present, availing themselves of that strength in order to overturn this Administration in order to put Mr. Townshend and General Conway at the head of the next, it was what he could never hear of.

[1] Grenville (J. M.) MSS.
[2] *Grenville Papers*, iv. 8. It was a mixture of Grenvilles, Bedfords, and Rockinghams, with Grenville at the Treasury and Rockingham or Newcastle named for Privy Seal. Lyttelton also asked whether 'a more consistent Ministry' might not be formed retaining only Charles Yorke of the Rockinghams.          [3] Grenville's Diary ; *ibid.* pp. 218-20.

Did Grenville then know of Rockingham's coquetting with Conway and Townshend? His 'extensive plan free from exclusions' is little different from Chatham's 'great and conciliating plan', or from the 'new Administration on a comprehensive plan' which Rockingham tried to form in July 1767. In short, the party leaders disclaimed the idea of party and professed to desire a union of the best of all parties : an indication that while party politics were practised they were also an innovation which had not yet acquired respectability.

The same day Rigby 'alarmed the Marquess greatly . . . by bringing Earl Temple forward',[1] and Albemarle, while professing to be 'in a great measure reconciled to Mr. Grenville', regretted 'we know so much of the Earl his brother' and concluded, 'I am afraid they want the Treasury in the hands of one of them'. But what did Rockingham want? Rigby told Grenville on March 27 that it was 'to have Lord Rockingham First Lord of the Treasury, Mr. Dowdeswell Chancellor of the Exchequer, Mr. Yorke Chancellor, and Mr. Charles Townshend Secretary of State'.[2] It is improbable that Rockingham thus specified his demands. Indeed, neither he nor Grenville openly claimed the Treasury although neither would have considered any other office : once again an implication that neither should command through party an office which the King should dispose of freely. But neither would leave the Treasury to the other, or consider seriously the idea of a compromise candidate. Grenville condemned these alleged demands of Rockingham, and proposed 'as a middle way' that one party should have the Treasury and the disposal of offices in the Commons and the other the Woolsack and a similar power in the Lords. It was quite clear which office Grenville had marked out for himself.

Albemarle, whose sister had married Lord Tavistock,[3] now began to despair of the union he so much wished. 'Earl

---

[1] Albemarle to Newcastle, March 27, 1767 ; Add. MS. 32980, f. 398.

[2] Grenville's Diary ; *Grenville Papers*, iv. 220.

[3] Tavistock's death on March 22 as the result of a hunting accident brought Albemarle into close and frequent contact with the Bedford family, and explains why Bedford himself took no part in these conversations.

Temple and his brother appearing as *principles* [*sic*]', he wrote
to Newcastle on March 29, 'has dampt my spirits. You
cannot in honour treat with *them*, your friends will not follow
you.'[1] And again on March 30 : 'I don't believe Grenville
wishes it, unless he or his brother has the Treasury'.[2] But
Newcastle, who could not bear the thought of the negotiation
breaking down, wished for a scapegoat and found one in
Rockingham, who did not attend sufficiently to the Duke's
advice. On March 29 he wrote to Albemarle :

> The Duke of Bedford will never come in heartily without
> George Grenville ; and I should blame him if he did ; for
> let my Lord Rockingham and his friends be ever so sanguine
> I will be bold to say, that his Lordship closely united with
> the Duke of Bedford's friends, exclusive of George Grenville,
> will not compose an Administration that will last six months.[3]

He saw Rigby again on April 1,[4] and learnt from him that 'the
whole now depended upon that single point of Mr. Grenville's
coming into the Treasury', and that Grenville never would
consent to Rockingham being there. Even Newcastle, eager
as he was for an agreement, could not stomach this and was
forced to admit, 'I am afraid there is an end of this negotiation'.
Even though Rigby argued 'that Mr. Grenville would never
think of renewing any of those measures which had been set
aside and overruled in my Lord Rockingham's Administration,
particularly with regard to North America' (was he authorized
by Grenville to give this pledge ?), Newcastle pleaded that 'our
best, most reasonable, and best disposed friends . . . would
not be brought to consent to Mr. Grenville's being brought
into the Treasury'. Sorrowfully he urged Rockingham not
to give up hope, but 'to go on with the negotiation and to
endeavour to bring it to a successful determination'. However,
by April 8 his resentment had got the better of his fears ; he
described as '*idle words* Rockingham's objection that *our
friends* will not agree' to union with Grenville.[5] Newcastle's
wish for union was not the product of conscious thought : his
busy tortured mind craved employment and without it he

[1] Add. MS. 32980, f. 422.    [2] *Ibid.* f. 438.    [3] *Ibid.* f. 424.
[4] Add. MS. 32981, ff. 1-4.    [5] To Mansfield ; *ibid.* ff. 65-6.

knew no peace. 'What a jealous head and restless mind that old man has!' wrote Albemarle.[1]

On March 31 Rockingham had laid down the conditions on which he would conclude an alliance.[2]

> To have a majority of friends in the Cabinet.
> To give the whole care of the West Indies and North America to my Lord Dartmouth, with the Seals as Third Secretary of State.
> To insist that Mr. Grenville should have nothing to do with North America.
> That the measures which were taken by his Lordship in the Treasury with regard to the trade and commerce in America and the laying taxes there, should be maintained and pursued.

Each of these conditions was designed as a barrier against Grenville's influence, and their effect would have been to make the Grenvilles the junior partners in the projected new Administration, and give the Rockinghams the privileged position they had hoped to hold under Chatham. They stood no chance of being accepted, but Rockingham was well content with what had happened. 'Upon the whole', he wrote to Charles Yorke on April 2, 'matters are now at a stand and in my belief not the worse that they are so.'[3] And to Lady Rockingham the next day : 'Negotiations stand as you wish them'.[4]

To sum up : Bedford in opposition would not give up the alliance with Grenville, and while Rockingham was prepared to work with Bedford, both in office and in opposition, neither he nor Grenville would yield the first place to the other. The union of opposition was as far away as ever, but what negotiations could not bring about co-operation in Parliament might.

---

[1] To Rockingham, April 3, 1767 ; Rockingham Papers, R2-61.
[2] Add. MS. 32980, f. 450.
[3] Add. MS. 35430, f. 71.
[4] Rockingham Papers, R156-10. Lady Rockingham was hostile to Grenville. See Dowdeswell's letter to her of March 20, 1768, in the Dowdeswell Papers at the William L. Clements Library. Part of this letter is printed in *Cavendish's Debates*, i. 582, as addressed to Rockingham.

(iii)

On April 10 the Duke of Bedford moved in the Lords for an
address to the King to take into consideration an Act of the
province of Massachusetts Bay for pardoning the rioters in the
Stamp Act disturbances. The motion was one that all opposition groups could support, for few even of those most sympathetic towards the colonies would defend this usurpation of
the Crown's prerogative of mercy. The King objected to the
motion because it 'tacitly implied a diffidence in the House of
my intentions on one of the most extraordinary Acts now sent
by the province of Massachusetts Bay'.[1] Grafton moved the
previous question and the motion was rejected by 63 votes
to 36.

The debate showed the opposition in a bad light, not
because they were defeated, but by their failure to co-operate
even on a matter where there was no strong difference of
opinion. Bedford had not thought fit to inform the Rockinghams
beforehand and they resented it accordingly. Rockingham
gave no lead to his followers and, while the Bedfords and
Grenvilles were solid in support of the motion, the Rockinghams
presented a remarkable spectacle of diversity of opinion.
Richmond spoke against the motion ; Rockingham, Dartmouth,
Monson, and Edgcumbe voted against it ; Newcastle,
Portland, Albemarle, Scarbrough, and Bessborough abstained;
Hardwicke and Grantham voted with the Bedfords.[2] Here is
Rockingham's account of this debate :

> Yesterday the Duke of Bedford made a motion in the
> House of Lords — the matter proper and what *we* might
> have concurr'd in, but upon the whole it rather appeared to
> me somewhat *unfair* or *uncandid to the Administration.* Many
> of our friends were desirous of joining in the question against
> Administration, and yet I felt as if our joining in it might
> have the appearance of peevishness and want of candour —
> of course I determined to vote with Administration. Many

[1] The King to Grafton, April 10, 1767 ; Fortescue, I, no. 501.
[2] Three Lords of the Bedchamber, Coventry, Eglinton, and Buckinghamshire voted against the Court. There is a division list in Add. MS.
32981, ff. 109-13.

of our friends staid and voted with me and many went away not to vote against. There was no tye upon us to vote with the Duke of Bedford for in fact they did not communicate with *us* on the matter. If they had and the question in all parts had been made suitable to our opinions *we* and *they* should have joined and I believe the consequence would have been a majority against Administration.[1]

This did not augur well, coming so soon after the failure of the conversations with Rigby, for the future of the combined opposition. The Court had little to fear from a party leader who did not wish to be 'unfair' or 'uncandid' to Administration, and whose differences with the other party leaders were such as to prevent union in a debate which he himself admitted they might have won. Newcastle complained to Sir William Baker,[2] with justice, that the division was bungled (April 12) :

I own I never was clearer in my life in opinion for any question than I was for that. I thought it would have had all the good consequences imaginable and no one bad one ; as nothing was said against it but that it was an imputation of neglect of duty in the Administration. If it was so I don't see any great inconvenience in that ; it would have shew'd my Lord Bute and my Lord Chatham (and there is my point) that, with the Duke of Bedford etc. we were masters of the House of Lords. It would have been paying a very innocent compliment to the Duke of Bedford, and might have been a means of union and concert during the remainder of this session, which is so necessary and so advisable for the whole.[3]

On April 14 Newcastle had a conversation with Bedford.[4] Bedford 'lamented the difficulties that prevented a most solid union and junction', which Newcastle ascribed to the deadlock over the Treasury. To Bedford's suggestion that Rockingham might be Secretary of State and Yorke Chancellor, with

---

[1] Rockingham to Lady Rockingham. Misdated April 10, 1767 ; it should be April 11. Rockingham Papers, R156-13.
[2] M.P. for Plympton. A strong pro-American.
[3] Add. MS. 32981, ff. 137-8. Grenville made the same motion in the Commons on April 13, but did not press it to a division.
[4] *Ibid.* ff. 156-9.

command over the House of Lords, Newcastle 'still adhered to the Treasury being the whole'.

The Duke of Bedford then hinted that Mr. Grenville was the most able man for it ; and why in an establishment which was to be solid and permanent should not the man the most conversant in the finances be put in the Treasury.

From this they went on to discuss the debate on Bedford's motion, and Newcastle excused himself for not voting against the Court but complained of 'the want of a proper communication'. Bedford

did not defend or condemn the want of communication ; but said the negotiation being broke off and a correspondence having been long kept up between my Lord Rockingham, Mr. Charles Townshend, and Mr. Conway, which he admitted might have been for some time at an end with Mr. Charles Townshend but he thought subsisted in its full force with Mr. Conway ; and the great intimacy and friendship subsisting between some of my Lord Rockingham's most intimate friends (meaning I suppose the Cavendishes) might have been the reason of the want of communication, lest Mr. Conway might have some notice of it.

When Newcastle showed his memorandum of this conversation to Rockingham

he said not one word upon it ; neither seem'd pleased nor displeased, but stopp'd at every place where George Grenville was named ; against whom and my Lord Temple (for he always puts them together) he seems more picqued than ever.[1]

Rockingham could scarce complain if his dealings with Conway and Townshend were regarded suspiciously by his would-be allies. And Bedford, who had also dealt with Administration, could not with justice censure Rockingham's relations with Conway and Townshend. But suspicions and recriminations were hardly conducive to forming a united opposition, and such a union was difficult when both parties had leanings towards the Court. Grenville, who had no

[1] Newcastle to Grantham, April 17, 1767 ; *ibid.* f. 197.

friends at Court and had never been invited to negotiate with it, was the advocate for opposition *à outrance* rather than Bedford or Rockingham. For his only chance of getting back to office was in the complete overthrow of the Administration.

A few days later there came an opportunity to undo the damage. On the East India inquiry at least all three parties agreed. The Committee was still hearing witnesses, negotiations were still carrying on with the Company, and no statement had come from the Cabinet on the policy they proposed to recommend to Parliament. On April 7 Sir William Meredith gave notice in the Commons that if within the next week Administration did not bring forward their proposals he would move to dissolve the Committee. The House was near rising for the Easter recess. 'It is thought to be right to press for some decision on this matter', wrote Rockingham to his wife on April 9, 'while the House is yet full.'[1] After Easter many of the country gentlemen would not return to London, and without their votes the opposition stood little chance of beating the Court. Rockingham asked his wife, then at Bath, to round up any stragglers there,[2] and the motion seems to have been concerted with the other opposition groups.[3]

Meredith made his motion on April 14, and at two o'clock in the morning it was rejected by 213 votes to 157. Rockingham wrote to his wife : 'Some of our friends thought the motion rather precipitate and divided against us'.[4] Or as Burke spitefully put it : 'Those who chose to be squeamish (not conscientious) were of opinion that the Committee ought to be suffer'd to sit in hopes that some proposition might be made ; this lost us some paltry people, but it lost the Grenvilles many more'.[5] In other words, the independents in the House thought they should await the issue of the negotiations before dissolving the Committee — a sensible point of view.

With Lady Rockingham, whose influence over her husband's politics was much greater than contemporaries realized,

---

[1] Rockingham Papers, R156-12.    [2] *Ibid.* and R156-11.
[3] Burke to Lady Rockingham [April 16, 1767]; *ibid.* R144-3. See also Newcastle's memorandum of his conversation with Bedford on April 14; Add. MS. 32981, ff. 156-9.    [4] Rockingham Papers, R156-14.
[5] To Lady Rockingham [April 16, 1767]; *ibid.* R144-3.

the Rockinghams made a point of disparaging Grenville. Burke took pleasure that Grenville had lost some support on Meredith's motion, while Meredith rejoiced because Townshend's Budget speech had a 'tendency to lower the rate of Mr. Grenville'.[1] But Newcastle, after Meredith had spent a night at Claremont, reported that he

> differs more with our friend the Marquess about union and coalition than your Grace [Portland] and I do. He thinks it so necessary that he intends (as he says) to set by George Grenville in the House of Commons *to use himself to it*.[2]

And Lyttelton thus reported to Grenville Hardwicke's conversation :

> Lord Hardwicke went so far as to say that he knew of no engagement that his brother and he were under to the Rockingham party that could prevent their holding offices in conjunction with Lord Temple and Mr. Grenville, especially as the Great Seal was not given to his brother when that party came into Government, though it might have been expected.[3]

And Whately wrote to Grenville on April 21 :

> Some large detachments of the Rockinghams, I hear, go still further ; and by the language they hold of the propriety and possibility of a junction with Mr. Grenville, are understood to intimate their inclination, at all events, to accomplish it.[4]

A division in the Commons always made the Rockinghams lean towards Grenville ; they could not do without him in opposition, though they hoped to do so in office.

### (iv)

Parliament reassembled after the Easter recess on April 28. During the next two months there was much to occupy the attention of both Houses — an unusual circumstance at this

---

[1] Meredith to Lady Rockingham, *ibid.* R144-1. Dated by Meredith, October 18, 1767, which is impossible : it should be April 18.
[2] Newcastle to Portland, April 27, 1767 ; Add. MS. 32981, f. 146.
[3] Grenville's Diary, April 11, 1767 ; *Grenville Papers*, iv. 223-4.
[4] *Ibid.* pp. 10-11.

K

time of the session. The Commons were busy with the East
India settlement and its accompanying legislation ; while in
the Lords an attack was launched against the Ministry which
at one time seemed certain to succeed, but was eventually
repulsed. It was an unhappy period for the Court. Grafton,
thoroughly rattled by the attacks of the combined opposition,
only just managed to hold his end up ; while in the Commons
Conway and Townshend deserted Administration on the East
India settlement.

By the beginning of May negotiations with the East India
Company were at the stage when an agreed settlement was in
sight. On May 1 when the Committee of Inquiry was resumed
Henry Crabb Boulton, a director of the Company, told the
Commons that negotiations were almost complete and the
Committee was adjourned to May 7. It seemed that nothing
was now wanting except the ratification of the General Court
and the House of Commons. Yet before the Committee met
again East India affairs were once more in turmoil ; and the
division in the Cabinet, patched over in March, broke out
afresh.

On May 6 the General Court, against the advice of the
Directors, raised the dividend to 12½ per cent.[1] When
Chatham took office it had stood at 6 per cent, and this was
the second increase since then. It was not a move concerted
with the parliamentary opposition, though individual members
such as Dempster and William Burke had taken part,[2] but was
planned and executed by elements within the Company
working for a rise in the price of stock. Politically, it endangered
the whole East India settlement and was an act of defiance
which the Administration dared not ignore. The East India
problem, which had seemed on the way to a satisfactory
solution, now supplied the opposition with a fresh weapon to
attack the Court.

On May 7 the Company were ordered to lay fresh papers
before the Committee of Inquiry together with an account of
the proceedings in the General Court, while the Chairman and

---

[1] For an account of how this was done, see Sutherland, pp. 169-72.
[2] Walpole, *Memoirs*, iii. 16.

Deputy Chairman were summoned to attend. The following day the Administration answered the General Court with a Bill to prohibit the Company from further increasing its dividend. The battle was on.

The East India settlement of 1767 was embodied in four Acts of Parliament. The agreement itself (7 George III, c. 57) was limited to two years' duration from February 1, 1767. During that period, the Company was confirmed in its territorial possessions, but had to pay the Crown £400,000 per annum. The cardinal point of Chatham's policy was therefore abandoned. In return for this payment the Company was granted concessions on the duty and drawback on tea (7 George III, c. 56). These measures passed with little opposition either in Parliament or in the Cabinet. It was otherwise with the restrictions on the Company imposed in consequence of the General Court of May 6. The Act 7 George III, c. 49, attempted to regulate voting in the General Court : previously the possession of £500 of stock had been the qualification; by this Act it was necessary to hold the stock for at least six months before an election. It proved ineffectual in stopping the abuse of splitting a large holding of stock to create faggot votes, but it was generally supported by all parties. Finally, the Dividend Bill (which became law as 7 George III, c. 48) restrained the dividend to 10 per cent, but only until the beginning of the next session of Parliament. It was this measure which caused the trouble.[1]

Yet the Bill passed the Commons much easier than might have been expected. There were several reasons for this. It was introduced at an unfavourable time for opposition : many of the independent members who might have been induced to oppose it had gone home for the Easter recess, and did not return during the remainder of the session. This was their usual practice, and had been noted by Rockingham as a reason for pressing Administration before the recess.[2] Secondly, the selfish and irresponsible behaviour of the General Court had turned opinion in the House against them, and there was a

---

[1] The Bill was most probably the work of Jeremiah Dyson.
[2] See above, p. 130.

feeling that restrictions of some kind were necessary. The opposition recognized this : they did not divide on second or third reading, but tried to amend the Bill in committee by raising the permitted dividend to 12½ per cent. In this they were supported by Conway and Townshend ; and though it was a point on which both Grenvilles and Rockinghams agreed, it was easily defeated.

Finally, the opposition had now decided to concentrate their attack in the Lords where it was believed the Court could be more easily defeated, and it was there that they hoped to amend the Bill.

### (v)

Hitherto Conway and Townshend had travelled on parallel tracks, though the motive power which propelled them was different. From the opening of the session they had formed an enclave within the Cabinet, a duumvirate differing in outlook and connection from their colleagues, which was offset by their position in the Commons. They had opposed Chatham's East India policy ; their idea of a negotiated settlement had been taken up by the Cabinet ; both had gained freedom to manœuvre through Chatham's withdrawal ; and finally both had showed an inclination towards the Rockinghams. They might have been rivals for the power which had dropped from Chatham's hands into Grafton's nervous and inadequate grasp. But Townshend preferred to insinuate, rather than force himself into power ; while Conway would not compete for the prize. So their paths had neither crossed nor diverged ; they had remained a duumvirate, united by circumstances not by inclination. Now those circumstances were changing.

During the early days of May, the bright flame of Townshend's genius burned higher and fiercer than ever before ; if he had desired to make a figure in the House then surely he now realized his ambition. On May 8, when Dyson moved for leave to bring in the Dividend Bill, he delivered his famous 'champagne speech', described by Walpole as 'a torrent of wit, parts, humour, knowledge, absurdity, vanity, and fiction, heightened by all the graces of comedy, the happiness of allusion and quotation, and the buffoonery of farce',[1] and by the prosaic Conway as one of 'the finest and most extraordinary speeches ever heard'.[2] Though Townshend was unable to get his way on the Dividend Bill, he found compensation in another sphere. In the American debates of May 13 and 15 he dominated the Commons and eclipsed even Grenville. But his day was almost spent. Major financial business was always completed well before the end of the session, and as the parliamentary battle shifted to the Lords he found fewer opportunities to shine. When Parliament was prorogued in July and negotiations began for new modelling the Administration Townshend took no part, and when death cut short his career he was a discredited and almost forgotten figure.

The abandonment of Chatham's East India policy eased Conway's position, but did not reconcile him to it. Though he still felt that he had liabilities towards the Rockinghams (and they were not likely to write them off or reduce them), at least he was no longer in fundamental conflict with the rest of the Cabinet. But that comparatively happy position did not last for long ; Conway in office never knew tranquillity. Rockingham's uneasy co-operation with Grenville challenged his position and outraged his feelings,[3] and there soon arose another question on which he felt obliged to make a stand in the Cabinet.

The repeal of the Stamp Act did not undo the mischief perpetrated by that measure. In America it gave expression to grievances and ambitions long concealed and perhaps only half felt, while in Britain the feeling was that a gesture had been made to which the colonies had not responded. Massachusetts Bay had pardoned those implicated in the Stamp Act riots, and New York had defied the Mutiny Act by refusing to provision the troops stationed there. In Britain Townshend

---

[1] *Memoirs*, iii. 17-18.

[2] Conway to the King [May 8, 1767] ; Fortescue, I, no. 508. Conway coupled together under this description the speeches of Grenville and Townshend. But Walpole ignores Grenville's speech.

[3] Grenville, writes Walpole, was 'the only man who had ever inspired him [Conway] with animosity'. *Memoirs*, iii. 9.

had pledged the Cabinet to raise a revenue from the colonies, and was now preparing a bill for that purpose. Conway preferred a mild policy when the rest of the Cabinet believed that a stand must be made against new and exorbitant demands. He refused to take the responsibility for introducing the Ministry's American measures in the Commons,[1] and that task was entrusted to Townshend, only too pleased to appear in the spotlight again.

The House was to go into Committee on the American papers on May 5, but as Townshend could not appear that day their consideration was postponed to May 13.[2] The Rockinghams had correctly conjectured what the Ministry intended to do, and also that Conway disagreed with it ; and Rockingham called a meeting of his advisers for May 4 to consider their tactics.[3] He wished to embarrass the Cabinet and gain advantage from its division, rather than to demonstrate in favour of the colonies or give support to Conway. He tried to consult Mansfield ; hoped for support from the Bedfords and Grenvilles ; and declared it was the 'mode' of the Ministry's plan that was 'improper', rather than its substance.[4] 'I think tomorrow may be a very useful day', he wrote to Charles Yorke on May 12, 'if a proper plan is fixed and well supported. Your assistance would have great effect on various denominations.'[5] Newcastle hoped that Dowdeswell 'would talk to Rigby or G. Grenville upon it', and added, 'It can do no hurt'.[6] It was not concern for the state of America which urged the Rockinghams to intervene in this debate.

On May 13 Townshend proposed three resolutions in the Committee of the whole House. The first declared that the province of New York had disobeyed the Mutiny Act ; the second condemned the provision they had made as inadequate ; and the third proposed that the Governor should be prohibited

[1] *Memoirs*, iii. p. 15.
[2] For the extraordinary story of why Townshend could not appear, see *ibid*. pp. 15 and 19.
[3] Rockingham to Charles Yorke, May 3, 1767 ; Add. MS. 35430, ff. 73-4.
[4] Rockingham to Newcastle, May 4, 1767 ; Add. MS. 32981, ff. 287-8.
[5] Add. MS. 35430, f. 77.
[6] Newcastle to Rockingham, May 13, 1767 ; Add. MS. 32981, f. 385.

from giving his assent to any Act of the province until they had complied. Conway contested the first resolution ; but the Rockinghams preferred to concentrate their fire against the third, and their objections were based on law rather than on policy. Hence the need to consult Mansfield and Yorke.

Townshend began by declaring that he spoke merely as a member of Parliament, 'that it did not belong to him, in respect of his office, to take the lead in the business'.[1] This, of course, was a hit at Conway who should himself have introduced these resolutions. But was there any more to it than that ? Bradshaw concludes his letter to Grafton : 'Mr. Townshend will meet your Grace in Grosvenor Square on Saturday evening at eight o'clock. He ask'd me if you seem'd to consider his resignation as decisive of the fate of Administration — I told him I had no reason to believe you did.' That same night Lord Suffolk wrote to Grenville :

> Since we parted tonight I have happen'd to hear, as credibly as these things can be heard, that the Duke of Grafton is sent for from Newmarket, and that it is apprehended Mr. Townshend's resignation is to be convey'd thro' him. Why it shd. be so, I don't see.[2]

Horace Walpole also mentions that Townshend threatened to resign about this time.[3] But Townshend does not appear to have entrusted Rockingham with his determination, and if it was such he soon changed it.

He did not confine his speech to the business on the order paper, but also outlined his scheme of American taxation and of the proposed American Customs Board. He was not extravagant, but made out a reasonable case for firm measures in America, such as appealed to the mood of the House and could not easily be refuted. The Rockinghams who spoke in the debate — Burke, Dowdeswell, Savile, John Cavendish, and

---

[1] All quotations are taken from Bradshaw's account of the debate. Bradshaw to Grafton, May 14, 1767 ; Grafton, *Autobiography*, pp. 176-8. Walpole, *Memoirs*, iii. 21-9, supplements Bradshaw, and does not contradict him on essentials.

[2] Grenville (J. M.) MSS.

[3] *Memoirs*, iii. 29.

Yorke [1] — were outmatched in interest by Grenville and Conway. Grenville 'attacked Mr. Conway with great violence', and 'talked of encouragement given to the colonies in their misbehavior and that impeachments might follow the authors'. Townshend's plan was not sufficiently strict for him ; the new duties were 'a subversion of the Act of Navigation under colour of a tax' ; finally, in an effort to outdo Townshend, he proposed that all office holders in America and all members of the colonial Assemblies should be compelled 'to subscribe a declaration to the effect of the Declaratory Act'.

Caught between Townshend and Grenville, with no support from the Rockinghams, Conway defended himself as best he could to an unsympathetic House. He represented the third resolution as 'violent, dangerous, and ineffectual, and stated the instance of disobedience as a trifling one'. Barré, Beckford, and Pownall also spoke for indulgence to the colonies, but could not take off the effect of Conway's isolation. Grenville's motion to amend the Mutiny Act was supported by the Rockinghams, but was rejected by 180 votes to 98, Conway and his relations voting against the Court.[2] 'I am quite tir'd of these factious proceedings', wrote Sir Charles Mordaunt to Sir Roger Newdigate on May 14, 'and wish myself in the country.' [3] There were others who felt as he did. When the resolutions were reported on May 15 Grenville's proposals were not supported by the Rockinghams, and were easily defeated.[4]

## (vi)

Conway and Grafton, in spite of their disagreements, kept on good terms with each other [5] — a fortunate circumstance,

[1] Yorke, according to Bradshaw, 'spoke very much in support of Mr. Grenville's arguments and adopted all his propositions'.

[2] Conway himself ; his nephew, Lord Beauchamp ; his cousin, Horace Walpole ; and his brother-in-law, Lord Frederick Campbell.

[3] Newdigate MS. B1840.

[4] One was an amendment to strengthen the first resolution by adding that the colonies still persisted 'in the open denial of the legislative authority' of Great Britain; this was lost by 150 votes to 51. The other was his motion 'that colonial officials should take an oath acknowledging the supremacy of Great Britain' ; this was lost by 141 votes to 42.

[5] Grafton, *Autobiography*, pp. 127-8.

as otherwise the Administration could hardly have survived. At this time it presented a spectacle of weakness and division rare, if not unique, in British political history. The nominal head of the Ministry had retired from business altogether ; the leader of the House of Commons had voted against the two principal ministerial measures ; the Chancellor of the Exchequer had also voted against one of these, and in addition seemed to regard the House merely as a stage on which he could exhibit himself in public ; while the Secretary of State for the Southern Department, with the American colonies and British foreign policy towards France and Spain under his control, was disliked and distrusted by his colleagues. Grafton neglected his work for horse-racing and was openly living with a woman of loose morals ;[1] Northington was thought to be dying ; Camden was timid and ineffectual ; while Granby and Hawke were ciphers outside their departments. Was this the Administration that had set out on that 'glad confident morning' of July 1766 to restore 'strength and dignity' to the King's government ? What hope was there from these men of a bold or generous policy ? Could not a vigorous and united opposition drive 'this weak and insufficient Administration' from office and replace it by the 'strong, united, national Administration' Chatham had so signally failed to form ? Yet during the last two months of the session the Court was never in serious danger in the Commons, and survived the assaults of the combined opposition in the Lords ; while Rockingham found it as difficult to construct 'a comprehensive Administration' as Chatham had done.

Conway made sporadic efforts to placate his 'old friends' with visions of a new Administration which they would be able to enter. Walpole busied himself a good deal in trying to learn from Richmond what it was the Rockinghams wanted,[2] and found they were haunted by the ghost of Bute — the proposed union with Bedford and Grenville was largely

[1] The first mention by one of Grafton's correspondents of 'Mrs. Haughton', better known as Nancy Parsons, is in a letter from Townshend docketed 'Ap. 23d 1767 Rx 24th', but probably written on April 24 ; Grafton MS. 452.

[2] One such attempt is described in his *Memoirs*, iii. 13-14.

dictated by unwillingness to rely on Bute's friends in any future Administration.[1] There was no substance behind Conway's overtures ; they were made solely to placate his uneasy conscience. The Rockinghams would not listen to any offer from Conway unless accompanied with his resignation ; only then would they be able to dictate both to the King and their allies. But Conway would not take the responsibility of dissolving the Administration and leaving the King in the lurch, who would be compelled to take the opposition on their own terms.

About this time Conway began to think seriously about retiring at the end of the session. Bradshaw mentions on May 14 'Mr. Conway's intended resignation',[2] and on May 23 Walpole told Grafton that 'my endeavours to prevent Mr. Conway's resignation are almost exhausted'.[3] On May 30 the King used 'the resolution of Lieut. General Conway to retire' as a spur to make Chatham see Grafton,[4] but Grafton does not seem to have spoken of it in his conversations with Chatham on May 29 and June 4, although the opposition knew of it by then.[5] It is difficult to say at what particular date he decided he would resign, for at no period was his determination absolute. He had been talking of resignation ever since December ; by May he had got round to naming the date — at the end of the session — and Walpole felt that affairs were passing out of his control. But not until the second half of June was Conway's intended resignation sufficiently accepted by all parties seriously to influence their conduct. By June 22 Conway had sent an 'official' notification to Rocking-

---

[1] The belief that Bute was a real factor in politics still controlling a number of members was not confined to the Rockinghams. Bradshaw wrote to Grafton on May 14 that Townshend 'had seen Mr. Worsley in the morning and told him of Mr. Conway's intended resignation : by the channel he made choice of it is easy to guess to what place he wish'd this information to be convey'd'. (Grafton, *Autobiography*, pp. 176-8.) Thomas Worsley, M.P., was a close friend of Bute, who had recommended him to Newcastle for a seat in Parliament. Many M.P.s believed that Bute still had a following in the House ; the Rockinghams were peculiar in believing that he was still a power behind the Throne.

[2] Grafton, *Autobiography*, pp. 176-8.        [3] *Ibid.* pp. 141-2.
[4] The King to Chatham, May 30, 1767 ; Fortescue, I, no. 521.
[5] Walpole to Grafton, June 4, 1767 ; Grafton MS. 778.

ham,[1] and on June 23 Whately (not prone to pass on mere rumours) told Grenville that Conway had actually resigned and 'now holds the seals only because he has been desired to keep them for a few days'.[2] This seems to be confirmed by the King's letter to Chatham of June 25 [3] which begins : 'Lieutenant General Conway has declared his intention of resigning as soon as the Parliament is prorogued'. Even so, when the session ended Conway did not resign.

Conway's indecision affected Grafton more than Rockingham. Rockingham had been waiting for Conway's resignation ever since December and was still hoping for it, but his tactics were no longer based on its immediate realization. The disagreements and jealousies of the three opposition leaders were put aside when they launched their attack in the Lords. Rockingham became so intoxicated with the battle that he forgot them and forgot Conway too. The united opposition which Bessborough had urged six months ago became a reality in May and June, but it was union in opposition only. Nothing was done to enable the three groups to become partners in Administration, and when Parliament was prorogued their union soon came to an end.

Grafton too became absorbed in the battle and had to work far harder than he had ever expected when he took office. But he could not ignore Conway's intended resignation : it affected his freedom to manœuvre but not that of Rockingham. If Administration triumphed, what would be its state without Conway to lead in the Commons ? To beat the opposition and then to have Conway resign would be a Pyrrhic victory.

One man at least never gave up hope that Conway could be induced to stay. Horace Walpole laboured incessantly with him, and kept Grafton fully informed of the state of feeling in the Rockingham party. On June 4, in sending him the substance of a conversation with Richmond, he wrote :

> What I have done has been in obedience to your Grace's commands. It does not become me, my Lord, to advise ; or I should wish to see the Parliament up before the treaty

[1] Hardwicke to Rockingham, June 22, 1767 ; Rockingham Papers, R1-504.　　[2] Grenville (J. M.) MSS.　　[3] Fortescue, I, no. 537.

is begun. Perhaps some overture flung out separately to Lord Gower, distinct both from Grenville and Rockingham, might be of use, as it woud prevent their leaguing together, which may happen if only one party is dealt with.

But, my Lord, forgive me if I say, that there is a point I have more at heart than all ; and that is, to have the fittest man remain in the Administration. I do not mean to flatter your Grace, it is not my turn ; but the great abilities your Grace displayed on Tuesday, the admiration you raised in men of all parties, your former conduct and talents, your firmness, and above all, your strict honour, are absolutely necessary to the King's and nation's service, and you must not, my Lord, you cannot in justice to the public, give yourself up to your ease and pleasures, when such men are so much wanted ; and so very few such to be found. And how unhappy is the country, if your Grace and Mr. Conway, at the moment when you may govern, with the approbation of the nation, persist in leaving it to the direction of weak and well-meaning men, or to the very worst men in it ! [1]

He had the sense to see that the best policy was to take the opposition at their word, throw the task of forming an Administration on them and wait to profit by the resulting bad feeling which would break out after their disagreements. In essence, this is the line Grafton took : he fought the opposition in the Lords, and, though hard pressed, finally beat them, and then he threw the ball at Rockingham's feet and waited for him to muff his shot.

(vii)

Throughout May, while the Commons were occupied with East India business, the opposition delivered a series of concerted attacks on the Ministry's American policy, which the Court barely managed to beat off. In June, when the East India business came into the Lords, the assault was turned on that, but by now the opposition had lost much of its *élan* and in some quarters its morale had slumped badly. It still retained sufficient fight to cause Adminis-

[1] Grafton MS. 778.

tration anxiety, and though finally defeated, it never struck its colours.

Rockingham and Newcastle flung themselves into the battle, oblivious of almost everything else. (The East India settlement passing through the Commons is never once mentioned in their correspondence during May.) Rockingham laboured with unaccustomed vigour, developed unsuspected powers in searching out possible votes, and so exerted himself that he had finally to take to his bed. His efforts were confined to rounding up supporters : he never spoke in any of these debates. Newcastle was in his element : this kind of bustle was the best possible substitute for the work of distributing the favours of the Crown which he loved so much. They were well supported on the flanks by Gower and Sandwich for the Bedfords, while Temple, closely followed by Suffolk and Lyttelton, led the Grenvilles. When the Dividend Bill came on they received valuable help from Lord Mansfield. But the man who really won his spurs in this contest, who first showed those powers which were later to make him so formidable in opposition, was the Duke of Richmond.

Charles Lennox, third Duke of Richmond, great-grandson of King Charles II, one generation nearer the blood royal than Grafton, was born in 1735 and succeeded to the title in 1750. He served in the Army, saw active service in Germany, and was present at the battle of Minden. He had deeply offended George III in a dispute over military appointments, yet had supported both Bute's and Grenville's Administrations. Ambitious of business, he accepted the embassy to France on the formation of the Rockingham Ministry, and in May 1766 succeeded Grafton as Secretary of State. He was outstanding among the followers of Rockingham for energy, intelligence, and resourcefulness. During Rockingham's absence from Parliament in 1771, he proved a far abler leader, and his campaign in the General Court of the East India Company in 1773 and 1774 was among the most vigorous ever waged in that battle-scarred arena. Like Sandwich, with whom he had much in common, he enjoyed administrative work : they both presided for a long period over a service department, Sandwich at the Admiralty from 1771 to 1782, Richmond at the Ordnance from December 1783 to 1795.[1] Without the detail of office to occupy his mind he speculated on constitutional reform, and developed ideas which were not acceptable to Rockingham and his friends. Towards the end of the American war Richmond became an advocate for parliamentary reform and annual parliaments, and proved an embarrassment to the Rockinghams when they returned to power in 1782. He disliked the frequent and profitless discussions of the party line which became the main occupation of the Rockinghams when they stood alone after 1771, and preferred hay-making at Goodwood, where he would take off his coat and spend days in the fields.[2] He was a man who might achieve much good in a strictly defined sphere, but much harm if permitted to range over the whole field of government, for though he had administrative ability he could not leave things well alone. His influence in his party was small, considering his rank; Portland, a man of infinitely less abilities and initiative, but with a greater electoral influence, was more valued than Richmond. His weaknesses as a politician were his failure to find an able spokesman in the Commons, and his excessive admiration for Burke, which frequently distorted his judgment.

The opening salvo was fired by Gower on May 6 when he moved for an address to the King to lay before the House the proceedings in Council on the Act of pardon of Massachusetts Bay. Rockingham was informed of the motion on May 3 and found it 'at first sight not improper'.[3] Mansfield's opinion was sought ; and the Rockingham peers seem to have discussed it at Newcastle House the night before the debate.[4]

[1] Sandwich also held the Admiralty from 1749 to 1751 and for a few months in 1763, and Richmond was at the Ordnance from March 1782 to April 1783.

[2] Edward Gibbon wrote to his stepmother on July 19, 1778, that Richmond (then with the Sussex militia) 'works like a Serjeant, a clerk, and a pack-horse'. (*The Private Letters of Edward Gibbon*, ed. by R. E. Prothero, i. 342.)

[3] Rockingham to Charles Yorke, May 3, 1767 ; Add. MS. 35430, ff. 73-4. Rockingham to Newcastle, May 4, 1767 ; Add. MS. 32981, ff. 287-8.

[4] Newcastle to Rockingham, May 4, 1767 ; *ibid.* f. 289. Rockingham to Newcastle, May 5, 1767 ; *ibid.* f. 295.

The motion was rejected by 52 votes to 43,[1] whereas Bedford's motion on the same subject on April 10 had been lost by a majority of 27. Richmond and Newcastle spoke for the Rockinghams; Gower and Sandwich for the Bedfords; Suffolk, Lyttelton, and Temple for the Grenvilles. A similar motion moved on the same day by Grenville in the Commons was rejected without a division; the Rockinghams would not extend to Grenville the same assistance which they gave to Gower. The King condemned as 'illiberal' the practice 'of making motions without giving previous notice',[2] this 'hussar-kind of war' as Walpole described it.[3]

This had been little more than preliminary practice, an opportunity to range the guns. Though the motion had long been prepared the 'whips' had not gone out on a wide scale — and yet the Court had been run to a majority of nine. That majority was made certain by the proxy votes, but a majority obtained only by proxies would be a humiliation, and the opposition soon carried their war into committee where proxies were not allowed.

The next thrust came from Richmond and was an attack on the Ministry's Canadian policy. It was discussed on May 11 by the Rockinghams,[4] and the decision was taken to address for papers. Newcastle and Rockingham went to considerable pains to inform themselves of the facts of the case:[5] copies were prepared of the relevant papers; a brief was drawn up and conned; and care was taken to see that argument would not wilt for lack of information. Richmond told Newcastle, 'Lord Rockingham . . . understands the matter thoroughly';[6] but Rockingham did not communicate his understanding to the House. 'I think we should summon

---

[1] There is a division list in Add. MS. 33036, ff. 451-4.

[2] The King to Conway, May 6, 1767; Namier, *Additions and Corrections*, p. 73.

[3] *Memoirs*, iii. 15.

[4] Rockingham to Charles Yorke, May 11, 1767; Add. MS. 35430, ff. 75-6. Rockingham to Newcastle, May 12, 1767; Add. MS. 32981, f. 367.

[5] See the correspondence between Newcastle and Richmond, Yorke, and Rockingham: *ibid.* ff. 369, 397, and 399; Add. MS. 32982, ff. 1, 3, and 46. Copies of the papers are *ibid.* ff. 5-30.

[6] Richmond to Newcastle, May 19, 1767; *ibid.* f. 77.

all our friends for Wensday', wrote Newcastle to Rockingham on May 17,[1] and he began to beat up for supporters on the episcopal bench. 'Our two new bishops don't seem disposed to vote at all', he complained the same day to the Archbishop of Canterbury; 'that is wrong.'[2] But Administration evaded battle by granting the papers in 'a very full House'.[3]

The Rockinghams now moved out of the front line and were relieved by the Bedfords. The mobilization for the Canada debate was not in vain, for the troops thus concentrated were thrown into battle on May 22, when Gower, persistently probing a weak spot in the best military manner, moved to refer the validity of the Massachusetts Bay pardons to the judges, and the Court's majority sank to four.[4] The opposition had two notable recruits this day : Mansfield, for the first time since the campaign had been launched, appeared in their favour ; and the Duke of York, as Grafton delicately put it, spoke 'for unanimity'.[5] The King, more able to show resentment, described this behaviour as

the extraordinary and highly improper step one of my family took when the state of the question and the arts used to bring persons down to the House manifested a more factious spirit in opposition than even has been shewn on any other occasion.[6]

The motion of May 22 was made in the committee to consider the American papers and was to be renewed on May 26. With proxies not permitted, the opposition stood a very good chance of beating the Court, and increased efforts were made by both sides to round up their supporters. While Newcastle scoured the episcopal bench (eight Bishops had voted in the minority on May 22), the King made his

---

[1] Add. MS. 32982, ff. 51-2.                    [2] *Ibid.* ff. 48-9.
[3] Grafton to the King, May 20, 1767 ; Fortescue, I, no. 511.
[4] The voting was 62 to 58. These are Newcastle's figures ; Walpole (*Memoirs*, iii. 34) gives the minority as 56. The opposition brought down 21 new votes. There is a division list in Add. MS. 33037, ff. 17-20, and two further lists of the minority (each with slight differences) in Add. MS. 32982, ff. 97-8 and Add. MS. 33037, ff. 41-2.
[5] Grafton to the King, May 22, 1767 ; Fortescue, I, no. 511.
[6] The King to Grafton, May 23, 1767 ; Grafton MS. 498.

brothers [1] go down and vote, and if Grafton's words are to be taken literally, peers were 'brought down from their very beds'.[2]   The opposition looked forward to a triumph ; Newcastle wrote on May 23 that 'the good appearance we made has done me so much good that I have not been so well or slept so well of some time as I did last night', and hoped that victory would give 'great encouragement to our friends . . . satisfaction to the nation and . . . a good preparation for a new Parliament'.[3]   But poor Rockingham, although thirty-seven years younger than the Duke, was compelled to stay in bed the next morning after 'the fatigue and heat of the House the night before'.[4]

Such a thorough whipping up was uncommon in the House of Lords, where the Court normally had a safe majority and the fate of Ministries was rarely decided.   Not until 1783 was there to be another division so critical.   For the debate of May 26 the opposition brought down ten new votes,[5] and the Court's majority sank to three.[6]   By how narrow a margin were the opposition denied their triumph!   Among the six peers who voted in the minority on May 22 and were absent on May 26 were Breadalbane (Hardwicke's father-in-law), Monson, and Scarbrough (pillars of the Rockingham party in November 1766 [7]).   Had the Rockingham party been as disciplined and united as Burke pretended they were, the opposition might have won.   But they did not have to win to intimidate Grafton.

[1] The Dukes of Gloucester and Cumberland.   The Duke of York was not present.

[2] Grafton to Chatham, May 29, 1767 ; *Chatham Correspondence*, iii. 257-9.

[3] Newcastle to Rockingham, May 23, 1767 ; Add. MS. 32982, ff. 95-6.

[4] Lady Rockingham to Newcastle, [May 24, 1767] ; *ibid*. f. 113.

[5] See Add. MS. 33037, ff. 51-4, for the division list.   Grafton in his report to the King (Fortescue, I, no. 514) says the opposition brought down 9 new votes, but it appears from the division list that the figure should be 10.   Grafton's report is carelessly drawn : he muddles the speakers (Newcastle and Temple spoke for the second motion, and Egmont against), and writes 'Winchester' for 'Winchilsea'.

[6] There were two divisions and the figures were the same on each, 65 to 62.

[7] See above, p. 49.

## (viii)

Eighteenth-century Administrations rarely fell through defeat in Parliament, unless defeat was brought about by revulsion of feeling consequent upon ill-success in war. Even so a strong Minister, such as Walpole, or a Minister artificially sustained by the Crown, such as North, could delay his fall even after a large section of parliamentary opinion had turned against him. It was only the timid and faint-hearted, such as Newcastle, who retired without making a fight. Grafton was of the type of Newcastle, rather than Walpole, and had to be propped up by the King in the same manner, but not to the same extent, as North.

Between April 10 and May 26 the Court's majority had fallen from twenty-seven to three. This indicates the efforts the opposition had put into their campaign, but gives no idea of the damage they had done. The campaign had put great heart into them, but it was on the other side of the House that its effects were really significant. 'For the profoundest truth of war', writes Captain Liddell Hart, 'is that the issue of battles is usually decided in the minds of the opposing commanders. . . . The best history would be a register of their thoughts and emotions, with a mere background of events to throw them into relief.'[1] The same is true of parliamentary warfare. The real success of the campaign of 1767 was that it utterly demoralized the Court's commander-in-chief, the Duke of Grafton.

He was not a fighter, and when he took office he had never bargained for warfare on this scale. The Court's slender majority in the Lords was at least as much the result of his neglect as of the opposition's efforts. A strong Minister would never have permitted that Assembly so to escape from his control. Even the Bishops had turned against him : nine of them voted in the minority on May 26. Grafton at the end of May, with his majority reduced to three, with Conway's resignation hanging over his head, with little assistance from the Cabinet, and with the biggest battle of all (over the Dividend

[1] *A History of the World War*, p. 111.

Bill) yet to come, felt he could go on no longer without Chatham's aid or advice. On May 27 he wrote to Chatham beseeching to be allowed to see him for 'one quarter of an hour', 'for the moment is too critical for your Lordship's advice and direction not to be necessary'.[1]

What did Grafton hope to get from a few minutes' conversation with his chief ? What 'advice and direction' could Chatham give that would not equally have occurred to Grafton himself ? The answer in part is that Grafton was never meant by character or temperament to be a politician ; he had no taste for the work, and had so neglected his duty that a crisis had developed which he had neither the courage nor the resources to face without a stimulant from outside to revive his confidence and animate his spirit. Like a child that has hurt itself, he ran back to his nurse for comfort and aid.

If Chatham's condition at this time was such as Walpole describes it,[2] Grafton went in vain. But in part also he went seeking Chatham's blessing for a concrete plan of action to relieve his distress — the idea of splitting the opposition by detaching the Bedfords.[3]

Chatham replied on May 27 declining to see Grafton on account of his health, but enclosing his proxy.[4] 'His Lordship's proxy sent me in this manner', writes Grafton, 'had something in it satisfactory, but nothing could take off from the disappointment Lord President and I felt on Lord Chatham's declining to receive me at North End.'[5] The Duke now turned to Northington for counsel and on May 28, after they had both seen the King, Northington drew up some notes and the draft of a letter which on May 29 Grafton used as the basis for a second letter to Chatham.[6] It is clear from these notes that Grafton contemplated retiring at the end of the session, and was already turning over in his mind the advice he should give to the King on the next Administration.

---

[1] *Chatham Correspondence*, iii. 255-6.    [2] Walpole, *Memoirs*, iii. 30-3.
[3] *Ibid.* pp. 36-7.    [4] Grafton, *Autobiography*, p. 133.    [5] *Ibid.*
[6] Northington's notes and draft comprise Grafton MSS. 14a and 14b, and are reproduced with errors of transcription and without the date in the *Autobiography*, pp. 174-5. Grafton's letter is in *Chatham Correspondence*, iii. 257-9 ; his copy is in *Autobiography*, pp. 134-5.

In this second letter Grafton laid his situation fully before Chatham as he had done before the King : 'deprived of an assistance which I never expected to have been without' ; 'factions united' preparing to intrude themselves upon the Closet ; Conway and Townshend 'acting from the beginning of the session in direct contradiction to all Cabinet decisions'; in the Lords 'brought to such a crisis as to carry questions in a very full House by majorities of three only'. 'The King was of opinion that your Lordship's presence and advice could still reinstate and give Administration some consistence again.' If Chatham had no suggestions 'for bettering the state of things', Grafton continued, 'all our powers and faculties having been tried, we see no possibility of serving his Majesty with effect, honor, or justice, to him or to the public'. 'Pray send me your commands,' he concluded, 'indeed, my Lord, your thoughts and advice in such a situation are due to the King and to those who have supported to their utmost in your absence every view of your's.' Chatham again declined to see Grafton, and could only suggest that he and Northington 'may not finally judge it necessary to leave the situation they are in'. (May 29.) [1]

Grafton sent Chatham's note to Northington and to the King. Northington described it as 'most extraordinary and as relative to ourselves most dangerous'.[2] He himself wanted to retire because of his health. The King, 'deeply concerned . . . and in the most agitated state of mind, yet ever harbouring the most affectionate esteem' for Grafton, asked him to come to Richmond Lodge 'this evening May 30 at any time convenient to you'.[3]

The King was now in the predicament he most dreaded — that of watching his Administration break up before he had had time to form its successor. It had been like that in May 1765 when Cumberland had failed to form an Administration and the King had been compelled to take back Grenville ; and

---

[1] Grafton, *Autobiography*, p. 135.
[2] Northington to Grafton, May 29, 1767 ; Grafton MS. 17. Grafton's letter to the King accompanying Chatham's note (Fortescue, I. no. 515) is a paraphrase of the one he had received from Northington.
[3] Grafton MS. 487. The draft is Fortescue, I, no. 517.

the same thing was to happen in February 1783 when Shelburne resigned after his defeat in the Commons, and the King had to accept the Fox-North coalition. Such a situation would have occurred in 1767 had Grafton resigned ; the King would have had to make the best terms he could with the opposition, unable to fall back on an alternative. He did not object to taking in some of those who had opposed, provided he still retained his freedom of action — that is, provided he had Grafton to fall back on if their terms were too high. Therefore at all costs he must persuade Grafton to stay, for he was the only defence the King had against a triumphant opposition.

On May 30 the King wrote to Chatham.[1] He began by regretting the necessity which compelled him to write, 'but the moment is so extremely critical that I cannot possibly delay it any longer'. After describing the situation in the Lords and the state of the Cabinet — 'the great coldness' of Shelburne, 'the avowed enmity' of Townshend, and 'the resolution of Lieutenant General Conway to retire', he declared his reliance on Chatham's 'firmness to act in defiance to that hydra faction'.

Tho' your relations, the Bedfords, and the Rockinghams are joined with intention to storm my Closet, yet if I was mean enough to submit, they owne they would not join in forming an Administration, therefore nothing but confusion could be obtained ; I am strongly of opinion with the answer you sent the Duke of Grafton, but by a note I have received from him I fear I cannot keep him above a day unless you would see him and give him encouragement ; your duty and affection for my person, your own honour call on you to make an effort, five minutes conversation with you would raise his spirits for his heart is good ; mine I thank Heaven want no rousing, my love to my country as well as what I owe to my own character and to my family prompt me not to yield to faction ; be firm and you will find me amply ready to take as active a part as the hour seems to require, tho' none of my Ministers stand by me I cannot truckle. I wish a few lines in answer as I am to have the Duke of Grafton

[1] *Chatham Correspondence*, iii. 260-2. The draft is in Fortescue, I, no. 521.

with me this evening and if you cannot come to me tomorrow I am ready to call at North End on my return that evening to this place.[1]

There could be no more convincing proof of the King's determination to stand by his Minister. Chatham, though 'totally incapable' from illness, agreed to see Grafton ;[2] but begged to be excused from attending the King, as 'the honour and weight of such an audience wou'd be more than he cou'd sustain in his present extreme weakness of nerves and spirits'.[3] Grafton saw Chatham twice — on May 31 and again on June 4.[4] In his *Autobiography*[5] he telescopes these two conversations into one, but there is no reason to doubt that he gives the substance of them correctly. He found Chatham's 'nerves and spirits . . . affected to a dreadful degree', and goes on to describe the conversations as 'truly painful'. His disorder then was clearly something more than physical. Much of Grafton's conversation was a repetition of what he had written in his letters, but the ground had to be gone over again — 'It was with much difficulty that I brought Lord Chatham to be sensible of the weakness of his Administration'. 'After much discourse and some arguing' Chatham entreated Grafton to remain at the Treasury, 'taking that method to strengthen the Ministry as should appear . . . to be the most eligible'. When asked whether the Bedfords or the Rockinghams should be applied to for the necessary 'accession of parliamentary strength', Chatham 'inclined to prefer entering into negotiation' with the Bedfords. Finally, writes Grafton,

Lord Chatham assured me, over and over, that I might depend on his giving all his support to the measures I should bring forward in his retirement ; and on a return of health, that he would smooth over any that he might have disapproved, knowing that they had arisen from the purest motives.

---

[1] Richmond Lodge.
[2] Chatham to the King, May 30, 1767 ; Fortescue, I, no. 518.
[3] Chatham to the King, May 30, 1767 ; *ibid*. no. 522.
[4] Chatham to the King, June 2, 1767 ; *ibid*. no. 524.  The King to Grafton, June 2, 1767 ; *ibid*. no. 528.  Grafton to Chatham, June 3, 1767 ; *Chatham Correspondence*, iii. 268-70.    [5] Pp. 136-9.

Fortified by these conversations Grafton returned to his duties in the Lords. There were two encouraging signs : Walpole's talk with Richmond on June 3 revealed how brittle were the chains which linked the opposition parties together,[1] and in the Lords the Court began at last to halt the progress of the opposition attacks.

### (ix)

On June 2 Richmond's motion of censure on the state of Canada was defeated by 73 votes to 61.[2] It was the Court's biggest majority since the campaign had begun : they had gained eight votes since May 26, while the opposition had lost one. Although the defaulters — Breadalbane, Monson, and Scarbrough — had been brought into line, the first signs appeared that the opposition attack was slackening. Mansfield was absent ; Harrington and Abercorn deserted to the Court ; and — quod di omen avertant — Lord Townshend, Charles's brother, voted for the first time in the campaign and voted with the Court. Time was not with the opposition : few peers cared to remain in London in summer merely to give a factious vote against the King's Ministers. The Whitsun recess was at hand : there would be many who would not return to Parliament, more from the opposition than from the Court side. Yet the Dividend Bill had to pass the Lords and great expectations were built on that. The opposition wisely decided not to divide on the second reading but to reserve their attack for the committee. Marshalled by Richmond they flung their troops into one last effort to take the citadel.

Their great hope was Mansfield. But poor Newcastle was so indiscreet as to tell him so :[3] the Duke forgot, in his zeal for 'the cause', that the Lord Chief Justice of the King's Bench was a very 'delicate man'. 'I have no idea of making a proposition of this kind a party flag', wrote Mansfield to Newcastle on May 29, 'the measure should stand singly upon what is right or wrong.'[4] Grenville was more cautious : he

---

[1] Walpole to Grafton, June 4, 1767 ; Grafton MS. 778.
[2] There is a division list in Add. MS. 33037, ff. 73-4 and 77-8.
[3] Newcastle to Mansfield, May 28, 1767 ; Add. MS. 32982, ff. 148-9.
[4] Ibid. ff. 160-1.

found Mansfield 'quite unappriz'd of the contents of the bill . . . but after much talk . . . he seem'd to be perfectly satisfy'd that the right way would be to restrain the East India Company's dividends to 12½%'. (May 30.)[1] 'This', added Grenville, 'has always been my idea.' Rockingham too trod carefully with Mansfield. 'A thorough consideration', he wrote on May 30, 'was all I could ask or wish of him.'[2] He also claimed credit for the idea that the permitted dividend should be 12½ per cent, and told Newcastle that he had suggested 'to some of the directors and proprietors' that they should present a petition to Parliament to this effect.[3]

On June 3 the Dividend Bill was read a second time in the Lords and the House rose for the Whitsun recess. During the holidays, Gower visited Grafton at Wakefield Lodge in Northamptonshire, and during this visit Grafton sounded him about joining the Ministry.[4] It is unlikely that any concrete proposals were made ; most probably Grafton merely attempted to feel the ground. But if he expected any response he was disappointed : this was not the moment for the Bedfords to desert the colours. There is no evidence that Gower communicated this conversation to his allies, the Grenvilles and the Rockinghams.

The offensive against the Dividend Bill was led by the Rockinghams and directed by Richmond. But he had to deal with an army that was losing its zest for battle : the Bedfords seemed to be tiring, and among the Rockinghams there was a tendency to question Richmond's leadership. The attack was made in two directions, and the opposition suffered the usual consequences of dispersing their strength, which was already melting away under the heat of a London summer. Dowdeswell suggested that before going into committee the Lords should demand a conference with the Commons to know their reasons for passing the Bill.[5] Both Rockingham and

---

[1] Grenville to Bedford, May 30, 1767 ; *Bedford Correspondence*, iii. 363-4.

[2] Rockingham to Newcastle, May 30, 1767 ; Add. MS. 32982, ff. 176-7.

[3] Rockingham to Newcastle, June 11, 1767 ; *ibid.* ff. 301-2.

[4] Walpole (*Memoirs*, iii. 41-2) describes this conversation ; his evidence is confirmed by Grafton's memorandum of July 3, 1767 (*Autobiography*, pp. 151-2).

[5] Rockingham to Newcastle, June 10, 1767 ; Add. MS. 32982, ff. 279-80.

Mansfield favoured the idea, and Newcastle consulted Joseph Wight, late Clerk to the House of Lords, as to whether it could be justified by precedent.[1]

But then Richmond, who had been eager for it before the recess, began to think it 'not . . . near so good a thing now'.[2] He pointed out that the main argument for such a conference was 'that we had no evidence whatever before us' for passing the Bill. But now that the House had agreed to hear counsel for the East India Company and evidence was to be laid before them, that argument could no longer be pleaded. Besides, Richmond would not move for the conference unless he could be certain of support and in particular of Mansfield's support, which was something Rockingham could not pledge in advance.

As to my moving this question for the conference *now* [wrote Richmond], it will greatly depend upon the support I shall be *certain* of having. Your Lordship may tell Lord Mansfield so, and that I was so much disappointed on the Quebec motion at his Lordship's not being even present, that before I undertake new matter, in which there is a prospect of his appearing and supporting, I must be *quite sure* of him. I don't mean but that motions may be made without him very easily. But when a dependance is had upon him, and that he fails, it does great harm. Pray touch him a little upon this, as gently as you please, but lett him feel it, for indeed any man that pretends to be a friend and hangs back, is in fact an enemy, and does great harm.

The opposition had not placed such stress on Mansfield's support during the earlier part of their campaign ; nor would they ever afterwards consider him 'a friend'.

Others besides Richmond began to doubt the wisdom of the measure. Newcastle, annoyed because he had not been consulted, questioned (with some justification) whether Rockingham and Dowdeswell had the experience to manage such a conference. 'I suppose', he wrote to Mansfield on June 13, 'my Lord Rockingham and Mr. Dowdeswell are aware that there are many previous points to be settled. I question

[1] *Ibid.* f. 209.
[2] Richmond to Rockingham, June 12, 1767 ; Rockingham Papers. R1-502.

whether either of them was ever present at such a conference.'[1] Hardwicke, too, thought that 'the precedents cited will certainly justifie that method of proceeding in the present instance, but I much doubt the expediency of it'.[2] He considered that the evidence to be offered to the House would be sufficient justification for amending or rejecting the Bill, and that the motion for a conference would not be well supported. He ended with one telling argument against a conference so late in the session : 'The saving some fatigue to us all, which the not multiplying debates and divisions will do, is no immaterial consideration at this season of the year'. And all seem to have forgotten that the division would be taken before the House went into committee, which would give the Court the advantage of the proxies.

Yet the opposition seem to have been very confident. Whately wrote to Grenville on June 11 : 'The East India proprietors are very sanguine that the Bill for regulating the dividends will be thrown out of the House of Lords'.[3] He quoted Rigby for the belief that 'the attendance on the part of opposition will be very great', and Townshend for a list of Court supporters who would certainly not attend ; and concluded 'the division will certainly be very near and depend upon an accidental absence of a Lord or two on one side or the other'. But Hardwicke's doubts proved to have been justified. Although Mansfield gave the support Richmond had desired the opposition were beaten by 73 votes to 52, while in addition the Court had twenty-five proxies against the opposition's five.[4] The King, pleased with this success, congratulated Grafton :

I am greatly rejoiced at the very happy turn of affairs this day, and flatter myself that it will put an end to the session,

[1] Add. MS. 32982, f. 325.
[2] Hardwicke to Rockingham, June 16, 1767 ; Rockingham Papers, R1-503.
[3] Grenville (J. M.) MSS.
[4] Grafton to the King, June 17, 1767 ; Fortescue, I, no. 534. Grafton makes two mistakes in this report : Bedford spoke for the amendment, not against it ; it was not Lord Essex whom the Court gained on this division, but Lord Sussex.

as opposition must see their united efforts are vain ; besides it will make what we talked of this day more feesible, as they must be convinced violence will not insure them success, I am the more pleased as this is solely owing to your ability and activity ; indeed there is no one more sincerely esteems you than I do.[1]

The note struck by the King in this letter is to be repeated over and over again in the next two years, as he desperately clung to the wavering Grafton and tried to convert him into a tower of strength.

The King was right : this defeat took the heart out of the opposition. The Lords heard evidence in committee for six days, and a lot of enthusiasm evaporated in the course of these sittings. Lyttelton was not the only one who was 'harassed by so many long attendances',[2] nor was Hardwicke alone in playing truant.[3] On June 25 the opposition launched their final attack and were beaten again by 59 votes to 44.[4] 'Fifteen is no very encouraging majority', wrote Hardwicke to Rockingham on June 25, 'considering the pains which have been taken.'[5] But this was sour grapes ; a better result had been expected.

### (x)

During the last days of the session, Conway made up his mind to resign when Parliament was prorogued, and Walpole gave up the struggle he had waged for the last six months to keep him in. 'I can now tell you but one point affirmatively', he wrote on June 30 to Mann, 'Mr Conway does quit. It is unlucky ; bad for the public, disadvantageous for himself, distressing to the King ; but he had promised his late friends.' It was taken for granted that the Administration would then be at an end, and the thoughts of politicians began to turn to the new one that must emerge from the chaos. On June 22 Hardwicke wrote to Rockingham :

[1] Grafton MS. 500.
[2] Whately to Grenville, June 25, 1767 ; Grenville (J. M.) MSS.
[3] Hardwicke to Rockingham, June 22, 1767 ; Rockingham Papers, R1-504.
[4] Walpole incorrectly gives the figures as 60 to 41. *Memoirs*, iii. 42.
[5] *Albemarle*, ii. 45-6.

Mr. Conway's notification to your Lordship of his determination to quit at the close of the session is very material and more than I expected from him after so much appearing irresolution. We shall see how far it will operate on Mr. Townshend ; he has always declared, that his resignation depended on the *others*, and that he was ready the moment Mr. Conway was. If these two gentlemen should go out I think this Administration cannot stand, but when another will be formed with power and confidence and ability sufficient I cannot tell.[1]

The same problem was being considered by the other opposition groups. The following day Whately wrote to Grenville :

Some imagine that there is a wish to make up to the Rockinghams, but I am persuaded they themselves do not or will not understand that any advances are intended, and the attempt is less likely to succeed than the others.[2]

He suspected that 'something has pass'd with the Bedfords', but had no fears of their deserting to Administration — 'Nobody indeed can be more round and fair than they are'.[3]

If only Townshend could be induced to follow Conway, how simple it would all be ! 'I am well convinced', wrote Hardwicke to Rockingham on June 25,

that if Charles Townshend can by any means be prevailed with to follow Mr. Conway's example, and to assign the true reasons of his resignation, this Administration cannot stand a month ; indeed his continuing to act with them, after the public disapprobation which the Ministers in the House of Lords have given to his conduct this session, will only reflect disgrace on himself, and he will find it impossible to go on, without recanting every opinion he has publicly given upon this business of the East India Company. . . .[4]

There are in the Grafton Papers three letters from Townshend to Grafton written about this time.[5] All deal with minor

---

[1] Rockingham Papers, R1-504.
[2] Whately to Grenville, June 23, 1767 ; Grenville (J. M.) MSS.
[3] Whately to Grenville, June 25, 1767 ; *ibid*.
[4] Albemarle, ii. 45-6.
[5] Grafton MSS. 455-7. All are undated, but are docketed by Grafton June 24, 25, and 27. It seems, however, that the third letter is docketed incorrectly, and that it was written on or before June 24.

government business and they do not read as if Townshend contemplated an early resignation. In one, docketed June 25, he writes :

> I never wish to have any mark of approbation separate from your Grace, and even in censure, I should have thought it an honor to have been of late attacked in the same manner and in the same papers with the Duke of Grafton.

Perhaps the Rockinghams were wrong in thinking that if only Conway could be brought to resign Townshend would follow. Would not Townshend see in Conway's departure an opportunity of jumping into his place as Minister in the House of Commons ?

While Chatham lay at North End sunk in inertia, and so lost to the world that for almost the first time since he entered Parliament in 1735 his name ceased to mean anything in politics, the King had retained a touching faith that he would soon recover and, as he wrote on June 20, 'that when you are able to come out all the difficultys that have been encountered will vanish'.[1] Since Grafton saw Chatham on June 4 the King had written three times inquiring about his health.[2] On June 13 Chatham was 'utterly incapable of the smallest efforts of thought' ;[3] on June 15 he excused himself from sending for the King's physician, Sir Clifton Wintringham, and declared 'his entire confidence is placed in Doctor Addington' ;[4] and on June 20 he contradicted the rumoured improvement in his health.[5] Yet the King did not despair but wrote again on June 25.

George III was neither strong nor self-reliant. The 'firmness' which was his panacea for all the ills of the body politic was often a simple refusal to face facts he did not like or implications he could not understand. His trust in Chatham was unsupported by logic or experience — it was the reflection of his need for help in a task which he found too difficult alone — and when Chatham could not come forth he resented it as desertion.

---

[1] *Chatham Correspondence*, iii. 274.
[2] On June 13, 15, and 20 ; *ibid*. pp. 271, 272, and 274.
[3] Fortescue, I, no. 531.    [4] *Ibid*. no. 533.    [5] *Ibid*. no. 536.

In his letter of June 25 [1] the King repeated the familiar catalogue of the Ministry's troubles, adding this time a new one — Townshend's demand that the Administration should be new modelled, not merely 'patched'. He asked again for Chatham's advice, Grafton 'tho' full of zeal' being 'unwilling to trace a plan'.

> I am thoroughly resolved to encounter any difficulty [he continued] rather than yield to faction, this is so congenial with your ideas that I am thoroughly persuaded your own feelings will make you take an active part at this hour, which will not only give lustre and ease to the subsequent years of my reign, but will raise the reputation of your own political life in times of inward faction even above it in the late memorable war ; such ends to be obtained would almost awaken the great men of this country of former ages, therefore must oblige you to cast aside any remains of your late indisposition.

The reference to Chatham's share in 'the late memorable war' which George III had so much abhorred is very suggestive, and so too is the assumption in the last sentence. The word 'any' merits particular attention ; only five days before Chatham had written that the report of an amendment in his health 'has unfortunately for the present arisen from some mistake'.

Chatham replied the same night [2] 'under a health so broken as renders at present application of mind totally impossible', and begged the King 'not to require of a most devoted unfortunate servant what in his state of weakness he has not the power to trace'. The only advice he could give was

> that if the Duke of Grafton can be prevailed upon to remain at the head of the Treasury, with a Chancellor of the Exchequer agreeable to his Grace success to your Majesty's affairs in Parliament and in the publick wou'd be insured ; *this being* in my poor opinion, the *vital and indispensible part of an Administration, likely to procure ease and stability*, to your Majesty's business, *namely, the Duke of Grafton remaining where he is.*

---

[1] *Chatham Correspondence*, iii. 275.    [2] Fortescue, I, no. 538.

The appeal to Chatham had failed ; Conway and Northington were leaving ; Townshend was no help ; only Grafton remained. Sadly the King turned to the task of building a new Administration — for the third successive summer — determined at all costs to retain Grafton.

# CHAPTER V

# THE NEGOTIATIONS OF JULY 1767

THE negotiations of July 1767 were a fitting climax to the first year of the Chatham-Grafton Administration. Twelve months of fierce party struggle and of divided counsels in the Ministry were crowned by three weeks of intense negotiations, before the politicians were allowed to go home for the summer ; and at the end of it all opposition and Administration stood to outside appearances just where they had been before. Yet something had changed : below the surface the parties had shifted their positions with regard to each other and the Court. These negotiations are the watershed between the period of short-lived Ministries which marked the first seven years of George III's reign, and the period of comparative stability under North. Their future sets the pattern of the Ministry which, after a rough launching, sails the political ocean until it is engulfed in the storms which follow the disasters of the American war.

There is a great deal of printed material available for the study of these negotiations — much of it, however, so badly edited as to make it essential to see the original documents — and valuable unprinted material in the papers of the chief negotiators. To read through these documents is a tiresome experience : the mind wearies with trying to follow the intricacies of time, place, and action ; and the discordant and jarring party manifestos and proclamations, self-righteous and intolerant like slogans at a General Election, numb the brain and finally cease to have any meaning. But place the documents side by side and read different accounts of the same incident ; best of all, compare the drafts of letters (fortunately preserved among the Grafton, Grenville, and Rockingham MSS. but not considered by the editors of those papers to be worth printing) with the letters as they were sent, and motives emerge, the fog lifts, and the negotiators are seen as armies on the field of battle, moving raggedly and in confusion, but controlled by purpose and will.

The King entrusted Grafton with the power to negotiate in order to keep him in office; he was prepared to take in part of the opposition if it would strengthen the Court's majority in Parliament or ease the Minister's mind, but wished to receive them as suppliants for favours not as conquerors in search of booty. They must accede to the Administration, not supplant it: the King wished to new model an old Administration, not form a new one. He apparently preferred to sound the Rockinghams first,[1] probably because he was afraid that if Bedford returned to office he would bring Grenville with him. At no time was he prepared to consider the return of Grenville to Cabinet office, nor did Grafton or Conway ever suggest it.

To Grafton and Conway the purpose of these negotiations was clear, though each hoped for a different outcome. They began by playing a familiar move in the parliamentary game — attempting to buy off part of the opposition. But while Grafton wished to approach the Bedfords[2] Conway preferred the Rockinghams, and had a 'firm belief' in the 'favorable disposition' of their chief. Conway had a stronger hand than Grafton, not only because his preference had the King's support, but also because Grafton wished to retain him as Minister in the House of Commons. Grafton had therefore to pay some consideration to Conway's wishes, however much he may have disliked them or doubted whether Rockingham was willing to come over to the Court. But Conway did not at first realize that if he prevailed on Grafton and the King to negotiate with Rockingham, and Rockingham either would not come in or pitched his terms too high, he would have incurred a moral obligation to remain in office. 'I told him', writes Walpole,

there were many independent men who would not sit still and see the closet taken by storm. No, he replied, it was

---

[1] Walpole, *Memoirs*, iii. 38.
[2] Grafton to Northington, July 18 and 19, 1767; *Autobiography*, pp. 146-148.

M

what he himself and the Rockinghams had come in two years before to prevent.[1]

This supplies the key to the elaborate tangle which followed. The turn the negotiations took arose from the need to persuade Conway that Rockingham would not come in except on conditions which the King could not grant. Once that was made clear it became incumbent on Conway to continue to defend the Closet, even against Rockingham. When the time came for his declaration of loyalty, Conway found that his allegiance was to the Crown, not to party.

The motives and wishes of the opposition were not so straightforward nor were they so clearly expressed. There were barriers between the parties which prevented frankness, while among the Rockinghams at least three separate courses of action were advocated. But underneath the tangled events of this month are certain assumptions peculiar to each party, never expressed in words but instinctive guides in action. If these assumptions are brought to the surface much of the complexity of the negotiations disappears.

Rockingham assumed from the very beginning that Chatham's Administration was at an end and that he was commissioned to form a new one. It is doubtful if he would have consented to negotiate at all except on this basis. In drafting his plan for a new Administration he had two principles in mind : to remove from the King's service those who had been connected with Bute or who Rockingham thought were friends of Bute ; and to prevent Grenville from having any influence in the Cabinet. Bedford's support was necessary because the Bedfords were to take the place of Bute's friends, Rockingham's own followers being too few to ensure him a stable majority in the Commons. He would have allowed some of Grenville's friends to occupy minor posts in the Administration, but was not prepared to admit either Grenville or Temple into the Cabinet if he could avoid it. To secure Bedford's support he had to make some pretence of consulting Grenville, but it was never more than pretence. In short, he aimed to form an Administration from his own group, the

[1] *Memoirs*, iii. 41.

Bedfords, and such members of Chatham's Ministry as he thought well-affected ; he was not prepared to accept the Grenvilles as equal partners though he would take some of them to please Bedford, and he was not prepared to enter the Administration with his own group only.

Rockingham thus claimed more than either Conway or Grafton, the servants of the Crown, could admit. His principle was not to trust to the Crown for support but to form a coalition so wide that the Crown would have no alternative but to accept it.[1] His ideas did not always find favour with some of his own friends. Newcastle did not share Rockingham's distrust of Grenville ; his disagreement over the issue of the negotiations arose largely from resentment at not having that deference paid to his judgment which he considered due to his age and experience, yet there was sound sense in his complaint that Rockingham should have gone all out to win Bedford even if that meant making some concessions to Grenville. He saw clearly that if only Rockingham could satisfy the Bedfords he need not worry much about Grenville. At the other end of the scale, Richmond was never easy about the alliance with the Bedfords and would have liked Rockingham to join Conway and Grafton alone. Rockingham's chief link with the Bedfords was Albemarle, eager for the alliance with Bedford and a determined enemy to Grafton. 'A union with the Bedfords is what I have most at heart,' he wrote to Rockingham on September 24, 1767, 'a union with the Duke of Grafton and Conway is what I most abhorr.'[2] His influence at this time was very great but rarely wise ; Newcastle and Richmond were much abler politicians, but were little heeded.

The behaviour of the Bedfords was the resultant of several forces brought to bear on the Duke, as well as his own prejudices and opinions. Although the alliance with Grenville was disliked by the Duchess and probably by Gower, it was never paraded so much as at this time. Rigby flattered Grenville and assured him of the Duke's loyalty and friendship, yet not

[1] Grafton saw this. See his letter to Northington of July 18 and 19, 1767 ; *Autobiography*, pp. 146-8.
[2] Rockingham Papers, R2-58.

to an extent or so openly as to put off Rockingham and Albe-marle. Rigby was the Janus of this negotiation : he appeared both to Grenville and Rockingham and his expression was different for each. He was the link of communication between them and contrived to garble their messages for his own purpose. He would not cast off Grenville until he was sure of coming into office, and he could not be sure of that until Rockingham had been received by the King. He therefore worked to retain Grenville's friendship until the last moment ; and if the negotiation did not succeed, to make a merit of it with him afterwards.

Finally there is Grenville, the *tertius gaudens* of this trio of opposition leaders. It could not have escaped Grenville's notice that while Bedford had thrice been solicited to enter the Administration, and while Rockingham had coquetted with Townshend and Conway, his assistance had never been requested. He knew well that Rockingham did not want him. Did he also know that Rigby's friendship would last only so long as it was expedient ? And did he guess that the King had placed a veto on his return to office as Minister ?

There can be no definite answers to these questions, but Grenville's attitude leaves little room to doubt. While pro-fessing his wish to see his friends return to office he disclaimed any thought of it for himself. He pointed out that the basis on which Rockingham believed himself authorized to construct a new Administration did not include Temple and himself ; he deduced from that (quite correctly) that the Court did not wish his return ; and he declared his resolution not to force himself upon the King. Under these circumstances he contented himself with wishing success to the negotiators, but explaining that he could only support the new Administration if it did not act contrary to his American policy. His attitude was detached and more disinterested than either of the other party leaders : a logical result of the terms of Rockingham's commission.

Disappointment is sometimes more illuminating than suc-cess. While Rockingham struggled with the problem of how to wean Bedford from Grenville, not realizing that their alliance held good in opposition only, Grenville divined that the projected Ministry Rockingham was trying to form was not desired by the Court, and that Rockingham was only allowed to try the experiment because neither he nor Bedford would come in alone. He saw that Rockingham's 'comprehensive Administration' was as fabulous as Chatham's 'union of the best of all parties', for there were not sufficient places to satisfy all. He preferred, therefore, not to join the scramble for power in an Administration which the King did not wish; and came nearest to realizing that 'the union of the best of all parties', which had so long been the ideal of politicians, could never be reached.

(ii)

On July 2 Parliament was prorogued, and the same day Grafton and Northington presented a memorandum to the King on the state of his Administration.[1] They declared 'the impracticability for them to form in the critical circumstances of this country a temporary Administration', and requested the King 'to ask of the Earl of Chatham whether he can devise any plan by which the immediate execution of government can be carried on'.

Grafton's position at this time is best described in the account of a conversation he had on July 3 with Sir Gilbert Elliot. Here is Elliot's account :

I saw the Duke of Grafton this morning (3rd July), and learnt in conversation with him that he had not seen Lord Chatham, nor heard from him since the 4th of June, that in his opinion there was no hope of his ever being a man again, that Lord President and himself had represented in writing to the King, how necessary it was in the present state of affairs, and in the present situation of Administration, that Lord Chatham should either appear and assist in filling up the vacancies that must immediately happen, or otherwise quit all thoughts of being Minister, as it was impossible to continue any longer in this state of suspense, or prevail with men of abilities to undertake a temporary plan, which might

[1] Fortescue, I, no. 542. It was drafted by Grafton the previous evening and corrected by Northington. See *Autobiography*, pp. 150-1.

be totally reversed, whenever Lord Chatham's health would permit him to act. The King transmitted this very paper to his Lordship but [by] the answer it appeared he wished Mr. Conway's place might be supplied, and the system still go on as it had done all the session. This his Grace seemed to think impossible ; he had expected that Lord Chatham would himself have given facility to the King to make an effectual arrangement, by declining upon account of his health to act any longer as Minister, as he had not for six months been able to attend so much as one Cabinet. But this reluctance to quit Ministry seemed to lay his Grace under great difficulty. Mr. Conway had quitted, the President of the Council was no longer able to go on, Mr. Townshend could not be depended on, Lord Shelborne [*sic*] was not trusted, so there remained for the Cabinet only the Duke himself, the Chancellor, and Lord Bristol,[1] nor was it to be expected that the Duke of Bedford or his friends would quit Mr. Grenville, and engage under the apprehension that Lord Chatham might soon control and overrule all that was done. It was also not altogether reconcileable to the delicacy of the Duke's own feelings to continue at the head of a government which was formed upon the ground of removing Lord Chatham, if not from his office, at least from all pretence to power.[2]

Clearly Grafton wielded unwillingly the power that had devolved on him and felt responsible to Chatham for the use he made of it. That is a tribute to the influence Chatham had over his followers, an influence derived solely from his character and genius. But at this moment it made Grafton's position very uneasy : if Chatham recovered and returned to command an Administration remodelled not according to his inclinations, the advantages so gained would be only temporary. He must be given a final opportunity to make his wishes known ; and it must be demonstrated beyond all doubt that he was incapable of an early recovery, before any of the opposition parties would negotiate seriously.

In the afternoon of July 2 the King sent to Grafton the

---

[1] Bristol was not in the Effective Cabinet.
[2] The Hon. George F. S. Elliot, *The Border Elliots and the Family of Minto*, pp. 402-3.

draft of a covering letter which he proposed to send to Chatham with Grafton's memorandum.[1]  Grafton writes in his *Autobiography* :

> His Majesty determined . . . to word a letter in such a manner to Lord Chatham, as either to incite him to exert himself to forward the measure he recommended by filling up the offices, in effect vacated ; or to draw from him an avowal of the necessity the King lay under of calling in other assistance.[2]

Grafton commented on the King's draft :

> that there appears to be omitted 'the necessity his Majesty will lye under of taking steps which Lord Chatham's declining to officiate will render inevitable'.  By this means his Lordship will see that the circumstances of the times will not allow that temporizing, which his last letters seemed to intimate as his wish, and at the same time must be convinced that if his infirmities make other assistance necessary, yet, that such a resource has not been thought of, but on the latest moment.[3]

The King accepted this suggestion and his letter was sent the same day.[4]  The earlier part of it is similar in content to the King's former appeals ; the letter ends :

> I earnestly call upon you to lay before me a plan and also to speak to those you shall propose for the most responsible offices ; you owe this to me, to your country, and to those who have embarked in Administration with you ; if after this you again decline taking an active part I shall then lye under a necessity of taking steps that nothing but the situation I am left in could have obliged me to.

Chatham's reply is also on familiar lines[5] ; it might have been written at any time in May or June.  The same words and phrases recur as they had done in every letter of his to the King since his illness.  Indeed, he might have saved Lady Chatham some of the fatigue of writing by anticipating the

[1] Fortescue, I, no. 540.
[2] Grafton, *Autobiography*, p. 151.          [3] Fortescue, I, no. 543.
[4] *Chatham Correspondence*, iii. 266-7.  Misdated by the King, 'June 2, 1767'.          [5] Fortescue, I, no. 541.

style of Mr. Jingle — 'duty and submission — unspeakable affliction — utter disability — cruel situation — ardent zeal — render'd useless'.

But there was a difference. Chatham's previous letters had only caused bewilderment and frustration; this one gave the signal for negotiations to begin.

## (iii)

On July 3 Grafton saw the King who communicated to him Chatham's letter. At this audience it was decided that an approach should be made to the Bedfords, and accordingly Grafton saw Gower that evening.[1] Gower was no more accommodating than he had been at Wakefield Lodge three weeks earlier. Though Grafton writes that the idea of Temple or Grenville 'in a great office was by no ways a hindrance in the King's mind', provided it bore 'the appearance of an accession to, and not a defeat of, the present Administration', Gower's demand that the new arrangements 'must bear to a considerable degree the marks of Lord Temple's weight'[2] was not encouraging. 'The situation in which the friends of the Duke of Bedford viewed the Administration', concluded Grafton, 'gave them such confidence as rendered them quite unreasonable.' The next day, when Grafton reported this conversation to the King, both 'considered it so much as the grounds of an Administration to be formed by, and under Lord Temple' as not to be worth further discussion.[3] 'Thus failed this attempt', wrote Grafton to Northington, 'which some moderation from that quarter might have brought to bear, and to have formed the best Ministry (in my opinion) which this country is now in a condition to receive.' He described his conversations with Gower as 'the communica-

---

[1] Grafton's memorandum; *Autobiography*, pp. 151-2. The original is misdated July 4. See also pp. 142-3, and Grafton to Northington, July 18 and 19, 1767, pp. 146-8.

[2] Made by Gower, according to Walpole, 'much against his will'. Walpole to Mann, July 20, 1767.

[3] Grafton's memorandum, *Autobiography*, p. 152. The original is dated July 4, which was subsequently changed to July 5, but the first date is correct.

tions of two old acquaintances who had a true regard for each other'; this regard was justified on Grafton's part, for Gower did not inform Rockingham of this overture.[1]

At the same time as Grafton tried the Bedfords, Conway was deputed to sound the Rockinghams; and the two conversations took place the same evening.[2] During the last few days, Conway had been dropping hints to Richmond and Rockingham that an offer would soon be made,[3] so it was no surprise to Rockingham when he was told 'that the Duke of Grafton would be ready to converse on the subject of forming an Administration'. Grafton was prepared to relinquish the Treasury, but wished Granby and Camden to be retained. Rockingham did not think Granby's retention 'would occasion much difficulty, as I have long known Lord Albemarle's sentiments on that matter'; but with regard to Camden he refused to give an opinion on 'vague and undefined propositions'. Charles Yorke, he knew, would not easily give up the prize for which he had contended so long. The Yorke family, wrote Newcastle, 'will never be satisfied till Charles Yorke has the Great Seal'.[4] Rockingham was assured that Chatham was considered as 'quite out of the question', and the prospect of his resignation was suggested. 'Indeed it was said to me', concluded Rockingham, 'that if we were shy and would not shew a readiness to treat, the probability was that treaty might be carried on elsewhere.'

[1] He does not appear to have informed Grenville either, but Whately got to know of it and gave Temple a distorted version. Whately to Temple, July 6, 1767; Grenville (J. M.) MSS. The Rockinghams only learnt about it after the negotiation with Rockingham had begun. Albemarle to Rockingham, July 10, 1767; Rockingham Papers, R2-52.

[2] For Rockingham's account of this conversation, see his letter to Newcastle of July 4, 1767; Add. MS. 32983, ff. 55-8. His account makes it clear that it was Conway with whom he spoke, and this is confirmed by Newcastle to White, July 6, 1767; ibid. f. 77. See also Whately to Temple, July 6, 1767; Grenville (J. M.) MSS.

[3] 'Your Grace knows', Rockingham wrote to Newcastle on July 4, 'for some days past it has been the conversation that the Duke of Grafton wished to see his old friends back in Administration and that it was his inclination to bring it about and at the same time wishing that those who held the conversation would try to sound our thoughts.' See also Newcastle to Portland, July 4, 1767; Add. MS. 32983, f. 67.

[4] Newcastle to Rockingham, July 4, 1767; ibid. f. 59.

The same evening a group of Rockingham's followers [1]
dined with him and Conway, and talked over the prospects.
They considered no answer could be given until it was known
'whether a general and solid plan was the object . . . in which
case . . . we should desire to talk with the Bedfords'. 'That
if it was only meant to make a few changes and not a solid
plan we would much prefer seeing any set or sets undertake
Administration on such a foot than be the undertakers ourselves.' That night Rockingham informed Gower and Weymouth. 'I don't think they received the information so
cordially as I wished', wrote Albemarle, but, he went on, 'we
parted very good friends at four this morning.' [2]   Gower did
not tell Rockingham that he had had a similar conversation
with Grafton that same evening ; perhaps this was the reason
why the Bedfords did not receive the news so cordially as
Albemarle hoped.

The next day (July 4) Albemarle got wind of the approach
to the Bedfords, and warned Rockingham to be on his guard
against Grafton.

> I have just learnt, and from the very best intelligence,
> that Lord Gower was with the Duke of Grafton in Grosvenor
> Square yesterday, or Thursday for a considerable time. I
> am glad we *saw* Lord Gower last night, what a rogue the
> Duke of Grafton is. I cannot say much for Lord Gower.
> Press Conway to be more explicit from the Duke of Grafton
> about Lord Chatham's situation, about the Earl of Bute,
> and about the King, and then declare on or off ; avoid
> nibling and entering into a negotiation of six months that
> can end in nothing but your discredit. They are such rogues,
> you are no match for them. [3]

He repeated this warning on July 10, when he was at Woburn.
'I have heard so much of the Duke of Grafton since I have
been here that I tremble when I think that a freind of mine is
so much in his hands as this negotiation has thrown you.' [4]

---

[1] They were Portland, Winchilsea, Albemarle, Dowdeswell, and the
three Cavendishes.

[2] Albemarle to Newcastle, July 4, 1767 ; Add. MS. 32983, f. 61.

[3] Rockingham Papers, R2-57.   One wonders who was Albemarle's
informant.                                      [4] *Ibid.* R2-52.

It was not Albemarle's fault that Rockingham did not reach agreement with Bedford.

On July 4 Conway saw Grafton and afterwards Rockingham; he told Rockingham that Grafton's ideas were 'nearer to what you seem'd to wish as to the method of proceeding', and asked him to call on Grafton the following morning.[1] Disappointed of the Bedfords, Grafton had no resource left but to follow up Conway's approach to Rockingham. However, he had not intended to go as far as this without the King's express command, and, wrote Conway to Rockingham on July 5, 'seem'd alarmed at the notion of *sending for you to his house* : which in his situation he thought was an air he shou'd not give himself : and that what had past he understood was *conversation* only : this would have the appearance of a *direct negotiation*'.[2] Moreover, Conway had received a summons to attend the King at Richmond, and he asked Rockingham to delay his visit to Grafton and 'wait to see if his Majesty has anything to say to me beyond common business'.

On the afternoon of Sunday July 5 Conway was received by the King and seems to have advised him to open a negotiation with Rockingham, even if Rockingham should demand the inclusion of the Bedfords. The King thought Conway's proposal required 'mature consideration before it is gone into, as I do dread there may arise evils from it that I am certain he does not foresee', and asked to see Grafton 'previous to any steps being taken'.[3] Grafton saw the King on July 6,[4] and it was then that it was finally decided to open negotiations.

On July 5 a group of the Rockinghams met at Claremont for dinner.[5] 'Little material passed', wrote Newcastle; indeed, there was little that could be said until a formal offer was made by the Court. Newcastle 'urged the necessity of

---

[1] Conway to Rockingham [July 4, 1767]; *ibid.* R1-542. Dated by Conway, 'Saturday night, at ten'.

[2] *Ibid.* R1 (undated letters). Dated by Conway, 'Sunday morning'.

[3] The King to Grafton, July 5, 1767; Fortescue, I, no. 545.

[4] Grafton to the King, July 5, 1767; *ibid.* no. 546.

[5] Those present were Newcastle, Rockingham, Winchilsea, Portland, Bessborough, Frederick Cavendish, and John Cavendish. Newcastle's account of this meeting is given in his letter to White of July 6, 1767; Add. MS. 32983, ff. 82-3.

taking the Bedfords with us', and found 'a good inclination
. . . in all the company to take in the Bedfords, tho' strong
declarations from some of them against George Grenville'.

Meanwhile Albemarle had gone to Woburn and found
the Duke of Bedford 'exceeding right'; 'his most sanguine
wish', he wrote to Rockingham on July 7, 'is that the Earl of
Bute may shew enough of his head to loose it'.[1] This was the
style of conversation Rockingham liked to hear. Gower had
'owned frequent conversations with the Duke of Grafton',
but found 'his Grace varying in every conversation, sometimes giving all up, at others saying they shall go on very
well'.

How had the Grenvilles taken the news of these openings ?
On July 6 Whately gave Temple an account of Gower's conversation with Grafton,[2] fairly accurate except in one particular — but then all Temple's correspondents made a point of
emphasizing how eager the Court was to regain his services.[3]
How strange, then, that the King should be so slow to send
for him ! — but probably Temple's correspondents knew their
man and sent him the news he wanted to hear. To Grenville
Whately wrote on July 7 that Sandwich had made 'professions
of attachment on the part of the Bedfords to you . . . as full
as words could express', and that Gower's behaviour was 'a
strong confirmation of all their professions'.[4] Soon Rigby's
voice would join in the devotional hymn. But one may well
ask, if the Bedfords were so devoted to Grenville, why did they
always find it necessary to emphasize their devotion every time
the way back to Court seemed to be open to them ?

(iv)

When Rockingham told Newcastle that he had been invited to
meet the Duke of Grafton he added : 'I shall try to be more
a hearer than speaker upon the occasion. . . . I do not expect

---

[1] Rockingham Papers, R1-506 ; part printed in Albemarle, ii. 47.
[2] Grenville (J. M.) MSS.
[3] See, for example, Augustus Hervey's letter to Grenville of July 21
1767 (*Grenville Papers*, iv. 67-70).
[4] Grenville (J. M.) MSS.

much to pass, but whether much or little, I shall send your Grace an account.'[1] Their meeting, at which Conway was also present, took place in the afternoon of Tuesday July 7. Here is the account Rockingham sent to Newcastle at seven o'clock that evening : [2]

> I met the Duke of Grafton at Mr. Conway's and begun by complimenting his Grace on the handsome part he had acted in this matter, and took occasion to say that last year our only difference arose in regard to Lord Chatham and that I attributed what had happened since to have ensued from the same cause.
>
> His Grace then opened what he was authorized to say from his Majesty and which amounted to a proposition that we should come into Administration along with the *remains* of the present Administration.
>
> That our friends should come into office and that his Majesty desired a plan might be formed to be laid before him.
>
> I desired to know whether we might try the Duke of Bedford's friends, and found that it was understood we would and no objection to it.
>
> In regard to G. Greenvile an implied exclusion. *Remains of the present Administration* I found particularly was relative to Lord Camden — tho' much caution in regard to others — by way of preventing at this moment it being said that his Majesty gave up A, B, or C.
>
> The Treasury offered to me — and the Duke of Grafton inclined either to take office or not according as it might appear to us advantageous for the Administration.

And this was Rockingham's conclusion :

> I can consider this only more as an opening, than as yet anything on which a judgement can be formed. The material matter is, how far his Majesty will incline to allow us to introduce a number sufficient to give real strength. If that can't be I own I shall have no desire to be a part.

---

[1] Rockingham to Newcastle, July 7, 1767 ; Add. MS. 32983, f. 125.
[2] *Ibid.* ff. 127-8.

Rockingham also wrote about this meeting to Albemarle,[1] to Dowdeswell,[2] to Charles Yorke,[3] and to Hardwicke.[4] And lastly, he drew up, presumably for his own use, notes of this conversation.[5] Though these accounts are substantially the same, different points were emphasized for the benefit of each recipient. To Albemarle, Rockingham wrote :

> Indeed my dear Lord if it is possible to persuade the Duke of Bedford and his friends to take a warm confidential part along with us in this matter, I should have great hope that a solid Administration might take effect.

He hoped that Bedford's answer might be such 'that might encourage me to pay his Grace a visit at Woburn'. He asked Dowdeswell to come to town 'because it is a very great ease and satisfaction to my own mind to have the assistance of your calm judgment within reach'. Yorke was also requested to come and give his advice, and this is what Rockingham had to say on the matter nearest to Yorke's heart : 'In regard to Lord Camden I avoided being explicit and was not pressed. You know my sentiments on that matter.' 'The idea of Presidency and peerage' which was 'thrown out' as a means of contenting Yorke, Rockingham knew very well would not do. Finally, in Rockingham's notes he mentions the indispensable preliminary without which he would not negotiate — 'Lord Chatham understood to be no part'.

'The Treasury offered to me' — this phrase occurs in every account Rockingham gave of these negotiations, and his friends and would-be allies took it for granted that it was so. In view of the interpretation the King put upon this offer, it

---

[1] The original letter does not seem to have survived. It is not among the Albemarle Papers, but Rockingham's draft is preserved among his papers at Sheffield (R1-543). It was dated 11 P.M., July 7. See *Grenville Papers*, iv. 227.

[2] July 8. *Cavendish's Debates*, i. 583. The draft is in Rockingham Papers, R1-511.

[3] July 8. Add. MS. 35430, ff. 85-6.

[4] Rockingham's letter is not in the Hardwicke Papers, but Hardwicke's reply, dated July 10, 1767, is in the Rockingham Papers, R1-513. It is part printed in Albemarle, ii. 48-9.

[5] Rockingham Papers, R9-4. The document is undated, but is often word for word with the account Rockingham gave to Newcastle.

is important to know what Rockingham understood by it.  His behaviour throughout shows that he understood it as an offer from the King.  But was it an offer from the King or only from Grafton ?  Had the King intended to make this offer, would he not have sent for Rockingham instead of trying to avoid sending for him ?  It is clear from Rockingham's audience of July 22 that the King did not think of the offer as coming from himself.  The policy of the Court was to persuade Rockingham to form a plan of Administration, without admitting that the present one was at an end.  Did Rockingham misunderstand Grafton ?  Or did Grafton deceive Rockingham ?  The truth probably is that both these things took place — that Rockingham was too quick to take the offer in the sense he wished to understand it, and that Grafton did not take care to make his message clear beyond doubt.  Such an interpretation fits the characters of both men, and accords with the King's sentiments.  Any other is difficult to substantiate.

This did not cause Rockingham any misgivings.  He was concerned to understand exactly what was meant by the phrase, 'the remains of the present Administration'.  Was this intended to restrict him in forming a new one, and did it imply that the Court wished the present one to continue ?  It was obviously essential to clear up this doubt before he saw Bedford, and in order to do so he wrote to Grafton on the evening of July 7.  Here is his letter.

I premised our conversation this morning with desiring your Grace to believe that no symptom of caution which appeared in me, was or could be occasioned by any want of confidence in your Grace and very truly professed my personal regard to your Grace and my sentiments on the very handsome part your Grace had taken in the present occurrence.

I had a difficulty of delicacy, when your Grace opened the matter, when your Grace conveyed as from his Majesty the question whether we would come into his service to form an Administration along with *the remains of the present Administration*.  Tho' your Grace had fully informed me of your own ideas on the personal subject of yourself yet I felt it difficult to press more explanation to what might be meant by *the remains of the present Administration*.

If it is his Majesty's intentions that a general plan for an Administration should be proposed, it should then be consider'd as a plan *de novo*, or if it is his Majesty's pleasure that it should not be so, it would be necessary to know with some precision what and who is meant by the *remains of the present Administration*.

Indeed my dear Lord it is no easy matter to form an Administration well composed in point of weight and abilities and well united from mutual confidence, but such a one is necessary and no consideration shall ever biass me to act in an Administration which in my opinion may be too weak effectually to serve the King and country.

If it is possible for me to be of any service, the duty I owe to his Majesty and the personal respect I bear him, would equally incline me to do the utmost that lies in my power.[1]

Although the letter as preserved in the Rockingham Papers seems to be a copy rather than a draft,[2] the original is not in the Grafton Papers ; no answer seems to have been sent by Grafton and there is no reference to the letter in subsequent correspondence. It seems clear, therefore, that it was never sent, and that Rockingham chose to understand that he was commissioned to form a new Administration (with the proviso that Camden should retain the Great Seal), and invited to become First Lord of the Treasury.

How did Rockingham's friends react to the news of the conversation of July 7 ? In a letter to Newcastle of the following day[3] Portland relates how he went to Grosvenor Square in the evening, and found there Richmond, Frederick and John Cavendish, Saunders, Keppel, and Burke,

who in general seem to think that the exclusion of George Grenville and his friends is pretended, either with a view

---

[1] Rockingham Papers, R1-508. It is dated 'Tuesday evening, seven o'clock'. The first sentence makes it clear that this was July 7, and that it was meant for Grafton.

[2] There is a draft of the last two paragraphs, in Rockingham's hand, *ibid.* R9-23.

[3] Add. MS. 32983, ff. 149-50.

to make our union with the Duke of Bedford and his friends impracticable, or . . . to have that party open for application at any future time when the Court might be dissatisfied with us, or have made such breaches or divisions amongst us, as I ventured to say would be the first object and immediate attempt they would make upon our coming into power.

Richmond favoured trying to win the Bedfords without the Grenvilles, or, if that would not do, to 'be ready to engage to support Mr. Grenville for any other employment that he or they can wish, except the Southern Department, provided it includes America'.

In this idea I think both the Cavendishes concurred . . . Keppel gave little advice . . . Burke was so constantly going to and fro that I could scarcely collect his opinion.

The Yorkes were not enthusiastic : if Camden was to stay, what benefit would they get from the new Administration ? Hardwicke told Rockingham that though he would come to town as requested, 'I cannot flatter myself that I can be of any use in adjusting so many difficult points, as will require to be settled, if this negotiation goes on'.[1]  To his brother Charles he explained that

in point of decency to our friends and real regard for your interests and those of the family, which are so much at stake, I think I ought not to decline the little trouble of the journey.[2]

Charles thought that the proviso that Camden should remain Chancellor 'has an ill grace and insincere aspect towards Lord Rockingham and all that party'.[3]  The Yorkes took little part in these negotiations.

Bessborough did not believe the negotiation would come to anything, but thought it would be useful,

because it will make such a union as must be exceedingly formidable, and by now having an opportunity of talking the whole over, as one united body, the true meaning must

---

[1] Hardwicke to Rockingham, July 10, 1767; Rockingham Papers, R1-513. Part printed in Albemarle, ii. 48-9.
[2] Hardwicke to Charles Yorke, July 10, 1767 ; Add. MS. 35362, ff. 124-5.
[3] Charles Yorke to Hardwicke, July 11, 1767 ; ibid. ff. 126-8.

N

be understood by the Bedfords and our friends, that the
grand and only *bien* is, to form a right strong and lasting
Administration of *Whigs*. . . . I think the offer has been in
hopes of getting the Marquis, your Grace and his friends to
join them without the Bedfords, but you have judged that
matter right, and you saw that such an Administration could
not last.[1]

He echoed the plaintive, heartfelt cry of the Rockinghams — 'I
wish Conway had resigned'. All their hopes for the last six
months had been built on this. Bessborough, like Albemarle,
put no trust in Grafton's sincerity — which was one of the
charges Rockingham was to make against Grenville.

Newcastle's satisfaction at the 'good prospect' of 'a stable,
national, united Administration'[2] was only marred by no
notice having been taken of him. Although he had just
entered his seventy-fourth year, he longed to have a leading
part and resented the limelight being thrown on Rockingham.
'It would not have been unworthy of his Lordship', he wrote
to Portland on July 8, 'if he had told the Duke of Grafton
that he must in the first place communicate every thing to the
Duke of Newcastle ; neither would it have been too much
condescension for his Lordship to have come down hither to
know my opinion before he had had this meeting.'[3] He had
spent the day writing 'volumes of advice' to Rockingham[4] on
the conduct of the negotiation, the choice of a suitable Secretary of State, the foreign policy of the new Ministry, together
with complaints of Conway's and Grafton's neglect. He
was profuse of advice — and of complaints that Rockingham
neglected it. It was not always the kind of advice Rockingham
liked to hear. 'I would submit to your Lordship's consideration', wrote Newcastle, 'whether a *total* exclusion of my Lord
Temple and his brothers, and of my Lord Lyttelton, will
quite answer the view and plan of settling a lasting Administration which should go on with ease and success.' It was the

---

[1] Bessborough to Newcastle, July 10, 1767 ; Add. MS. 32983, ff. 193-4.
[2] Newcastle to Albemarle, July 8, 1767 ; *ibid.* ff. 147-8.
[3] *Ibid.* ff. 151-2.
[4] These 'volumes of advice' comprise Add. MS. 32983, ff. 137-42 and
144-5.

general opinion among Rockingham's intimates that the Duke
had gone over to the Grenvilles.

Then there was Lady Rockingham, not without influence
on her husband's political behaviour, and with her own
sharply defined views. On July 9 she began a letter to Lord
Scarbrough :

> I have stipulated to be secretary *only* for the Home
> Department, not to have anything to do with *foreign* corre-
> spondants, for I am dull and can only form my pen to one
> kind of stile, a stile between old acquaintances and sincere
> friends . . .[1]

and ended it : 'I must own I shall not weep many tears if
we speedily afterwards jogg off merily for Yorkshire'. And
on July 11 in another letter (probably to Lord Dartmouth),
after saying that Rockingham would send 'clearer accounts' on
his return from Woburn, she wrote : 'to take off considerable
uneasiness of my mind and make me compleatly happy these
accounts must be to inform you that all is at an end, and we
setting out for Yorkshire'.[2]

In the evening of July 8 there came a reply from Albemarle
to the account Rockingham had sent him of his conversation
with Grafton.[3] Albemarle described Bedford as 'very sensible
of your civility', and as sincerely wishing 'to join with you
in the great plan of removing the favourite and his friends
from Court'.

> This end his Grace thinks cannot be attained without the
> junction and hearty concurrence of Mr. Grenville, and asked
> me if you would have any objection to treat with Mr. Gren-
> ville. I ventured to say that you certainly would not,

---

[1] Rockingham Papers, R147-5. Misdated, 'June 9 1767'.

[2] *Ibid.* R147-4. The letter is undated, but was obviously written on
July 11.

[3] *Ibid.* R1-507, part printed in Albemarle, ii. 46-7. It is dated July 8,
half-past twelve. Since Rockingham received it late that night (see his
letter to Newcastle of July 9, 1767, Add. MS. 32983, ff. 166-7) it was presumably written at 12.30 P.M. 'I was extremely ill when I wrote it', wrote
Albemarle to Rockingham on July 10, 'and in a situation I never was in
before, so nervous from the sudden and unexpected news that I could
hardly join my letters, in a room full of people, it was chiefly dictated by the
Duke of Bedford.' Rockingham Papers, R2-52.

provided it was through his Grace as one of his friends.
Rigby will meet you at White's at ten tonight. He is very
sanguine in his wishes. The Treasury they look upon *as
yours*. A little giving up in other points, and civility to
George Grenville, will secure the Bedfords thoro'ghly, and
if Grenville is unreasonable, I dare say they will not support
him ; but they are afraid, and with reason, that unless he is
satisfied, he will join Bute, and with the support of the
Court will be too strong for you all. As the Treasury is
*yours*, I hope every other objection will be easily removed.

Rockingham described this letter to Dowdeswell as 'an
answer which in part I like'.[1] Yet although Grafton's offer
was 'not to extend to G. Greenvile' he could not, without
offending the Bedfords, refuse their request to communicate
with him. But when Rockingham saw Rigby in the evening
of July 8 —

I explained to him that in correctness I thought it would
not be proper that any messages from me should go to
Mr. Greenvile — that the proposition was to us and in-
clusive of the Duke of Bedford's friends, but seemed limited
there. But that in the present state it appeared very proper
for the Duke of Bedford and his friends, if thought proper
to communicate with Mr. Greenvile and that great good
might arise, if thro' the Duke of Bedford any insight might
be got on what plan and how a general junction of the three
parties might be made. That I thought the Duke of Bedford's weight would be a means of procuring moderation in
that quarter.[2]

Rigby professed to be satisfied with this and said Bedford
would not contest Rockingham's claim to the Treasury.

In talking to Albemarle at Woburn Rigby went further,
and said (Albemarle wrote to Rockingham on July 10),

that the Treasury was now indisputably *your own*, that if
Grenville did not give it up he would be very unreasonable,

[1] Rockingham to Dowdeswell, July 8, 1767 ; *Cavendish's Debates*,
i. 583.
[2] Rockingham to Newcastle, July 9, 1767 ; Add. MS. 32983, ff. 166-7.
The words from 'and that great good might arise' to the end of the sentence
were underlined by Newcastle.

that there was a connection between G. Grenville and the Duke of Bedford but not so strong as to prevent his Grace's friends from going to Court till Mr. Grenville was Prime Minister, in which situation he hoped never to see him. That he thought the Duke of Bedford could not in decency avoid the communicating of this business to him, and asked me if you would have any objection to treat with him, he hoped not he said, that though he liked the appearance of things the Duke of Bedford could not in honor enter into any negotiation 'till he, Mr. Grenville, had been informed of it. If he was wrong headed, that then they could, and would treat without him.[1]

Rigby also stated his price for leaving Grenville : he asked Albemarle if Rockingham would give him the Pay Office. 'I said I believed you would', wrote Albemarle.

But what did Rigby say to Grenville ? Rockingham had arranged to go to Woburn on July 11, while Rigby was to see Grenville and return to Woburn to report. On July 10 Rigby went to Wotton, whither Grenville had just returned from his 'Western progress', 'to endeavour to prevail upon him to support (if not take a part) in an Administration', formed from the Bedford and Rockingham parties.[2]

Rigby began by informing Grenville of Grafton's opening to Gower ; Grafton 'had expressed a desire that the King should send to the Duke of Bedford and Lord Temple to make a part in a new Administration'. Next, he gave Grenville a résumé of Rockingham's letter to Albemarle of July 7, but with a difference ; this is the account Rigby gave of Rockingham's conversation with Grafton :

After some civilities, the Duke told him [Rockingham] he had a message to deliver to him from the King, 'to desire that he and his friends should compose a new Administration,

[1] Rockingham Papers, R2–52.
[2] Albemarle to Newcastle, July 10, 1767 ; Add. MS. 32983, ff. 191–2. Grenville's Diary (Grenville Papers, iv. 227–31) contains a long account of this conversation. A careful study of it, against the background of Rigby's dealings with Albemarle and Rockingham, throws considerable light on his part in these negotiations.

his Lordship holding again the office of First Lord of the Treasury'.[1]

Thus Grenville was not accurately informed how the negotiation had begun : Grafton had not 'expressed a desire that the King should send to the Duke of Bedford and Lord Temple' ; he had broken off the contact because Gower had pushed Temple too far.  Nor had Rockingham been requested to 'compose a new Administration' — his projected letter to Grafton of July 7 shows that he was uncertain how far his commission went, although he afterwards acted as if he had full powers.  But Grenville does not seem to have taken the negotiations seriously, and had justifiable doubts how far Rockingham was authorized to form a new Administration.

> Everything is in a state of great uncertainty [Grenville wrote to Lord Buckinghamshire on July 14], nor does it seem clear to me to what degree the King means to authorize Lord Rockingham.  A week has already elapsed, and not only nothing is done but he has not even seen the King which, if it is intended to succeed, is surely very extraordinary.[2]

And this is what Rigby told Grenville of his conversation with Rockingham on July 8 :

> Mr. Rigby expressly declared to him, that the Duke of Bedford and his friends would do nothing but in concert with Mr. Grenville, and that for his own part, he should never depart from his opinions with regard to America, and that he knew Mr. Grenville's ideas were the same on that subject as they had ever been.

In Rockingham's account of his conversation with Rigby,[3] Rigby is made to say that 'it was necessary and incumbent on them to communicate with Mr. Grenville', but there is nothing about America.  That would not have been the right way to

---

[1] The inverted commas are in Grenville's Diary, and it appears as if the phrase were a quotation from Rockingham's letter to Albemarle.  But in Rockingham's draft the phrase is 'to desire to know whether we and our friends were inclined to come into Administration with the remains'.  The qualification in the last three words was not explained to Grenville.

[2] *H.M.C., Lothian MSS.*, pp. 277-8.

[3] Rockingham to Newcastle, July 9, 1767 ; Add. MS. 32983, ff. 166-7.

approach Rockingham. Had Rigby told Rockingham 'he should never depart from his opinions with regard to America', he might have destroyed the chances of union ; to do so with Grenville was improving them.

Grenville saw that no offer had been made to him, and in these circumstances cared more for preserving his 'consistency' than for forcing his way back into office. This was his reply to Rigby :

> To all this Mr. Grenville said, after acknowledging the friendship and attachment shown to him by the Duke of Bedford and his friends, that it seemed scarcely to amount to a proposition, and that in all probability all that was meant by it was to endeavour to divide the opposition ; that as there was no message to him, so he could give no answer, nor would he have given one without Lord Temple, but that in general, if the King thought fit to call Lord Rockingham into his government, upon a great and extended plan, carried on with vigour, and asserting the sovereignty of Great Britain over her colonies, he had no factious dispositions to disturb it, but that he could never alter his opinion on the subject of America ; that with regard to the forming the Administration, he only desired that no pretensions of his should in any way stand in the way of his friends ; that, on the contrary, he was willing to waive them entirely, provided he could see his friends properly placed ; that he would never on any account or in any situation obtrude himself upon the King, and earnestly desired that his name might not even be mentioned for any office whatever.

To Lyttelton on July 14 Grenville wrote : 'I am very glad that the failure of it can never be imputed to the ambitious, or interested views of Lord Temple or myself'.[1] Was this genuine, or was he merely trying to make the best of his disappointment ?

## (v)

On Saturday July 11, Rockingham, accompanied by Admiral Keppel, arrived at Woburn, and so did Rigby, just back from Wotton. Rockingham informed the company (which included

[1] Robert Phillimore, *Memoirs and Correspondence of Lord Lyttelton*, pp. 721-2.

Gower and Albemarle) of his conversation with Grafton, and Rigby described 'the good temper of mind in which he found Mr. Grenville, with regard to any Administration which could be formed to defeat the secret influence of Lord Bute, and where measures should be pursued conformable to his sentiments about America'.[1]   Rigby, according to the story he told Grenville the next day, 'marked to Lord Rockingham the moderation and temper' of Grenville's words (Grenville had not mentioned Bute) ; and 'alarmed' him 'on the manner in which all this was transacted' by showing him 'the indispensible necessity of his seeing the King himself'.

In the morning of July 12 Rigby went to Stowe to consult Temple.   The message he was to carry back to Woburn is given in one sentence of Grenville's Diary : 'Lord Temple and Mr. Grenville still desired to waive their own pretensions, and desired to be at liberty to support or not, according to the measures'.   This last declaration followed logically from Grenville's condition that 'measures should be pursued conformable to his sentiments about America'.   But did Rigby carry this message back to Woburn ?   Bedford says nothing about it in his diary ;[2] Albemarle does not mention it in his letter to Newcastle of July 12 ;[3] Rockingham, in a letter to Newcastle written at two o'clock in the morning of July 13 — immediately on his return to London — describes how 'the result of Rigby's visit at Wooton and Stowe adds much to the general promising aspect' ;[4] he wrote to Charles Yorke in the afternoon of July 13 that there was 'the greatest cordiality imaginable at Woburn and much smoothness elsewhere'.[5] Finally, this is how Hardwicke described Rockingham's mood on his return :[6]

Lord Rockingham is come back with flying colors from Woburn, a most successful negotiator ; *his Grace and company* in the best dispositions imaginable, perfectly satisfied with Lord Rockingham's being at the head of the Treasury,

---

[1] Bedford's Diary ; *Cavendish's Debates,* i. 604-5.
[2] *Ibid.* p. 605.          [3] Add. MS. 32983, ff. 223-4.
[4] *Ibid.* ff. 225-6.          [5] Add. MS. 35430, f. 81.
[6] Hardwicke to Charles Yorke, July 13, 1767 ; Add. MS. 35362, ff. 129-130.

for a *thorough* concert in, *or out*, and will be very reasonable in their pretensions. . . . He is vastly pleased with his reception at Woburn, and the confidence which his Grace showed him, and is determined to make *cause commune* with that set. Who would have expected this three months ago ?

It is difficult to believe that Rockingham would have been so satisfied with his diplomacy and so convinced that Grenville would not be an obstacle to the union with Bedford if he had heard the declaration that Grenville considered himself at liberty 'to support or not, according to the measures'. But it was Rigby's interest to maintain the connection with Rockingham in case he should be admitted to office, and yet to keep open the line to Grenville in case he should not. It would not do to alarm Rockingham too much, and equally it would not do to give Grenville the impression that the Bedfords were prepared to come into office without him. Rigby had a delicate game to play ; but as the link between two men who would not communicate with each other, he was well placed for playing it.

Rockingham's visit to Woburn lifted the negotiations on to a more serious plane. Satisfied that the Bedfords would co-operate with him, he was now able to tell Grafton that he could prepare a plan of Administration. But nothing had been done to make that co-operation lasting : neither policy nor places appear to have been discussed at Woburn. The Bedfords had agreed to Rockingham having the Treasury, apparently the only point about which he was concerned ; but who was to hold the vital office of Minister in the House of Commons ? Practical questions such as this were not discussed. In short, Rockingham's visit merely gave grounds to hope that a united Administration was possible. 'I had always hoped', wrote Newcastle to Rockingham on July 13, 'that when you came to understand one another, the difficulties would not be so great as was apprehended.'[1] He did not know that the difficulties had not yet been approached.

On July 13 Rockingham's 'Shadow Cabinet' met in

---

[1] Add. MS. 32983, f. 236.

Grosvenor Square, heard his report on the mission to Woburn, and decided on the next step.

That my Lord Rockingham, having learnt the opinion of his own friends and also that of the Duke of Bedford, and some of his Grace's friends ; and the Duke of Bedford having learnt also the sentiments of my Lord Temple and Mr. Grenville, my Lord Rockingham has found an equal disposition in all to assist and support an Administration for carrying on the affairs of this kingdom with zeal and activity ; my Lord Rockingham desires to know whether it was his Majesty's intention that he should prepare a *comprehensive* plan of Administration for his Majesty's consideration ; that, if *that* was his Majesty's intention my Lord Rockingham should desire to have the honor to attend his Majesty, to receive his *more particular* commands upon a subject of that high importance.

The view of this was, that if there was no intention to form such an Administration as would be able to do the King's business and that of the nation with ability and credit, that then my Lord Rockingham would decline taking any share in it.[1]

Rockingham saw Conway the next day but nothing material passed ;[2] late that evening Grafton returned to London (he had spent the last week at Newmarket) and agreed to see Rockingham on July 15.[3]

The second conversation between Rockingham, Grafton, and Conway took place at Conway's house on Wednesday morning, July 15.[4] Rockingham told Grafton that he had

---

[1] Newcastle to White, July 14, 1767 ; *ibid.* f. 109.
[2] Rockingham to Newcastle, July 14, 1767 ; *ibid.* f. 246.
[3] Conway to Rockingham [July 14, 1767] ; Rockingham Papers, R1-469.
[4] Rockingham wrote an account of this conversation to Bedford at 1 A.M., Thursday July 16. The letter is printed in *Bedford Correspondence*, iii. 374-6, incorrectly dated 'Thursday night, 1 o'clock, July 17, 1767'. It was incorrectly dated by Rockingham 'Thursday morning, 1 o'clock, July 17, 1767', but docketed by Bedford, 'shd. be 16. Rx by his servt. at 8 A.M.' The original is Woburn MS. lv. f. 180. The same day Bedford received another account of this conversation from Weymouth. In the evening of July 15 Rockingham met Weymouth at White's, told him what had happened with Grafton, and said he did not intend to write to Bedford. So Weymouth sent a letter to Rigby at nine o'clock that evening, and this

consulted Bedford and through Bedford had learnt Grenville's opinions, and now wished to know whether it was the King's intention that he should prepare 'a comprehensive plan of Administration'. If this was so, he expected an audience of the King to receive his commands. Grafton was troubled by the word 'comprehensive' and wanted to know if it implied the dismissal of all those now in office. Rockingham condemned this as 'violent' and 'imprudent'; when asked if he was prepared to accept Camden as Chancellor, he answered 'that till a comprehensive plan was prepared and digested it was impossible and unnecessary to answer to any particular matter'. Grafton said that the King had a 'very great facility' to take in the Bedfords and the Rockinghams, but Rockingham insisted that 'the comprehensive plan was what we should abide by'. Grafton left to report their conversation to the King, and it seems to have been understood that he would reply in writing.[1]

It was not an easy letter to write. Conway had urged the King to negotiate with Rockingham, believing that Rockingham would come in alone ; Grafton, not so credulous, had apparently thought that the opposition would not be able to agree and that from their squabbles the Court might derive some profit. But now Rockingham had apparently succeeded in getting the Bedfords and Grenvilles to follow his lead, and was

probably reached Woburn before Rockingham's. Rockingham wrote to Bedford after being pressed to do so by Weymouth (see Lady Rockingham to Newcastle, July 16, 1767 ; Add. MS. 32983, ff. 258-9) ; he seems to have found it a difficult letter to write. There is a draft in the Rockingham Papers (R9-25) in Rockingham's hand, with many corrections ; he made six attempts to draft the first sentence. While Rockingham was writing to Bedford Lady Rockingham sent a note to Newcastle (Add. MS. 32983, ff. 258-9), and this was followed by a more detailed account from Rockingham, written at 7 A.M., July 16 (ibid. ff. 267-70). There are also in the Rockingham Papers (R9-5) some notes in Rockingham's hand, apparently drawn up before the conversation with Grafton. These notes and Rockingham's letters to Bedford and Newcastle are very similar, and sometimes identical in phrase. Grafton's account is given in his letter to Northington of July 18 and 19 (Autobiography, pp. 146-8), in which he jumbles together the conversations of July 7 and 15 ; and in a brief passage of the Autobiography (p. 143), based on this letter. Grafton's version is not so full as Rockingham's and does not contradict it.

[1] This may have been the reason why Rockingham delayed writing to Bedford.

demanding an audience of the King. If his request were granted, it would be conceding his claim that the Administration was at an end and authorizing him to form a new one ; if the audience were refused, the negotiations would collapse and the opposition would be more united than before. The Court had a difficult line to follow : it must persuade Rockingham to attempt to form a new Administration, in order to keep the negotiation going and in the hope that the parties would quarrel over the disposal of offices ; but it must not admit Rockingham's claim for an audience and thus concede his demand to form a new Administration. These were the motives behind the exchange of notes which followed between Rockingham and Grafton, in which each tried to outmanoeuvre the other. These notes deserve very careful study.

## (vi)

In the evening of July 15 Grafton, helped by Conway and Hertford, drafted the letter to Rockingham. This draft does not appear to have survived, but this is the text given by Walpole in his *Memoirs*.[1]

> After having delivered to his Majesty the answer which your Lordship communicated to General Conway and myself this morning, I was commanded to acquaint your Lordship that the King will expect to receive from your Lordship the plan on which you and your friends would propose to come in, in order to extend and strengthen his Administration, that his Majesty may be enabled to judge how far the same shall appear consistent with his Majesty's honour and the public service.

It was shown by Hertford to Walpole that evening, who criticized it as too harsh : it would not do to give Rockingham an excuse for breaking off the negotiations. Here is Walpole's draft :

> After having delivered to his Majesty the answer which your Lordship communicated to General Conway and myself this morning I was commanded to acquaint your Lordship

that the King wishes your Lordship would specify the plan
on which you and your friends would propose to come in in
order to form an extensive and solid Administration that his
Majesty may be inabled to judge how far the same may be
advantageous to his Majesty's and the publick service.[1]

In trying to make the letter more acceptable to Rockingham
Walpole had gone too far : Grafton could not admit the
phrase 'to form an extensive and solid Administration', with
its implication that the present one was at an end. He restored
his original phrase, 'extend and strengthen his Administration',
made one other slight alteration,[2] and forwarded the letter to
Rockingham who received it between 10 and 11 A.M., July 16.[3]

Meanwhile, Bedford had written to thank Rockingham for
his account of the conversation with Grafton.[4]  His letter is full
of phrases dear to Rockingham's heart : the opposition were
united 'to rescue his Majesty and this country out of the hands
of the Earl of Bute . . . in one common cause for rooting out
that maxim of favourites who have got too great an ascendancy
over the minds of princes, of *divide et impera*', etc.  If this
was the sort of talk Rockingham heard at Woburn, no wonder
he returned so pleased.  And this was Bedford's appraisal of
the state of the negotiations :

> I think, and I hope your Lordship and your friends will
> agree in opinion with me, that the present negotiation is
> over, unless his Majesty shall immediately send for you, in
> order to receive a plan of Administration, consonant to what
> was agreed to at this place ; and I flatter myself, that your
> Lordship has that favourable opinion of the honor of those

[1] The original, in Hertford's hand, is Grafton MS. 20.  There are
differences in spelling from the text as given by Walpole in his *Memoirs*,
iii. 52, and the words 'to him' in line 5 of Walpole's text are not in the
original.  It is docketed in Grafton's hand, 'Copy to Ld. Rockingham from
the D. of G. tho' in Lord Hertford's hand writing'.

[2] 'To specify', instead of 'would specify'.  In Walpole's draft these
corrections are in Grafton's hand.

[3] The original is Rockingham Papers, R1-515.  It bears the date July
15, but as Rockingham did not receive it until between 10 and 11 A.M.
July 16, and in view of the redrafting described above, the correct date
should probably be July 16.

[4] *Ibid.* R1-521.  It is dated 8 A.M. July 16.  Bedford's copy, identical
with the original, is printed in *Bedford Correspondence*, iii. 373-4.

who gave assurances of giving the same answer as you shall
have done, to any future offers that may be made to them,
as to leave no doubt remaining in your mind, about their
religious observance of their engagements.[1]

On the same day (July 16) Rigby forwarded to Temple
copies of Weymouth's letter of July 15, Rockingham's letter
written at 1 A.M. July 16, and Bedford's reply, quoted above,[2]
and asked him to send them on to Grenville. It does not
appear that Rigby sought Rockingham's permission to do this,
and the first intimation Rockingham had that copies of his
correspondence had been sent to Grenville and Temple was
when he saw Bedford on the morning of July 20.[3] Temple
professed himself 'much edified' by the perusal of this correspondence and invited Rigby to spend a few days at Stowe ;
originally, the invitation was extended to Rigby 'or any of the
joint friends', but Temple had second thoughts and deleted
this phrase.[4] While Temple thought 'a real storm is brewing
against Lord B. and the Court',[5] Grenville made no reference
to Bute but pointed out that Rockingham's letter ignored 'the
capital measure of asserting and establishing the sovereignty
of Great Britain over its colonies',[6] an essential condition of
his support. 'As to whatever else may have passed', he wrote
to Rigby, 'concerning Lord Rockingham's other intentions
either at Woburn, or in the conferences with the Duke of
Grafton in London, as I [am] ignorant what they are I can give
no opinion about them, 'till I learn them from the Duke of
Bedford or you.' 'If it is true', he wrote to Temple the same
day (July 16), 'that Lord Rockingham stated to Mr. Rigby
that his powers were unlimited, 'with the single exception of

---

[1] It must be remembered that Bedford wrote this before he knew of
Grafton's reply to Rockingham.

[2] Rigby's covering letter, together with these copies in Rigby's hand,
are in the Grenville (J. M.) MSS.

[3] See Dowdeswell's memorandum, Rockingham Papers, R1-536.

[4] Temple's letter to Rigby, dated 5 P.M. July 16, is printed in *Bedford
Correspondence*, iii. 371-2. His draft is among the Grenville (J. M.) MSS.
It was sent to Grenville for his approval.

[5] Temple to Grenville, 5 P.M. July 16, 1767 ; Grenville (J. M.) MSS.
This is the covering letter to Temple's draft of his answer to Rigby.

[6] Grenville to Rigby, 10 P.M. July 16, 1767 ; *Bedford Correspondence*,
iii. 369-71.

your Lordship and myself', we might have saved ourselves the trouble of insisting that we should not be named for any office.'[1] But he insisted that Rockingham had overrated his powers, and 'that the Duke of Grafton acted exactly the same part both with Lord Gower and with Lord Rockingham, with the same view of disuniting and getting some individuals'. Grenville had a shrewd idea of the Court's intentions. 'I understand', wrote Grafton to Northington on July 19,

> that they are now employed in making out their plan to be offer'd to his Majesty's consideration, a work, which before it can be brought to birth, seems open to so many accidents, that I am, I own, not without thinking it possible, that it may disunite parties freshly and loosely cemented, and that some one among them may find it for their interest, as well as credit, to fall in honorably with the present Administration.[2]

Between 10 and 11 A.M. July 16, Rockingham received Grafton's letter, with its request 'to specify the plan' on which the opposition would take office. 'I don't like the Duke of Grafton's answer', commented Newcastle (and his opinion may be taken as general amongst the opposition), '*extending and strengthening the present Administration*, I apprehend, is not our object'.[3] Nor did Rockingham like it : it did not contain the expected summons to see the King. He went to Grafton, pressed for an audience, and tried to show that the letter did not require a written answer. Grafton insisted that he must have a reply in writing 'to avoid any mistakes', and evaded the request for an audience.[4] Rockingham went home to draft his reply ; here it is, dated 2 P.M. July 16 :

> I have the honour of your Grace's letter by which your Grace acquaints me *that his Majesty wishes me to specify the*

---

[1] *Grenville Papers*, iv. 53. Cf. William Gerard Hamilton to Temple, July 13, 1767 : 'To Mr. Rigby, I understand, Lord Rockingham stated, that he had the power of forming any Administration he thought proper, with the single exception of your Lordship and Mr. Grenville'. *Ibid.* p. 46. This letter was sent by Temple to Grenville on July 15. *Ibid.* p. 52.
[2] *Autobiography*, pp. 146-8.
[3] Newcastle to Lady Rockingham, July 16, 1767 ; Add. MS. 32983, f. 277.
[4] Rockingham to Bedford, 11 P.M. July 16, 1767 ; *Bedford Correspondence*, iii. 368-9.

*plan, on which I, and my friends would propose to come in, in order to extend and strengthen his Administration.*

I hope your Grace will do me the honour to explain to his Majesty, that the principle on which I would proceed should be to consider the present Administration as at an end, notwithstanding the great regard and esteem which I have for some of those who compose it.

If his Majesty thinks it for his service to form a new Administration on a comprehensive plan, the general idea of which has already been opened to your Grace, I should then humbly hope to have his Majesty's permission to attend him, in order to receive his commands, it being impossible to enter into particulars till I have his Majesty's leave to proceed upon this plan.[1]

Thus Rockingham stated categorically his basic principle — that he was negotiating to form a new Administration — which Grafton could not deny without breaking off altogether. He sent a note to Rockingham to say that the letter had arrived too late to lay it before the King that day ;[2] but Rockingham's belief that this was merely to gain time[3] was probably true. There is in the Rockingham Papers a note by Burke, written during the afternoon or evening of July 16.[4]

I just saw the D. of Grafton go in to Horry Walpole's. I dare say it is to try to work upon Conway to stay in. If yr. Lordship should not have a very speedy answer from his Grace of Grafton would it be amiss to send the D. of Bedford the copies of the two letters which passed this morning.

Burke's suspicion may be correct ; but Grafton also wanted to consult Walpole on the reply to be sent to Rockingham.

Rockingham took Burke's advice and at 11 P.M. July 16 sent Bedford copies of the letters which had passed with

---

[1] Grafton, *Autobiography*, p. 144. The original is Grafton MS. 19. There are three drafts of this letter in the Rockingham Papers, R1-544, R9-10, and R1-516. The second paragraph occurs only in the third draft.

[2] Grafton to Rockingham, July 16, 1767 ; *ibid.* R1-520.

[3] Rockingham to Bedford, 11 P.M. July 16, 1767 ; *Bedford Correspondence,* iii. 368-9.

[4] Rockingham Papers, R8-9G. It is undated, but the reference to 'two letters which passed this morning' shows that July 16 is the date. It must have been written between the time Rockingham wrote to Grafton (2 P.M.) and the time he wrote to Bedford (11 P.M.).

Grafton and a short account of his conversation with Grafton that day.[1]  This correspondence was also sent by Rigby to Temple and Grenville the following day.[2]  Bedford fully approved Rockingham's answer and his demand for an audience. 'I think the Court is trifling with your Lordship', he wrote, 'and do therefore advise that your Lordship should see the King imediately.'[3]  Temple and Grenville also approved ;[4] while Hardwicke wrote: 'If the Duke of Grafton's answer should be dilatory or not explicit, I hope your Lordship will not continue the correspondence.'[5]

There is no reason to doubt Walpole's statement that he drafted Grafton's second letter to Rockingham.[6]  His part in the drafting of the first letter has been shown by evidence in the Grafton MSS., and material in these and other papers testifies to the influence he had on these transactions through his friendship with Conway.  It was, as Rockingham admitted, 'a well turned letter'.[7]  It side-stepped Rockingham's demand for an audience, but did not refuse it ; it did not admit that the present Administration was at an end, but, by saying that the King was 'willing to appoint such a one as shall exclude no denomination of men attached to his person and government', appeared to welcome the comprehensive plan and yet in words so vague that they did not pledge the Court to accept. Here is the letter :

I have laid your Lordship's letter before his Majesty, and have the satisfaction of acquainting your Lordship, that the King's gracious sentiments concur with your Lordship's in regard to the forming of a comprehensive plan of Administration, and that his Majesty desirous of uniting the hearts of all his subjects, is most ready, and willing to appoint such

[1] *Bedford Correspondence*, iii. 368-9.

[2] Rigby's letter to Temple, dated '17 July 1767, twelve o'clock', together with copies of Rockingham's correspondence in Rigby's hand, is in the Grenville (J. M.) MSS.

[3] Bedford to Rockingham, 9.30 A.M. July 17, 1767 ; Rockingham Papers, R1-522. Printed in *Bedford Correspondence*, iii. 379-80.

[4] Temple to Rigby, 3 P.M. July 17, 1767 ; *ibid.* p. 379. Grenville to Rigby, 7 P.M. July 17, 1767 ; *ibid.* p. 372.

[5] Hardwicke to Rockingham, July 16 [1767] ; Rockingham Papers, R1-517.    [6] *Memoirs*, iii. 53.

[7] Rockingham to Newcastle, July 17, 1767 ; Add. MS. 32983, ff. 288-9.

a one as shall exclude no denomination of men attached to his person and government.

When your Lordship is prepared to offer a plan of Administration formed on these views his Majesty is willing that your Lordship should yourself lay the same before him for his Majesty's consideration.[1]

Rockingham seems to have been satisfied with this letter ; after seeing Weymouth he decided not to insist on an audience with the King, but thought 'it should be pressed and rather in conversation than by *letter*'.[2] The part that pleased him was Grafton's apparent acquiescence in the thesis that the present Administration was to be considered as dissolved. 'Your Grace will also observe', he wrote to Newcastle on July 17,

> that the acknowledgment of the present Administration's being at an end is also avoided, but this letter coming in answer to my very explicit letter of yesterday in which I said *the principle on which I would proceed would be to consider this Administration at an end* I think the very being order'd to proceed is in fact tho' not in words an acknowledgment.

Hardwicke and Charles Yorke both seemed to agree that the demand for an audience should not be pressed, but believed that the Court 'flatter themselves that the difficultys in forming the plan may overset it'.[3] Hardwicke cautioned Rockingham : 'No more writing to his Grace of Grafton which only produces these artificial epistles'.[4]

---

[1] Rockingham Papers, R1-523. Identical with the text given in Grafton's *Autobiography*, pp. 144-5, except for the word 'those' instead of 'these' in line 11. There are unimportant verbal differences with the text in Walpole's *Memoirs*, iii. 53. The letter is dated July 17, and was received by Rockingham before 8 P.M., at which time he sent a copy to Newcastle. A copy was sent to Bedford at 10 P.M. the same evening (*Bedford Correspondence*, iii. 376-8) ; and Rigby sent a copy, together with the correspondence of Rockingham and Bedford on July 17 and 18, to Temple and Grenville on July 18 (*Grenville Papers*, iv. 57-8). These copies are in the Grenville (J. M.) MSS.

[2] Rockingham to Newcastle, July 17, 1767 ; Add. MS. 32983, ff. 288-9.

[3] Hardwicke to Yorke, July 17, 1767 ; Add. MS. 35362, f. 135. Yorke to Hardwicke, July 17, 1767 ; Rockingham Papers, R1-518. Hardwicke sent this letter to Rockingham who did not return it.

[4] Hardwicke to Rockingham, July 17, 1767 ; *ibid.* R1-519.

Rockingham forwarded to Bedford a copy of Grafton's letter at 10 P.M. July 17, and told him that he thought the demand for a previous audience should not be pressed.[1]  His first intention had been to go to Woburn himself, but he dropped this idea and instead asked Bedford to come to London.  'I hope your Grace will communicate what has passed to Lord Temple and Mr. Greenvile', he wrote, 'and will inform yourself of their ideas. What their wishes are for their friends should be particularly known.'[2]  This was the first time Rockingham had made such a request : he had hitherto insisted that his negotiation was with Bedford only, and he now asked not for Grenville's assistance but for a list of those followers whom he would like to see in office.  The serious business — the bargaining over the disposal of offices — was about to commence.  'I think your Lordship is in the right', replied Bedford on July 18, 'in proceeding in the negotiation notwithstanding you are not yet admitted to see the King.'[3]  He promised to be in London the next day, informed of Grenville's and Temple's ideas.

Rockingham had asked particularly for a list of Grenville's followers, but Rigby merely wanted to know 'the sentiments of Lord Temple and Mr. Grenville upon the present crisis, in any manner they choose to convey them'.[4]  This was not at all the same thing.  Rigby knew that Grenville had never promised support to the comprehensive Administration, but had declared he would judge it by its American policy ; while Rockingham had persuaded himself (or been persuaded by others) that Grenville's support was secured.  He was now to feel the disadvantages of negotiating with Grenville via an interested intermediary.  Grenville complained to Temple that 'no notice is taken that we have insisted only upon measures, and that we have expressly declined being named for any office.  This makes it necessary to be cautious, lest our true

---

[1] *Bedford Correspondence*, iii. 376-8. A draft is in the Rockingham Papers, R9-11.

[2] Judging from the draft, Rockingham found these sentences difficult to phrase.

[3] *Ibid.* R1-525. Printed in *Bedford Correspondence*, iii. 381-2.

[4] Rigby to Temple and Grenville, July 18, 1767 ; *Grenville Papers*, iv. 57-8.

ground should be mistaken.'¹ Rigby had taken care that Rockingham should take no notice, and Rockingham had been so relieved at Grenville's waiving the Treasury that he had not considered the possibility of disagreement upon measures. 'Mr. Grenville and Lord Temple', Grafton admitted, 'have been those who in this affair have acted as the wiser politicians.'² Grenville, proscribed by the Court, thought only of policy ; Rockingham, flattered by the Court, thought only of office.

In the evening of July 18 Temple went over to Wooton and the brothers drew up a joint letter to Rigby.³ This is the substance of their manifesto :

> They refer themselves for their precise ideas to Mr. Gren-
> ville's letter of the 16th instant to Mr. Rigby ; they wish all
> success to the present negotiation upon those public prin-
> ciples, and when they are informed of the further particulars
> contained in the plan to be proposed by Lord Rockingham
> to the King and of his Majesty's consent to its taking effect, if
> an honourable and becoming share shall be allotted to their
> friends, they will be ready to manifest the sincerity of their
> intentions by using their good offices to induce them to
> accept. They will be glad to hear that previous to any plan
> of particular persons, stated to his Majesty for particular
> employments, the King may have been prevail'd upon to
> explain his intentions, as that would give great facility to this
> transaction and prevent many future ill consequences.⁴

All this was happily concealed from Rockingham ; he had not troubled himself about what Grenville and Temple were thinking and Rigby did not try to enlighten him. In the evening of July 17, after he had received Grafton's second letter, he called on Grafton and told him,

> that the previous audience was a point in which I owned I
> felt much interested, on various reasonings. That I called

---

¹ Grenville to Temple, July 18, 1767 ; *ibid.* pp. 59-60.
² Grafton to Northington, July 18 and 19, 1767 ; *Autobiography*, pp. 146-148.
³ *Bedford Correspondence*, iii. 380.
⁴ 'Those public principles' were, of course, 'a plan of measures to our satisfaction and particularly the capital measure of asserting and establishing the sovereignty of Great Britain over its colonies.'

upon him merely to suggest to his Grace that it was a matter
on which I doubted and that some consideration must be
had upon it, which would take time and longer than ought
to be, if an answer to his Majesty for the gracious sentiments
expressed in the Duke of Grafton's letter, were to remain
unnoticed till the other matter was decided.[1]

But Grafton insisted that the King 'neither designed nor
ought to grant that request',[2] and Rockingham pressed it no
further.

After this conversation Rockingham went to his house at
Parson's Green (then in the country), to rest after the 'continual
hurries' of the last few days.  He was due to dine at Claremont
on Sunday July 19, and would have preferred to excuse himself
but knew how easily Newcastle took offence.[3]  He felt pleased
at the way the negotiations had gone and seemed to think
they would end well.  On July 19 he wrote to Conway :

> I think I have tolerably digested in my own thoughts,
> the principles on which we should proceed in the arduous
> task of forming an Administration on a comprehensive plan.
> The great object is to restrain and put an end to that
> mischievous power, which has occasioned all the confusions
> and divisions, which have tore and perplexed this country
> for some years past.
> The avowed maxim of one side has been *divide et impera*
> — the only wise rule to be adopted in those who have or
> mean to resist the effect is to conciliate and unite.
> I don't despond — indeed I should not when I think
> appearances are much more favourable than any expectation
> could have justified.  The Duke of Bedford comes to town
> tonight — I hope fully informed of the sentiments and
> opinions of Lord T. and G. G. and in his own ideas I have
> every reason to believe warmly and well inclined.
> By this time tomorrow I shall probably be well enabled
> to judge, and if upon the whole such a system and plan is

[1] Rockingham to Charles Yorke, July 18, 1767; Add. MS. 35430,
ff. 83-4.
[2] Grafton to Northington, July 18 and 19, 1767; *Autobiography*,
pp. 146-8.
[3] Rockingham, however, does not seem to have gone to Claremont, nor
for once did Newcastle take offence.

adopted as will give content and satisfaction to those I
esteem, and will bid fair for general approbation in the
publick, I shall be very happy indeed.[1]

### (vii)

Meanwhile Grafton had taken fright and thrown the Court
into confusion. Conway had decided to resign on July 22,
and Grafton told the King he would not remain at the Treasury
without Conway to lead the Commons. The King was now
faced with the prospect of losing his alternative to the combined
opposition, just at a time when they seemed to have sunk
their differences. On July 17 he wrote to Lord Hertford what
Walpole rightly describes as 'a most pathetic letter', begging
Hertford to use his influence with Conway to prevail on him
to stay.

Indeed your brother has it now in his power to extricate
me out of all my difficulties by lending himself at least for a
time to my civil service ; if he will but one moment cooly
reflect, he must see he has most scrupulously fulfilled his
unguarded promise to those who have not acted by him as
he has towards them ; for he has persuaded me to cast my
eyes towards them, they have upon this made most indecent
demands, which must inevitably oblige me to go through
any difficultys rather than submit to their chains ; if he thinks
of his duty it must teach him that he must continue the
chief Minister in the House of Commons, as it will encourage
the Duke of Grafton to remain, and consequently prevent
every evil that otherwise may arise ; if he feels a delicacy
that would make him easier in holding another province
than that of the North, I will erect a Secretary of State for
America, and will undoubtedly give him the command of the
very lucrative and honorable regiment I hinted to you the
other day whenever it shall become vacant. Succeed in this
and you may depend on it I shall remember your conduct.[2]

Walpole had also been asked by Grafton to induce Conway
to change his mind and he describes in his *Memoirs*,[3] with

---

[1] Rockingham Papers, R1-535. He also wrote on July 18 in a similar
strain to Charles Yorke ; Add. MS. 35430, ff. 83-4.
[2] Fortescue, I, no. 548.          [3] *Memoirs*, iii. 53-8.

pride in his diplomacy and tact, the tortuous stratagems he used. The King had been persuaded by Conway to negotiate with Rockingham ; Rockingham had rejected what had seemed to Conway a fair opportunity of returning to office and proposed to force his way back with the aid of Bedford and Grenville, a procedure and combination most distasteful to Conway. There was sense and justice in Walpole's argument that Rockingham's terms were unreasonable, and that Conway was 'bound in honour to extricate the King from the difficulties in which he had, by his promise of resignation involved him'. For Rockingham, his eyes dazzled with the vision of the comprehensive Administration as the only barrier to Bute's influence, had forgotten that half his strength lay in Conway. If Conway, revolted by Rockingham's behaviour, broke with him and acted whole-heartedly with Grafton, the Rockinghams would no longer be so formidable in the face of a united Cabinet.

Walpole claims that on July 18 he persuaded Conway to stay : he was to resign the Seals, as he had intended, on the 22nd and then to resume them without the salary, 'to show he did not act from interest, and to strike a great stroke in character'. 'We agreed to keep this a secret from all the world', writes Walpole, 'and I was only to give the Duke of Grafton and Lord Hertford hopes.' His account is supported by evidence from the documents. Here is a passage from Grafton's letter to Northington, written on July 19 :

Mr. Conway sees the extension of Lord Rockingham's connexions in the same light as myself, and I believe there is nothing he would not do to prevent such a Ministry from taking place under the certainty of bringing the country into fresh difficulties. He presses me much not to retire. My only answer has been that which your Lordship knows : however by the King's most gracious proposals to these different sets of men, so *strangely* receiv'd by them all, I think the case greatly alter'd, and that there is a great deal to justify those, who shall endeavour to carry on Administration on a narrower ground than they could wish. I have told the King on his repeated requisition to me to remain at the

Treasury, that one previous point must be attained to make it possible and that, even then, it would labor to a great degree, perhaps too much to move forward. That previous point in such case must be Mr. Conway's retaining the lead in the House of Commons. In consequence of this his Majesty has much employed his brother to press him to do so : and though he is determined to resign, which he will do on Wednesday, it is not impossible but they may still prevail on him ; so much he apprehends the consequences of the other event. Your Lordship sees that my fate remains still undecided, or rather dependent on what Mr. Conway can bring himself to.[1]

And here are the relevant parts of Conway's letter to Rockingham of July 20 :

I have, as the Duke of Grafton told your Lordship, resolved to ask his Majesty's leave to resign the Seal on Wednesday next, and have desired his Grace and my brother to apprize his Majesty of it : I confess that from his Majesty's personal kindness to me and his desire to keep me I am apprehensive I may thereby give him some offence, but my situation is so awkward, the more as this has seem'd the desire and expectation of your Lordship and others, I wish to call my friends, that I was resolved to press it. So I hope to compleat it on Wednesday ; and shall then with the utmost freedom give your Lordship, if you do me the honour to allow it, my full and fair opinion upon the plan you will have to offer to his Majesty. There was one you know I approv'd ; for the rest I must suspend my judgement. I agree perfectly with your Lordship in the idea of restraining the power you mention, but in the mode of doing it I am not sure we agree. I wou'd do what was necessary for that purpose and no more ; and I wou'd take care the world shou'd see that alone was intended and that other views and purposes were not substituted to it ; for I think too much may be done, as well as too little, towards that right purpose, and may even succeed the less to that very end.[2]

Rockingham had lost the battle for the soul of Conway ; he was now to be disappointed in his vision of a comprehensive Administration.

[1] Grafton, *Autobiography*, pp. 146-8.    [2] Rockingham Papers, R1-532.

(viii)

In the afternoon of July 20 Rockingham had a long conversation
with Bedford, and it was decided that there should be a meeting
of the two parties at Newcastle House that evening.[1]  It was
now that Rockingham saw for the first time the correspondence
which had passed between Rigby and the Grenvilles, and
particularly Grenville's letter of July 16 and the joint letter
of July 18.  Relying on Rigby's assurances, he had taken
Grenville's co-operation for granted.  Now, confronted with
Grenville's manifesto, which could admit of no comfortable
interpretation, all his distrust awoke and clouded the favourable prospect.

There is in Rockingham's papers a document in his own
hand,[2] which seems to have been drawn up between this
conversation with Bedford and the meeting at Newcastle
House.  It is a draft of the points he wished to make at that
meeting.  'That the conduct of Lord Temple and Mr.
Greenvile', he writes, 'has not been so fair and open as our
conduct towards them required.'  Yet he still hoped to reach
agreement with Bedford ; this is his sketch of the principles
on which this agreement should be based.

That a plan of arrangements should be proceeded in
that we may see how far the Duke of Bedford's friends and
ours can be accomodated.

That some of Mr. Greenvile's and Lord Temple's friends
should still be included tho' they have thrown a point of such
difficulty by not naming them and their objects particularly
upon the Duke of Bedford, and indeed on all of us.

The Duke of Bedford and General Conway absolutely
necessary.

Necessary to undermine Lord B. by supplying any degree
of animosity against persons of much weight and who otherwise from anger and revenge may be drove herafter to take
a part tho' not under yet servicable [sic] to Lord B.

---

[1] The conversation began about one o'clock (Bedford's diary ; *Cavendish's
Debates*, i. 606) and ended at near four o'clock (Rockingham to Newcastle,
July 20, 1767 ; Add. MS. 32983, f. 335). Rockingham proposed either
Bedford House or Newcastle House as the venue for the meeting, and Bedford
chose Newcastle House.                                    [2] R9-20.

That in forming our plan we should always have it in view that it may in a short time be published at Charing Cross and therefore it should be a wise, prudent and admitting of as much moderation as security can allow.

The meeting began at nine o'clock in the evening of July 20 and lasted till almost two o'clock in the morning. In addition to the party leaders there were present Newcastle, Richmond, Portland, Keppel, and Dowdeswell of the Rockinghams ; and Weymouth, Sandwich, and Rigby of the Bedfords. Five of those who took part wrote accounts of this meeting, and there is general agreement as to what was said. The interest of these accounts is not what the writers include, but what they omit. They were each written from a different point of view and for a different purpose, and from them much can be learnt of the motives and wishes of their authors.

Newcastle's account,[1] afterwards circulated to a select group of friends and sympathizers, is the journal of a disappointed man. Newcastle had set his heart on the success of these negotiations and could not bear the thought that it might be impossible to reconcile conflicting views and ambitions. Failure could not be inherent ; it must be due to mishandling ; a scapegoat had to be found and Newcastle found him in Rockingham. He had felt aggrieved that Rockingham had been entrusted with the negotiation while he had been ignored by the Court ; while sincerely wishing Rockingham success, and prepared to rejoice with him if it came, he regarded failure as the consequence of neglecting his advice. He judged Rockingham severely but not unjustly, and did not sympathize with his distrust of Grenville.

Rockingham, too, needed a scapegoat : he did not care to admit that the comprehensive Administration was an unattainable vision, with no solid roots in the political earth, and he blamed 'the intrigues and chicane of the Cobham school' for its failure.[2] His account is given in a letter to Hardwicke of

---

[1] Add. MS. 32983, ff. 351-63.
[2] The phrase is used by Rockingham in the draft of a letter, probably written on July 21. Rockingham Papers, R9-22. The draft is unfinished, and it is not clear for whom the letter was intended.

July 26.[1] There is also in the Rockingham Papers another and much fuller account of this meeting and that of the following day.[2] This appears to be by Dowdeswell, and can be taken as reflecting Rockingham's views.[3]

On the Bedford side, there is Rigby's letter to Grenville of July 21 and 22.[4] The negotiation having failed, Rigby was concerned to demonstrate his fidelity to Grenville and to widen the gap between the Rockinghams and the Bedfords. What Rigby says tallies very much with the other accounts : but what he omits is very instructive. Finally, there is a short and matter-of-fact entry in Bedford's Diary.[5] Unlike the others, it is not an apologia ; Bedford at least felt no need to defend himself and needed no scapegoat for what he had done.

The conference was opened by Bedford who outlined the replies which had been received from Temple and Grenville. Then Rockingham began a long recapitulation of the events since the negotiations had begun : the initial overtures were

[1] *Ibid.* R1-539 ; part printed in Albemarle, ii. 50-4.    [2] R1-536.
[3] My reasons for believing it is by Dowdeswell are : (1) In his Memorandum, 'Thoughts on the present state of publick affairs and the propriety of accepting or declining Administration', written on July 23 and 24, Dowdeswell writes: 'With this view it was that Administration was lately offer'd to Lord Rockingham. He endeavour'd to form a plan as comprehensive as was possible. He fail'd. . . . Why it fail'd . . . is consider'd in another paper.' Evidently Dowdeswell did write an account of the conferences of July 20 and 21. (2) This account must have been written before the 'Thoughts on the present state of publick affairs', *i.e.* before Conway's offer to Rockingham to come in with his own party was rejected. The account I take to be Dowdeswell's deals only with the events of July 20 and 21. (3) It is written in the third person, a clumsy form for Rockingham to adopt when his own speech is so much the subject-matter, but natural to a third person. (4) The document describes how Dowdeswell declined Bedford's suggestion to become Minister in the House of Commons, 'for many reasons which he then gave, and for many more which he kept in his own breast'. This also suggests Dowdeswell as the author. (5) In Rockingham's letter to Hardwicke he writes on the declaration requested by Grenville, that Rigby 'seemed to think that nothing would content Mr. George Grenville, but an assent to the words as they stood'. This is confirmed by Newcastle's account, and had Rockingham written a second account, he would surely not omit such a point against Grenville. (6) There is a precision and fullness in the account which suggests Dowdeswell rather than Rockingham. (7) The similarity in phrasing between this account and Rockingham's letter to Hardwicke is no proof that Rockingham was the author : he could well have used the account of so orthodox a follower as Dowdeswell as the basis of this letter.
[4] *Grenville Papers*, iv. 80-6.    [5] *Cavendish's Debates*, i. 606.

to himself and his friends only, he extended it to include the Bedfords, and Bedford desired to consult Grenville. Rockingham declared that although his commission did not include Grenville, he had no objection to Bedford consulting him ; indeed, 'if Mr. Grenville cou'd be induc'd to concurr it wou'd be still better, because the system wou'd become the stronger by it', although 'he has reason to think he is not the better in the Closet for having made his plan so comprehensive'. After all this, he complained

> that Lord Temple and Mr. Grenville shou'd create difficulties by starting questions on America for immediate discussion, the answer of which must depend on future and uncertain events ; shou'd claim honourable and becoming portion of office for their friends without saying who those friends were, nor to what extent that portion shou'd be ; shou'd press the insisting on an audience in the Closet when it was agreed in general by the Duke of Bedford as well as the rest that that was not a point to be insisted upon ; and shou'd both of them avoid coming to London, where their presence might be so necessary to the speedy determination of this matter, though they even knew that the Duke of Bedford wisht one of them to be in town ; that upon the whole of this matter, and from the knowledge he had of those persons, he cou'd not but conclude that they meant to obstruct instead of facilitating, and did in his own mind foresee an unhappy event to this great and important business.[1]

The argument turned on the meaning of Grenville's phrase, 'asserting and establishing the sovereignty of Great Britain over its colonies', which he stipulated as a *sine qua non* of his support and which Rockingham saw as questioning his good faith and intentions. Bedford, according to Newcastle, 'endeavour'd to soften and reconcile things in a most amicable and prudent manner' ; declared he was perfectly satisfied with Rockingham's assurances ; but that Grenville, disappointed in his hopes of the Treasury, might be 'a little sore' and 'fling out some expressions which otherwise he might not have done'. He was sure that Grenville meant nothing unreasonable, but 'might have his doubts, especially as Lord

[1] Dowdeswell's memorandum ; Rockingham Papers, R1-536.

Chatham, the Lord Chancellor and Lord Shelburne had all of them denied this sovereignty'.

The mention of Chatham, and the assumption that Rockingham's opinions were similar to his, only made Rockingham more indignant. According to Dowdeswell's narrative,

Lord Rockingham appealed to the conduct of himself and his friends whether there was the least doubt of his and their intentions to maintain the sovereignty of Great Britain over her colonies, that he did not think himself answerable for what had been said by Lord Chatham, the Lord Chancellor, or Lord Shelburne ; that after the publick proof given of him and his friends' intentions he thought neither Lord Temple nor Mr. Grenville had the right to put such a question to him, that he wondered they dared do it, that he did not think it worth an answer, his opinions and intentions being so well known, and that he would not permit Lord Temple and Mr. Grenville or any man to question his sincerity.

Rigby now intervened and pleaded 'that it was not so material how Mr. Grenville' understood the words 'asserting and establishing',

as what the Duke of Bedford thought of them and what might be his intentions upon them ; that Mr. Grenville and we were very opposite, that the Duke of Bedford was the middle man between us and the arbiter to decide in cases where we differed ; that if Mr. Grenville put an improper construction on them, or called upon us to do a wrong thing in consequence, the Duke of Bedford, as the arbiter, would step in and tell Mr. Grenville that he was wrong and join against him.

Naturally Rigby says not a word of this in his letter to Grenville ; instead he rejoices at being accused 'of showing too much partiality to you and your opinions, which I think does me infinite honour'.

Finally Bedford was persuaded to explain the sense in which he understood Grenville's words, and Dowdeswell took down his statement in writing. Here it is :

That with regard to the American colonies no new measures shou'd be understood to be agreed upon at this meeting, unless new matter arises, but if new matter shou'd arise the sovereignty of this country shou'd be asserted and established with firmness and temper.[1]

Bedford's statement was found 'very satisfactory' by all the company, and it was agreed that it should be submitted to Grenville. Here a divergence appears in the narratives : Dowdeswell says that Bedford, while willing to transmit his statement to Grenville, 'could not answer for him'. This point is not made by any other witness, and is of little importance since the question did not arise.

Rockingham admits that he became 'warm' over this matter, and Bedford says that Rockingham afterwards apologized to him in the presence of Keppel, 'alleging the warmth of his temper and his resentment of Earl Temple's former behaviour to him'. Newcastle speaks also of 'much warmth from the Duke of Richmond' ; he is the only one who mentions Richmond as having had any part in the dispute.

The statement on American policy, made by Bedford and accepted by Rockingham, is a middle way between the extremes of Grenville and Chatham. It shows how far the Rockinghams were from appreciating the nature of the dispute with the colonies, and indicates how little they would have been able to prevent a separation had they returned to office. Rockingham was thinking in terms of persons not of policy : he resented Grenville's interference at all points, not merely on the American problem. He next went on to complain about Grenville's wish that Rockingham should have an audience with the King, and about 'the honourable and becoming portion of office' which Grenville demanded for his friends, and about his refusal to attend the meeting (although no indication had been given that he would be welcome there). In short, the dispute grew to such a point that both Bedford and Rockingham began to have little hope of a happy issue.

[1] Rockingham Papers, R9-7. There is also another version of this in Rockingham's hand (R9-6), the second part expressed even more positively : 'That there ought not nor can be a doubt that it is the intentions of this company to support the rights of Great Britain over its colonies'.

These wrangles took up the greater part of the time, and it was late before the question of places was entered upon. When it was, it soon terminated the discussion. Rockingham first proposed that Grafton should be invited to take office, which was not vetoed by Bedford, although his lack of enthusiasm was noted and resented by the Rockinghams. But when Rockingham named Conway, Bedford gave an absolute refusal and the argument started afresh. Bedford, while wishing Conway preferment in the Army,[1] refused to consider him as Minister in the House of Commons and complained that his inclusion had never been once suggested. Rockingham was equally insistent that Conway must be included.

What was discussed when Rockingham visited Woburn ? Apparently neither men nor measures. Or was it that Rockingham, having secured Bedford's approval of himself at the head of the Treasury, assumed that the main bone of contention was removed ?

Both sides refusing to budge from the positions they had taken, the conference ended at near two o'clock in the morning.

On July 21 Newcastle wrote to Bedford, begging 'to have the honour of some discourse . . . to see whether it may not be possible to set things right'.[2] 'My disappointment', continued Newcastle, 'is beyond what I can express, and therefore must be an excuse for the liberty I now take.' Bedford replied that he would visit Newcastle that afternoon, but before he could do so Rockingham called. 'Lord Rockingham was very much to the same purport', wrote Bedford in his diary,[3] 'and very much in praise of General Conway's abilities ; to which I did by no means give my assent. It concluded on both sides in thinking the negotiation at an end.' Newcastle feared so too but wished to make one more attempt, and he prevailed on Bedford and Rockingham to meet again that evening. Both Newcastle and Bedford thought a small meeting was more likely to achieve success ; indeed, it would

[1] In Bedford's words, 'a promise of the best regiment in the King's service' ; in Rigby's, 'such preferment as the King might think proper to bestow upon him'.
[2] Woburn MS., lv. f. 224.
[3] Cavendish's Debates, i. 606-7.

have been more sensible to have kept down the numbers at the first meeting, for most of those who attended did so as a tribute to their rank in the party rather than for any contribution they could make to the discussion. At this second meeting (also at Newcastle House) the arrangements resembled those for a boxing match or a duel : Bedford and Rockingham had their seconds, Rigby and Dowdeswell, and Newcastle acted as referee. (He had tried to get Mansfield to attend but that prudent man had refused.[1]) Bedford went a long way towards a compromise : he admitted Rockingham's argument that the First Lord of the Treasury should have a Minister in the House of Commons whom he could trust, and proposed Dowdeswell. But Dowdeswell declined, and insisted that Conway was the only man qualified to lead the Commons. The only result of this meeting was that the old ground was re-trodden and the two sides remained further off agreement than ever, for they ended (much to Newcastle's sorrow) with a declaration that each should be at liberty to take whatever part they pleased in the future. The knell of the comprehensive Administration seemed to be rung at last.

(ix)

On July 22 Rockingham had what he described as 'a truly gracious audience' with the King. He began by explaining why he thought a comprehensive plan necessary and why he had extended it 'beyond what his Majesty *originally had intended*'. It was 'to unite the hearts of all his subjects' (or in other words, to keep out Bute's friends).

> I said that when I had the honour of being in his Majesty's service, the measures of Administration were thwarted and obstructed by men in office, acting like a corps ; that I flatter'd myself it was not intirely with his Majesty's inclination, and I would assure him it was very detrimental to his service.[2]

[1] See the letters which passed between Newcastle and Mansfield on July 21 ; Add. MS. 32983, ff. 400 and 406.
[2] Rockingham to Hardwicke, July 26, 1767 ; Rockingham Papers, R1-539.

He laid the blame on the Grenvilles for the failure of the negotiation [1] and concluded with admitting that he could not now form a Ministry. The King said that he had not offered him the Treasury.

Grafton and Conway were waiting outside the Closet, and to them Rockingham recounted what had passed. Grafton appeared surprised that the King had not asked Rockingham to form an Administration 'upon his own bottom', and suggested that they should meet in the evening to discuss this. But Rockingham saw no purpose in such a meeting, and Newcastle counselled him against it. Albemarle also was afraid that Rockingham had engaged himself so deeply 'as to be obliged to undertake the forming of an Administration without the Bedfords'.[2] The Rockinghams seem to have admitted, at least tacitly, that Conway could not resign ; and Richmond saw that it would be very difficult for them to oppose with decency.[3]

Now the wheel turned once more, and one negotiation having ended another began. The Rockinghams had broken with Bedford on Conway, and he felt under a greater obligation to them than before. Walpole counselled Grafton to offer the Treasury again to Rockingham, it being understood that it was not to extend to the Bedfords and the Grenvilles. This was Conway's wish in the first place, before Rockingham had gone chasing after that elusive creature the comprehensive Administration. It was the obvious policy for Grafton, now the opposition was divided, to try to detach a part of it. And the need to retain Conway resulted in the offer being made to Rockingham. If he refused, Conway would have quit himself of his obligations and the way would be clear for the Bedfords. They would not boggle at the ghost of Bute as Rockingham did.

---

[1] He had not Dr. Johnson's charity. In his celebrated conversation with George III in February 1767 Johnson, when asked his opinion of Dr. Hill, said he was 'an ingenious man, but had no veracity'. 'I now', said Johnson, when telling the story to his friends, 'began to consider that I was depreciating this man in the estimation of his Sovereign, and thought it was time for me to say something that might be more favourable.' But Rockingham could not depreciate Grenville any further in the estimation of George III.

[2] Albemarle to Rockingham, July 23, 1767 ; Rockingham Papers, R1-533.        [3] Walpole, *Memoirs*, iii. 60-1.

P

On July 23 Grafton saw the King, and that evening he and Conway offered 'that if Lord Rockingham would now come into the Treasury, he and all his friends should be provided for'.[1] Rockingham declined, 'because from everything he had seen both in the Closet and out of it, he could not persuade himself that the King was very anxious to have him undertake the Administration'.[2] 'I said I did not see the practicability in the present moment', he wrote to Hardwicke on July 26,

and rather wished that our *old friends* who were in, would come out to us than chuse to go in with our friends to them ; that if we did we must still be subject to the same power as we had been to before, and I wished them to remark that if we thought that even if we all went in that still we should not be sufficiently strong to check that power we had reason to be attentive to, they being but a few who were in must still be more at the mercy than we should be.[3]

The warning and the invitation both went unheeded, and Rockingham rejected for the last time what Walpole rightly describes as 'the only rational plan, a junction with the Administration, without insisting on the pre-eminence of Rockingham'.[4]

That evening (July 23) Conway made a last effort to get Rockingham to come in and sent Richmond[5] to him 'with reiteration and pressing'.

Upon which Lord Rockingham desired the Duke of Richmond to tell Mr. Conway for his own information, but to be made such use of as it might be necessary, that after

---

[1] Conway's invitation to Rockingham to attend at his house that evening is in the Rockingham Papers, R9-13, dated 'Thursday, past three'. For the events of this and the following day, see the memorandum in the Rockingham Papers, R1-537 ; Rockingham to Hardwicke, July 26, 1767 (*ibid.* R1-539) ; Rockingham to Newcastle, July 24, 1767 (Add. MS. 32984, ff. 34-5); Walpole, *Memoirs*, iii. 63-5.

[2] Rockingham Papers, R1-537.

[3] Rockingham to Hardwicke, July 26, 1767 ; *ibid.* R1-539.

[4] *Memoirs*, iii. 62.

[5] Richmond wished Rockingham to come in. He wrote to Burke on November 15, 1772 : 'Had my opinion of taking Administration by ourselves, when our negotiation with Bedford House broke off in 1766, (or 1767, I forget which year,) been followed, things would have been very different from what they are at present'. (*Burke Correspondence*, i. 369-72).

all that had happened he could not undertake Administration but upon full power given him by the King himself; that if his Majesty would please to impower him to form it wherever he could he would undertake it; that in that case, he would endeavour to renew the treaty with the Duke of Bedford and would offer such terms as would put the Duke exceedingly in the wrong if he refused to agree; that if the Duke did put himself thus in the wrong he should think himself justified in undertaking the Administration upon narrower ground and would do it.[1]

Conway 'was a good deal hurt at the idea of renewing the treaty with the Duke of Bedford as he lookt upon it as an exclusion of himself', and 'was confident that his Majesty would give no power until he saw a plan'. Neither he nor Grafton considered Rockingham's proposal worth putting to the King, and nothing came of it.

There is in the Rockingham Papers a document headed 'Thoughts on the present state of publick affairs and the propriety of accepting or declining Administration'.[2] It was written by Dowdeswell on July 23 and 24, for Rockingham's information only and 'for Lady Rockingham if she will take the trouble of reading it'.[3] The original does not seem to have survived; the document is a copy in Lady Rockingham's hand. Rockingham's reception of Conway's offer accorded with the principles set out in this paper. It is of the highest importance for the history of the Rockingham party.

Dowdeswell begins by lamenting 'the present distemper'd state of publick affairs', the shortness of Administrations, and the divisions that have resulted therefrom. 'All mankind cries aloud for union and permanency . . . let there be permanency in Administration whatever hands it may happen to be placed in.' Rockingham has attempted to cure these evils by forming 'a plan as comprehensive as was possible'. He has failed; what should he do now to 'enable him to be useful to his King and country'?

Rockingham can only accept Administration on two conditions:

[1] Rockingham Papers, R1-537.        [2] *Ibid.* R1-538.
[3] Dowdeswell to Rockingham, July 24, 1767; *ibid.* R1-534.

First, that the King should send for him to give him his powers from his own mouth without the interposition of any of his Ministers.  This will give him weight, and is absolutely necessary at this time there having been in the former negociation a point not rightly understood, tho' no less essential than whether he was to be at the head of the Treasury.

Secondly, at his audience he must give the King to understand as tenderly as he can, but at the same time as truly, the real cause of all the public misfortunes.  They must be imputed not to the influence of particular persons but to the prevalence of a political principle which says that the power of the Crown arises out of the weakness of the Administration.  The public misfortunes necessarily resulting from that weakness should be set forth and the distress of the Crown in its income and its honour.  At the same time that these representations are made with all possible deference and submission there should appear a manly resolution not to maintain the pageantry of Administration an hour after it is divested of its necessary weight in the Closet, and its necessary power in other places.

If these conditions are fulfilled, 'he should not fall into a common error that the removal of a particular set supposed connected with the prevailing influence either gives or marks the power of an Administration'.  Removals there should be for example's sake, but 'there are others who belong to other corps'.  Then Dowdeswell reverts to the idea of the comprehensive plan ; Rockingham should apply to Bedford, but must first 'remove those stumbling blocks which were in his way in his former negociation'.  Bedford cannot be treated with 'on a par', and Grenville must have nothing to do with the forming of the Administration.  Conway is no longer to be insisted upon for Secretary of State ; Townshend is to be offered it, provided he will be 'confidential' ; if not, then Dowdeswell will take it himself.  It should be made clear to Bedford that Rockingham

must consider himself as the former of an Administration and answerable for its success and would therefore preserve in all offices of business a manifest superiority for his own friends, but that if his Grace would make a list of his friends with the nature of his wishes for them he would find Lord Rockingham as earnestly as he could wish in giving all possible proof of his desire of what might be perfectly satisfactory.[1]

Grenville will be allowed no share in the disposal of offices ; but if he gives to Bedford a list of his friends everything will be done to include them ; and if there should be competition between Bedford and Grenville, so much the better — 'the event of such a struggle must do some good'.

But Rockingham should take care to be so liberal to his associates 'that the sincerity of his intentions for an union may be manifest beyond contradiction'. Every effort should be made to make the Administration 'broad and comprehensive' ; only such a one will be able to stand against 'the intrigues of the Closet'. 'A new Parliament should certainly be call'd, by which not only the number of Lord Rockingham's particular friends might be encreased but our one of speakers also enlarg'd.'

Finally, Dowdeswell considers what should be done if this plan be thought 'too great and impracticable'. Should Rockingham engage to come in 'on his own bottom' ? 'To do it, would be so contrary to all our former assertions that unless some great good is to be got by it, or some great evil prevented, it is surely a thing not to be thought of.' It would be a weak Administration and a short one ; 'it can do no good, it cannot enterprize, it would not probably be allow'd to hold to the General Election, it would not dare to shorten the continuance of this Parliament, it would be insulted at home and despised abroad'. After a long review of the arguments he concludes it would be neither desirable nor practicable.

And here is his conclusion :

[1] The same idea was expressed, in less straightforward language, by Burke in *Observations on 'The Present State of the Nation'* : 'It is, however, false that the idea of an united administration carries with it that of a proscription of any other party. It does indeed imply the necessity of having the great strongholds of government in well-united hands, in order to secure the predominance of right and uniform principles ; of having the capital offices of deliberation and execution of those who can deliberate with mutual confidence, and who will execute what is resolved with firmness and fidelity.'

What then can be done ?   Nothing but to finish with
honour.   We have hitherto acted with the strictest honour.
If our friends will not joyn us it is impossible for us to joyn
them. . . .

I confess that I see no fair prospect before us.   Standing
still is the only thing we can do.   This may possibly weaken
us as a party, it depends upon the virtue of our friends whether
it will or will not but I am sure it will do us honour as
individuals.

In these unhappy times when we find ourselves well in
the opinion of mankind the wisest thing we can do is to
stand still and enjoy the reputation which we have, not risque
it for something new the chances of which are so much
against us.

This is the doctrine of the Rockingham party in 1767, as
laid down by the man who had most influence with its leader.
How little does the idea of party appear, so eloquently
expounded by Burke less than three years later, in his *Thoughts
on the Cause of the Present Discontents* !   How much survives
from the past — that government is the King's, that his
Administration should be formed from the best of all parties,
that union not division is the ideal state !   How little does
ideology divide the parties !   Yet underneath it all new roots
are growing.   For Rockingham could have come in in 1767
had he conceded to Grafton the pre-eminence which the King
wished him to have.   While implicitly acknowledging the King's
right to choose his Minister, Rockingham wished to confine
that choice to himself.   While refusing to come in without
the support of the Bedfords and the Grenvilles, he did not
wish that support unless they accepted his own supremacy.
And by remaining outside he compelled Grafton to turn to the
Bedfords to stabilize his Administration, and weighted the
balance in the Cabinet against a conciliatory policy in America.

(x)

The politicians were leaving London and would not return
until November.   On July 25 Conway took a sad farewell of
Rockingham.

I understand [he wrote] you think of going out of Town
today, or tomorrow. I am going till Monday or Tuesday.
The Duke of Grafton is also gone to the same time and the
Duke of Richmond goes today. From all this I despair of
any change in the present disagreable situation of things :
and I write this short word only to say that I most cordially
and sincerely lament it, after having done and said all I
possibly cou'd to prevent it. There is a moment left and I
shou'd be happy indeed if your Lordship cou'd on reflexion
take it to bring what still depends absolutely on yourself,
and you do reflect that if you and your friends don't come in,
there is, as I think, no one good alternative. For surely that
which you seem alone to have any taste for is impracticable :
the Bedfords have shut the door for any junction with them
to your Lordship and they have barr'd it to me.

I dread anything that looks like a separation, even a
political one from your Lordship and your friends. But I
have the misfortune to differ widely as to the present determination and have no plea nor pretence to take the part you
seem inclin'd to take.

I shall trouble your Lordship no further ; I have done it
too much with my vain and insignificant thoughts already.
You have others that advise you better, and much more
forcibly.[1]

On July 31 Grafton notified Lady Chatham, with the request
that she would inform her husband, 'that General Conway
has given him authority to say, that, though the particular
situation is not fixed on, he is determined to stand forward in
the House of Commons to carry on the King's business'.[2]

It was just a year and a day since Chatham had kissed
hands for the Privy Seal.

[1] Rockingham Papers, R9-21. Dated 'Saturday morning'.
[2] *Chatham Correspondence*, iii. 281-2.

# CHAPTER VI

# PARTY IN THE AGE OF GRAFTON AND CHATHAM

CONSTITUTIONAL monarchy and its prerequisite, government by party, are England's peculiar contributions to the art of politics. Yet the history of English parties has never been written : too much attention has been concentrated on biographies of their leaders, and histories of the ideas they were held to enshrine. Instead, when parties became respectable in the nineteenth century, they were provided with mythical pedigrees like those found in older editions of peerage genealogies. Just as almost every noble family was traced back to some ancestor who landed with William the Conqueror, so the two great English parties were found to have sprung from the divisions of the Long Parliament on the Grand Remonstrance. From that event was derived an unbroken, apostolic succession. The Whigs were derived from the Roundheads and the Exclusionists of Charles II's time ; under Walpole and the Pelhams the party became corrupt ; purified by the long exile from office under Rockingham and Fox, it emerged in 1832 as the party of liberty, reform, and progress. Similarly, the Tory pedigree was traced from Clarendon, through Bolingbroke, North, and the younger Pitt, to Liverpool, Peel, and Disraeli. When the Labour party became respectable in the twentieth century it in its turn was provided with a forged pedigree, and the Diggers and Levellers of Cromwell's day were found to be the ancestors of modern British Socialism.

Party history is not so straightforward as this : the parties do not have a continuous history stretching over three centuries. Just as a peerage can become extinct, to be revived in a different family connected by marriage or often not connected at all with the original holder, so party names are assumed at different periods by different groups and interests : it is the name that survives, not the party. The constantly changing class structure of English society is reflected in the development of parties. As new problems come to the front in politics, so new parties spring up to grapple with them, and new principles and new men shelter behind old names. Though Rockingham called himself a Whig, it was North who inherited both the principles and personnel of the Pelhams. The history of party in the eighteenth century tells how little groups, clustered first round a great nobleman or prominent politician, blossom into maturity and then die ; evanescent creatures, they live for a day, but their place is quickly taken by others. In the 1760's there were parties led by Bute, Grenville, Bedford, and Rockingham ; later there emerged the City Radicals and the party grouped round Shelburne ; while towards the close of the American war Charles Fox built his own party within the Rockingham enclave. He, more than any man, may be deemed the founder of the Whig party of the early nineteenth century, yet how little did he inherit from Walpole or Newcastle, or even from Rockingham.

'Party divisions', wrote Burke in 1769, 'whether on the whole operating for good or evil are things inseparable from free government.' [1] And in *Thoughts on the Cause of the Present Discontents*, published in 1770, he defined party as 'a body of men united for promoting by their joint endeavours the national interest upon some particular principle in which they are all agreed'. To what extent did these pronouncements find general agreement among Burke's contemporaries ? How far did party influence the voting of members of Parliament ? How many considered themselves as belonging to a party, and on what principles did the different parties seek to promote the national interest ?

When a nation is agreed on the fundamentals of government, and when the service of government is open to all classes or interests capable of the work ; when the extent of government's activity is restricted to the maintenance of order, the defence of property, and the conduct of foreign affairs, conditions are

[1] *Observations on 'The Present State of the Nation'.*

not suitable for the growth of parties. To win mass support, especially where political mass action is not the rule, and to preserve continuity longer than the lives of their leaders, parties must enshrine principles or represent interests, both of which are threatened or need to be advocated or defended. These conditions did not exist in the eighteenth century. There were no constitutional or religious issues to cause deep rifts in the nation as in the previous century. Socially, there was a remarkable degree of harmony : there was no great divergence of interests between the landowning and mercantile classes. Indeed, the spheres of 'moneyed' men and landed men interlocked and overlapped, and there was no barrier against intermarriage (the acid test of social distinctions) between the mercantile classes and the peerage. The unenfranchised classes, not yet herded into towns, were hardly aware that political action might be a remedy for their grievances, economic rather than political in their nature. There was no mass electorate, and no need for party programmes. The story of party in the eighteenth century centres in Parliament rather than in the constituencies.

The electoral system, though heavily weighted in favour of the owners of land, was yet sufficiently elastic to allow merchants, civil servants, service officers, professional men, and men of letters to enter the House of Commons. The majority of members owed their seats neither to the Crown nor to a party leader : consequently they could be independent of both. Politics was not a profession, and to enter Parliament did not necessarily make a man a politician. 'There are many honest well-meaning country gentlemen', Burke told Dr. Johnson in 1778, 'who are in Parliament only to keep up the consequence of their families.' [1] Eighteenth-century politics are too often seen from the point of view of London and the men who directed their course. London was the centre of political gossip and intrigue, the Mecca of all who wished to make a figure in the world whether in politics, literature and the arts, or social life. The great memoir and letter writers — Lord Hervey, Horace Walpole, Boswell, Gibbon, Fanny

[1] Boswell's *Life of Johnson* (ed. by Birkbeck Hill and Powell), iii. 234.

Burney — depict the life of the salons and coffee-houses of London, of the lobbies of Westminster and the waiting-room at St. James's. But scattered all over Great Britain, living in their country houses and on the rentals of their estates, were the country gentlemen, not as a rule an articulate class. Many of them entered Parliament and for six months of the year enjoyed the social and political life of London without ever becoming part of it. Their roots were in the country ; yet they were an important element in the calculations of politicians, and deference was paid to their prejudices and respect to their interests. Though they left few literary memorials, their tastes and habits can be studied from the fiction of the second half of the eighteenth century, where they stand as the prototype of the typical Englishman.

Their interests were personal rather than political, local rather than national. They did not aim at place or influence ; they had few favours to ask of government beyond that it should leave them alone, and that its cost should not weigh too heavily upon them. Their politics were of the county rather than of Westminster ; local government was their province, and Parliament a final court of appeal for local issues. Each year measures were added to the statute book promoted by these men or relevant to their needs : bills to enclose land or reclaim waste, to enable canals to be cut or roads to be constructed, to levy rates for the building of county gaols or shire halls, measures concerning the militia or the poor law, originated in the counties and were sanctioned at Westminster. Divisions on these matters led to the rise of parties in the counties and these parties transferred their contests to Parliament, where each side lobbied for the support of friends and friends' friends. Election petitions were often of this nature : they arose from a struggle for supremacy in a constituency ; this was decided in the House of Commons, the final court of appeal.

Much of the time of Parliament was spent on local business, and for many members it was the real stuff of politics. In addition, there were personal matters sufficiently important to require the seal of parliamentary authority : divorces, alterations of marriage settlements, and matters concerning the disposal of land were effected by Act of Parliament. Such private and local business receives much space in the statute book, in the Journals of the two Houses, and in the correspondence of country gentlemen, but is not reflected in the writings of politicians and consequently rarely in those of historians.

Though a member might owe his seat to his local standing, and though his interests centred in his locality rather than at Westminster, once in the House he shared its life and work, and entered the wider world of the politician and administrator. On the burning questions of the day, by which the politician gauged the rise and decay of parties or reputations, the country member had a vote and not infrequently an opinion. That opinion was rarely dictated by party, but it could be moulded by a good case skilfully presented ; and the independent member deemed it his duty to give a critical support to government measures. The independent attitude to party squabbles was described by Mansfield in a letter to Newcastle of October 10, 1767.

> The only conclusion I make is, that the present sett are too weak, in every sense of the word, to serve or do any good either to the King or publick, but will baffle parliamentary resistance, and may be helped by honest men, who may think the whole ought not to be thrown into confusion, and who may wish to leave to the King the power of giving the Treasury to any of the competitors rather than see him forced and held in subjection by any.[1]

But their support could not be relied upon : it had to be won by debating skill and merited by sound and frugal administration. The presence of a large number of members in the House not inclined to embarrass Administration without serious cause, and whose attendance was never continuous to the end of the session, retarded the growth of party.

The way in which Parliament did its work also affected the development of party. Parliament's task was to watch over the state of the nation, and in particular the way in which its money was spent, rather than to legislate. The

---

[1] Add. MS. 32985, ff. 421-2.

common law, interpreted by Westminster Hall, was held to be sufficient for all normal purposes. Public legislation was an emergency measure designed to cure a specific evil, and introduced reluctantly, tentatively, and often for a limited period. This was especially so where the government dealt with matters not hitherto the subject of legislation, and for which there were no precedents. The East India settlement of 1767 was initially for one year only ; the Regulating Act of 1774 was another temporary measure ; and it was not until 1784 that a more permanent settlement was adopted for the problem Chatham had first brought to the notice of Parliament eighteen years earlier. Parliament did not thrust legislation on the country ; it waited until matters grew to a point when its interference was essential. Such legislation was empirical rather than dogmatic ; *laissez-faire* was the rule in politics long before it was accepted in economics.

The function of the House of Commons resembled that of a jury, and they sprang from the same origins. But the verdict of a jury must be unanimous, and there long lingered a tradition that on legislation the decision of the House should be unanimous. General principles of policy were considered by the Committee of the whole House before specific measures were introduced ; and it was in Committee, rather than in the House, that the debate took place. Finance was dealt with in the Committees of Supply and Ways and Means : resolutions were there considered which, when embodied in legislation, passed usually without debate or division. With non-financial public legislation the usual procedure was to move for a Committee of Inquiry or to lay papers before the House. This was how Chatham proposed to deal with the East India problem : the House was to resolve itself into a Committee of Inquiry, hear and examine witnesses, and consider resolutions previously drafted by the Cabinet. It did not work out this way because of opposition from Conway and Townshend and the absence of Chatham : the House heard the witnesses, but before any resolutions were considered the Company increased its dividend, and the Dividend Bill was hastily introduced to meet an unexpected situation. But the normal procedure was followed over the Administration's American policy. Papers were laid before the House and resolutions debated in Committee on May 13, 1767 ; the resolutions were reported on May 15. On both days the House sat till one o'clock in the morning, and on both days there were divisions. The bill framed on the basis of these resolutions was introduced on May 27, read a second time on June 1, committed on June 11, reported on June 12, and read a third time on June 15. There was no division at any of these stages ; the bill passed through the House almost automatically and without opposition. But, of course, this procedure was not always followed. When a measure excited more controversy than usual there would be debates and divisions on the bill itself as well as on the preparatory resolutions (*e.g.* the bill to repeal the Stamp Act). When a bill was introduced to meet a new situation or was thought to be urgently needed (*e.g.* the Royal Marriage Bill), or was not introduced by Administration (*e.g.* the Nullum Tempus Bill), it was not, of course, preceded by resolutions.

When a bill was the subject of debate the House fell naturally into two sides — those for and against. Intermediate positions were possible but not easily taken, and two parties tended to emerge. But when papers were read or the House was in Committee of Inquiry the debate ranged far and wide : the House was like a jury, which hears evidence and then delivers a verdict. Its verdict took the form of resolutions framed by Ministers, but its proceedings were more like a discussion than a debate. Members could suggest amendments or propose alternatives, take up intermediate positions between acceptance or rejection of the Ministry's proposals, ventilate their grievances or urge their panaceas. The picture of opposing parties becomes blurred, and instead there emerge little groups and individuals, sometimes uniting, sometimes falling apart — a true likeness of the House.

(ii)

In the eighteenth century unity rather than division was the ideal. 'To unite the hearts of all his Majesty's subjects' was the professed aim of every politician — of Rockingham in opposition as well as Chatham in office. Even those foremost in opposition decried the idea of party and prayed for union. On May 9, 1769, when Burke was composing his pamphlet in defence of party and of the Rockingham party in particular, he was present at a dinner at the Thatched House tavern attended by members of Parliament who had taken part in the opposition to Wilkes's expulsion. One of the toasts drunk on that day, after a session of fierce party strife, was 'May all personal, party, and national distinctions be lost in the publick good!'[1] When George III talked of 'that evil called connection' he was expressing, as he often did, the opinion of most of his subjects. Men took pride in the balance and equilibrium of the British constitution, which they regarded as the bulwark of their freedom. King, Lords, and Commons shared political power: freedom was in danger if one of them achieved supremacy in the State, but such an attempt would be checked by the union of the other two. Horace Walpole, who had feared the tyranny of the aristocracy under George II and the tyranny of the Crown under George III (both imaginary fears), lived to see the French Revolution and to fear the tyranny of a representative assembly which had overthrown both Crown and aristocracy.

Co-operation between these three elements was essential to sound and stable government. Executive power belonged to the Crown but could not be exercised in a manner contrary to the will of Parliament; the Crown had the choice of its Ministers, but they had to be acceptable to Parliament. The House of Commons was a check upon the Crown's abuse of its power, but not a drag upon its limited and legitimate employment. The duty of a member of Parliament was to give general support to the measures of the Crown, but also to guard the privileges of Parliament and the rights of the people. Opposition was not ruled out, but a distinction was drawn between opposition to specific measures for conscientious reasons and 'formed opposition'. 'Formed opposition' was condemned by politicians of all parties as indecent and offensive. Each

[1] The list of those present and the toasts drunk is in *Chatham Correspondence*, iii. 359-61.

time Newcastle left office — in 1756, 1762, and 1766 — he protested that he would not go into 'formed opposition'; Walpole told Grenville in 1764 that 'he would not find Mr. Conway engaged in any regular opposition'; [1] Rockingham in 1766 wished his friends to be 'quiet', and was not eager to oppose.

But men did go into 'formed opposition' in spite of their protestations. It was always understood that those who did had no right to expect favours from the Crown; but the contrary was also true — that those who aspired to, but did not receive, favours from the Crown, went into opposition. In any representative assembly an opposition is bound to arise unless that assembly is to degenerate into an organ for registering the decrees of the executive. Under a system of responsible government opposition is desirable as an alternative Ministry. But a system of responsible government did not exist in the eighteenth century : the prerogative of the Crown was a reality, though its limits had never been precisely defined.

When government could only be carried on by co-operation between Crown and Parliament it was essential for the Crown to have its own following in Parliament. The Ministers of the Crown were the leaders of this party. But the power they wielded as Ministers and as party leaders was derived from, and entrusted to them by, the Crown. Most of their followers had no connection with them in any other capacity, and would not follow them outside its service, as Newcastle found in 1762 and Chatham in 1770. 'I will have nothing to do with any persons who mean to act independent of the King', wrote George Selwyn on September 5, 1767, 'for let my circumstances be what they may, I will belong to nobody else.' [2] But though the King was the real head of the Court party he could not exercise direct command : that task was delegated to his vicegerents in Parliament.

The Court party — 'Those who have always hitherto acted upon the sole principle of attachment to the Crown' [3] — re-

---

[1] *Memoirs*, i. 273.

[2] *Letters to Henry Fox, Lord Holland*, ed. by Lord Ilchester, pp. 281-2.

[3] 'Observations on the probable dissolution of Lord Rockingham's [first] Administration'; N. S. Jucker, *The Jenkinson Papers, 1760-1766*, pp. 404-8.

quired some 'person to accept of a Ministerial office at the head of them'. The other parties began with a leader, who collected a group of followers round him ; the Court party began with the followers, and had to find a leader. Hence arose the difficulties of 1766 to 1767 : the Court party had no leader. Chatham was ill ; Grafton was incapable ; Conway was ineffective. The Court normally had numbers sufficient ; its task was to find someone to lead them.

The difficulty was not simply that the leader must be acceptable to both Crown and Parliament : it was that he should remember his position, and not try to substitute himself for the Crown at the head of the party. Every Minister made such connections or conferred such obligations during his tenure of office as to be able to convert office perquisites into heirlooms. The amount he could thus alienate depended on personal qualities and on how long he had been in office. The strength of his position on leaving office depended on how much he had alienated and on the acceptability of his successor. Grenville entrenched himself so deep in the party of the Crown that he was able to take many of its followers with him into opposition ; Rockingham won so little support that he barely survived a year. All depended on men and circumstances : George II could not retain Walpole in 1742 nor George III North in 1782, though he had discarded Newcastle twenty years earlier with little difficulty.

When the Crown was so closely identified with Administration, opposition took on a tinge of disloyalty. This was veiled in the reign of George II by opposition blending its cause with the personal quarrel of the heir apparent with his father, though the two were separate and could exist independently. Opposition now took on the guise of the Ministry in reversion : loyalty to the Crown was preserved, but not to the wearer of it. From 1727 until the death of Frederick Prince of Wales in 1751 there was always a Prince's party, though its numbers and personnel varied at different times. A body of opposition legend grew up to justify this combination of interests : it was pretended that the King was 'a prisoner in his Closet', the slave of his Ministers, and not responsible for their policy.

Q

The point of the attack was always urged against the Ministers, not against the Crown. The King was irremovable except by death.

The death of the Prince broke up his party, and temporarily put an end to this type of opposition. Though the new heir-apparent in his turn came to dislike and despise George II and his Ministers, he did not become an active politician until he mounted the Throne. There gathered at Leicester House a knot of men who hoped for favours in the next reign ; and it was known that Bute, the Prince's favourite, would stand highest. But there was no parliamentary party grouped round the Prince, as there had been round his father, to oppose the coalition of Newcastle and Pitt. While George II was alive they did not fear serious opposition from Leicester House, but they did speculate over, and try to prepare for, what would happen when he was dead.

Every politician who went into opposition tried to win support from the independent members. They were a reserve of uncommitted troops, holding the balance between sets of politicians : the Court depended for its majority on their support or acquiescence. If sufficient of them could be enticed away the Court might be compelled to treat with the opposition and admit part into office. Hence the opposition's programme was framed to appeal to independent opinion and flatter 'country' prejudices. On February 8, 1748, the Prince of Wales, 'thoroughly convinced of the distresses and calamities that have befallen and are more likely every day to befall his country from party and faction', appealed to 'all well wishers to this country and constitution to unite and coalize with him'.[1] He promised first 'to abolish for the future all distinctions of party'. For it was one of the ironies of the situation that the opposition, to make its appeal attractive to the independent members, must condemn party (which these hated) as an evil element in political life. The remainder of the programme was designed to remedy the supposed grievances of the time : a militia was to be set up, junior officers of the Army and Navy were to be excluded from the Commons, the

---

[1] *Bedford Correspondence*, i. 320-3.

Civil List was to be reduced. The Prince's followers promised to support 'his wise and salutary purposes, that the Throne may be strengthened, religion and morality encouraged, faction and corruption destroyed, the purity and essence of Parliament restored, and the happyness and welfare of our constitution preserved'.

Only the naïve or the gullible fell for these promises. They were trite and insincere, and were made to attract the independents but to benefit the politicians. The effectiveness of opposition was more related to the mistakes of the Court than to its own promises. It was only dangerous when it could take advantage of the genuine resentment aroused by mishandling of a popular question. Walpole's excise scheme, George II's partiality for Hanover, even the unpopularity of Lord Hardwicke's Marriage Bill, had served this purpose during the reign of George II. Successful oppositions, such as those which triumphed in 1742 or 1782, were combinations of politicians, intent on forcing themselves into office, and of independent members, not desirous of office but genuinely alarmed at the policy of Administration. Even so, it needed the disillusionment of ill-success or failure in war to sweep them into power.

The new reign killed old controversies but bred new ones. During the early years of George III, the cause of John Wilkes provided opposition with a popular question. It was not an ideal one : Wilkes's profligacy, violence, and popularity with the London mob disgusted respectable men. Pitt and the Rockinghams distinguished between the man and the cause : they condemned Wilkes and refused to palliate his conduct, but held that the principles involved in his case and not the fate of the man were the real issue. In this they were largely successful : Wilkes fled to France, and his person ceased to be an important factor in the parliamentary struggle. Although there were precedents for the use of general warrants the principle could not be justified, and when opposition launched their full-scale attack on February 18, 1764, Grenville's Administration had a majority of only fourteen votes.

Wilkes's return to England, his election for Middlesex in

1768, his repeated expulsions from the House of Commons, and finally the decision that his defeated opponent was duly elected, made that demagogue again the subject of political controversy. The issues involved were more exceptionable and more easily comprehended than in 1763, but greater finesse was required to present the case in Parliament. Wilkes had now become the idol of the London mob, and his cause was taken up by a group of City politicians whose radicalism frightened the Rockingham party. But the problem was badly mishandled by Grafton and North : the issue was not decided twelve months after Wilkes's first election, and the declaration of Luttrell as the duly elected member for Middlesex though he had obtained fewer votes than Wilkes seemed to strike at the rights of electors. Many independent members who disliked Wilkes, distrusted City radicalism, and feared the London mob, could not stomach this negation of the free-holder's vote. Had Wilkes been returned by a small or even medium-sized borough, or had a man of some standing in the county been his opponent, probably little offence would have been given ; but the case was far different when the county representation seemed to be at stake. The Rockinghams received considerable support from the independent members, and were joined by their old enemies, Chatham and Grenville. The Wilkes affair dominated Parliament in 1769 and seriously worried the Court, but it died away when foreign affairs became threatening in 1770. It shook the Administration and discredited Grafton, but never looked like bringing the Rockinghams back into power.

From 1771 to 1774 were quiet years : North's Administration had settled down, and few questions arose on which the Rockinghams could expect independent support. Their opposition sank so low and seemed so contemptible that they seriously considered abandoning Parliament. Those were the years when discontent in America was developing towards armed revolt. When war broke out it became an issue in British politics. There were many who asserted the supremacy of Great Britain over the colonies and were exasperated by the behaviour of the Americans, but were horrified at the advent of civil war. Yet the outbreak of war lost North's Administration little support ; their failure to conduct it efficiently and to end it quickly lost them much more ; and the surrender at Yorktown overthrew them. Charles James Fox was only the most prominent of those who had supported North and Grafton over Wilkes and who in 1782 were acting with Rockingham. More significant than the desertion of politicians was North's failure to retain the support of the independents, and when they abandoned him in 1782, the end had come. The American war was as fatal to North as the Norway campaign was to Neville Chamberlain.

The American war was of great significance for the development of party. Hitherto parties had existed only in Parliament, with no roots in the nation at large, and little moral support to reinforce their claim to office. Apart from the City of London, opinion outside Parliament was seldom sufficiently self-conscious or articulate to influence events at Westminster. But the petitioning movement of 1780, the most significant development in the history of party since the Revolution, began in the provinces and aimed to mobilize support outside and, if necessary, against Parliament. Sprung from deeply felt but inchoate discontent at the disasters of the American war, its aims were radical and cut across those of the parliamentary parties. Reduction of expenditure and reform of the abuses of Court and Administration had been the watchwords of the Tory country gentlemen of George II's reign, and had been adopted by those politicians who had angled for their support. But parliamentary reform was a new demand outside the City of London, and disconcerting and alarming even to opposition leaders at Westminster. Still more significant was the mobilization of opinion outside Parliament, and the growth of party organizations in the counties. The petitioning movement of 1769 was artificial, stirred up by the politicians for their own ends ; that of 1780 was spontaneous, and it confounded the politicians by having ends of its own. The Rockinghams, accustomed to play the party game in a limited sphere, feared a movement which threatened to make party a popular element in politics.

Rockingham returned to office against the King's wishes, because he was the only effective alternative to North. His party had produced their apologia before the American crisis became acute, and opposition to the American war was not solely their *raison d'être*. In the early years, in the absence of a reversionary interest, they had to find a new basis for opposition : they could not become respectable by putting the heir apparent at their head. A new legend was needed to justify what was felt to be unjustifiable, and give their cause a moral basis.

The Rockingham legend was elaborated in Burke's pamphlet, *Thoughts on the Cause of the Present Discontents*, published in 1770. Originally, their opposition had been to Bute, the reputed secret adviser behind successive Administrations. By 1770 this story was threadbare : Bute had been abroad during most of 1769 and 1770 and could hardly have controlled Administration from Italy, and though simple souls like the Duke of Portland considered that Burke had dealt too leniently with him,[1] and though the story of his influence with the Princess Dowager was so stimulating to Walpole's imagination that he could not bear to discard it, the Bute bogy no longer frightened. Over three hundred new members had entered the Commons since Bute's resignation, and they required a more topical explanation of 'the cause of the present discontents'.

Burke was too intelligent not to see that the old myth had served its purpose, and had imagination sufficient to create a new one. Besides, he had never been thoroughly infected with the Bute virus : he did not enter Parliament until 1765 and his enmity was directed rather against Chatham, the man who had refused to support Rockingham and had eventually supplanted him, than against Bute. His imagination was as vivid as Walpole's, and he had had little experience of government or the Court to control it ; but their fantasies, each characteristic of its author, were vastly different. Walpole wrote a sham Gothic romance, with an ambitious, adulterous

[1] Portland to Rockingham, December 3, 1769 ; Rockingham Papers, R1-694 (part printed in Albemarle, ii. 145-7).

mother as the villain ; Burke, who preferred to work behind
the scenes of the Rockingham party and who venerated its
leaders too much to appear openly as their equal,[1] invented 'a
cabal of the closet and back-stairs' — the real power behind
the Cabinet. Supporting the cabal in Parliament was a Court
party which engrossed the favours of the Crown. So Burke
builds up his theory of the 'Double Cabinet' and the 'King's
Friends' as the pretext for the Rockingham opposition.

How much of this hotch-potch was accepted by Rockingham's followers it is difficult to say. Rockingham certainly
believed it — the surest way to gain his confidence was to talk
of 'secret influence' ; Portland and Richmond apparently,
and Burke himself presumably, did so. It is doubtful, however,
if the rank and file swallowed it. Moreover, by 1780 opposition
was beginning to revert to the older, traditional pattern. The
Prince of Wales was now a man and about to become a politician, on bad terms with his father and inclined towards
opposition. In 1780 when Admiral Keppel, the hero of
opposition, was elected M.P. for Surrey,[2] he told Rockingham
how

> the Prince of Wales and Prince Frederick took the most
> undisguised pains to express to every friend of mine their
> extream satisfaction upon my success, and to one friend, I
> believe to more than one they said, *we* have had a most com-
> pleat victory. . . .[3]

By 1783 the Prince and Fox had become close friends ; there
was once again a Prince's party ; and Burke's fictions were
no longer necessary to justify opposition. His pamphlets could
now pass into honourable retirement as classics of political
philosophy.

[1] Richmond once rebuked Burke for this. 'The only part of it [Burke's
letter] which I disliked', he wrote on September 2, 1769, 'was the excuses
you made for giving your opinion freely ; this I take rather ill, for it was
supposing me very absurd to think them necessary. I had asked your
opinion, how could I take it amiss that you should give it ? Indeed this
was very ill placed modesty.' Rockingham Papers, R8-2.

[2] He had been defeated at Windsor, where the King had intervened
against him.

[3] Rockingham Papers, R2-114. 'The Prince of Wales took great part
for Keppel', wrote Walpole, and declared his victory 'the happiest event
he had ever known.' (*Last Journals*, ii. 329-30.)

(iii)

In the eighteenth century a party rarely created an Administration ; an Administration always created a party. Grenville and Rockingham were not appointed to the head of the Treasury because they were party leaders ; [1] but they were party leaders when they were dismissed, and they were able to take some of their followers into opposition. A Minister made friends and attracted followers, some of whom, when he left office, chose to remain with him rather than with the Court. The explanation of this phenomenon is personal and individual rather than political and general. Of Grenville's Secretaries to the Treasury, why did Whately prefer to remain in opposition with his chief, while Jenkinson seized the first opportunity to return to Court ? Neither Conway nor Dowdeswell were connected with Rockingham before 1765 : why did Dowdeswell follow him into opposition and Conway remain with Chatham ? Why did Shelburne and Camden join Chatham in opposition in 1770, while Bristol and Grafton supported North ? No answers can be given to these questions without a thorough knowledge of the men — their characters, and the nature of their relations with their leaders. There was no convention to guide them : they determined their course by the light of their own inclinations. Party history in the eighteenth century is the study of men : their friendships, their connections, their ambitions, their interests.

About the time Burke was writing *Thoughts on the Cause of the Present Discontents* the word 'party' had not yet acquired respectability : it was used as a term of abuse, synonymous with 'faction'. The political groups were commonly referred to as 'Lord Rockingham's friends', 'the Duke of Bedford's friends', etc.[2] Even in the early nineteenth century the term 'Mr. Pitt's friends' was used. There was sense and truth in this method of nomenclature, for the relation between the leader and his followers was personal rather than political.

[1] This refers to Rockingham in 1765. In 1782 he came to the Treasury because he was a party leader.

[2] Chatham once called the Rockinghams, 'the remnant of the late Duke of Cumberland's party'. (Walpole, *Memoirs*, ii. 282.)

Even so, it was not always direct, and the term 'Lord Rocking-ham's friends' is inaccurate if taken literally. Most of the rank and file of the Rockingham party were followers not of Rockingham but of his associates, and their relation to their leader was indirect. Indeed, in 1766 men spoke of 'the Duke of Newcastle's friends' as a separate and distinct body from 'Lord Rockingham's friends'. The party magnates had each their small group of followers, based usually, though not necessarily, on personal friendship, borough interest, or family connection. A party was really a coalition of small groups, each group connected with the others by the friendship of the magnates with the party leader. Grenville's party came nearest to being monolithic in structure ; even the Chathamites were divided between the City radicals and the friends of Chatham and of Shelburne.

This structure can be seen clearest when the 'whips' were sent out for an important division. Rockingham did not send out his 'summonses for attendance' direct to his followers : he sent them to the deputy leaders, who transmitted them to those of the rank and file for whom they were responsible. With this indirect channel of communication it was often difficult for the rank and file to know what was party policy or strategy : when Newcastle complained on November 20, 1767, that 'nobody knows what to do', he was merely describing the usual state of affairs in the Rockingham party at the opening of a session.[1] Hence the importance of the 'man of business', the confidant of the party leader, whose task it was to keep the deputy leaders in touch with each other. Burke performed this service for the Rockinghams, Rigby for the Bedfords, and Whately for the Grenvilles. These men of business developed a common understanding, and could work together in Parlia-ment even though their chiefs were rivals. The 'man of business', part 'whip', part secretary, could exert the greatest influence. Rigby was the real director of the strategy of the Bedford party in 1767 ; it was Whately, rather than Grenville, who led his party into collaboration with the Rockinghams in

---

[1] Newcastle to Admiral Keppel, November 20, 1767; Add. MS. 32987, f. 63.

1769. That Burke had not the same influence was not due to his lack of opportunity but because he failed to use it : he had too much deference for Rockingham to take an independent line. During the summer recess of 1767, Burke visited Newcastle, Richmond, and Albemarle to learn their views ; was in touch with Portland and Dowdeswell ; and yet could propose no strategy for the opening of the session in November. Neither Rigby nor Whately would have neglected such opportunities to further their party's cause and to increase their political stature.

Such unity and coherence as a party had depended on the leader and lasted for his life only : no leader could bequeath his followers to a successor. The Prince's party was dissolved in 1751 by the death of Frederick. Temple could not succeed to the command of Grenville's party after his death : Grenville's followers had no connection with Temple. Bedford's party was scattered after his death in 1771 : some followed Gower, some Sandwich, some merged into the Court party, some drifted back into opposition. Only the party of the Crown possessed continuity, for its leader never died.

An Administration was built up round the Court party, with one or more of the political groups added, and with the goodwill of the independents.[1] The political groups gave the Administration the façade of being founded on party, which disguised the fact that its majority was based on the party of the Crown. It was desirable to include as many groups as possible to reduce the quality of the opposition, but since their leaders could only be accommodated in the highest offices some had to be left out. Administration had to have a party façade, though party alone could not make an Administration. It was the perpetual dream of the independents (never to be realized) to support an Administration comprehending all the parties, and the party leaders paid at least lip service to this ideal.

Burke, in a well-known passage in his speech on American taxation (April 19, 1774), thus described the Ministry Chatham formed in 1766 :

[1] See Sir Lewis Namier's Romanes Lecture, 'Monarchy and the Party System reprinted in *Personalities and Powers* (1955)

He made an Administration, so checkered and speckled ; he put together a piece of joinery, so crossly indented and whimsically dove-tailed ; a cabinet so variously inlaid ; such a piece of diversified mosaic ; such a tesselated pavement without cement ; here a bit of black stone, and there a bit of white ; patriots and courtiers, King's friends and republicans ; Whigs and Tories ; treacherous friends and open enemies ; that it was, indeed, a very curious show ; but utterly unsafe to touch, and unsure to stand on.

This is the language of rhetoric, but it has been quoted to show how unrealistic Chatham was in not basing his Administration on party. But Burke's description fits every Administration of the period : that which Cumberland formed with Rockingham at the head of the Treasury in 1765 ; the one Rockingham himself tried to form in 1767 ; the one he did form in 1782. It was not Chatham's fault that his Administration was 'checkered and speckled' ; it was inevitable under eighteenth-century conditions, when no one party, nor indeed all combined, could take on Administration by themselves. And surely Chatham never created such 'a piece of diversified mosaic' as Fox and North did in 1783.

In discussing party and its place in politics I have not used the words Whig and Tory. There is little point in doing so. 'Am not I, Lord Camden, and Lord Shelburne Whigs ?' said Chatham.[1] If Rockingham claimed to be a Whig, so too did Bedford ; while North never renounced the name. What politician did not call himself a Whig ? What politician ever called himself a Tory ?[2] These names do not explain or differentiate the parties, and they foster the illusion that parties were stable, coherent bodies. There were parties in the eighteenth century, but they were like meteors, flashing across

[1] Walpole, *Memoirs*, ii. 261.
[2] Boswell called himself a Tory, but his use of the word shows what little meaning it had in the years of the American Revolution. 'I never differed from you in politicks', he wrote to Johnson on February 28, 1778, 'but upon two points, — the Middlesex Election, and the Taxation of the Americans by the British *Houses of Representatives*. . . . As I am a steady and warm Tory, I regret that the King does not see it to be better for him to receive constitutional supplies from his American subjects by the voice of their own assemblies, where his Royal Person is represented, than through the medium of his British subjects.' (*Life of Johnson*, iii. 221.)

the sky and then gone.   There could be no party system when
the King himself was the first of the party leaders.

(iv)

How many were of the parties, and who were they ?   It is
impossible to be precise :  blacks and whites cannot be exactly
enumerated when so many were pigmented.   Some members
were so closely connected with party leaders that there can be
no doubt :  Burke and Dowdeswell were obviously followers
of Rockingham, and so (in a different category), was Savile
Finch, who sat for Rockingham's borough of Malton.   But
John Mostyn, the other member for Malton in 1767, was not :
he owed his seat to a family, and not to a political connection.[1]
A great deal of knowledge is required about most members
before party connection can be determined, and even then it
often changes.   In 1767 Newcastle counted Charles Barrow
(M.P. for Gloucester) as a Tory, but a year later Dowdeswell
described him as 'a very good friend of our's'.[2]   He voted in
Parliament with the Rockinghams :  can he therefore be considered as of the party ?   Harbord Harbord (M.P. for Norwich)
was claimed as a friend by both Rockingham and Newcastle
in 1767 :  yet he was sufficiently well-disposed towards
Administration to solicit patronage from Shelburne.[3]   From
1768 onwards he voted in Parliament with the Rockinghams :
can he be considered as of the party ?[4]   Party connection did

[1] He was first cousin to Rockingham.  Mostyn followed the Court ;
he had been a Groom of the Bedchamber since 1746, and in February 1768
was appointed Governor of Minorca.  Rockingham refused to return him
for Malton at the General Election of 1768.

[2] In a letter to Newcastle, dated March 4, 1768, asking him to secure
Lord Gage's interest for Barrow at Gloucester.  (Add. MS. 32989, f. 35.)
Although Gage was of the Court party he gave his interest to Barrow.

[3] There are three letters from Harbord to Shelburne in the Lansdowne
MSS. concerning small patronage business :  they are dated March 19, 1767,
June 11, 1767, and June 5, 1768.

[4] A politician in opposition was not always debarred from the favours
of the Crown.  In 1768 James Harris (M.P. for Christchurch), a follower
of Grenville, secured the appointment of his son (later Lord Malmesbury,
the well-known diplomatist) to the secretaryship of the Madrid Embassy.
This was effected through Lord Hyde, also a follower of Grenville, but on
friendly terms with Shelburne (Hyde to Shelburne, September 7, 1768 ;
ibid.).  Personal friendship sometimes cut across party connection.

not follow logically on political opinion : Bedford described Sir John Hinde Cotton (M.P. for Cambridgeshire) as 'my friend . . . with whose conduct in Parliament I had reason to be contented',[1] and gave him his interest in Cambridgeshire at the General Election of 1768. Yet neither Newcastle nor Rockingham reckoned Cotton as a follower of Bedford. They were correct : he was an independent country gentleman, a friend of Bedford's and of similar political opinions, but who would have scorned to be the follower of any party leader. Neither would Savile, closely connected though he was with Rockingham, have considered himself a member of the Rockingham party. Chatham told Richmond in 1771 that 'there were many excentric men who would not belong to a party' and that 'they were the real strength of opposition' ; [2] while Conway claimed in 1779 that though he 'disliked party . . . all was so ill-conducted, everybody ought to join against the Ministry'.[3] To be in opposition was not to belong to a party.

Party connection was sufficiently comprehensive to include several different types. The Rockingham party included Burke, a professional politician for whom party was a trade, and also Sir Edward Astley, independent of a patron and not playing for office. It comprised small men like John Norris and Nathaniel Cholmley, who had no parliamentary interest of their own and could only secure a seat through a patron ; and also Sir William Meredith and George Dempster, sitting on their own interest and considerable figures apart from their party connection. The degree of attachment to the party varied with the individual, his connections, his interest, or his opinions, and can rarely be accurately measured. The party stratum was threefold : there was, first, an inner circle of men so closely identified with the party leaders as to have made common cause with them, and who were consulted on all important occasions. Then there was a second rank, those equally committed but not of sufficient importance or not

---

[1] Bedford to Granby, April 17, 1767 ; Woburn MS., lv. f. 72.
[2] Richmond to Rockingham, February 12, 1771 ; Rockingham Papers, R158-44.  [3] Walpole, *Last Journals*, ii. 258.

sufficiently interested to be consulted on party tactics : younger brothers and dependants of peers often fell into this class. Lastly, there are those on the fringe of the party : acting from genuine conviction, they never identified themselves with a party or sought to profit from it. They are not easy to classify ; they cannot be neatly ticketed and distributed on the shelves ; their parliamentary conduct could never be taken for granted. It requires a fine degree of judgment to separate those who were of the party from those who acted with it, and may often depend on the chance survival of private papers. Much of the material needed for the study of party has been lost or lies undiscovered in family archives, and without it judgment has often to be qualified or suspended.

Then there are those who went from one party to another. Since party connection was not a qualification for membership of Parliament and independence was extolled and respected even by the parties, consistency is not to be expected. During the years of the American revolution honest conviction more often determined party allegiance than has generally been admitted. 'I have often and severely censured the faults of Administration', wrote Gibbon to Edward Eliot on September 8, 1780, after Eliot had refused to re-elect him for Liskeard, 'but I have always condemned the *system* of opposition, and your judgment will allow that in public life, every man is reduced to the necessity of choosing the side which upon the whole appears to him the least reprehensible.'[1] Convinced of 'the justice of the American war' (though not sanguine of success), he believed the dangers from party to be greater than those from war.

In 1767 both Newcastle and Rockingham counted Eliot as of the Court party, nor did their judgment seem wrong. He commanded six seats in the House of Commons,[2] for which he had hitherto returned members friendly to Administration ; and he had been a Lord of Trade since 1760. Though a placeman and ambitious of a peerage, Eliot was not typical of the Court party : he voted against Grenville's Administra-

---

[1] *The Private Letters of Edward Gibbon*, ed. by R. E. Prothero, i. 388-90.
[2] For the boroughs of Liskeard, Grampound, and St. Germans.

tion on General Warrants ; from 1766 till the outbreak of the American war rarely attended Parliament;[1] and in 1775 went into opposition. Both Newcastle and Rockingham were well acquainted with Eliot, yet their classification of him in 1766 was incorrect ten years later. This was not unusual when party composition was so fluctuating and party allegiance still a novel element in political life.

## (v)

There is in the Rockingham Papers a list of the House of Commons arranged according to presumed party connection.[2] It seems to have been drawn up in December 1766, and has been corrected to February 1767.[3] There is in the Newcastle Papers a similar list, dated March 2, 1767.[4] What can be learnt from these lists of the state of parties, and, equally important, what their leaders imagined it to be ?

Rockingham classifies 553 members of the House of Commons [5] in ten categories : 'Bute'; 'Chatham'; 'Swiss' (presumably those who enlisted under any Administration which rewarded them) ; 'Tories, ministerial, Bute'; 'Tories, perhaps not ministerial' ; 'Bedford' ; 'Grenville' ; 'Whigs' (*i.e.* Rockinghams) ; 'Doubtful' ; 'Absentees'. Newcastle's list (of 547 members) has only five categories : 'For the Administration' ; 'Friends to the last Administration' ;

---

[1] Gibbon wrote to J. B. Holroyd on September 10, 1773, that Eliot spent nine months of the year in the country. (*Ibid.* p. 194.) Between 1766 and 1768 he attended only 27 out of the 268 meetings of the Board of Trade. His name does not appear in any of the division lists I have found for the 1768 Parliament.

[2] R86.

[3] There is nothing to prove that it was drawn up by Rockingham, but presumably it was prepared under his direction.

[4] Add. MS. 33001, ff. 357-63. This was probably the work of Newcastle himself.

[5] Rockingham's list contains 558 names, but two must be removed and two appear twice. John Stanwix died in October 1766, and Lord Lorne received a British peerage in December 1766 : their successors are included in the list. Lord George Lennox and William Burke appear twice : Lennox both times as 'Whig' ; William Burke first as 'Swiss', then (after he had resigned his place of Under-Secretary of State) as 'Whig'. I have counted him among the 'Whigs'. The four members whom Rockingham omitted were : Richard Burton, John Damer, Archibald Douglas and John Grey.

'Bedfords and Grenvilles'; 'Tories'; 'Doubtful or Absent'. Rearranging Rockingham's list to correspond with Newcastle's, the following comparison emerges :

|  | Rockingham | Newcastle |
|---|---|---|
| For the Administration | 225 [1] | 232 |
| Rockinghams | 121 | 101 |
| Bedfords and Grenvilles | 52 [2] | 54 |
| Tories | 86 [3] | 91 |
| Doubtful or Absent | 69 | 69 |
|  | 553 | 547 |

At first sight it seems that there is a large measure of agreement between these two lists. But there appears much less on comparing the personnel of the groups. Take, for example, the 121 members whom Rockingham lists as 'Whigs' — here they are, as classified by Newcastle :

| Friends to the last Administration | 77 |
|---|---|
| Doubtful or Absent | 17 |
| For the Administration | 14 |
| Tories | 8 [4] |
| Bedfords and Grenvilles | 4 |
| Not classified | 1 |
|  | 121 |

Only two-thirds of those whom Rockingham termed 'Whigs' were considered so by Newcastle. What is the other side of the medal like ?

Here is Rockingham's classification of the 101 members whom Newcastle considered to be 'Friends to the last Administration' :

[1] Those described as 'Bute', 'Chatham', and 'Swiss'.
[2] 35 Bedfords, 17 Grenvilles.
[3] 'Tories, ministerial', and 'Tories, perhaps not ministerial'.
[4] The eight members whom Rockingham termed Whigs and Newcastle Tories were: Charles Barrow, Edward Bouverie, Thomas Cholmondeley, Sir Edward Dering, Samuel Egerton, Samuel Eyre, Philip Rashleigh, and John Tuckfield.

| | |
|---|---|
| Whigs | 77 |
| Doubtful | 13 |
| Swiss | 4 |
| Grenvilles | 3 |
| Tories | 2 |
| Chatham | 1 |
| Bute | 1 [1] |
| | 101 |

Almost three-quarters of Newcastle's list was accepted by Rockingham.

Putting these results in another way, more than one-third of Rockingham's list of friends was rejected by Newcastle, and about a quarter of Newcastle's list was rejected by Rockingham. Yet the two lists were drawn up within three months of each other. Here, then, are the leaders of a party unable to agree upon who were their followers. What value can be given to their lists of the other parties if they do not know their own ? And what kind of a party was it whose leaders did not know their own followers ? Rockingham once said 'that he was responsible to a large body of people for his conduct'.[2] But how many of those to whom he claimed to be responsible would have acknowledged his lead ? Let us apply the acid test of a division to these lists.

On February 17, 1768, Sir George Savile moved for leave to bring in the Nullum Tempus Bill, to prevent the Crown from raising claims to landed property which had been alienated for more than sixty years. The motion arose out of Sir James Lowther's claim upon part of Portland's Cumberland estates ; [3]

[1] Lord Downe. Three months later Downe was a 'Whig'. He wrote to Rockingham on March 9, 1767 : 'Your Lordship may depend on my attendance this day ; and I wish my abilitys were greater, that I might be more useful to your Lordship, that is, to my country, for no person living is more thoroughly persuaded than myself, that all your Lordship's views, both during your late Administration, and before and since you presided at the Treasury, are directed to the benefit of that single object'. (Rockingham Papers, R158-132.)

[2] Charles Lloyd to Temple, July 16, 1767 ; *Grenville Papers*, iv. 54-5.

[3] Inglewood Forest and the Manor of the Socage of Carlisle Castle. The property had come into the Bentinck family by grant from the Crown in William III's reign. It was one of those grants against which the Commons protested in 1698. Lowther petitioned for a lease of property which he claimed was not included in the original grant.

R

it deeply concerned the Rockingham party, and had been carefully prepared by its legal members. The 'whips' went out to all who were believed to be in any degree sympathetic, but the motion was withheld from them in order to catch the Court unawares. 'I hardly ever knew a more important question agitated in Parliament', wrote Rockingham ;[1] and on February 14 he described to Newcastle his efforts to round up votes :

> I hope we shall make a good figure in the House of Commons on this occasion. . . .
> I take all the pains I can to send and speak to all and every one where I have a chance of being persuasive, for really I am so fully convinced both of the propriety and of the necessity of this revival of the principle of the bill that I am exceedingly anxious for its success and I am persuaded that if we make a great figure upon it this year in one or two years this bill will be forced by the publick upon the Ministers.[2]

In short, he did all he could to achieve success, and only narrowly failed : the motion was defeated by 134 votes to 114 (excluding the tellers).

There are three lists of those who voted in this division. In Almon's *Debates and Proceedings of the British House of Commons, 1743-74*,[3] there is a list both of the majority and minority ; there is a similar list in the Burke Papers ;[4] and in the Rockingham Papers there is an incomplete list of the minority, grouped under presumed party allegiances.[5] By collating these lists we obtain the names of the 116 members

---

[1] Rockingham to Perry Wentworth ; undated, but shortly after February 17, 1768. Rockingham Papers, R1, undated letters.

[2] Add. MS. 32988, ff. 307-8.

[3] Vol. VII, pp. 365-70.

[4] Burke Papers, Sheffield City Library. I refer to it as Burke's list, although there is nothing to prove that it was compiled by him. It is not in his hand. The list of both minority and majority is roughly alphabetical : the first name in the minority list, however, is Lord John Cavendish ; the first names in the majority list are Sir George Warren and Francis Reynolds. These names are written much larger than the others. It seems that this list was drawn up for use at Lancaster at the General Election of 1768, where Cavendish, Warren, and Reynolds were the candidates.

[5] Rockingham Papers, R91-218. It is in Rockingham's hand.

who voted for Savile's motion (including the tellers),[1] and 97 out of the 136 (also including the tellers) who voted against it.[2] The following table compares the votes of Rockingham's 'Whigs', Newcastle's 'Friends', and the members common to both lists.

| | Voted for Savile's motion | Voted against Savile's motion | Votes not recorded | Not in the House |
|---|---|---|---|---|
| Rockingham's 'Whigs' (121) | 56 (46·3%) | 5[3] (4·1%) | 59 (48·7%) | 1[4] (0·9%) |
| Newcastle's 'Friends' (101) | 59 (58·5%) | 2[5] (1·9%) | 40 (39·6%) | ... |
| Common to both lists (77) | 50 (64·9%) | ... | 27 (35·1%) | ... |

[1] Almon's list contains 116 names (the full number); Burke's 115; and Rockingham's 107 (with the names of 6 'Absent Friends'). There is a curious circumstance about these lists: Dowdeswell's name does not appear in any of them, nor in Rockingham's list of 'Absent Friends', although he was present at the debate and spoke for Savile's motion. (See Rockingham to Newcastle, February 18, 1768, Add. MS. 32988, ff. 369-70; and West to Newcastle, February 17, 1768, ibid. f. 357.) If he voted in the minority it is difficult to believe that all three lists, which seem from internal evidence to have been compiled independently of each other (and one of which was drawn up by Rockingham himself), should omit him. Yet the alternative seems equally incredible — that Dowdeswell, the leader of the Rockingham party in the Commons, should have spoken for a motion which the party considered to be so important and yet gone away without voting. I take Burke's list to be more nearly correct, and add Dowdeswell's name to make the full total. But for Armstead Parker (who followed the Court, and is not included in the minority by Almon and Rockingham) I read John Parker (included by both Almon and Rockingham); and for Thomas Duncombe (included in Almon's list of the majority) I read Velters Cornewall (included in the list of the minority by both Almon and Rockingham). It is impossible to check the discrepancies between these three lists. Yet these discrepancies would have to be considered and the balance of probabilities weighed if the lists were to be used for determining the votes of individual members; in a statistical analysis, where the margin of error is not critical, they may be ignored.

[2] Almon's list contains 89 names, Burke's 86. I take Almon's list as correct, and add the following from Burke's: Lord Brownlow Bertie, Charles Sloane Cadogan, John Calcraft, Thomas Calcraft, Lord Frederick Campbell, John Dodd, James Grenville senior, and Richard Price. This makes 97 names, including the tellers — 39 short of the full number.

[3] John Dodd, Welbore Ellis, George Jennings, Thomas H. Medlycott, and Frederick Vane. All were listed by Newcastle as 'Administration'.

[4] John Tuckfield, who died December 6, 1767.

[5] Richard Myddleton (listed by Rockingham as 'Doubtful') and Thomas Pelham (listed by Rockingham as 'Swiss'). Newcastle wrote to Rockingham on February 13 that 'my good and tender friend Tom Pelham

Tried by this division Newcastle was a better judge of who were or who were not 'friends' than Rockingham : perhaps there was some justification for his many complaints against the 'young men' who were 'ruining the party'. But one-third of those whom both described as friends did not vote on Savile's motion or voted against it.[1]   Among these were : Connolly, the Duke of Richmond's brother-in-law ; William Keppel, younger brother of Lord Albemarle ; William Plumer, who sat on Newcastle's interest at Lewes ; etc.   These men had close ties with the magnates of the Rockingham party.   If all claimed as friends in both lists had voted for the motion it would have been carried.   But a party leader could not count on the votes of even his closest followers ; while those in the outer circle had to be wooed with affection and persuaded with tact.

Lastly, here is a table to show the composition of the minority of February 17, 1768, according to these two lists.

|  | Rockingham's list | Newcastle's list |
|---|---|---|
| Rockinghams | 56 | 59 |
| Tories | 21 | 24 |
| Bedfords and Grenvilles | 11 | 10 |
| Administration | 12 | 11 |
| Doubtful or Absent | 12 | 8 |
| Not classified | 4 | 4 |
|  | 116 | 116 |

---

. . . will be sure to be with you' (Add. MS. 32988, f. 301).   Rockingham replied on February 16 :

'I told Mr. Pelham very fully my thoughts on the matter and indeed I could not do less either from the feeling I had of the dissapointment it would be to your Grace if he did not vote and also because I am so convinced on the propriety and real publick utility of the matter moved for.

'When he left me, he was much distressed and rather doubtful what to do.   His difficulty arises from, as he says, having declared that he would not *in office* vote against Administration.

'The only light in which I am grieved at this event, is, from the dissapointment your Grace would feel in an expectation that gave you pleasure, but I wish you would not disturb yourself about it and so far you certainly may rely, that Tom Pelham's not voting according to your wishes (if it should so happen) can not proceed from any want of regard to your Grace but from some cause which he perhaps has not strength to get over.'   (*Ibid.* ff. 333-5.)

[1] The list of the majority is short of 39 names, and among these may have been some 'friends'.

And here, for comparison, is my own analysis :

| | |
|---|---|
| Independents | 49 |
| Rockinghams | 40 |
| Grenvilles [1] | 17 |
| Court | 10 |
| | 116 |

'I think all our able friends will exert themselves', wrote Rockingham to Newcastle on February 14, 'and I much rely that the real goodness of the question will operate strongly on many persons in the House who may have the least inclination of favour towards us.' [2] Had he been compelled to rely on the support of his friends only, he would have made a poor figure : on his own classification they accounted for less than half of the minority.

It was 'the real goodness of the question' which made the minority respectable. The point at issue was one on which landed men might be expected to be sensitive, and where the legal position did not correspond to justice and fair dealing. The Court did not oppose the motion with a direct negative,[3] and ten of the Court party voted with the opposition. With the support of the independents the Nullum Tempus Bill eventually became law ; only with their support could the parties hope to defeat the Court.

[1] The Bedfords had gone over to the Court in December 1767.
[2] Add. MS. 32988, ff. 307-8.
[3] Lord North moved for the orders of the day, and it was on this motion that the division was taken.

# CHAPTER VII

# THE PARTIES IN JULY 1767

## The Chathamites

IN Shelburne's autobiographical fragment there is a sketch of Chatham which deserves careful study : Shelburne was a shrewd observer, and had many opportunities of getting to know his subject. Here is what he has to say about Chatham as a party leader :

He did not cultivate men because he felt it an incumbrance, and thought that he could act to more advantage without the incumbrance of a party. . . . What took much from his character was that he was always acting, always made up, and never natural, in a perpetual state of exertion, incapable of friendship, or of any act which tended to it, and constantly upon the watch, and never unbent. He told me that, independent of the consideration of his health, he should for reasons of policy have always lived as he did a few miles out of town. I was in the most intimate political habits with him for ten years, the time that I was Secretary of State included, he Minister, and necessarily was with him at all hours in town and country, without drinking a glass of water in his house or company, or five minutes conversation out of the way of business. . . . I never found him when I have gone to him, which was always by appointment, with so much as a book before him, but always sitting alone in a drawing-room waiting the hour of appointment, and in the country with his hat and stick in his hand.[1]

Pride ? Or shyness ? A shy man may affect a degree of *hauteur* that will repel those who wish to be friendly.

Chatham is an incongruous figure beside the other politicians, for he did not claim to be a party leader and

---

[1] Fitzmaurice, *Life of Shelburne*, i. 58-61.

professed to scorn the idea of party. Yet, as one of 'Cobham's cubs', he had played the party game under George II, and had successfully 'stormed the Closet' in 1756. From 1757 to 1761 Chatham had the good fortune to enjoy the support of a following of independent members in the House of Commons, without the drudgery of tending it. It was a spontaneous testimony to the confidence felt in his ability to lead the nation to victory : a replica, on a smaller scale, of the mass support Sir Winston Churchill received in Britain's darkest hour. The country gentlemen, disgusted with Newcastle's incapacity to conduct war, suspicious of Fox's intrigues and hating his jobbery, turned to the one politician untainted by office and with resolution to face and overcome the crisis. Their trust was not misplaced and was fully reciprocated. Chatham's direction of the war was vigorous, courageous, and successful. He pushed forward the plan for a militia against the dislike and obstruction of Newcastle and his followers, and gave the country gentlemen local responsibility and command. Excluded from office by their own choice, not by any formal barrier, they yet resented their exclusion. In the militia they exercised authority and responsibility without having to go to Court : a psychological substitute for office.

Out of office Chatham could no longer command the support of the country gentlemen. They began to count the expense of a war which they had not grudged when victory was still uncertain or incomplete. Chatham censured a peace which they approved, and adopted an attitude towards the colonies they did not share. The things they wanted from government — economy, sound administration, freedom from foreign entanglements — were not in Chatham's programme. Moreover, peace had lowered his stature : he was no longer above the politicians, merely the *primus inter pares*. When Chatham returned to office in 1766 it was without the enthusiastic following of ten years earlier.

Rockingham's list of Chatham's followers contains fifty-eight names. This number is an exaggeration. While he remained in office it was academic to distinguish between his personal following and those who were his friends only because he was Minister.  Rockingham's list had a pragmatic purpose, and was not an exercise in determining party connection.  John Shelley may fairly be reckoned a follower of Chatham in 1766 : had not Chatham alienated the Rockingham party to make Shelley Treasurer of the Household ?  Yet Shelley remained in office after Chatham had gone into opposition, and when removed in 1777 was solaced with a pension.  In 1766 Thomas Walpole (M.P. for Ashburton),[1] a close friend of Camden, was one of Chatham's staunchest supporters ;  yet he too remained with the Court after 1770, and rejoined the opposition only on the eve of the American war.  Grafton's friends — Richard Hopkins (Dartmouth), Hugo Meynell (Lichfield), Charles Fitzroy Scudamore (Hereford), and Lord Villiers (Aldborough) — supported North until Grafton's resignation of the Privy Seal in 1775, while his brother Charles Fitzroy (Bury St. Edmunds) continued with the Court even then and finally obtained a peerage in 1780.  On the other hand, Lord Granby, who had served every Administration since 1760, although he could not in 1766 be reckoned a follower of Chatham, resigned in 1770 and went into opposition.  Neither Sir Piercy Brett nor Sir George Yonge were connected with Chatham in 1766 ; both voted with the Court to confirm Luttrell's election for Middlesex (May 8, 1769) ; both resigned in January 1770.  At what point, if any, do they become followers of Chatham ?

These men have at least a party tinge.  It would be ridiculous to count as followers of Chatham in 1766 all who jumped on the waggon because there was room for them, and remained there after the driver had fallen off and another had assumed the reins.  When a party leader was in office his followers and those of the Court were often indistinguishable.  His withdrawal from office is the only test which will separate them.  I have, therefore, limited Chatham's friends to those who had some personal connection with him, who supported Administration until 1769 or 1770, and who then went into opposition.  They are few, and hardly merit the name of a party.

Shelburne was represented by his brother, Thomas

---

[1] In this chapter the constituency named is the one the Member represented at the dissolution of Parliament in 1768.

Fitzmaurice (M.P. for Calne), and Isaac Barré (Chipping Wycombe). In 1768 they were joined by James Townsend (West Looe), son of the government contractor Chauncy Townsend (Westbury), but himself a zealous and uncompromising City radical; and at the General Election by John Dunning (Calne), one of the first men at the Bar, but not of a comparable stature in Parliament; and Lauchlin Macleane (Arundell), a rascally Irish adventurer, whom Shelburne had made Under-Secretary of State, and who trafficked with his patron's credit in East India stock. Shelburne's interest in the affairs of the East India Company brought him a few followers, such as Laurence Sulivan and Robert Palk. But for these the politics of Westminster were subservient to the politics of India House.

Barré was Shelburne's confidential 'man of business', and had been connected with him since at least 1761. Barré had made his parliamentary début with a violent and unfair attack upon Pitt, but in 1763 he followed Shelburne into opposition. In 1766 he was given the well-paid sinecure of joint Vice-Treasurer of Ireland, but he was never at ease except in opposition. On February 18, 1767, the King expressed 'some surprize' that Barré still remained 'a silent spectator', and wrote to Conway: 'I should imagine considering the unmerited favours he has received he ought to be zealous in supporting my Administration'.[1] Barré resigned with Shelburne in 1768, remained with him throughout the American war, and was rewarded in 1782 with a pension of £3000 per annum. He was then going blind, and his career was virtually ended when Shelburne resigned in 1783. There was a great deal of the bravo and the bully in him: his speeches in Parliament were frequent, coarse, and abusive, and repelled moderate men.

In 1767 Chatham's following numbered some strange characters. Square pegs who could not fit into round holes attached themselves to him: he was one himself. There were, for instance, John Calcraft (M.P. for Calne), and his brother Thomas (Poole). An amusing and instructive monograph

[1] Fortescue, I, no. 68.

could be written about John Calcraft, and it would have to delve deep into the undergrowth of eighteenth-century politics and business. He had been the right-hand man of Henry Fox, whom he deserted in 1763 for Pitt. His speciality was under-cover activity — Walpole describes him as having 'the best head for intrigue in the whole party'.[1] He arranged the reconciliation between Chatham and Temple in 1769, and persuaded Granby (with whom he had great influence) to resign in 1770.

There were also William Beckford (M.P. for London), restless, noisy, and voluble ; and George Cooke (Middlesex), like Beckford a Tory under George II but a radical under George III. Cooke was made joint Paymaster-General in 1766 and died in 1768.

Sir Lewis Namier has pointed out [2] that Chatham's family connections would have formed the basis for a good parliamentary interest, had he been able to work with men. In fact, after 1761 he was generally on bad terms with one or other of his brothers-in-law, and it was only in opposition that they could all agree. James Grenville was the only one who consistently supported him, but even he seems to have tired of Chatham's eccentric and unpredictable course. His name does not appear in any of the division lists on Wilkes's case, and in January 1770 he resigned his place of joint Vice-Treasurer of Ireland ('unwillingly', writes Walpole, 'to gratify the violence of his brothers'[3]), and shortly afterwards left Parliament. Perhaps the line he would have taken had he remained can be deduced from that of his son, James Grenville junior. He entered Parliament in 1765 as M.P. for Thirsk, and supported Chatham's Administration. He was not returned at the General Election of 1768, but re-entered the House for Buckingham in 1770 on the death of his uncle George. Although he voted with the opposition on the Spanish Convention (February 13, 1771), he is marked as 'Friend' in the King's list of the division of February 9, 1773.[4] On the outbreak of the American war he went back into opposition.

[1] *Memoirs*, iii. 184. By 'the whole party' Walpole means the whole opposition. He was writing of 1768.    [2] *The Structure of Politics*, i. 14.
[3] *Memoirs*, iv. 37.    [4] Fortescue, II, no. 1193.

In 1766 Chatham was supported by many independent men who would have formed a strong party in opposition had he cultivated them.   Sir John Griffin Griffin (M.P. for Andover) is a typical example.   An Army officer and Colonel of the first troop of Horse Grenadier Guards, he had voted against General Warrants and supported the repeal of the Stamp Act.   Descended through his mother from James, second Lord Griffin, and James Howard, third Earl of Suffolk and Lord Howard de Walden, he had obvious claims to a peerage, but was told by Chatham on August 19, 1766, that the King would 'probably not be easily moved to create many'.[1]   He supported the Court on the Land Tax motion, but voted against Wilkes's expulsion.   His interest in horse-racing brought him into frequent contact with Rockingham, and it was extended to include politics.   'I am very happy at receiving your letter', wrote Rockingham to Griffin on February 23, 1769, 'which gives me the satisfaction of seeing in every instance, how kindly you are inclined to weigh and consider the matters which arise, wherein I feel a warm wish.'[2]   On May 5, 1769, Rockingham wrote to request Griffin's attendance on the Middlesex petition against Luttrell's election, but not in the style of a party leader to one of his followers :

> I have hopes that your opinion is not with the then majority [3] and . . . I must express how much I wish that you would be present at the debate on Monday, and I shall be very happy if your sentiments on this matter concur with many of my friends who are very eager on this affair.[4]

Although 'no friend to the resolution of the House of Commons which gave Colonel Lutterell [sic] his seat there', business had called Griffin into Essex ; he could not attend, but hoped Rockingham would put 'the kindest constructions' on his absence.[5]   He continued to vote with the opposition and to receive Rockingham's requests for attendance : it is clear from

[1] Braybrooke Papers (Essex Record Office), D/DBy C8/74.
[2] Ibid. C8/91.
[3] On the motion to postpone hearing the Middlesex petition, April 29, 1769.
[4] Ibid. C8/92.
[5] Griffin to Rockingham, May 9, 1769 ; Rockingham Papers, R1-653.

their nature and repetition that his vote was not given automatically. In short, Griffin was an independent, connected first with Chatham and then with Rockingham, but not a party man.

Lastly, there is Robert Pratt (M.P. for Horsham), Camden's nephew : his politics conformed to his uncle's, but he was of no weight in the Commons.

When Chatham recovered from his illness in the summer of 1769 he made known his disagreement with the decision of the Commons on the Middlesex election, and put out feelers towards the Rockinghams. They were received warily and suspiciously. But when Chatham reappeared in the Lords in January 1770 Grafton's Ministry seemed on the point of dissolution, and Chatham and Rockingham put aside their differences in the face of this sanguine prospect. On January 22 Chatham spoke in the Lords of the 'cordial' and 'indissoluble' union between himself and Rockingham.

It barely lasted a year. Rockingham had deeply resented Chatham's conduct in 1765 and 1766 and never forgave it, while Chatham was as difficult to work with as ever, even had Rockingham been eager to do so. By February 1771 they were at each other's throats again. Differences on American policy did not facilitate a joint front against North : Rockingham stood firm by the Declaratory Act,[1] while Chatham would not admit that Britain had a right to tax the colonies. Nor, when war broke out, was their union any easier : Rockingham was prepared to grant American independence, which Chatham refused to concede. No wonder men continued to support North, even when it was clear that the colonies could not be subdued — the opposition's personal and doctrinal feuds did not promise any better alternative.

But when war broke out Chatham was of little consequence in politics : he was never the figure in the Lords he had been in the Commons ; his most important followers in the Commons were dead (Granby and Beckford died in 1770,

[1] In 1777, two years after fighting had broken out in America, Richmond proposed to Rockingham to move the repeal of the Declaratory Act, but his suggestion does not seem to have been favourably received. (Richmond to Rockingham, November 2, 1777 ; *ibid.* R1-968.)

Calcraft in 1772) ; he was an old and tired man. A new generation had entered politics since 1766, and those who went into opposition found their inspiration in Charles Fox. Shelburne built up his own party : he inherited no followers from Chatham. It is sad to see a great man die, with his greatness far behind him and his wisdom little heeded, but such was the fate of two of the greatest British war ministers — Chatham and David Lloyd George.

### The Bedfords

The Bedford party was a family group : most of its members were followers of peers connected by marriage with the Duke. It was compact, small, and united : a useful ally to the Court, but not the core round which an Administration could be built. The real strength of the Bedfords lay in the Lords, but their twenty votes in the Commons were not negligible. Voting there was rarely high : in only two divisions between 1766 and 1770 did the numbers exceed 400 out of a House of 558.[1] Only 373 members voted on May 8, 1769, on the motion which confirmed Luttrell in his seat for Middlesex. Between July 1766 and the dissolution in March 1768 there were fifteen divisions in the Commons on motions dealing with public business (excluding those in Committee) : in only four divisions did more than 300 members vote, in four the Court's majority was less than fifty. When voting was so low, even twenty members were a welcome addition to the party of the Crown.

Six of the party were Bedford's personal followers and sat on his interest in Parliament : Richard Vernon (M.P. for Bedford) ; Lord Upper Ossory (Bedfordshire) ; Thomas Brand (Gatton) ; Alexander Forrester (Okehampton) ; Richard Neville Neville and Richard Rigby (Tavistock).

Neville had been connected with Bedford since at least 1748,[2] and had been his secretary when he went to Paris in 1762 to negotiate peace. In 1763 he was made Paymaster of

---

[1] These were on the motion to hear Wilkes's counsel (January 27, 1769), 409 ; and the motion on the Civil List debts (March 1, 1769), 419.

[2] He was Under-Secretary when Bedford was Secretary of State, 1748–51.

Pensions, but was dismissed in 1765 to make way for Lord Gage who had 'suffered' for Newcastle. By 1766 Neville had dropped out of the inner circle of the party : Bedford made no demands on his behalf in the negotiations with Chatham, and he was not provided for in 1767. On October 23, 1768, Neville asked Bedford to recommend him for the office of joint Postmaster-General, as 'an honourable retreat from Parliament, but an ample compensation for the loss of a place' which, through Bedford's 'kind testimony and recommendation had been given as a reward for services. . . .' [1] Bedford replied on October 24 :

> I am much abused, by the enemies of the present Adminis-
> tration, for having (as they are pleased to call it) forced many
> of my friends into publick employments, and I am appre-
> hensive that many of the Duke of Grafton's old friends,
> look upon my influence on his Grace, with a jealous eye. [2]

He concluded :

> I must therefore hope, that you will think it reasonable to
> concur with me in this opinion, and wait till some more
> proper opportunity may present itself, for my being of service
> to you, especially as you are in such circumstances, as not
> to need any such assistance.

The 'proper opportunity' never came, and Neville obtained no further preferment. He continued to vote with the Court after 1768, and left Parliament in 1774.

Thomas Brand had married Lady Caroline Pierrepoint, daughter of Evelyn, first Duke of Kingston, and half-sister of Lady Evelyn Pierrepoint, mother of the Duchess of Bedford. He too had long been connected with Bedford, who was one of the trustees of his marriage settlement. [3] Brand's ambition was a peerage, and it had been one of the terms Bedford had proposed to Chatham in December 1766. When, after the failure of that negotiation, Lord Lorne obtained a peerage by direct application to Chatham, Brand proposed to do the same ; Bedford refused either to approve or disapprove, and

---

[1] Woburn MS., lvii. f. 186.    [2] *Ibid.* f. 190.
[3] A copy of the proposals, dated October 1748, is in *ibid.* xxii. f. 41.

Brand dropped the idea. He wrote to Bedford on December 18, 1766 :

> I was so provoked by the Minister's behaviour in a late instance that I meant if I could to distress them by making the claim of a promise at this time, to which they must have given some answer and I could think of nothing more hostile than to reproach them with breech of their word in a proper manner.[1]

A peerage for Brand was one of the terms of the treaty by which the Bedfords entered Administration in December 1767. It was the subject of an acrimonious interchange of letters between Bedford and Grafton in March 1769, Bedford claiming Grafton's promise that Brand should be made a peer at the end of the session, while Grafton only acknowledged that he 'was to be among the first of the peers to be created without a specification of time'.[2] 'If Mr. Brand's health, my Lord,' wrote Grafton to Bedford on March 23, 'is the only circumstance that makes him so pressing, I am very ready to carry his request to the King . . . that his son should be equally certain of the rank he desires, if any accident should befall the father.' Brand seems to have taken his disappointment to heart : his name does not appear in any division list after 1768. He was closely connected with Lord George Sackville,[3] who was in opposition to Grafton's Administration. On April 11, 1769, Rigby (well satisfied with his own share of the bargain the Bedfords had made) wrote to Bedford :

> I hear from many quarters of Mr. Brand's great warmth of expression towards the Duke of Grafton upon the present *mal-entendue*. I am certain that can tend to no good end, and it is an ill-judged piece of resentment that will hurt nobody so much as himself. He is disappointed and angry, and is not aware that he is going to tramp it about the town

[1] Correspondence between Brand and Bedford, December 16, 17, and 18, 1766 ; *ibid*. liv. ff. 176 and 184.

[2] Correspondence between Bedford and Grafton, March 22 and 23, 1769 ; *ibid*. lviii. ff. 24 and 28.

[3] Walpole writes of the time of Sackville's disgrace after the battle of Minden : 'I, Sir John Irvine, and Mr. Brand had been the only three men in England who had dared to speak to or sit by Lord George in public places'. (*Last Journals*, ii. 49.)

more for Lord George Sackville's ill-humour than his own. He was with Lord George to day at the House of Commons, and all last Saturday night at the opera ; any prospect of a disagrement between your Grace and the Duke of Grafton will be nuts to Lord George and Lord Temple, and Brand, I am afraid, does not see that he will be the dupe to their malice.[1]

Brand's connection with Bedford did not procure him a coronet : he died in 1770, nor was his son made a peer.

Richard Vernon, a great racing man and gambler, had married Evelyn, daughter of John, first Earl Gower, and sister of the Duchess of Bedford. He was important because of his connection with Grafton through Grafton's friend, Hugo Meynell. Vernon's wife was the widow of John Fitzpatrick, first Earl of Upper Ossory. Her son, the second Earl, succeeded his friend Lord Tavistock as M.P. for Bedfordshire in March 1767, and in December helped to negotiate the entry of the Bedfords into Administration. His brother, Richard Fitzpatrick (who entered Parliament in 1770 as M.P. for Okehampton), was the intimate friend of Charles James Fox ; the Fitzpatrick brothers, who had hitherto supported the Court, went over to the opposition with Fox in 1775.

Thomas Gilbert (M.P. for Newcastle-under-Lyme) and Edward Thurlow (Tamworth) were connected with Gower, and sat on his interest in Parliament. Lord Charles Spencer (Oxfordshire) was the brother of the Duke of Marlborough, Bedford's son-in-law. Robert Wood (Brackley) had been the tutor and companion of the Duke of Bridgwater, Bedford's nephew, on his grand tour. He had been under-secretary when Pitt was Secretary of State, and resumed that post when Weymouth took the seals in 1768. Timothy Caswall (Hertford) was also connected with the Duke of Bridgwater, who brought him into Parliament for Brackley in 1771. Henry St. John (Wotton Bassett) was the brother of Lord Bolingbroke, who had married Lady Diana Spencer, sister of the Duke of Marlborough. Bolingbroke divorced her in 1768 because of

[1] Woburn MS., lviii. f. 36 ; part printed in *Bedford Correspondence*, iii. 408.

her adultery with Topham Beauclerk, Dr. Johnson's friend. Her conduct seems to have led to strained relations between Bolingbroke and Marlborough. On November 12, 1766, Bolingbroke applied to Grafton for a Lordship of the Bed-chamber.

> I voluntarily gave it up [he wrote] to oblige a man [Marl-borough], from whom I have in return received the most unmerited behaviour. Any connection therefore with him, my Lord, is what my pride will for ever make me avoid ; the same pride, my Lord, makes me wish to owe to his Majesty's goodness, without the shadow of owing it to the Duke of Marlborough, the honour of again being in his Majesty's family as I was before.[1]

Nothing came of this application, and on May 11, 1767, Bolingbroke offered Bedford his vote in the Lords, 'either in person or by proxy'.[2] He was made a Lord of the Bedchamber in 1768.

Lord Sandwich had four followers in the party : his son, Lord Hinchingbrooke (M.P. for Brackley) ; Lord Carysfort (Huntingdonshire) ; John Stephenson (Mitchell) ; and Robert Jones (Huntingdon), an East India director and Sandwich's parliamentary link with the Company.

I do not know how Weymouth came to join the Bedfords : he frequented the gambling circles at White's, where Rigby and Gower were members, and this may have led to a political connection. He had two followers in the party : his brother, Henry Frederick Thynne and William Lynch, both of whom sat for Weymouth's borough of Weobley. Weymouth had married the Duke of Portland's sister, but family alliance did not necessarily imply political connection in the eighteenth century. He remained on good terms with Portland in spite of their political differences, and the link with the Rockinghams proved useful in 1782 : although Conway could not save his brother, Lord Hertford (Lord Chamberlain since 1766), from being dismissed, Weymouth (who had twice been Secretary of State under Grafton and North) was made Groom of the Stole in the second Rockingham Administration.

Grafton MS. 327.              [2] Woburn MS., lv. f. 92.

S

Lastly, there was Sir Laurence Dundas (M.P. for Newcastle-under-Lyme), and his son Thomas (Richmond). Sir Laurence had been brought into Parliament by Gower ; father and son supported Grenville's ministry and opposed Rockingham's. Sir Laurence, a close friend of Wedderburn, was connected with both Grenville and Bedford, and so long as the two followed the same path did not have to choose between them. But in 1767 Rigby seems to have attempted connecting Dundas more closely to the Bedfords, as if preparing for a separation from Grenville. In September 1767 Wedderburn wrote to Whately : 'I wish Mr. Grenville would take some opportunity of writing to Sir Laurence Dundas ; the Bedfords are extremely attentive to him, and he is apt to be taken with attentions'.[1] Grenville appears to have done little, and on December 4, on the eve of the Bedfords' return to Court, Whately suggested to him 'that it may be proper to call on Sir Laurence'.[2] Neither Dundas nor his son is recorded as having voted on the Nullum Tempus Bill (February 17, 1768), and Whately did not give them up without a struggle. On October 14, 1768, he wrote to Grenville :

> I have a letter from Wedderburn, who asks whether you have written lately to Sir L. D. Tho' he is more satisfied than ever with his language, yet he wishes a civility were now and then thrown in to prevent any impression, by the great attention paid him from another quarter. The least compliment from you will, he says, go further than all their adulation.[3]

In 1769 Dundas and Wedderburn separated politically : Wedderburn followed Grenville over Wilkes, and resigned his seat for Richmond (Dundas's borough) in consequence. Still Whately persisted in regarding Dundas as a 'friend'. On June 2, 1769, he wrote to Grenville that Dundas was buying East India stock,

> at the desire of Administration, who intending to make a push at the directors next year, prevail'd on him to provide such a quantity of the stock for qualifications. He is a zealous freind, but unlucky in his manner of showing it.[4]

[1] *Grenville Papers*, iv. 160-2.    [2] Grenville (J. M.) MSS.
[3] *Ibid.*    [4] *Ibid.*

He was indeed ! From the beginning of 1769 Dundas voted regularly with the Court until about 1780, when he began to drift towards the Rockinghams. He died in 1781, having, in his twenty years in Parliament, worked with almost every party.

In 1766 Bedford numbered at least three other Scotsmen among his followers — Lord Lorne (M.P. for Dover), his brother, Lord Frederick Campbell (Glasgow Burghs), and Lord Garlies (Morpeth). Lorne and Garlies were seeking peerages, and, as eldest sons of Scottish peers, could not afford to wait long.[1] Bedford stipulated a peerage for Lorne as one of his terms for entering Administration in December 1766, and when the negotiation broke down Lorne applied direct to Chatham and Conway (his brother-in-law), without informing Bedford. More fortunate and better connected than Brand, he obtained a British peerage with remainder (failing his own issue) to his younger brothers. Garlies, 'very angry at Lord Lorne's having got a peerage', and believing that 'being in a constant opposition will weaken the interest of his family', begged Marlborough (with whom he seems to have had a special connection) to intercede with Bedford to make a peerage for himself a *sine qua non* of the party's return to office.[2] 'It is my *omnium*,' he wrote, 'the only thing in life I wish for, and the only thing I can be materially obliged in.' Marlborough testified that Garlies had been 'exceedingly steady', but Bedford refused his request ; and Garlies set off to see Chatham at Bath.[3] He was unlucky, and had to wait until 1796 for his 'omnium'. Both he and Lord Frederick Campbell voted with the Court on the Land Tax motion.

The desertion of Bedford's Scottish followers had an important political effect. There is a marked contrast between

---

[1] Before 1782 a Scottish peer could not be created a peer of Great Britain, but his eldest son could. Nor could the eldest son of a Scottish peer sit in the Commons for a Scottish constituency : hence both Lorne and Garlies sat for English constituencies.

[2] Garlies to Bedford, December 1, 1766 ; Marlborough to Bedford, December 29, 1766. Woburn MS., liv. ff. 140 and 192.

[3] Bedford to Marlborough, December 31, 1766 ; Garlies to Bedford, January 5, 1767 ; Marlborough to Bedford, January 8, 1767. *Ibid.* f. 192, and lv. ff. 2 and 12.

the Duke's attitude towards Chatham's Administration in 1766, when he was so eager to return to Court and so lukewarm about opposition, and his attitude in 1767, when he was active in opposition and refused all Grafton's offers. He had taken offence at Lorne's obtaining a peerage from Chatham when that request had been refused to himself. 'This has given me a disgust', he wrote to Marlborough on December 31, 1766, 'to any farther negotiations with the King or his Ministers.' Neither the Duchess nor Gower shared that disgust, but it was welcomed by Rigby ; and the Bedfords spent 1767 in opposition, until circumstances were more favourable for their return to Court.

## The Grenvilles

Grenville, unlike Bedford, was not the head of a parliamentary family. Out of office he could not ensure the return of a single member of Parliament : he depended on his brother, Lord Temple, for his own seat at Buckingham. His followers in the House of Commons included only one closely related to him by blood,[1] and only one (his brother-in-law, Lord Thomond) closely related by marriage. Nor, like Rockingham, was he dependent on the followers of peers : only George Hobart (brother of Lord Buckinghamshire) and Thomas Howard (uncle of Lord Suffolk) fall into this class. Lastly, his party owed little to his brother : Temple's only connection in the party was William Gerard Hamilton, and Hamilton was not obliged to Temple for his seat in the House.[2]

Grenville built up his party while he was First Lord of the Treasury. Of the remainder of his followers in July 1767 eight had held office under his Administration : Bamber Gascoyne, James Harris, Augustus Hervey, Thomas Orby Hunter, Sir Fletcher Norton, Thomas Pitt, Henry Seymour, and Thomas Whately. All, except Hervey, left office in 1765. Four others had been supporters of Grenville's Administration : Lord Catherlough, James Edward Colleton, Lord Fife, and Alexander Wedderburn. John Sargent and William Hussey

---

[1] Thomas Pitt and Grenville were first cousins once removed.
[2] Hamilton was also closely connected with Calcraft.

owed their seats to Grenville's recommendation while he was
First Lord of the Treasury.[1]  Henry Shiffner had been given
a secret service pension by Grenville.  Only two of Grenville's
followers in July 1767, Lord George Sackville and John Irwin,
had voted with the opposition over General Warrants.

After 1765 Grenville was the foremost advocate of parliamentary supremacy over the colonies : he never allowed his
opinions on America to be influenced by considerations of
party tactics.  Did his followers agree with those opinions ?
How far did his party have an ideological basis ?  Seventeen
out of the twenty-five who remained in July 1767 had voted
against the repeal of the Stamp Act.  Yet ideology could not
hold the party together after Grenville's death.  Sixteen of his
followers were still in Parliament when the American war
broke out : four (Hamilton, Hussey, Pitt, and Seymour)
opposed the war from the beginning, and three (Hervey,
Fife and Norton) ended by opposing it.[2]

In addition there is the Clive group.  In 1763 Clive had
offered Grenville the support of his followers in Parliament
in return for Grenville's help against Sulivan at India House.
In July 1767 Clive had three followers in Parliament :  his
father, Richard ;  his cousin, George ;  and his relative by
marriage and agent, John Walsh.  In February 1768 they were
joined by John Carnac, and at the General Election by William
Clive and Henry Strachey.  Grenville in opposition could be
of little help to Clive at India House, and on November 25,
1767, Walsh wrote to Clive : 'I shall go to the Duke of Grafton's
levee, as you desire to shew we are not in opposition : every
mark of respect though not of servility to H.M.'s Ministers is
conformable to, nay essential in the independent plan you
mean to support'.[3]  Clive, it is clear, did not intend his followers to acknowledge any leader but himself.  Yet he and

[1] For Sargent, see Grenville to James Buller, December 11, 1764 ; for
Hussey, see Grenville to Edward Eliot, June 23, 1765.  Copies of these
letters are in Grenville's letter books among the Stowe MSS. in the Henry
H. Huntington Library, San Marino, California.

[2] Sargent, who left Parliament in 1768, sympathized with the colonies.
He was a friend and correspondent of Benjamin Franklin, and remained
on good terms with him after the colonies had become independent.

[3] Powis Castle MSS.

Grenville seem to have had a sincere respect for each other ; Grenville cultivated him more than any other man ; and the Clive group voted with the opposition over Wilkes in 1769 and 1770.

The circumstances of Grenville's dismissal in 1765 helped to prolong his party's life in opposition.  The Rockinghams, determined to show that they did not owe their power to Bute and wishing to restore those who had suffered in 1762, dismissed many who had hitherto had no party connection with Grenville.  Their numbers were increased by resignations in minor offices — not usual on a change of Administration. Many were annoyed and bewildered that a settled Administration had been dismissed for no cause that they could see, and despised the inexperience and dilettantism of the new Ministers. Those who resigned or were dismissed went into opposition, which helped to create the belief that Grenville had a formidable party — which he himself seems to have entertained.

When Chatham replaced Rockingham this illusion was exposed.  There was an inclination to return to office on the part of men whom Grenville seems to have expected to remain with him in opposition.  Chatham proscribed nobody (except Lord George Sackville), had only a handful of friends to be preferred, and, professing a wish to abolish party distinctions, gave office both to supporters of the Stamp Act and of its repeal.  Grenville found he could no longer count on those whom he had favoured or promoted, and, when Parliament met, his hopes of a vigorous opposition were soon blasted.  In the two divisions before Christmas 1766, though joined by the Rockinghams, he cut but a poor figure.  On January 27, 1767, when his followers alone divided on the report of the Army estimates, he mustered only nineteen votes.  It was clear that he could not hope to do much better unless he co-operated with Rockingham.  And co-operation with Rockingham meant compromise on the American question, with at least an implication that the policy behind the Stamp Act was mistaken.

When did Grenville realize that the King had vetoed his return to office ?  Probably slowly and by stages.  He does not seem to have been aware of it in November 1766 ; he certainly

was in July 1767. This, added to the distaste Grenville had
for working with the Rockinghams, and suspicion that the
Bedfords wished to return to Court, changed his attitude to
parliamentary politics. He grew resigned to his exclusion from
office, and ceased to shape his tactics to this end. He relaxed
his hold on the party, made few efforts to seek recruits, or even
to communicate with those remaining supporters who were
not his personal friends. He neglected the politicians, and
began to appeal to the independents.

Even when Minister, Grenville had been heard with respect
by the country gentlemen. On February 21, 1764, three days
after the General Warrants motion, Newdigate wrote in his
diary :

> Mr. Grenville's Levy, where I met most of the country
> gentlemen by agreement.
> Mr. Grenville First Lord of the Treasury's Levy, the
> first time I was ever at a Minister's Levy.

Here is the entry in Grenville's Diary for February 27, 1767,
the day of the land-tax victory : 'The joy in the House of
Commons was very great, all the country gentlemen coming
round Mr. Grenville, shaking him by the hand, and testifying
the greatest satisfaction'.[1] Newdigate, in the House of
Commons on March 27, 'professed he had never admired any
Administration but Grenville's'.[2] And on April 12 Grenville's
Diary contains the entry : 'Great industry is being used to
detach the country gentlemen from Mr. Grenville'.[3] He
abandoned his position as a party leader, but maintained his
standing in the House.

This change can be seen in Grenville's relations with Sir
Fletcher Norton. Norton had succeeded Yorke as Attorney-
General in 1763, but was dismissed in 1765. He went into
opposition, and had maintained his connection with Grenville.
Although Chatham talked of some opening for Norton nothing
was done for him in 1766, and he remained a potential member
of the opposition. He was a coarse though able speaker ; a
lawyer of standing ; and an important man in the Commons

---

[1] *Grenville Papers*, iv. 211-12.          [2] Walpole, *Memoirs*, ii. 312.
[3] *Grenville Papers*, iv. 224.

whether in or out of office. On November 6, 1766, Grenville
was informed that Norton desired to act with him.[1] The next
day he noted that Norton's 'language was great anger and
disgust at the ill-treatment he had met with, but yet did not
seem inclined to take any active part'.[2]  It was too early to
commit himself to opposition. Did Grenville foment the
'anger and disgust', or encourage Norton 'to take any active
part' ? On December 3 his diary reads : 'Sir Fletcher Norton
and Mr. Wedderburne as yet remain firm to Mr. Grenville'.[3]
The wording is significant : so too is the entry for December 5
— 'Sir Fletcher Norton and Mr. Wedderburn supported
Mr. Grenville'.[4] But after this date there are no entries of any
consequence concerning Norton, nor did he take part in the
opposition to the East India inquiry.

On March 13, 1767, Grafton wrote to Chatham : 'If your
Lordship could see Sir Fletcher Norton for a few minutes, I
have great reason to think you might quite fix him'.[5]  But
Chatham was even less disposed than Grenville to court men,
and on March 25 Norton 'firmly denied' the rumour that he
had 'made up matters with Administration'.[6]  In July 1767
Wedderburn told Rockingham that Norton had no other
connection but with Grenville ; [7] yet he was not among those
to whom Grenville or Whately sent an account of the negotiations.  Norton was a man of too much consequence to remain
neglected for long : Grenville did not consult him, he had no
connection with Bedford, Rockingham was his declared enemy
— he naturally returned to Court. A Minister more capable
than Grafton would have snapped him up before 1769.[8]
The case of Wedderburn, another lawyer and able House

---

[1] *Grenville Papers*, iii. 380-1.       [2] *Ibid.*       [3] *Ibid.* pp. 393-4.
[4] On the report stage of the Indemnity Bill. *Ibid.* p. 395.
[5] *Chatham Correspondence*, iii. 232.
[6] Rockingham to Newcastle, March 26, 1767 ; Add. MS. 32980,
ff. 384-5.
[7] Whatley to Grenville, July 20, 1767 ; *Grenville Papers*, iv. 66-7.
[8] In justice to Grafton it must be remembered that Norton had been
connected with Bute, and was *persona non grata* with the Rockinghams.
Conway, to maintain his reputation for 'consistency', would certainly have
opposed bringing him into office. (See Walpole, *Memoirs*, ii. 268.)  In
1769 Grafton could afford to ignore Conway's scruples ; he could not in
1767.

of Commons man, who had links with the Bedfords through Sir
Laurence Dundas, provides a similar example of how Grenville
neglected his party. Contact with Wedderburn was maintained,
but more by Whately than by Grenville. He was, for example,
informed of the progress of the negotiations of July 1767.
Wedderburn also had a link with Rockingham : he was the
friend and companion on the Northern Circuit of John Lee,
intimately connected with Rockingham. Soon Wedderburn
was invited to visit Wentworth, became intimate with Burke,
and took his place in the councils of the Rockingham party.
He helped to draw up the Yorkshire petition of 1769, and was
consulted by Dowdeswell on legal aspects of the petitioning
movement.[1] When he resigned his seat for Richmond because
of his vote on Wilkes, Rockingham offered to bring him into
Parliament again.[2] In 1769 and 1770 Wedderburn can almost
be classed as a follower of Rockingham's. But he was ambitious
to rise in his profession, and in 1771 he accompanied other
followers of Grenville into North's Administration.

Lord George Sackville, Wedderburn's friend, provides a
further illustration. Since Sackville's disgrace in 1759 he had
been an outlaw in the political world. Yet he was an able
man, and had two friends in the Commons.[3] Sackville was
rehabilitated and made respectable by Rockingham : short of
speakers in the Commons, Rockingham made him joint Vice-
Treasurer of Ireland, and though he voted against the repeal
of the Stamp Act, he seems to have been grateful to his
benefactor.[4] But in 1766 Sackville was inclined rather towards
Grenville. Grenville's Diary for November 27 contains the
entry : 'Lord George Sackville sent to Mr. Grenville to
devote himself to him, and came to him that evening'.[5] This

[1] Dowdeswell to Rockingham, September 5 and October 11, 1769;
Dowdeswell Papers.

[2] Whately to Grenville, May 13, 1769 ; Grenville (J. M.) MSS.

[3] General Irwin and Sir Charles Farnaby (M.P. for East Grinstead).
But I am doubtful about Farnaby, though Sackville mentions him among
his 'particular friends'. (In a letter to Irwin, dated August 20, 1766, in
the Germain Papers in the William L. Clements Library.) Farnaby did
not follow Sackville after 1768.

[4] Sackville to Rockingham, August 2, 1766 ; Rockingham Papers,
R1-419.                           [5] Grenville Papers, iii. 390.

connection was maintained : Grenville informed him of the outcome of the negotiations of July 1767.[1] He remained in opposition, and like Wedderburn was drawn into the Rockingham orbit. In 1771 he was so closely connected with that party that he was one of three consulted by Richmond on policy and tactics during Rockingham's absence at Bath.[2] But Sackville too tired of opposition, and went over to the Court in 1775.

Here are three men, two of whom were to achieve the Cabinet and the third of Cabinet stature, whom Grenville permitted to slip through his fingers to other parties. If he took such few pains to retain the services of men of the first rank, it is hardly surprising that he took none for those of the second. Bamber Gascoyne had been made a Lord of Trade by Grenville in 1763. On standing for re-election at Maldon he was defeated, and Grenville arranged a seat for him at Midhurst. He resigned office in 1765, and opposed the Rockingham Administration. Although wishing to remain in Parliament, he could not find a seat at the General Election of 1768. The only way he could get back was by going over to the Court, and the way was opened for him by Lord Hillsborough, his old chief at the Board of Trade. In 1769 Gascoyne used his influence to stop a petition which had been begun in Essex ; and in 1770 resumed his post at the Board of Trade, and re-entered Parliament for Lord Weymouth's borough of Weobley.

Under these circumstances it may seem surprising that so many of Grenville's followers remained faithful. Of the twenty-five whom I classify as followers of Grenville in July 1767, Sargent and Shiffner left Parliament in 1768, and Hunter died before Grenville. Of the remainder, only Catherlough, Gascoyne, and Norton had gone over to the Court when Grenville died. It is a tribute to Grenville's personal and political character that so many should remain faithful when no hopes of office or favours were held out to them. It

---

[1] Grenville to Sackville, July 26, 1767 ; *H.M.C.*, *Stopford-Sackville MSS.*, i. 71.

[2] The others were Dowdeswell and John Cavendish. (Richmond to Rockingham [January 22, 1771] ; Rockingham Papers, R158-46.)

is a tribute also to the fidelity and hard work of his 'man of business', Whately. The active management of the party passed almost completely into Whately's hands : he rounded up supporters (using Grenville's name) ; sought out topics for motions ; pressed Grenville to write to this follower or call upon that ; and took upon himself the drudgery which Grenville would not do. Whately also directed party strategy : he led it into collaboration with the Rockinghams, and formed connections with Burke and Dowdeswell. It was he who prolonged the life of the Grenville party after its leader had tired of it.

Lastly, here is an amusing example of the difficulty of drawing hard and fast lines between the parties and how easily a slippery man may dodge them.

There were three Herveys in Parliament in 1766 : Lord Bristol, who professed himself a follower of Chatham ; [1] and his brothers, Augustus and William. The Hervey brothers were notorious for their quarrels with each other, and were rarely on the same side in politics. They were like spirited and highly trained horses at the beginning of the Derby : first one would rear and threaten to throw its rider, then another would turn itself the wrong way, and when these had been quieted the third would lash out with its hooves and threaten its neighbours. But in July 1766 the Hervey brothers appeared to be in line, presenting a joint front in support of Chatham. It was an illusion, and the tale of Augustus Hervey's antics at the starting post can be told from his letters to Grenville.

Augustus was a naval officer, who, although a Groom of the Bedchamber, was reckoned a follower of Grenville. On July 10, 1766, he told Grenville of the domestic bliss which reigned in the Hervey family, in spite of his brother and himself being on opposite sides in politics.

I have the pleasure to tell you [he wrote] my brother has *requested* of me *to be for Bury* next Parliament and with the

---

[1] In language so fulsome that the reader is sickened. These passages are usually omitted from Bristol's letters printed in the *Chatham Correspondence*.

assurances that I am *ever* to be at *my own liberty as to what measures I shall pursue*.[1]

Then came the 'joyfull bustle' of the change of Administration, and Augustus, assuming that Temple was to have 'the settling all with *Mr. P.*', staked out his claim. He wrote to Temple 'to lightly throw . . . before him' his wish to be at the Admiralty Board, though he did not doubt that Grenville had mentioned his name.

Two days later (July 21) he wrote again to Grenville :

You'll be tired seeing my hand, but last night my brother recieved a long very kind letter from *Mr. P.* inviting him *in* and *to everything* he can wish and desire, but telling him *Ld. T.* had again declined and gone to Stowe. My brother is gone this day to Town to be with *Mr. P.* to morrow, but I do not think 'tis yet clear he will come in, as his health is his objection, tho' *Mr. P.* presses very much, which obliged him to go rather than write, and yet I own I wish him to be something as I think the only thing likely to stir the most dejected mind and worst spirits I ever saw, and which at times I knew not what to think off, and vexes me much. In short, I do not think he will accept of anything whatever. I may be mistaken. He has been very kind thro' out to me about it all. This morning on taking leave of me he told me, Well brother, I am sorry none of *your friends* are to be included. I said, I was sorry that only *one* would probably be. He said, If I accept, I hope you'll take a seat at the Admiralty as I know you wish it. I beg to be excused. I said, brother, I wish'd it had my friends come in with yours. But all I desire is that I may not be offer'd it, because I'll refuse. If this is ask'd you, or if you intended to make this your terms too, assure yourself you'll only hurt me. I am determined to take nothing whatever. But if you go in, I'll not oppose and by that means shew that 'tis for you alone. But if you remember you have ever promised to leave me at liberty and not to let it break us. He seem'd very well pleased but said he wished if he came in I would take a seat at the Admiralty, but I absolutely (before my sister) insisted on my not being named, but if *Mr. P.* did, to refuse it for me.

[1] The letters from Hervey to Grenville from which I quote are in the Grenville (J. M.) MSS.

I thought I would let you know, my dear Sir, how all stood, and hope you will be satisfied with my part. I see and know *qu'il ne tient qu'à moi* to have him and myself both in. But I never will take but one part, and I told him this morning. I am sure he must have a better opinion of me for it. I suppose I shall have another attack when he has seen *Mr. P.*, if he should accept, but I am very staunch.

Clearly party allegiance should give place to fraternal affection, and no one could blame Augustus for accepting a seat at the Admiralty Board in order to please his elder brother. But no such offer was made, and on July 28 he renewed his 'deliberate and steady perseverance of those sentiments and principles which must attach a disinterrested mind and pure heart' to Grenville, 'both in . . . publick and private life'.

Then Bristol accepted the post of Lord Lieutenant of Ireland ('the King . . . told him that he *has long wished* to put him at the head of that government'), and asked Hervey to go with him as his secretary. Hervey did not want to go — office was the last thing in the world he wished — and only agreed because of his devotion to his brother. On August 30 he sent Grenville an account of Bristol's audience with the King, and then continued :

This my brother told me after the audience and surprized me, as ill health, inabilities and *other things* had made me determine not to go, and to remain quiet as I was. I told him this and declined it, but had you seen the effect of it and how impossible it was for me to persist after what he said, you would both applaud and pity the determination. So there I am embarked in what I know nothing of, nor like. For 'tho he says 'tis inconceivable what Ld. Chatham told him of me, and how much he wished that very thing, yet I do assure you I am vex'd to death about it. No emoluments can avail to one of my way of thinking, and *now* my way of living, and unconcern about affluence if I have what is requisite, which thank God, none can rob me of.

While continuing to profess his attachment to Grenville he did not neglect the other side. In October he suggested to Shelburne that Sandwich should be offered the embassy to

Madrid — 'as a friend to Administration he thought it might accelerate further arrangements'.[1]    Devotion to Grenville, then, was not incompatible with an attempt to seduce the Bedfords, Grenville's allies.

Hervey, as a man in office and the brother of Chatham's friend, was asked to second the Address at the opening of the session.    Here is the entry in Grenville's Diary for November 10, 1766 :

> At the Cockpit meeting Lord Lisburne was called upon, having promised to move the Address, but he excused himself, saying he was ill, and found himself utterly unable : this a little disconcerted Mr. Conway, but he immediately meant to have recourse to Mr. Augustus Hervey, who had been induced by Lord Bristol's earnest and peremptory solicitation (though very much against his will) to second the Address, and accordingly his name was echoed round the room, but in vain, for he was playing at Quadrille with Mrs. Grenville instead of attending the meeting.[2]

The next day he moved the Address with what Grenville's Diary calls 'a direct *opposition* speech'.    But it is strange that Walpole, who would have noted such a contretemps, does not mention it in his *Memoirs*.

William Hervey voted with the Court on the Land Tax motion, but Augustus abstained.    In the spring he went to Bath.    But the Court had had sufficient experience of the political confusion that could result from drinking the waters, and he was hastily recalled.

> I was wrote too [he told Grenville on April 4, 1767] to desire I would come to Town, *that the Closet canvass'd over rigidly every absentee, and that it became me to act with more circumspection and more vigor than the rest, least I should be suspected to be waiting the cast of the dye, when it was so well known I was so strongly and avowedly attached to those two brothers who were the declared antagonists of that one which he was determined to support* ; and therefore press'd again to return.

[1] See above, p. 37.    [2] *Grenville Papers*, iii. 382.

The sick man set off,

> little careing for the suspicions of the *Closet*, because if any one can suspect me of a design in this I despise them. I repeated to him, that even my friend Mr. Grenville knows and approves my determination to support my brother in preference to himself, and he, (my brother) knows it is, to support Mr. Grenville in preference to every one else but my brother.

'Poor indeed, my dear Sir,' he concluded, 'must their G[overnmen]t be to need every invalid's risking his health to prove his zeal.'

This summons, of course, had come from brother Bristol. The harmony between the two brothers had now lasted almost a year, and was due to break at any moment. The story can be told in the letters which passed between Augustus and Bristol, copies of which Augustus sent to Grenville.[1] On July 1, 1767, he wrote to ask Bristol 'the reason of the very great alteration' towards him, which had determined him to resign his office.

> It was only the report and probability that prevails of your not going to Ireland which prevented my doing so before, as that office would then have dropp'd with your own, and I should have avoided the only disagreeable but necessary part your conduct has obliged me too, of troubling his Majesty of my reasons why I do ; I owe it to the King from every consideration, as I do that constant support I have given and will continue to give his Government, and which not even this step will make me vary from ; and I hope will at length make you regret the treating me as you have done for the sake of others, whom I wish you may always find deserve as well of you.
>
> I shall enter into no further discussion, because I have a right to expect it of you in person ; I do not mean it by way of justifying myself because I feel nothing that requires it ; nor do I ask it by way of any reperation, because you can make me none for having let those succeed whose interest and business it has been to withdraw your confidence from

---

[1] And which Hervey also showed to the King. (Hervey to Grenville. July 4, 1767 ; *Grenville Papers*, iv. 29-30.)

me, and endeavour to separate us : but I owe it to myself from other motives ; I do not mean political ones, altho' in them I think myself wounded by your suffering it to be insinuated that your conduct to me proceeds from my not supporting the King's Administration, which is false in who ever dare to tell you the untruth or to propagate it. I have nothing more at present to add than that you'll please to recollect this is the second time, you have sacrificed the warmest affection, and most disinterrested attachment that any man can have for another in

your brother

A. HERVEY

Bristol replied the same day :

I have received your letter by Sir Robert Wilmot acquainting me with your desire to resign the office you hold of my Principal Secretary. I can have no objection to the informing you in person with the change of my behaviour, which will be a repitition of what I shall now set down ; that I cou'd not submitt to the reproaches of the world that accus'd me of taking advantage of Lord Chatham's ill state of health, to carry on through your means, a private intercourse between his opponents and myself, and altho' I was conscious of my own innocence, yet I had no other method of disculpating my conduct than by breaking off all communication between yourself and

your brother

BRISTOL

Perhaps it was just as well the brothers never went to Ireland.

During the negotiations of July 1767 Augustus was all zeal for Grenville and Temple, and professed to believe that the Court was also. He told Grenville of a conversation he had had with Grafton's brother, Fitzroy, in which Fitzroy had said that Grafton 'had avoided any personalities against Lord Temple' or Grenville, 'and knew no man so fit to be at the head' of the Commons.[1] William and Augustus voted against the Court on the Nullum Tempus Bill, and though Augustus continued to profess his attachment to Grenville he voted with the Court over Wilkes (May 8, 1769).

---

[1] Hervey to Grenville, July 21, 1767 ; *Grenville Papers*, iv. 67-70.

When Chatham resigned in October 1768 the Privy Seal was offered to Bristol. Before accepting, he sought Chatham's approval. 'Do you choose, my Lord,' he wrote on October 29, 'that I should hold it till your health will permit you to resume the reins of Government? Be assured, my Lord, that on such terms I shall relinquish the office with infinitely more satisfaction than I can enter into it.' [1]  Put that way, who could refuse his sanction? Not Chatham. 'I beg to decline', he replied on October 30, 'any way entering into arrangements of office. Allow me, my Lord, at the same time to entreat, that the idea of your Lordship's holding the Privy Seal only for an interim may not, on any account, be further thought of by your Lordship.' [2]

When Chatham went into opposition in January 1770 his friends stood by him : Camden resigned the Great Seal, Granby the command of the Army — and Bristol exchanged his office of Lord Privy Seal for that of Groom of the Stole, which he held until his death in 1775. Augustus came back in 1771 with others of the Grenville party : he was made a Lord of the Admiralty, and remained there until he succeeded his brother in the earldom when he resigned his offices. In the last years of his life he went back into opposition, becoming a staunch supporter of Keppel in his quarrel with Sandwich. In 1766 Sandwich had been Hervey's friend, but since then they had sat together four years at the Admiralty Board.

A study of the Hervey family is recommended to those who believe there were organized political parties in the eighteenth century.

### The Rockinghams

Lord Macaulay, in his essay *The Earl of Chatham*, thus described the Rockingham party :

They were men worthy to have charged by the side of Hampden at Chalgrove, or to have exchanged the last embrace with Russell on the scaffold in Lincoln's Inn Fields. They carried into politics the same high principles of virtue which regulated their private dealings, nor would they

[1] *Chatham Correspondence*, iii. 347.          [2] *Ibid.* p. 348.

T

stoop to promote even the noblest and most salutary ends
by means which honour and probity condemn. Such men
. . . we hold in honour as the second founders of the Whig
party, as the restorers of its pristine health and energy after
half a century of degeneracy.

The Rockinghams were fortunate above all other parties of
this period : their apologia was written by Edmund Burke.
His pamphlets and speeches on their behalf have been admitted
into the canon of English political science, and have taken
their place among the classics of English literature. He won
for the Rockingham party a posthumous reputation for political
wisdom and honesty ; nineteenth-century historians saw them
as the forerunners of Liberalism, the ancestors of the party of
Russell, Palmerston, and Gladstone.[1] The Rockinghams had
a longer life than any of their contemporaries : in 1766
Rockingham was the youngest of the party leaders, and he
outlived the others. Moreover, he was in opposition for the
best part of his political career. The Rockinghams, therefore,
give most scope for a study of the composition of party and
the practice of opposition in the second half of the eighteenth
century.

Macaulay believed that the Rockinghams were *sui generis*
among eighteenth-century parties. In another passage of his
essay on Chatham he illustrated the difference between the
use and abuse of party by comparing them with the Bedfords.
The Bedfords had 'no principle whatever', except to win the
favours of the Crown : they acted in concert because they
thought 'that they should fetch a higher price jointly than
singly'. But the Rockinghams, though 'desiring by honest
and constitutional means, the direction of affairs', refused to
accept it 'on any terms inconsistent with their principles'.
'The Rockingham party', Macaulay concluded, 'was, in our
view, exactly what a party should be.'

Yet the structure of the two parties was the same. The
Rockinghams, like the Bedfords, consisted of a handful of

---

[1] They are referred to as the 'Liberal' party by Sir Denis Le Marchant,
in a footnote to Walpole's *Memoirs*, ii. 18 ; and by Lord Albemarle, in his
*Memoirs of the Marquis of Rockingham*, ii. 209.

peers, with their followers placed at varying distances from the centre. Just as Bedford, Gower, Sandwich, and Weymouth each contributed their quota, whose connection was with their patron rather than with the group, so Rockingham, Portland, Newcastle, Albemarle, and Richmond had their followers, and the only band of union was the friendship of the magnates. From the point of view of Parliament the Bedfords had the superior organization. Bedford, Gower, and Sandwich were among the first men in the House of Lords ; only Richmond among the Rockinghams could compare with them, and apart from Newcastle the party had no other reliable speaker there. They had more votes and better speakers in the Commons than the Bedfords, but the effect of superior numbers was countered by the difficulty of getting them into the division lobby : Rigby marshalled his troops better than Burke. And in an age when travelling was difficult, and the parliamentary recess lasted from early summer till November or December, it was easier to keep a party in line from Bedfordshire than from Yorkshire.

Six of the eleven who can be counted as Rockingham's personal followers were from Yorkshire : Sir George Armytage (M.P. for York) ; Nathaniel Cholmley (Aldborough) ; [1] Lord Downe (Cirencester) ; Fountayne Wentworth Osbaldeston (Scarborough) ; Sir George Savile (Yorkshire) ; and William Weddell (Kingston upon Hull).[2] None, except Savile, were of any mark in Parliament ; and their adherence to Rockingham was more in consequence of his standing in the county than his position as a party leader. Armytage, who sat on Rockingham's interest at York, pleaded ill-health for refusing to stand in 1768 ; while Downe, on October 16, 1770, repeated a request made to Rockingham the previous spring that he should be permitted to resign his seat because of his health.[3]

---

[1] Cholmley sat in Parliament on Newcastle's interest, at Rockingham's recommendation. (Newcastle to Rockingham, December 22, 1767 ; Add. MS. 32987, ff. 397-8.)

[2] Weddell married in 1771 Elizabeth, daughter of Sir John Ramsden, 3rd Bart., and half-sister of Lady Rockingham.

[3] Rockingham Papers, R1-750. He was then M.P. for Rockingham's borough of Malton.

Osbaldeston died in 1770, and Downe and Cholmley left Parliament in 1774 ; only Savile and Weddell remained when the American war broke out.

Savile was the outstanding figure in the Rockingham group : one of the most independent, disinterested, and public-spirited men in the House of Commons. A close friend of Rockingham, together they were supreme in Yorkshire politics : no other interest could stand against them. When, in 1774, Savile considered retiring from Parliament, Rockingham thought of leaving politics altogether. 'My whole thoughts are absorbed in the ruin and confusion which will ensue', he wrote to Savile on August 9, 1774, 'if you should persist in the idea of declining to be representative of this county in the next election.' [1] The Rev. John Fountayne, Dean of York, 'exceedingly concerned at the possibility of the event', had warned Savile of 'the horrid confusion such a step would throw this county into'.

I have an absolute horror of the approach of York races [Rockingham continued] least anything should tempt you either to make any declaration or indeed to let such an idea generally transpire. I earnestly wish that you would let us all meet again in London before you take any step of such general importance. Let us have the opportunity of talking it over with some of the most considerable of our publick friends. I am indeed doubly interested in this, for assuredly if you give up the county, and I must add the publick, I have nothing to do but fairly to retire and relinquish all late ideas relative to Yorkshire, or of being of any service to the publick.

Yet was Savile a party man ? He could have had almost any office he wished in 1765 or 1782, yet he took none. He refused to vote on the land tax division,[2] and wrote to Rockingham of the East India inquiry :

I am sure I sincerely wish the set I wish the best to, to do nothing. If injustice is attempted against the E.I. Co. oppose it, protest against it. If so good a bargain is not made as should be, shew the weak parts or if the mode be bad or the offer too good to be trusted. . . . It is a reasonable thing for me to ask, and yet perhaps an unreasonable thing to expect to obtain from men in some of your situations that you will forget where propositions come from.[1]

Nor was he forward to take the lead on the Nullum Tempus Bill, although it was a just and reasonable measure. 'His diffidence of his own abilities', wrote Rockingham to Newcastle on February 7, 1768, 'and the uncertain state of his health made him for a long time positive that he could not undertake to be the *mover*, though every sensation of his mind made him anxious to do his utmost on the matter.'[2]  A leading figure in the opposition to Wilkes's expulsion and to the American war, he was never accused of faction.  He took no side in the struggle for power between Shelburne and Fox in 1782–3, and in a list of the House of Commons drawn up in March 1783 his name appears in the column 'Country gentlemen and doubtful', with the remark 'Absent'.[3]  His connection with party had ended on Rockingham's death.

Others in the party connected closely with Rockingham were Savile Finch (M.P. for Malton), George Dempster (Perth Burghs), Sir William Meredith (Liverpool), and Frederick Montagu (Northampton).  Finch was a small man, who readily gave up his seat in Parliament in December 1780 when it was required for Burke.  The others, however, were considerable figures in the party and in Parliament, yet they also had connections with other groups.

Dempster was closely connected with the Johnstone family, who played a large part in the affairs of the East India Company : he was a frequent speaker in the Commons on East Indian affairs.  He seems originally to have been attached to Shelburne : he consulted Shelburne in 1765 'whether he should engage with the Duke's Administration, with Lord Rockingham at the head of the Treasury'.[4]  Rockingham appointed him Secretary to the Order of the Thistle, and

[1] Savile to Rockingham, March 26, 1767 ; Rockingham Papers, R1-489.
[2] Add. MS. 32988, ff. 204-6.
[3] Dundas Papers, National Library of Scotland.
[4] Shelburne to Barré, July 7, 1765 ; Fitzmaurice, *Life of Shelburne*, i. 233.

gained a loyal follower. 'It will give me pleasure', he wrote
to Rockingham on November 8, 1766, 'to regulate my parliamentary conduct in whatever shape is agreeable to you. Let
me say even more pleasure now than when your Lordship was
at the head of the Treasury.'[1]  Yet Dempster seems to have
retained some regard for Shelburne : he voted with Shelburne's
Administration on February 18, 1783, and did not vote on the
second reading of Fox's East India Bill.

Montagu was close to both Rockingham and Portland, yet
he had strong connections with other politicians.  On November 8, 1763, Lord Halifax, second cousin to Montagu, recommended him to Grenville as 'a most unexceptionable worthy
man' ;  he asked on his behalf for the seat at the Board of
Trade vacant by John Yorke's resignation.[2]  Two days later
he wrote again :

> My credit as one of the principal servants of his Majesty,
> and yours, as a friend to me, will suffer, if a seat at the one
> or the other of the Boards be not given to my near and dear
> relation.  I lay in my pretensions thus early, which I am
> confident you will think most reasonable.[3]

But Grenville 'had not had the disposal of one single House
of Commons office since those he named when he was First
Commissioner of the Treasury, and consequently could not
yet have provided for any friend of his own'.[4]  The place was
given to Jeremiah Dyson.

Montagu was not one of those who voted against Grenville's
Administration on General Warrants.[5]  In November 1764 he
refused the place of Groom Porter, 'saying it was no office of
business, which was the line in which he wished to move.
Lord Halifax was much displeased at his refusal. . . .'[6]  By
now he was on bad terms with Halifax, and in the next few
months shifted his allegiance to Rockingham.  By 1768 he

---

[1] Rockingham Papers, R1-445.          [2] Grenville (J. M.) MSS.
[3] Ibid.
[4] Grenville's Diary, November 10, 1763 ; Grenville Papers, ii. 221.
[5] He also canvassed for Sandwich when he stood for High Steward of
Cambridge University in 1764. (Walpole, Memoirs, i. 315.)
[6] Grenville's Diary, November 1, 1764 ; Grenville Papers, ii. 520-1.

was close to Rockingham, who returned him for Higham Ferrers at the General Election.

Sir William Meredith had been prominent in the opposition to Grenville's Ministry, and was closely connected with Rockingham and Portland. In 1767 there were few men whose loyalty seemed so dependable, yet it soon began to waver. Towards the end of 1770, when relations between Chatham and Rockingham were becoming strained, he was suspected of deviating from the pure Rockingham doctrine ; and in the House of Commons on March 7, 1771, he supported Chatham's opinions against Dowdeswell's on the rights of juries. Soon his deviationism became more pronounced and more reprehensible. In 1774 he took office as Comptroller of the Household, but, opposing the American war, resigned in 1777 and went back into opposition. But the lost sheep never returned to the Rockingham fold : such inconsistency could not be forgiven.

The other magnates — Portland, Richmond, and Albemarle — had their followers. But since they had never held the Treasury their attractive power was not so great as Rockingham's : ties of blood, marriage, and personal friendship counted for more with them than political connection. In July 1767 Portland had four followers in the Commons, including a brother, a brother-in-law, and a cousin ; [1] Albemarle had four, two of whom were his brothers ; [2] and Richmond two — his brother Lord George Henry Lennox (M.P. for Sussex), and his brother-in-law Thomas Connolly (Malmesbury). There was also the Verney group : Lord Verney (Carmarthen), and the two Burkes, whom he had brought into Parliament — Edmund for Wendover and William for Great Bedwin. Edmund Burke, as the party's mouthpiece and Rockingham's 'man of business', had very close relations with all the party magnates, and after 1766 was never dependent on Verney for a seat in Parliament. Yet he did not forget his former obligations, and watched over Verney's interests

[1] Lord Edward Bentinck (Lewes), Lord Grey (Staffordshire), John Bentinck (Rye), and Henry Curwen (Carlisle).

[2] Augustus Keppel (Windsor), William Keppel (Chichester), Sir Charles Saunders (Hedon), and Sir Samuel Cornish (New Shoreham).

with care, even when they were not supported by the party leaders.[1]

For forty years Newcastle had been one of the leaders of the Court party ; his survival as a political figure after 1762 was incidental to the development of parties, and affected neither their course nor their nature.  He could not take with him into opposition the political principles he had learnt as a Minister of the Crown, nor the friends he had served with the patronage of the Crown.  The advice he gave to the King at his final audience in 1766 was 'to keep as many of the last Administration as he could, his best and truest friends'.[2]  His former followers had learnt their lesson well : on September 2, 1769, Richmond told Burke why he could not promote a petition from Sussex — 'the long habit in which the late Duke of Newcastle had brought the Whigs of approving all measures of the old Court'.[3]  A whole generation of politicians had been taught that lesson by Newcastle ; the party Rockingham built up had to be formed on different principles and with new men.

Newcastle himself and a handful of his friends, too old or too attached to him to accommodate themselves to the new régime, followed Rockingham ; but the men on whom he had depended in the days of his greatness went with the Court. Consider, for example, those who had sat with him at the Treasury Board — usually considered his particular protégés. By 1766 three were dead (Lord Darlington, H. B. Legge, and Henry Furnese), and one had left politics (Lord Dupplin).  Five of the remainder adhered to the Court after 1766 (Robert Nugent, Lord North, James Oswald, Lord Barrington, and Sir Gilbert Elliot) ; two followed Grenville (Sir George Lyttelton and Lord Thomond) ; and one followed Chatham (James Grenville). Only Lord Duncannon, now Earl of Bessborough, accompanied Newcastle into the Rockingham party.  But Bessborough's attitude to politics was of the old school; he had little sympathy with the practice of opposition moulded by Dowdeswell or the theory preached by Burke ; and he took little part in politics

[1] See below, p. 337.
[2] 'Considerations for my behaviour to the King, upon my giving up'; Add. MS. 33001, f. 271.
[3] Rockingham Papers, R8-2.

after 1768.[1] Relatives greatly favoured by Newcastle—Shelley, Lincoln, Thomas Pelham, and Onslow — remained with the Court throughout the American war. When the House of Commons divided on March 15, 1782, on the motion of no confidence in North's Ministry, there were no Pelhams or Yorkes with the opposition.

By July 1767 the number of Newcastle's followers had diminished to six : these were the only votes he could command in a House of Commons chosen while he was head of the Treasury and the Crown's chief election agent. Only one remained of his numerous City friends on whom he had depended for advice on commercial and financial business — Sir William Baker (M.P. for Plympton Erle), a rich merchant, with extensive business dealings with the colonies, and strongly pro-American. He retired from Parliament in 1768, and was succeeded at Plympton by his son (the negotiation for the seat was conducted through Newcastle), and William Baker junior became one of Rockingham's most reliable followers.

John White (M.P. for East Retford) was an old friend of Newcastle's and, after the death of Hardwicke and Devonshire in 1764, the chief recipient of the Duke's anxious confidences. His Whiggism was so pure and undefiled that Burke thought of dedicating to him *Thoughts on the Cause of the Present Discontents* ; and David Hartley, had he been successful at Callington at the General Election of 1768, proposed to vacate his seat in favour of White.[2] But White's Whiggism was detached and independent. The difference between the Whiggism of the Pelhams and the Rockinghams can be seen in the Rockinghams' attitude to White and Mansfield. White, who had never fitted into the Pelham system, was revered by the Rockinghams as the representative of a purer age : his Whiggism was out of date in 1754, and almost extinct in 1768. Mansfield was Rockingham's uncle ; he had guided the young Rockingham's first faltering steps in politics ; to him Newcastle had almost gone down on his knees in 1756 to induce him to

---

[1] Except for a brief appearance in 1773 on the occasion of the Irish absentee land tax, when his personal interests, like Rockingham's, were affected.

[2] Hartley to Portland, March 14, 1768 ; Portland MS. 295.

stay in the Commons. Rockingham never lost his respect for Mansfield in spite of their political differences, yet during the American war his followers believed Mansfield to be the King's secret adviser — the leader of the junto behind the Cabinet. Yet Mansfield was a typical product of the Pelham régime (though far above its general level in ability and intelligence), while White was not. The Rockinghams inherited a great deal from the Tories of the first half of the eighteenth century, far more than they realized or than historians have been willing to admit.

By 1767 Newcastle was grateful for the fidelity of small men, and praised and magnified their goodness to himself. Of this kind were John Norris (M.P. for Rye), and John Offley (Orford). Norris had been returned for Rye in 1762 at Newcastle's recommendation ; his father had also represented the borough from 1727 to 1733. On July 24, 1767, Norris senior wrote to Newcastle :

> If any credit may be given to publick reports, your Grace is going again to be employed in the service of the Crown ; I reflect with concern both with regard to your Grace and the human heart, how few among the many you have rewarded have proved faithful in the day of tryal, and beg leave to observe that among the few my son and myself have given the clearest proofs of our attachment to your person and interest. Be pleased my Lord now to reward this our attachment in the person of my son. . . .[1]

Unfortunately Newcastle was unable to do so. A few months later young Norris laid in a fresh claim to the Duke's gratitude. Here is the story as told by Newcastle to Rockingham (November 17, 1767) :

> At a time when I am so cruelly used by some of my friends, I will give your Lordship a most uncommon instance of zeal and friendship, in one who has no other obligation to me than bringing him into Parliament at Rye, young Norris ; his father is dead ; and his seat is vacated by the reversion of his father's place in the Customs, called always

[1] Add. MS. 32984, f. 30.

700£ pr. annum, but is not near so much as that. Your Lordship has heard that the Duke of Grafton's attempt at Rye was rejected by the chief man in the town. I think it probable that his Grace will now renew his attempt if there should be a vacancy. Norris is gone down this day to Rye ; and if he finds that they will not resist all temptation and chuse whomsoever I shall recommend to them he is determined (and it was all his own act) not to accept the place.[1]

The place was incompatible with a seat in Parliament, so 'honest Norris' went to the Duke of Grafton and resigned it (and also the offer to name his successor), 'with thankfull decency but with a firmness that . . . an old Roman would have approved'.[2] 'My dear friend,' wrote Newcastle to Norris on November 22,

for that I am sure you have shew'd yourself to be, in such a generous manner, as can never be forgot by me or any of my friends. . . . *Honor* it will certainly be to you ; and I hope in time you will have no reason to be sorry for it *in any respect*.[3]

Norris was returned again for Rye in 1768. Whether he ever regretted his action is not easy to say : he soon ran into financial difficulties, but remained in opposition until he left Parliament in 1774.

John Offley was connected with Newcastle's 'ungrateful nephew', Lord Lincoln, and in Newcastle's list of the House of Commons (March 2, 1767) is placed among the 'Doubtful or Absent'. In the autumn of 1767 he sprang into high favour with the Rockinghams when he refused the place of Master of the Household, 'offer'd him in the handsomest manner by the Duke of Grafton'.[4] But he performed his greatest service to 'the cause' at the General Election of 1768 when, as a candidate for East Retford acceptable to both Newcastle and Lincoln, he enabled the Duke to save his face there.[5] 'Mr. Offley is no party man', wrote Newcastle to Mansfield on

[1] Add. MS. 32987, ff. 14-18.
[2] West to Newcastle [November 21, 1767] ; *ibid.* f. 69.
[3] *Ibid.* f. 83.
[4] Newcastle to Rockingham, November 22, 1767 ; *ibid.* f. 77.
[5] See below, p. 343.

December 7, 1767, 'and has no particular attachment to any. He has constantly acted honorably with his friends, and will certainly continue to do so.' [1] Offley voted with the opposition on the Nullum Tempus Bill (February 17, 1768), but his name does not appear in any division list after 1768, and he left Parliament in 1774. Perhaps, after all, he was no party man.

Only one man who had held office while Newcastle was at the Treasury remained with him to the end — James West (M.P. for St. Albans), formerly Secretary to the Treasury. There is something rather touching about West's loyalty, for Newcastle was querulous and exacting to an almost unbearable degree during the last months of his life, yet West never complained. He was a man whom it was worth while to keep in the party : he had considerable influence with his son-in-law, Andrew Archer (Coventry), and with Archer's brother-in-law, Lord Winterton (Bramber), both of whom generally voted with the Rockinghams.

Yet West had a grievance against Rockingham which, in the case of a lesser man, would have rankled and served as the pretext for a timely desertion. He had left office with Newcastle in 1762, had joined the opposition to Bute and Grenville, and naturally hoped for restitution in 1765. Newcastle pressed Rockingham to make West Secretary to the Treasury once more : Rockingham refused, but told Newcastle West was to be Treasurer of the Navy and even appointed a day for kissing hands.[2] But that office was given to Lord Howe, and a Lordship of the Admiralty was suggested for West.[3] Yet the matter dragged on, and on July 24, 1765, Newcastle wrote to Rockingham : 'Sure, you will have seen West. For Godsake, don't let the poor man be publish'd every day in the papers, when it is not intended that he should have the office.' [4] 'I saw Mr. West yesterday', replied Rockingham on July 25, 'and must commend his behaviour. I mentioned whether he would

[1] Add. MS. 32987, ff. 194-6.
[2] Rockingham to Newcastle, July 17 and 19, 1765 ; Add. MS. 32968, ff. 33-4 and 84.
[3] Note by Rockingham [July 21, 1765] ; *ibid*. ff. 185-6.
[4] *Ibid*. f. 212.

like to be at any of the Boards, which he declined, and I must say I was not sorry.'[1] On July 26 Newcastle made another effort to get something for West :

> I saw poor West [he wrote to Rockingham]; he was very reasonable, but as you must know very much mortified. He says your Lordship told him, he had a great many enemies ; but he little thinks (poor man) who they are. He wishes to have some mark of his being not quite disgraced, he goes so low as to propose a Groom of the Bedchamber for his son, and to pay the salary of it to anybody. He says he is known to be rich ; and that his enemies say he got it all by corruption, whereas he had £1,000 per annum from his father, and one hundred thousand pounds by his wife. Those facts, I dare say, have drawn the imputation upon him.[2]

The next day (July 27) West saw Rockingham, who could only give him hopes that 'something might be done that would be agreable' to him. 'I am stopped by every Member I see', he told Newcastle, 'to know what is done for me, to which I can only answer *nothing yet*.'[3]

West's behaviour was dignified and manly : he did not press Newcastle importunely but relied on the Duke's good faith, nor did he upbraid or threaten when nothing was done for him. He supported Rockingham's Ministry, and followed Newcastle into opposition in 1766. During the last two years of Newcastle's life, he made frequent visits to Claremont,[4] and regularly sent him reports of debates in the Commons. Newcastle appreciated these attentions and tried to show his gratitude : he brought West's son into Parliament in 1767, and returned West at the General Election.

In December 1767 Newcastle had a paralytic stroke, from which he only partially recovered. He seems to have pressed Rockingham to a reconciliation with West, and to have urged him to make the first move. On January 24, 1768, Rockingham invited West to call on him in Grosvenor Square.

---

[1] *Ibid.* ff. 240-1.
[2] *Ibid.* ff. 264-7.
[3] West to Newcastle [July 27, 1765] ; *ibid.* f. 299.
[4] Newcastle loved to have company at Claremont, but most of his friends were bored by the old man and tried to dodge his invitations.

Mr. West immediately went to wait on his Lordship [wrote West to Thomas Hurdis [1]] who received Mr. West with great condescension and affability, hoped all former matters were forgot, and that he had long been very sorry for it and was ready to make the *amende honorable*. To which Mr. West replied that he should never think of it more. Lord Rockingham . . . complimented Mr. West for his invariable attachment to Whig principles and to the Duke of Newcastle and hoped for Mr. West's and his friends support.

Mr. West thanked his Lordship for his kind opinion of him, that he believed Lord Rockingham's principles and his were the same, that his attachment to the Duke of Newcastle and his obligations to him were such that he could never vary from during life and that all his actions and interest, had and should always be under his Grace's directions, and assured his Lordship of his respect for him, and his principles, and that he should at all times have the greatest pleasure in endeavouring to obey his commands.

Lord Rockingham repeated his thanks and great professions of acknowledgements, and with shaking hands reiterated his promises of friendship, and appeared perfectly happy.

West supported the Rockinghams in Parliament until his death in 1772. He seems to have been genuinely fond of Newcastle, and the relations between the two men did them both honour. With all Newcastle's absurdities, he had many fine and even lovable qualities, and it is to West's credit that he recognized them.

The names of Cavendish [2] and Yorke [3] in the list of

---

[1] January 25, 1768 ; Add. MS. 32988, f. 72. 'Honest and faithful Hurdis', Newcastle's domestic chaplain and amanuensis, is a man to whom all students of eighteenth-century history are deeply in debt. He kept Newcastle's papers, made copies (in copperplate handwriting) of his letters and memoranda, and docketed or dated his correspondence (which Newcastle rarely bothered to do).

[2] There were four Cavendishes in the Rockingham party in July 1767 : three sons of the third Duke of Devonshire — George (M.P. for Derbyshire), Frederick (Derby), and the most active, John (Knaresborough) ; and Richard (Wendover), a grandson of the first Duke. Sir Anthony Abdy (Knaresborough) was closely connected with the Cavendishes : he was legal agent for the Burlington estates, which passed into the family by the marriage of the fourth Duke to Charlotte, daughter and heiress of Richard, third and last Earl of Burlington.

[3] Charles (Reigate) and John (Higham Ferrers), sons of Philip, first Earl of Hardwicke.

Rockingham's friends helps to create the illusion that his party had roots in George II's reign, and that he had inherited the personnel of the Pelham régime. But the Cavendishes were much more than followers of the Pelhams : the fourth Duke of Devonshire was too big a man for his relatives and dependants to be in close political connection with anyone but himself, and his relations with Newcastle were very different from those of Murray or Kinnoull, or even of Hardwicke.

The Yorkes, if left to themselves, would have made terms with the new reign : they were dragged into opposition, reluctantly and half-heartedly,[1] a sacrifice to their father's friendship with Newcastle, for which they never forgave the Duke. Typical products of the Pelham school, they were not opposition material : their aim was to advance the interests of the family, and their politics were concentrated on one object — to obtain the Great Seal for Charles Yorke. His rivals in the succession to the highest legal office were the enemies of the Yorke family (hence their dislike of Chatham who sponsored Camden) ; those likely to promote their object were their allies. Rockingham had greatly respected and admired the first Lord Hardwicke,[2] and he transferred these feelings (with much less justification) to Charles Yorke. Had Rockingham been able he would have made Yorke Chancellor in 1765, as he would also in 1767. The Yorkes knew their goal would be reached if Rockingham ever came to power again : their only doubt was how long they would have to wait.

In 1766 and 1767 the Yorkes favoured any policy which threatened to bring down Chatham : they were strong advocates, therefore, for the combined opposition and the comprehensive Administration. They did not share Rockingham's distrust of Grenville : their own ideas on American policy did not differ radically from his, while Grenville had no candidate for the Great Seal and was well disposed towards

---

[1] Meredith, in a letter to Portland of December 21, 1764, included Charles Yorke among those 'who have no regard for the party they are bound to, but as it is the ladder to their own ambition and interest'. (Portland MS. 406.)

[2] 'I honoured and loved the late Lord Hardwicke', wrote Rockingham to Charles Turner in 1772. (Rockingham Papers, R77-1.)

Charles Yorke.  Hardwicke later censured Rockingham's handling of the negotiations of July 1767, and considered that his brother had been neglected ; [1] while the return of the Bedfords to Court and the break-up of the combined opposition was as great a blow to him as to Albemarle.

The Yorkes, brought up in a legal atmosphere, had no sympathy with Wilkes's cause or the opposition's attitude towards it.  Charles told Rockingham that if the petitioning movement succeeded, and 'if the King was prevailed with to dissolve the Parliament on this point, he could never recover the least degree of authority for his whole reign'.[2]  But he would not, though urged by his brothers, Hardwicke and John Yorke, declare his opinion in Parliament.  Though Rockingham seemed to be advancing farther and farther into the wilderness of opposition, to break with him was to block one avenue to the Woolsack.  Charles Yorke was a timid man, and feared to commit himself.  In the autumn of 1769 his uncertainty increased with rumours of Camden's dissatisfaction.  His brothers urged him to prepare for a vacancy on the Woolsack, and to make clear his position with respect to the Rockinghams, 'that the world might not have run away with the idea that he particularly belonged to that connection'.[3]  But Yorke could not resolve his doubts or banish his fears — to stay with Rockingham or to take service with a Ministry apparently on the brink of dissolution — and when the offer of the Great Seal was made in January 1770 he was still undecided and apprehensive.  After his death his brothers, who had no longer any motive for remaining in opposition, went over to the Court and supported North to the end.

To complete this survey of the personnel of the Rockingham party there is a group of thirteen Members, most of whom sat on their own interest in Parliament.  Dowdeswell is the most important : he had two friends in the party — his brother-in-law, Sir William Codrington (M.P. for Tewkesbury), and Charles Barrow (Gloucester).  The others were : Aubrey

---

[1] Hardwicke's 'Memorial of Family Occurrences' ;  Add. MS. 35428, f. 13.                [2] *Ibid.* f. 17.                [3] *Ibid.* f. 18.

Beauclerk (Thetford) ; [1] Wenman Coke (Okehampton) ; [2] Sir Mathew Fetherstonhaugh (Portsmouth) ; [3] Harbord Harbord (Norwich) ; [4] John Hewett (Nottinghamshire) ; [5] James Murray (Wigtownshire) ; William Plumer (Lewes) ; and John Plumptre (Nottingham). Sir George Colebrooke (Arundel) and James Scawen (Mitchell) were on the fringe of the party in 1767 : after 1768 they became more deeply committed.

In 1767 the parties led by Chatham and Grenville were moribund : their leaders had passed the zenith of their influence in politics. Bedford's party was soon to be merged into that of the Court, never to be re-formed. But the Rockingham party had only entered upon its career : its existence stretched before it, full of endless possibilities. Its nature and principles were moulded by these early years : it developed, but within a framework constructed between 1766 and 1768.

The significance of these years in the history of the Rockingham party is that they prepared the ground for the more momentous crisis of 1782–3 : the seed sown when Chatham was Minister ripened under Shelburne. Rockingham learnt from the negotiations of July 1767 that if ever again he were invited to come into office, the Treasury and the disposal of subordinate offices must be in his hands before he could accept. He had failed to form a comprehensive Administration in 1767 (so he believed) because he did not have direct authority from the King which he could employ in negotiations with Bedford and Grenville. He never claimed that any future Administration should be formed from his friends only : he was always prepared to admit other parties, provided they would acknowledge the supremacy of his own group. The symbol of that supremacy was the Treasury in Rockingham's hands.

[1] Lord Bessborough's son-in-law. In 1768 Grafton refused to re-elect him at Thetford ; he was returned by Newcastle for Aldborough.

[2] Described by Newcastle as 'a particular friend of mine . . . who has constantly voted with us in Parliament'. (Newcastle to Lord Winterton, October 17, 1767 ; Add. MS. 32986, f. 32.) Coke contested Norfolk with Sir Edward Astley in 1768, but was defeated.

[3] A Sussex country gentleman, friendly with Newcastle and Richmond. He was a considerable proprietor of East India stock, which he put at the service of Clive at India House elections.

[4] See above, p. 238.          [5] Savile's brother-in-law.

U

This proposition, initially put forward by Dowdeswell [1] and later elaborated by Burke, was bound to be challenged by the King and the other parties. The King regarded it as an encroachment on his right to choose his Ministers freely : it was one thing to grant of his own accord full powers to Chatham ; quite another to yield them to Rockingham as a condition of his forming an Administration. It appeared to the King that the Rockinghams were attempting to change the constitution against the will of Parliament. It was natural also that the other parties should resist these claims : neither Grenville nor Chatham would admit Rockingham's supremacy, or condescend to serve as his auxiliary.

Hence it was not easy for Rockingham and Chatham to work together in opposition, or for Rockingham and Shelburne to work together in office. Hence also Fox's demand on Rockingham's death that the Cabinet should nominate the new head of the Treasury. But doctrine rarely governs action in politics : power is the end of the parliamentary game, and consistency is a luxury few politicians can afford. In 1782 Richmond and Keppel, two of Rockingham's closest colleagues, remained in office with Shelburne after Fox and his friends had resigned ; while one may well wonder whether Fox would have insisted on the Cabinet's being consulted had he been chosen for the Treasury.

The events of 1766 to 1768 stamped the Rockingham party as anti-Chathamite. Chatham, by withholding his support, had wrecked the first Rockingham Administration ; Chatham had profited by its fall ; Chatham had insulted the party in December 1766. Rockingham had been prepared to work with Bedford and Grenville in 1767 in spite of their differences on America, but only on the basis of Chatham being no part. He and his followers distrusted Grenville, but they feared and disliked Chatham.

By 1774 even the most ardent of the Rockinghams, such as Richmond, or the most devoted, such as Dowdeswell, were wearied by the futility of opposition. Dowdeswell, in one of his last letters to Rockingham (June 8, 1774) wrote : 'Impossi-

[1] See above, p. 214.

bility of doing good in opposition, and despair of being able to do it if we were again called into Administration, has long left me hopeless in politics'.[1] The American war saved the Rockingham party from extinction. It was an issue of principle (the first considerable one since the Wilkes case), which brought over to Rockingham's group some independents, then — as disasters accumulated — the turncoats. The Rockinghams were anti-Court and anti-war — a rallying point for all who felt the weight of the 'present discontents'.

Charles Fox was the most considerable recruit who enlisted under the Rockingham banner. In 1775 Dowdeswell died ; his place in the Commons was filled by Fox. It was Fox, not the colourless Rockingham, who attracted men to the party. He built up his own following, independent of Rockingham but enlisted under his banner. The survival of Rockingham after 1775, like the survival of Newcastle after 1766, was incidental to the development of the party. Fox was the driving force; Rockingham the symbol of unity and aspiration.

Shelburne after 1768 was Chatham's closest disciple and eventually his political heir : he inherited and aggravated the dislike the Rockinghams had felt for his master. The anti-Chathamite tradition was hidden during the American war, but remained only just below the surface ; it oozed up every time the Court tried to negotiate with the opposition, and it burst out like a torrent in 1782. By conceding the primacy to Rockingham Shelburne enabled the two groups to work together for a few weeks, but when Rockingham died their collaboration was at an end. Rockingham's party was not dissolved by his death : so many of his followers owed allegiance primarily to Portland or Fox, and the anti-Chathamite tradition was by now the main force which bound them together.

There was much to keep Fox and Shelburne together in 1782, had they been guided by reason and policy. But the histories of parties, like the lives of men, cannot be written in terms of reason and policy : conscious and subconscious fears and jealousies influence groups as well as individuals. There

[1] Dowdeswell Papers.

were many factors at work in 1782–3 : Fox's personal dislike of Shelburne ; the resentment of men who, after sixteen years of opposition, had enjoyed office for only three months ; and the anti-Chathamite tradition. These were all turned against Shelburne.

The Fox-North coalition was much more than a piece of political chicanery on the part of men anxious for office. This unnatural coalition was really most natural — it gave expression to the deepest tradition in the Rockingham party, one which had governed it since 1766. The Rockinghams joined North to oust the successor of Chatham, just as they had been prepared to join Bedford and Grenville to oust Chatham himself. The comprehensive Administration, so eagerly desired in 1767, at last materialized in 1783 as the Fox-North coalition.

What of the King ? In 1783, as in 1767, the politicians forgot the King and ignored his wishes. Here is part of Shelburne's speech in the House of Lords on July 9, 1782, reported in *oratio obliqua* :

> These being his principles, it was, he said, natural for him to stand up for the prerogative of the Crown, and insist upon the King's right to appoint his own servants. If the power which others wished to assume, of vesting in the Cabinet the right of appointing to all places, and filling up all vacancies, should once be established, the King must then resemble the King of the Mahrattas, who had nothing of sovereignty but the name : in that case the monarchical part of the constitution would be absorbed by the aristocracy, and the famed constitution of England would be no more.[1]

We are back where we started : the British constitution in the eighteenth century was a combination of King, Lords, and Commons ; and in 1784, as in 1767, the power of the Crown was greater than the power of the parties.

---

[1] Fitzmaurice, *Life of Shelburne*, ii. 162-3.

# CHAPTER VIII

# THE ENTRY OF THE BEDFORDS

During the summer and autumn of 1767 the Rockingham party held a protracted post-mortem on the corpse of the comprehensive Administration. They finally concluded that it was not dead but in a state of suspended animation, and that it would revive once Parliament had met. In the course of this inquiry Rockingham's policy was challenged by Newcastle and Richmond, but accepted passively by the rest of his followers ; yet there was a feeling that somehow or other a great opportunity had been missed. Rockingham maintained constantly that he had been right, and since the only alternative policy — put forward by Richmond — was not acceptable to the party's 'shadow Cabinet', he won his point. But the return of the Bedfords to Court at the end of the year showed that he had badly misjudged both men and events.

Newcastle was the first to take up the attack : at seventy-four, and still unreconciled to retirement, he could not afford to see many opportunities thrown away. On July 25, 1767, when all was over, he wrote a long letter to Rockingham [1] complaining of the way the negotiation had been conducted and finally broken off. There was the familiar complaint of neglect — he was 'most sensibly mortified' because Rockingham had not visited Claremont before leaving for Yorkshire ('What an appearance it must have to the world !') — but beneath his peevishness was a foundation of sound sense. Fifty years' experience had not helped him to bear disappointment or to cease to fear neglect, though it had given him a shrewd insight into politics. 'When, if ever, all that has passed in this negotiation shall come to be known', he wrote, 'I flatter myself that those who are real friends to your Lordship

[1] Add. MS. 32984, ff. 36-42.

and this country will think that if my wishes had been followed it might have been better *for both*.' His criticisms were : that Rockingham's suspicions of Grenville's honesty and sincerity were excessive, and had been allowed to clog the negotiations ; and that Rockingham should not have insisted on Conway as Minister in the House of Commons.

Newcastle maintained that 'the declaration proposed by Mr. Grenville . . . was so whittled down by the Duke of Bedford that it could not *finally* have made any difficulty', and that Rockingham should have 'left all this altercation with Mr. Grenville to the Duke of Bedford'. He insisted that 'Conway's remaining the Minister in the House of Commons' was the 'great point' on which the negotiation broke down.

> When I heard of it [Newcastle wrote] it did indeed surprize me as much as it did the Duke of Bedford. I took the liberty then to tell your Lordship that I believed the Duke of Bedford would not agree to it. And also that I knew, and do know now, that some of your Lordship's best friends would not approve of it.

These were the Keppels : Albemarle had already told Rockingham that though they 'agreed that the Grenvilles did not mean that the negotiation should take place', yet 'wished it had broke off upon North America instead of Mr. Conway'.[1] Lastly —

> The great thing, my Lord, that hurt me the most was the strong declaration your Lordship made to the Duke of Bedford and his Grace's assent to it, that each party were at full liberty to take what part they pleased, without consulting or considering what the sentiments of the other party might be, and that your Lordship should acquaint the King with your having done so.

Rockingham was annoyed at this letter — not without reason — which he described as 'much too captious'.[2] Newcastle was a tiresome old man, and though Rockingham was

---

[1] Albemarle to Rockingham, July 23, 1767 ; Rockingham Papers, R1-533.
[2] Rockingham to Newcastle, July 25 or 26, 1767 (dated Saturday, July 26, which was a Sunday) ; Add. MS. 32984, ff. 49-53.

very patient his temper sometimes gave way. The remark
that many of his best friends disapproved of his insistence
on Conway was true, and hurt. He did not attempt a detailed
reply to Newcastle — he was just setting out for Yorkshire
— but defended his conduct in setting Bedford and Grenville
free 'from their declarations in regard to [the] comprehensive plan'. 'The Duke of Marlborough after the battle of
Hocksted', commented Newcastle to Mansfield on receiving
Rockingham's reply, 'could not be more vain of his conduct
than my Lord Rockingham . . . or expect more applause
from it.'[1]

Newcastle was not alone is his disagreement with Rockingham. Albemarle, though he would not complain openly but
preferred to insinuate his criticism, was deeply disappointed
at the failure to form a close alliance with the Bedfords, and
begged Rigby to assure the Duke of his 'constant regard and
attention to him and his family'.[2] Charles Yorke would have
gone far to reach agreement with Grenville : he told Hardwicke
that Newcastle was 'for taking Grenville along in *cordiality*',
and added, 'but he durst not speak out'. 'Your Lordship
knows', Yorke wrote, 'I have often talked *freely* to the Marquess
of Rockingham in that style in *private*.'[3] Richmond, on the
other hand, leant towards Conway and Grafton. 'As to the
Bedfords', he wrote to Newcastle on August 7, 'I must say I
saw, and was sorry to see that they were *then* entirely governed
by Mr. Grenville's politicks, and I think the surest way to have
got them would have been for the Marquis to have agreed with
the Duke of Grafton.'[4]

Throughout August Newcastle grumbled to his friends,[5]
and on September 11 wrote another long letter to Rockingham,[6]

---

[1] Newcastle to Mansfield, July 26, 1767 ; *ibid*. ff. 55-7.
[2] Albemarle to Rigby, July 23, 1767 ; *Bedford Correspondence*, iii. 387-9.
'Monday evening' should be 'Thursday evening'. The original (Woburn
MS., lv. f. 232) is docketed by Rigby : 'Buxton July 23d 1767 thursday
evening. Recd. the 24th.'
[3] Yorke to Hardwicke, July 27, 1767 ; Add. MS. 35362, ff. 139-42.
[4] Add. MS. 32984, ff. 208-9.
[5] See his letters to Portland (August 7), *ibid*. ff. 191-9 ; White (August
7), ff. 201-2 ; and to Albemarle (August 21), f. 307.
[6] Add. MS. 32985, ff. 72-80.

which he submitted in draft for Mansfield's opinion.¹ His disappointment had to some extent worn off, and he was consoled by 'a happy circumstance' — Grenville's friends had said '*that the three corps are not at all broke by what has passed*'. His criticisms had not changed (and he repeated them at great length), but he was now more concerned to look forward than backward, and thought there was a fair prospect for a comprehensive opposition. 'I have had a long letter from the Duke of Newcastle', wrote Rockingham to Dowdeswell on September 14, 'whose hurries and impatience and want of steadiness to adhere strictly to what in my judgment appears to be *one* of the fundamental principles ² on which we have acted perplexes me very much and requires full consideration.' ³

Characteristically, his apologia was addressed to Dowdeswell, from whom he could expect sympathy, rather than to Newcastle, his critic.⁴ It was both a survey of the past and a prospect of the future. 'Some difference of opinion among those who *we* denominate *our friends*', wrote Rockingham, 'in such uncertain times as the present is to be expected . . . but I hope no difference will ensue that could be so material as to become matter of rupture among ourselves'. He wished to restate 'the two fundamental principles' of the Rockingham party — opposition to Bute (*i.e.* Chatham) and opposition to Grenville, and believed the only difference could arise 'from variety of opinion in regard to the most probable mode of accomplishing those objects'.

To enter into any more discussion on these obvious principles is needless, but it may be right occasionally to

¹ Newcastle to Mansfield, September 4, 1767 ; *ibid.* ff. 13-15. Mansfield to Newcastle, September 5, 1767 ; *ibid.* ff. 21-2. Mansfield's comment was characteristic : 'If I advise I make it a point of honour . . . to examine what is proper for the person to whom I give the advice, not strictly what I would say or do. . . . I think your Grace's letter proper, honest, and wise. . . . I am not sure that it will please.'

² Opposition to Grenville.          ³ Rockingham Papers, R1-556.

⁴ Rockingham to Dowdeswell, September 9, 1767 ; *ibid.* R1-551. This is Rockingham's original letter, docketed by Dowdeswell. Rockingham's unfinished draft is *ibid.* R9-1. Rockingham's letters to Dowdeswell appear to have been returned after Dowdeswell's death ; there are a number of them in the Rockingham Papers, docketed in Dowdeswell's hand. In the Dowdeswell Papers are many of Dowdeswell's original letters to Rockingham.

resort to, to revive, and to fix these acknowledged principles in the minds of our friends, least from other new and more immediate motives of passion and resentment, they may lose sight of the original good foundation, and adopt and pursue a conduct on a line in which the publick may not be so ready to go along with them, and may attribute the motives not to be of publick service, but of private interest.

I firmly beleive that no set of politicians ever acted a more unbiassed part in point of interest than we and our friends have done, and as I firmly hope and trust we shall always adhere to it. Indeed we have generally been acting the part which time serving politicians conceived was not attended with any very pleasing *prospects*. You know I never disguised to our friends on trying occasions that I consider'd them as a forlorn hope, but that the maintenance of character and credit was in honour incumbent upon them, and would in the first place be a comfort to their own minds, and tho' it might appear improbable in present, yet it was not impossible but that such conduct would ultimately prove perhaps the better policy.

Was 'the maintenance of character and credit' all that Rockingham had to offer his party ? If so, it was a poor outlook for those who had other aims in politics and were not afraid of risking their 'character and credit' to attain them. Even Keppel, no astute politician, saw 'the inconveniences attending a protracted opposition from the craving demands of friends and dependents, who will very little enter into the motives of a conduct which stand between them and all their wants and expectations'.[1]

Such a policy did not suit Richmond. He feared 'that the corps which will neither unite with the other squadrons in opposition, nor accept the offers made by Administration, must, in the nature of things, be dissolved very speedily, and perhaps not very reputably'.[2] In a letter to Rockingham of October 4 [3] he posed a series of rhetorical questions which cut at the roots of Rockingham's policy.

[1] Burke to Rockingham, August 18, 1767 ; *Burke Correspondence*, i. 138-44.          [2] *Ibid.*          [3] Albemarle, ii. 59-63.

Is it not impossible to form a junction of the whole? Would there be places enough if the different politicks and passions of the parties could agree? Are not the Ministry distressed to keep, and the Bedfords distressed to gett, their places? Must not therefore each of them be ready to joyn your Lordship? If you cannot unite the whole, which should you preferr joyning with, in point of consistency as to measures and in point of prudence? First, as to security of their attachment to you; and, secondly, as to probability of success in the Closet? Have the present Ministry any favourite measures in view to which they require your compliance? Have the Bedfords none as to America, and are their notions of trade and foreign affairs likely to be submitted to your Lordship, particularly Mr. Grenville's? Is it most prudent to trust to the sincerity of Mr. Rigby, Lord Sandwich, Lord Gower, Lord Temple, and Mr. Grenville, or to the Duke of Grafton and General Conway? As to success in coming in, is it most likely to take place from a junction with Bedford House and the Grenvilles, or with the Duke of Grafton and Conway? Is not the King likely to do every thing he can to support the present Ministry against a junction of your Lordship with the Bedfords and Grenvilles? Cannot the present people hold out at least till the elections are over? Is it not a condition of the union with Bedford House that Conway shall not be the leader of the House of Commons? Is not this the very same point you broke upon before? Is not this plainly setting him aside as a Minister that you may have no House of Commons man to stand in competition with Mr. Grenville? Is the condition of the other side of keeping Lord Camden Chancellor, tho' bad enough, of so bad a tendency as this? Might not that condition now be withdrawn by the Court? If it was, are you very sure that Yorke is not already leaving you for Grenville? If you joyn the Bedfords and Grenvilles and of course separate from Conway, will they not outrate you in speakers both in the House of Lords and in the House of Commons? Can you suppose that a party which has the best speakers in both Houses will submit to remain inferiors to another party, and act in subordination or even upon an equality with it? Must not Conway or Grenville have the lead in the House of Commons now that

Townshend is no more ?  Can you believe that Grenville
will be Dowdeswell's second ?  If Grenville does support
Dowdeswell for a session, can it be supposed it will remain
so ?  Will not even his supporting Dowdeswell insensibly
gett the House of Commons to be his and not Dowdeswell's ?
Must not this end in Grenville's taking the lead himself ?
Who would then be Minister ?  Would he not in that situation require the powers of the House of Commons and
under that name ingross all those of the Treasury ?  Or
would your Lordship divide them with him ?  Would
Conway require any powers ?

If the support of Lord Bute's friends which you would
have if you join'd the present Ministers frightens you, I
suppose you mean never to come in but when you have them
in opposition to you.  If so I would ask your Lordship if
you think you can ever come in but by force ?  How long
may you think it will take to bring that about ?  Whether
when brought about you will not have the King in his heart
your enemy and hating you ?  Whether it is pleasant to be a
Minister in such a situation ?  Whether 'tis a safe situation,
when you can expect no other treatment than to be turned
out the first unpopular measure you are engaged in, and
cannot depend on your new friends for support ?  I come
now (and it is time) to my last question which I think is a
very material one.  Will you be most likely to carry with
you your friends in the City and those who are attached to
you from principle and opinions when you joyn with the
Bedfords and Grenvilles, or with the Duke of Grafton and
Conway ?

Richmond's   questions   remained   unanswered   when
Rockingham visited Goodwood on October 9.  'His mind is
not quite at ease', Rockingham wrote to Dowdeswell on
November 9, 'but I have no fears about him, tho' I think he
will have some difficulties now and then.'[1]  But Richmond
sank into one of his occasional fits of apathy, and showed
little interest in politics until roused by the excitement of
the Wilkes case in 1769.

[1] Rockingham Papers, R1-558.

(ii)

'For Godsake, my dear Lord, don't loose sight of the Duke of Bedford,' wrote Albemarle to Rockingham on July 23, 'I hope you have not parted upon such bad terms as to make your meeting again impossible or difficult.'[1] The Bedfords continued to occupy the pivotal position between the parties, and hopes of effective opposition remained centred on them. But Rockingham was not quite so keen on cultivating their alliance as he had been before the negotiations. 'I am very clear in opinion', he wrote to Newcastle on July 26, 'that it is right to keep up a good understanding with the Duke of Bedford and his friends, but I do not think that it is at all necessary to be too *courting*.'[2] He smarted from his disappointment : pride would not allow him to appear too eager when he believed himself as necessary to the Bedfords as they were to him. But Newcastle and Albemarle thought every opportunity should be taken to renew the alliance and smooth over any ill feeling or resentment. 'I am so sincere a well wisher to your Grace and your family', wrote Newcastle to Bedford on August 21, when congratulating the Duke on the birth of Lord Tavistock's posthumous son, 'that nothing can happen to your Grace in which I do not take a part.'[3] 'This welcome news made everybody happy at the races yesterday', wrote William Keppel to Bedford on August 22, 'and I thought once the Duke of Newcastle would have danced on the occasion.'[4] 'I don't repeat all the great attachment and violent love for the Duchess of Bedford and your Grace', wrote Rigby to Bedford about his conversation with Newcastle of October 11, 'suppose all that in the superlative degree and I may save myself the trouble of writing and you the reading it.'[5] Newcastle tried to live up to his protestations : he did all he could to support the interest of the Duchess's nephew, John Frederick Sackville, who was standing for Kent at the General Election ; flattered Rigby ; entertained the Duke and Duchess at Clare-

[1] Rockingham Papers, R1-533.      [2] Add. MS. 32984, ff. 49-53.
[3] Woburn MS., lvi. f. 52.      [4] *Ibid.* f. 56.
[5] Rigby to Bedford, October 12, 1767 ; *Bedford Correspondence*, iii. 391-4.

mont ; and pushed the Bedford alliance with Rockingham for all he was worth.

So did Albemarle : he made it his business to try to get Rockingham and Bedford talking again, but he knew that to hustle Rockingham would defeat his end. Neither he nor Newcastle seemed to consider that the Bedfords might have other and more hopeful plans than joining with Rockingham in opposition ; both thought that Conway was the only stumbling-block, and that Rockingham must be persuaded to give him up before any good could result. 'I have seen Rigby', wrote Albemarle to Newcastle on August 28,

> who is eager for opposition. . . . He has asked me, and *from himself*, if the Marquess was clear of Mr. Conway, and all connections with the present Administration, to which I could not give a positive answer. . . . It will be very necessary to have that point thoroughly known before any steps can be taken towards the renewal of a negotiation with the Duke of Bedford and his friends.[1]

Newcastle, who had a conversation with Bedford at Princess Amelia's house at Gunnersbury on September 4, found him

> in the very disposition . . . that every true friend of this country could wish . . . expressing the same ardent zeal for a most thorough *union and friendship* with *my Lord Rockingham* and instead of imagining that Mr. Grenville intended or wished to break off the negotiation with my Lord Rockingham mentioned some circumstances . . . that shew'd that G. Grenville was determined to acquiesce. . . .[2]

'In short,' he concluded, 'the single point is Mr. Conway ; if my Lord Rockingham waves that proposal of Mr. Conway's remaining Secretary of State and at the head of the House of Commons, I am very much mistaken if the Duke of Bedford does not make every thing else *easy*.'

There is a lack of direct evidence of what the Bedfords were thinking : most of the information comes from Albemarle or Newcastle, both of whom welcomed and magnified the

---

[1] Add. MS. 32984, f. 301.
[2] Newcastle to Portland, September 9, 1767 ; Add. MS. 32985, ff. 45-51.

slightest disposition towards union. There was little contact between Bedford and Grenville at this time ; Grenville had set out on a series of visits to friends in the country, and had no correspondence with either Bedford or Rigby until the approach of the new session of Parliament. Nevertheless, there are signs that the Bedfords wished to strengthen the link with Rockingham, and even indications of what were their motives.

The news of Rockingham's rejection of Conway's offer to come in with his friends alone had spread round the political world ; Whately heard of it from Mansfield on July 30,[1] and Walpole talked openly of it.[2] What would have been the Bedfords' position had Rockingham accepted ? Rigby admitted to Bessborough that 'he wished to have an employment'.[3] What if a fresh overture were to come from Conway and this time be accepted ? The Bedfords knew that some of Rockingham's followers wished to reunite with Grafton and Conway, and feared a renewal of the offer to Rockingham. They were very uneasy about Rockingham's partiality for Conway. Here is Newcastle's account to Portland of a conversation he had with Bedford and Rigby on September 7 :

> The Duke of Bedford and Rigby expressed the same wish and zeal for a most thorough union with us ; but they are under great apprehensions from something that Mr. Conway said to Major-General Keppel when he resigned his place of Equerry to the King. Conway said to him, What is this ? Opposition ? Keppel answer'd very well, I am too old and too heavy for a riding galloping Equerry. Conway said, *Opposition now — the door is open.* My Lord Rockingham and his friends may come in if they please.
>
> The Duke of Bedford is strongly of opinion that a young friend of our's and a near relation of his Grace's [4] is not a friend or well-wisher to the union between the Duke of

---

[1] Whately to Grenville, August 1, 1767 ; *Grenville Papers*, iv. 138-46.
[2] Whately to Grenville, August 20, 1767 ; *ibid.* 150-5.
[3] Newcastle to Princess Amelia, November 4, 1767 ; Add. MS. 32986, ff. 243-6.
[4] Lord John Cavendish. Their relationship was not so near. William, second Duke of Devonshire (grandfather of Lord John Cavendish) had married Rachel, daughter of William, Lord Russell (son of the first Duke of Bedford and grandfather of the fourth Duke).

Bedford and my Lord Rockingham ; and he thinks he has great weight with my Lord Rockingham. . . .

They also suspect that a regard and attention to the Duke of Richmond makes my Lord Rockingham more difficult about General Conway. I own I do not suspect that ; I thought it proceeded singly from the Marquess's regard for Conway himself, he thinking him a certain friend to him. If there should ever be a difference between my Lord Rockingham and the Duke of Bedford, and most eminently so whenever Mr. Grenville is in the question, and for that reason, I am afraid my Lord Rockingham will suspect Mr. Grenville to be concerned in every thing, whereas the way not to have him concerned is not to be always thinking about Mr. Grenville, but leaving him entirely to the Duke of Bedford's management.[1]

The Bedfords need not have worried. Rockingham, incensed at the account of the negotiations which Almon published in his *Political Register*, had thought of writing to Grafton to clear himself of the suspicion of having supplied the material for it. But (he wrote to Dowdeswell on September 9), 'It might be conster'd [construed] that I was paying Court'.[2] Rockingham would pay Court to neither Bedford nor Grafton.

Thus arose a game of cross-purposes. Rigby took advantage of Newcastle's and Albemarle's eagerness for a renewal of the alliance for his own ends. He encouraged their belief that Conway was the only obstacle and that the Rockinghams must make a clean break with the Court. At present there was no disposition on the part of Grafton to negotiate with opposition, but, when Parliament met, the need for allies would be felt : if the Rockinghams had broken with Conway, to whom could Grafton turn ? In the spring Rigby had urged the necessity of taking in Grenville : now he dropped all mention of him. When Rigby wished to oppose he turned to Grenville ; tiring of opposition, he neglected him. The signs were there, could Rockingham read them.

Rigby attempted to work upon Rockingham through Albemarle.[3] He began by 'lamenting that the negotiation

---

[1] Newcastle to Portland, September 9, 1767 ; Add. MS. 32985, ff. 45-51.
[2] Rockingham Papers, R1-551.      [3] *Ibid.*

broke off', assuring Albemarle 'that the Duke of Bedford was most strictly sincere in wishing success to it and exculpating himself as having been thought to have acted with too much partiality towards G. Greenvile in it'. Rockingham told Dowdeswell he believed Bedford was sincere (nothing was said about Rigby's sincerity). 'Rigby then wished that Lord Albemarle would set about opening a new communication between the Duke of Bedford' and Rockingham.

The preliminary of an union [wrote Rockingham] was to be a declaration of *my* and *our* having no communication with the present Administration, and a renuntiation of General Conway in particular was required. This done Rigby said the Duke of Bedford would be ready to converse and communicate and concert a plan for the operations of the ensuing campaign, and to try to agree on some leading points in regard to arrangements to take place whenever the opposition succeeded. Their idea of opposition was to be warm and well supported and to begin the very first day Parliament met.

But Rockingham was very cautious and determined not to be tricked. No mention was made of Grenville, and he also wanted to know whether the renunciation extended 'to all those who were usually called our old friends'. The position of those members of Rockingham's Ministry who had been allowed to remain in office with Chatham was peculiar : Rockingham had counted on them for his comprehensive Administration, but if he were now to league with Bedford against Conway and Grafton would he not lose their support ?

It becomes therefore [he continued] matter of consideration how far in the present moment this would be adviseable, and I think howsoever provocative the conduct of *our old friends* have been, yet some prudential consideration should be given, whether we in fact really gain anything essential, by sacrificing the remains of regard which may still exist in many of us for some or other of them.

I freely avow that even exclusive of other reasons from feelings — I think in case of any future arrangement taking place, *our old friends* might be useful as some strength to us against the weight which otherwise under different descriptions *G. Greenvillians* might be foisted into office.

He concluded that the best policy was 'rather to think than to act'. Union with Bedford would be 'very adviseable and very desireable', but was as necessary for the Bedfords as for the Rockinghams. In order 'to carry any of the public opinion along' with them, the appearance should rather be that the Bedfords acceded to the Rockinghams than vice versa. Rockingham had refused to enter office as junior partner to Grafton ; could it be expected that he would join with Bedford on any other terms than those of recognized pre-eminence ? But what if Grafton, instead of renewing his offer to Rockingham, were to make it to Bedford ? Which would the Bedfords choose — junior partnership to Grafton in office or to Rockingham in opposition ? Bedford could not expect many years of active political life — his eyesight was already so bad that he could barely see to write his name — and his followers were weary of opposition. Was it not his duty to make a bargain with the Court while his influence still had weight ? And would Rockingham, so full of scruples, make an effective partner in opposition ?

These considerations do not seem to have occurred to Rockingham : they may well have occurred to Rigby and Bedford.

(iii)

There were three clearly defined policies advocated in the Rockingham party during the autumn of 1767. Newcastle and Albemarle pressed for the Bedford alliance at the expense of Conway ; Richmond and the Cavendishes preferred an alliance with Conway and Grafton at the expense of the Bedfords ; while Rockingham and Dowdeswell trod the middle way — hoping for the Bedford alliance they were wary of Grenville, and not wishing to lose touch with Conway they would not go to Court without the Bedfords. Their policy prevailed : and the Rockinghams lost Conway without gaining Bedford.

At the end of July Burke had a conversation with Conway. Here is the account which he sent to Rockingham :

x

I never knew him talk in a more alert, firm, and decided tone. There was not the slightest trace of his usual diffidence and hesitation. He lamented your Lordship's mistake in not coming into Administration at this juncture. But, I declare, his conversation did, to me, more thoroughly justify your non-acceptance, than any thing I had heard, either from yourself or others, on that subject, as it laid open more clearly the ideas upon which they went in treating with you. Their plan, in short, was that your Lordship, with a few only of the chief of your friends, should take offices ; and that the rest should wait those vacancies which death, and occasional arrangements might make in a course of time. . . . I told him that your Lordship's opinion of the duty of a leader of party was to take more care of his friends than of himself ; and that the world greatly mistook you if they imagined that you would come in otherwise than in *corps* ; and that after you had thought your own whole bottom too narrow, you would condescend to build your Administration on a foundation still narrower ; and give up (for that it would be) many of your own people, in order to establish your irreconcilable enemies in those situations which had formerly enabled, and would again enable them to distress, probably to destroy you. That, beyond this, he was not less fond of a system of extermination than you were. I said a great deal, and with as much freedom as consisted with carrying on the discourse in good humour, of the power and dispositions of the Bute party, the use they had made of their power in your time, and the formidable increase and full establishment of that power, which must be the necessary consequence of the part which our former friends in office seemed just now inclined to take. This discourse had no sort of effect. The Bute influence had lost all its terrors. An apprehension of Grenville's coming in was the ostensible objection to every thing. Much moderation towards the King's friends, and many apologies for every part of their conduct. In the end he said (I think, directly, but I am sure in effect), that as long as the Duke of Grafton thought it for his honour to stay in, he could not resign.[1]

But what did Conway say ? More than three-quarters of Burke's account deals with his own share of the conversation,

[1] *Burke Correspondence*, i. 132-7.

and repeats the arguments which had been current in Rockingham's circle for months. Whom was he trying to convert? While condemning Conway's behaviour ('Conway is gone fairly to the Devil' [1]). Burke told Newcastle that Rockingham's honour was 'concerned in not dropping Mr. Conway . . . or suffering him to go out to the Army'.[2] He added that Rockingham was 'in the right in all the objections' he made to Grenville ; brushed aside Conway's 'apprehension of Grenville's coming in' ; yet censured Richmond's 'leaning to Conway' and 'dislike of the Grenvilles'. In short, Burke tied himself in knots in trying to make sense of Rockingham's irritation and *malaise*. His master's voice ! Or his master's parrot ?

Poor Conway ! For a brief time this ineffective man continued to be a key figure in politics, not because of his character, abilities, or influence, but rather through his vacillation and indecision and the failures of others — the breakdown of Chatham and the weakness of Grafton. How he longed to break through the chains of party and settle down in some quiet backwater of military administration ! When Lord Townshend was made Lord Lieutenant of Ireland in August 1767 Conway took his place as Lieutenant-General of the Ordnance, and continued to hold the seals of Secretary of State without the salary — but he did not thereby gain credit with the Rockinghams for disinterestedness.[3] 'Lord Albemarle and many of our friends', wrote Rockingham to Dowdeswell on September 9, 'are very much offended with General Conway's having continued in office. . . . My own thoughts are that General Conway's conduct has been both unfortunate for himself and for us and no one in particular was probably to be more affected by it than myself. . . .'

Meanwhile Conway, unable to persuade the Rockinghams

---

[1] Burke to Rockingham, August 18, 1767 ; *Burke Correspondence*, i. 138-44.

[2] Newcastle to Albemarle, September 29, 1767 ; Add. MS. 32984, f. 358.

[3] A scheme was on foot to make Conway Secretary of State for the Colonies, but the lawyers advised against it. (Walpole, *Memoirs*, iii. 69-71.) By 4 and 5 Anne, c. 8, the holder of a newly created office could not sit in the House of Commons : it was held that to divide the Southern Department would be to create a new office.

to come in as a party, seems to have resolved to offer places to individuals, probably less with a view of detaching them from Rockingham as in the hope of quieting his conscience and softening their animosity.  At the end of August he offered the embassy to Russia to Lord George Lennox, Richmond's brother ;[1] it was refused, and Richmond apparently did not inform Rockingham.  But a similar invitation to a more considerable person could not be kept quiet, and only further provoked the Rockinghams.

Burke had warned Rockingham on August 1 that Lord Edgcumbe was 'wofully impatient', and had suggested that a word from Rockingham 'to set the matter to rights, as to the rupture of both negotiations, might be useful with regard to him'.  But Rockingham apparently did nothing : in spite of the fuss made about Edgcumbe in November 1766 he was only on the fringe of the party.  In October 1767 Conway offered to make Edgcumbe joint Paymaster-General :  Edgcumbe was about to accept but was dissuaded by Bessborough, 'who let him understand that his friends who had resigned on his account could never forgive his accepting'.[2]  Edgcumbe, wrote Bessborough to Newcastle on October 22,

was convinced by the G[eneral]'s letter that there would not be any opposition *from our friends*, till he received my letter to the contrary.  Had that been the case I see no sort of objection to his taking an employment, for all would be open and every man might shift for himself as well as he could, and of course strengthen the present Ministry as much as they could desire.  I believe some of our friends that talked in that idle way (of there being no opposition intended) to the General, did not see the consequences.  I hope nothing of that kind will happen again.  It certainly was the most impolitical conversation that could be to a Minister, and what most naturally he would make use of, which was the case, and was upon the brink of succeeding, for there was a pretty strong inclination in our friend to accept.[3]

[1] *H.M.C., Bathurst MSS.*, p. 695.
[2] Whately to Grenville, November 5, 1767 ;  *Grenville Papers*, iv. 183-7.
[3] Add. MS. 32986, ff. 82-3.

The Rockinghams were virtuously indignant at Conway's behaviour. Burke 'was outrageous with Mr. Conway for the means he had used to draw in poor Lord Edgecombe'; [1] Keppel's 'language was violent and spirited opposition, with great virulence against Conway, for whom, however, he said the Cavendishes have still a strange partiality'; [2] Saunders said Edgcumbe 'ought to have asked Mr. Conway what reason he had to think him a scoundrel'.[3] After all this Rockingham's comment was mild: 'it does not do General Conway much honour according to the opinion of many'.[4]

Edgcumbe's eagerness to accept was so patent that the Rockinghams had no reason to hope that he would remain with them very long. In 1770 he returned to office as joint Vice-Treasurer of Ireland, and broke off all connection with Rockingham.

(iv)

There can be little doubt that Grafton was sincere when he told Lady Chatham on July 31 that he only remained in office 'in order to wait the return of Lord Chatham to the head of affairs'.[5] But how long would he have to wait? Chatham's condition held out no hopes of an early recovery. Here is a letter written on August 5 by Thomas Nuthall, Chatham's friend and solicitor, to Camden:

I found the Earl of Chatham in his garden, and had some conversation with her Ladyship before he came in, to whom I delivered your message; she desired me to inform your Lordship, that from the time of the last attack about three weeks ago, when there was a necessity of letting blood twice, Lord Chatham had never been so well as he had been before, that he had now a good deal of fever upon him and was extremely weak and nervous, yet Mr. Graham, his apothecary, had assured her yesterday that he saw no danger, but on the contrary was satisfied he would get well, tho' it would be a work of time. This your Lordship sees is

[1] Newcastle to Princess Amelia, November 4, 1767; *ibid.* ff. 243-6.
[2] Whately to Grenville, November 5, 1767; *Grenville Papers*, iv. 183-7.
[3] *Ibid.*
[4] Rockingham to Dowdeswell, September 9, 1767; Rockingham Papers, R1-558.          [5] Grafton, *Autobiography*, p. 154.

the old tale, but upon viewing attentively and conversing with Lord Chatham I think I see a visible alteration for the worse, his hands tremble more, he is paler and thinner in the face, and I am persuaded much emaciated in his body and thighs within these three weeks since I saw him last, and on talking over some particulars of the estate he was more than once bewildered, and say'd his head was so much confused that he scarcely knew what subject he was speaking upon, and there were two or three things I could not make him understand, wch. her Ladyship cut short by saying she did, and would explain to him another time. His Lordship beg'd I would present his most affectionate wishes to you, and was glad you had got over the fatigue of business. When we were alone, he fell into a desponding strain, and say'd he now saw it impossible he should be well, that he was in a fever all over him ; he desired me to feel his hand, wch. was very hot and dry indeed. Upon the whole I am satisfied he is very much worse, and in my opinion dangerously ill. He is miserable beyond conception in his own mind with respect to his state of health, and I should not wonder if he should soon sink under this horrid dejection of spirits. I promised to tell your Lordship the whole truth, tho' truly sorry I am to relate it.[1]

Camden sent this letter to the King, who commented : 'the seeing a man that has appeared in so very great a light fall into such a situation is an abasement of human nature'.[2]

In August Chatham was advised to go into Somerset ; and Grafton was compelled, against his inclination and temperament, to assume responsibility as head of the Ministry.

Administration had seemed at the beginning of July to be falling to pieces. But by negotiating with the opposition groups it had gained a tactical victory : the attempt to form a new Administration had been too much for their apparent unity. The combined opposition was dissolved ; the meeting of Parliament was four months away ; and Grafton had time to take stock of the new situation. His first task was to

[1] Camden MSS. I owe this reference to the kindness of Sir Lewis Namier. The letter is dated 'Wednesday, 5 o'clock' ; the King's letter of August 6, 1767 (Fortescue, I, no. 552), shows that it was written on August 5.
[2] Ibid.

strengthen his Ministry by taking in part of the opposition. Fortune, and the blindness of the Rockinghams, favoured him.

Though Townshend had not been consulted during the negotiations, and though it had been clearly demonstrated that his standing was not as great as Conway's, his prospects in the summer of 1767 seemed favourable.    It was plain that Conway would not long remain Secretary of State, and Townshend seemed his obvious successor.    In August his wife was created a peeress, and his brother made Lord Lieutenant of Ireland. But he did not long enjoy these favours or this pleasing prospect, for he died on September 4.

'The amazing abilities', wrote Rockingham, 'joined to a manner and to a good humour which made everything so agreable in Mr. Townshend's conversation, will make his loss irreparable to those who from alliance or from friendship had frequent opportunities of enjoying his company.' [1]   A naïve and superficial judgment.  'As a man of incomparable parts', wrote Walpole with more insight, 'and most entertaining to a spectator, I regret his death . . . but in a political light, I own I cannot look upon it as a misfortune.  His treachery alarmed me, and I apprehended everything from it.  It was not advisable to throw him into the arms of the opposition. His death avoids both kinds of mischief.' [2]   In the shifting politics of the early years of George III's reign Townshend had shown his untrustworthiness and want of judgment : they were not the least of the difficulties the Court had to face in consequence of Chatham's illness.  His death was a fortunate event for Administration :  it removed the main source of unrest in the Cabinet.

Walpole took it for granted that North would now become Chancellor of the Exchequer, and Grafton seems to have thought of no one else.  In his *Autobiography* [3] he justified his choice as that of 'the person Lord Chatham desired to bring to that high post'.  It was true that he did — but not as the stepping-stone to the Treasury.  North was summoned to

---

[1] Written in Rockingham's hand on a loose sheet of paper ; Rockingham Papers, R78-40b.
[2] Walpole to Conway, September 9, 1767.               [3] P. 166.

London; pressed by Grafton and the King to accept, but declined.[1] His reasons seem to have been genuine unwillingness to accept ministerial responsibility (it was apparently understood that the offer extended to a seat in the Cabinet [2]), and concern at his father's poor state of health.

'In a hurrying moment' Grafton offered the Exchequer to Lord Barrington, Secretary at War, an experienced and able administrator rather than a politician, and not of Cabinet rank, who 'accepted the offer through duty and gratitude to his Majesty'.[3] But on September 10 North told Grafton that his father's health was much improved; if there was 'any real difficulty in disposing of the seals' he was 'ready to obey any call from his Majesty', although he preferred to remain where he was.[4] Barrington yielded willingly. Since Conway was so ill at ease, and Granby and Hawke, the other commoners in the Cabinet, sat only in right of their departments, North seemed also to have the reversion of the lead in the Commons.

North had entered Parliament in 1754, and first held office under Newcastle as a Lord of the Treasury. He had served under Bute and Grenville without attaching himself to either, but had refused office from Rockingham. He was a frequent speaker in the Commons, a useful man in minor office, but not hitherto considered as ambitious of, or suitable for, high office. He soon came to win the respect of the House; his steadiness, good humour, and coolness in the face of criticism carried him through the difficult session of 1769, and established him as a successful leader of the Commons. As a Minister he had the knack of selecting able subordinates; but his dilatoriness and his chronic indecision at times of crisis, as yet unper-

[1] Grafton to the King, September 9, 1767; Fortescue, I, no. 556. The King to Grafton, September 9, 1767. Grafton MS. 507.

[2] North was at this time joint Paymaster-General, an office of standing and emolument, but not of ministerial responsibility. The Chancellor of the Exchequer had hitherto been no higher in the ministerial hierarchy, and was not hitherto in the Effective Cabinet. From 1767 this became normal practice. But when the First Lord of the Treasury was a commoner he continued to hold the office of Chancellor of the Exchequer: Peel in 1841 was the first who did not, and as late as 1880 Gladstone held the two offices at the same time.

[3] Grafton, *Autobiography*, pp. 166-7.    [4] *Ibid.* p. 167.

ceived, made him totally unfit for the supreme direction of affairs.

(v)

In the middle of September Rockingham assembled a 'conciliabulum' of his chief advisers at Wentworth, to consider what line to take towards the Bedfords.[1]  Portland recommended that Conway should be dropped, and that discussions should be opened with the Bedfords.  He told Newcastle that he found Rockingham 'in the very disposition . . . his real friends could have desired'.[2]

Conway was given up by everybody [wrote Portland] fully and explicitly, except Lord J. Cavendish who was silent. A desire of union, nay even the necessity of union was as strongly urged, a general free unlimited communication of plans and intentions with regard to proceedings in Parliament deem'd equally necessary and adviseable, and in short every preliminary agreed to that might engage the Duke of Bedford and his friends, and prove to them our wishes of uniting and becoming a corps.  A considerable employment was talk'd of for G. Grenville, and I rather think Lord Rockingham himself mention'd and certainly acquiesced in the idea of the Cabinet for Mr. Grenville, with or without an office.

Towards the end of the month Rockingham went to Newmarket for the races, hoping also to have some conversation with Rigby and Gower.  'You will neither see Lord Gower nor Rigby', wrote Albemarle on September 24, 'but you will see the Duke of Grafton.  Beware of him, they are baiting the trap for you that they have got in themselves.'[3]  But Rockingham found 'very little politics stirring at Newmarket';[4] and in the interval between the two race meetings he visited his

[1] Dowdeswell, John Cavendish, Portland, and Burke attended, and there may have been others.  Dartmouth was invited (Rockingham to Dartmouth, August 15, 1767; *H.M.C.*, 13th Report, Appendix 10, p. 57) but apparently did not come.  Newcastle was not invited.

[2] Portland to Newcastle, October 20, 1767; Add. MS. 32986, ff. 58-60.

[3] Rockingham Papers, R2-56.

[4] Rockingham to Newcastle, October 1, 1767; Add. MS. 32985, ff. 306-307.

party colleagues, calling on Albemarle, Newcastle, Bessborough, and Richmond.

Albemarle, who was going abroad for his health, wished to pay his respects to Bedford at Woburn ; and to take the opportunity to reopen political discussions. Newcastle complained that he went 'but half charged' ;[1] his instructions were that Conway was not to be given up 'with precipitation', and 'a digested plan of arrangements' was not to be discussed since it 'would be attended with much danger of offence to individuals'.[2] The Bedfords were to be kept at arm's length.

Upon the full discussion of what appeared [wrote Rockingham to Dowdeswell on November 9] and the particular time in which the hurry was — that we were to be desired to be explicit, it did occur that there was a possibility it might arise from its being then thought (on Charles Townshend's decease) that some *overtures* might again come *to us* and that therefore there was some policy in the wish at that time to get us to be active in shutting the door against ourselves, being the persons most probable to be applied to, or indeed into whose hands a negotiation from some part of Administration was most likely to be thrown.

Albemarle went to Woburn on October 3, but nothing resulted from his visit : the conversation was confined to generalities and platitudes. Bedford, Albemarle wrote to Newcastle on October 4,

did not think it adviseable to talk of any arrangements now, that it would weaken the opposition, as it would disgust some part or other of it, that the Treasury was the great and material object, which should be determined by the King. I said that I hoped that choice would fall upon the Marquess of Rockingham, and that Mr. Dowdeswell would be his Chancellor and leader of the House of Commons, and that I was persuaded if that was the case every thing else would be easily settled, that I was afraid nothing else would do. His Grace closed the conversation by saying that he hoped we should all go into opposition.[3]

[1] Newcastle to Bessborough, October 4, 1767 ; *ibid*. f. 343.
[2] Rockingham to Dowdeswell, November 9, 1767 ; Rockingham Papers, R1-558.
[3] Albemarle to Newcastle, October 4, 1767 ; Add. MS. 32985, f. 360.

Rockingham did not seem disappointed : while Albemarle cried 'Forward' and Richmond cried 'Back',[1] he probably thought it best to stay where he was, a policy that suited his own convictions and character. He still believed that the Bedfords danced to Grenville's tune, and that until they repudiated him nothing could be done. He wrote to Burke on October 31 : 'I have no idea that the Duke of Bedford will take any step in that matter but just merely according to the directions he may receive from George Grenville'.[2] And to Dowdeswell on November 9 :

> I think if it appeared to many of the *Bedfordians* that G. G. was a bad game it would be the first step towards a real union with us, and I am not without hopes that with some management the Bedfordians may be learn't to think that G. G. and Ld. T. were (as I have always insisted) the cause of the late negotiation not taking effect.[3]

Meanwhile, Rigby continued to press the need for vigorous opposition, but found little enthusiasm outside the ranks of the converted. On October 11 he visited Claremont.

> I told the Duke of Newcastle [he wrote to Bedford on October 12] that it was my opinion we shou'd all unite in opposition to this Ministry, if we mean to shew the world that we really thought them so insufficient and incapable as we were fond of saying we did, and take our chance for the consequences in case we succeeded so as to drive them out ; that we had given sufficient proofs to shew we were tractable and reasonable, and that it lay upon them to give at least such a proof as uniting in opposition with us, which would still be far short of the sacrifice we had made.[4]

To Bessborough he went even further.

> Mr. Rigby told my Lord Bessborough in decent terms, 'That he owned he (Rigby) wished to have an employment ; it would be very convenient for him ; but that he would not accept one but upon honourable terms with his friends ; that he most earnestly wished a most cordial union between the Duke of Bedford and our friends ; that in case there

---

[1] See above, p. 300.  [2] Rockingham Papers, R153-1.
[3] *Ibid.* R1-558.  [4] *Bedford Correspondence*, iii. 391-4.

was such a union once made he (Rigby) would not only for himself but he would engage that the Duke of Bedford and his friends should and would give up Mr. Grenville and remain thoroughly united with us, in case Mr. Grenville should not behave as he ought to do, or give any just cause of complaint'.[1]

But Rockingham was content to let events take their course. He did not have long to wait.

## (vi)

There had been no contact between Bedford and Grenville during the summer : they had not seen each other, nor do they appear to have exchanged letters. Neither had Rigby tried to keep in touch with Grenville. But as the meeting of Parliament approached, Bedford tried to pick up the threads. On November 5 he wrote to Grenville, regretting he had not been able to see him and hoping for an opportunity 'of talking fully . . . on the present state of political affairs and of the steps it may be proper to take at the beginning of the ensuing sessions'.[2]  Grenville, never reluctant to explain his 'thoughts on the present state of political affairs', did so at his accustomed length and with his accustomed flatness.[3]  Peace must be maintained ;  Administration should be 'settled, moderate, and frugal' ;  'the lawful authority of the King and Parliament' should be asserted 'over every part of our dominions in every part of the world' ;  right measures could not be taken 'until the King's mind be possessed with a serious conviction of the danger, or the people be brought to open their eyes on the brink of a precipice before they fall into it'.  'My plan however', he concluded, 'will be at all events to acquit myself of what I owe to them, and to my friends, as well as to my own character and opinions, but I believe that our attendance will be very thin in the House of Commons, from a variety of circumstances.'

[1] Newcastle to Princess Amelia, November 4, 1767 ;  Add. MS. 32986, ff. 243-6.                    [2] *Bedford Correspondence*, iii. 394-5.
[3] Grenville to Bedford, November 6, 1767 ;  *ibid.* pp. 396-9.

Little inspiration could be drawn from these banalities. It was clear that Grenville meant to take his own line, independent of Bedford, Rockingham, or the Court, without any regard to political expediency. On November 21 he saw Bedford in London, and his diary records :

> Mr. Grenville came to town ; saw the Duke of Bedford in the evening, whose language was most perfectly friendly to him, and agreeing entirely in his political ideas, but taking no notice whatever of the last letter he wrote to his Grace from Wotton.[1]

Parliament met on November 24. Bedford, according to Keppel, was 'very hostile to the present Administration' ;[2] Rockingham inclined to 'some demonstration' to show his party was 'not quite in so passive a disposition as has been industriously propagated'.[3] Yet he had neglected to send out his 'summonses for attendance'. The 'demonstration' took the form of (in Conway's words [4]) 'a very insignificant amendment' to the Address, regretting there was no mention in the King's Speech of measures to increase trade. The Rockinghams hoped by this to show that they meant vigorous opposition, and the topic had been chosen as one which could give no offence to the Bedfords (or, indeed, to anyone). But Grenville was in no mood for trifling ; seizing upon a reference in Dowdeswell's speech, he launched out into a full-blooded denunciation of the Rockinghams' American policy. There is in the Newcastle Papers a document which purports to give 'the substance, tho' not the words' of what Grenville said.[5] Grenville,

> after declaring his sentiments about America, and of the necessity of enforcing (supposed to mean by some new Act) the superiority of this country over the colonies ; that there were persons of contrary sentiments (turning his eyes towards Mr. Dowdeswell) whom he never would support in power

---

[1] *Grenville Papers*, iv. 232. Grenville's last letter was of November 6, quoted above.
[2] Keppel to Newcastle, November 19, 1767 ; Add. MS. 32987, f. 37.
[3] Rockingham to Newcastle, November 22, 1767 ; *ibid*. ff. 75-6.
[4] Conway to the King, November 24, 1767 ; Fortescue, I, no. 566.
[5] Add. MS. 32987, f. 113.

or cooperate with ; and that he would hold the same distance from them that he would from those who opposed the principles of the Revolution.

This to Rockingham was the last straw — a confirmation of all he had felt about Grenville. 'It is no comfort to me', he wrote to Newcastle in the early hours of November 25, 'to have had this full proof that my ideas had not been ill founded for some time past.' [1]   Many of his friends, he claimed, were 'hurt and warm with what Mr. Grenville had done' ; they complained also that the Bedfords had neither repudiated Grenville nor defended Dowdeswell ; and called for 'a most full and explicit declaration and explanation from the Duke of Bedford's friends on this matter'.

In the evening of November 24 Rockingham saw Weymouth (who told him he intended to move in the Lords to consider the state of the nation), and pointed to the indignation and anger Grenville's speech had aroused among his friends. Weymouth's defence, though probably sincere, was not considered satisfactory.

> Ld. Weymouth said [wrote Rockingham to Dowdeswell on November 25] that he was not informed what George Greenvile had said in the House — that there was always much distinction to be made between what G. G. did and what they (the D. of Bedford's friends) did. That they were separate corps — that Mr. G. might have ill blood towards *us* — which was entirely contrary to their wishes and system and upon the whole seem'd in a good deal of concern.[2]

Rockingham also saw Rigby that evening — 'he seemed rather to avoid conversation'. Perhaps he was thinking of something else.

On November 25 the Rockinghams met in council, and drew up a paper which Newcastle was to communicate to Bedford.

> The Duke of Newcastle will complain to the Duke of Bedford of Mr. Grenville's hostile speech, declaring he

[1] Add. MS. 32987, ff. 87-8.
[2] Rockingham Papers, R1-559. The letter was written in the early hours of November 25, but dated by Rockingham November 24.

would have nothing to do with us ; and of the want of support from the Duke of Bedford's friends to Mr. Doweswell's motion. It will be necessary to know the Duke of Bedford's thoughts and resolutions upon that declaration of Mr. Grenville before we can determine our conduct.

As to my Lord Weymouth's motion, the Duke of Newcastle can say nothing till we know upon what points they intend to go.[1]

Newcastle did not expect much from his conversation with Bedford. 'I shall see the Duke of Bedford this morning', he wrote to Sir William Baker on November 26, 'but I despair of any good being done.'[2] What did the Rockinghams expect Bedford to say ? It seems that nothing would have satisfied them short of a complete break with Grenville.

On November 26 Newcastle saw Bedford and 'read the paper over distinctly'. Here is his account of their conversation :

As to Mr. Grenville's speech, and particularly that of the second day,[3] which he had heard was much the worst, his Grace said that he entirely disapproved it, thought it very wrong in prudence and in every light ; but that Mr. Grenville justified himself by the declaration which he understood my Lord Rockingham had made against him at Newmarket.[4] That if my Lord Rockingham would say anything to the Duke of Bedford to explain that supposed declaration in any manner that could be satisfactory he (the Duke of Bedford) would undertake to talk strongly to Mr. Grenville, and should then have good grounds to go upon ; and that if then Mr. Grenville should act in an improper manner he

---

[1] Add. MS. 32931, ff. 270-1. This document, and some others concerning this affair, have been misplaced among Newcastle's papers, and appear in a volume for 1761. There is a slightly longer version of this paper, headed 'Paper proposed by D. of N.', in Add. MS. 32987, f. 111.

[2] *Ibid.* f. 125.

[3] On November 25 Grenville had aggravated his offence by engaging in 'a hot altercation with Dowdeswell and Burke on their different ideas of what ought to be done with respect to America'. (Walpole, *Memoirs*, iii. 84.)

[4] Lyttelton, in a letter to Temple of November 25, 1767, wrote that Bedford had said 'that Lord Rockingham was stark mad, that he had told the Duke of Bridgewater, who talked to him about a union with his friends, *that he would hear of nothing in which there was a Grenville*'. (Phillimore, *Memoirs and Correspondence of Lord Lyttelton*, pp. 734-41.)

(the Duke of Bedford) would not support him in it, and that his Grace would exert all his weight to bring about a thorough union and concert with us.

That as to Mr. Rigby and his friends not speaking, he thought they did very wrong ; tho' Mr. Dowdeswell's motion had not been communicated to them [1] he thought it was very right and should have been supported by Mr. Rigby : but Mr. Rigby's excuse was that Wedderburn had spoke so well that there was nothing left for him to say ; that Mr. Rigby and some of George Grenville's own friends, particularly Mr. Wilbraham the lawyer and Mr. Gray of Colchester,[2] did all they could to prevail with him not to speak, but Mr. Grenville was obstinate.

That as to future arrangements it was pretty clear that if our joint party should prevail the King would certainly chuse my Lord Rockingham for his Treasury, and in that case they (meaning Mr. Grenville) would acquiesce in it.

The Duke of Bedford was extremely civil and cordial to me, and hoped that in all events (meaning whether we agreed or not in publick affairs) the same intimacy, friendship, and cordiality would remain between us two, of which I assured his Grace in the strongest manner that that was my wish and intention, but that at the same time I was sure that his Grace neither wished nor expected that I should leave my old friends with whom I had hitherto constantly acted. To which he replied he had never such a thought, but wished only that sometimes I would exert myself a little more with them.

That as to my Lord Weymouth's motion when the time for the consideration of it came on, he proposed that each side should acquaint the other what they intended to bring on : but did not think that we were yet upon a foot to come to previous concerts at the first setting out.[3]

[1] According to Rockingham, he had asked Keppel to inform Bedford of Dowdeswell's amendment. (Draft of a letter by Rockingham probably to Albemarle, written after November 25, 1767 ; Rockingham Papers, R5-28.)

[2] Randle Wilbraham (M.P. for Newton, Lancs) and his son-in-law, Charles Gray (M.P. for Colchester). They were listed as Tories by both Newcastle and Rockingham : their connection with Grenville was not of a party nature.

[3] 'Substance of what passed this morning with the Duke of Bedford', November 26, 1767 ; Add. MS. 32931, ff. 289-92.

Rockingham seemed quite satisfied with this. 'Upon the whole state of what has passed', he wrote to Newcastle in the early hours of November 27, 'I can not but see the improbability of that junction between the Duke of Bedford's friends and ours, which we have so long wished, and to attain which we have taken such pains and acted so fairly.' 'But if after all', he concluded, 'such is the ascendancy of Mr. Greenvile it may be happy that we see it now rather than it should have appeared some time later, when after acting together and an increasing appearance of thorough cordiality we might have felt a reverse — the severer from being less to be expected.' [1]

By November 27 the break was complete. Newcastle drafted a letter to Bedford, but Bedford called on him that morning and Newcastle read him the letter. Here are the relevant paragraphs :

I take the liberty to acquaint you that I have made a very faithful report to my Lord Rockingham and some of his friends of what passed in the conversation I had the honor to have with your Grace the other day, and have nothing to trouble your Grace with that seems to me the least material upon it ; and have consequently now only to lament the ill success of all my endeavours.

I have desired my Lord Rockingham and must desire your Grace to excuse me from giving either of you any farther trouble upon a point in which I see I can be of no service. I always fear'd that Mr. Grenville's hostile speeches would have this consequence. I heartily wish any expedient could have been found, but I do not see any probability of it.[2]

And here is Newcastle's account of the conversation which followed :

He took it with much more coolness and temper than I could have expected ; and instead of flying out he was for going on and seeing whether we could not agree in measures, and by that defeat the present Administration ; and tho' he often said he looked upon the union as over, he as often shew'd a strong inclination not to understand it so.

He assured me in the strongest manner that there was no inclination or intention in the Committee upon the State

[1] Add. MS. 32987, ff. 119-20.    [2] Add. MS. 32931, ff. 301-2.

Y

of the Nation to bring on any fresh affair relating to America which could possibly be disagreeable to us ; he said it was not so he was sure, but what it may be now after the breach he could not say, tho' he would answer for himself and his friends — Lord Gower, Lord Weymouth, the Duke of Bridgewater, and I think he named Lord Sandwich — what others may do he could not tell.

The Duke of Bedford seem'd extremely to wish that we might act together in measures against this Administration, which might produce that union he so much desired.[1]

This was Newcastle's last political transaction in a career which had spanned the years from Queen Anne to George III. And though the poor old man had faithfully carried out the instructions given him by Rockingham, he could not escape giving offence.

I must decline meddling [wrote Keppel to Newcastle on November 27] or appearing in any thing that may be disagreable to the Duke of Bedford, I mean in regard to any thing that may be offer'd for his consideration, and I cou'd have wish'd your Grace had not thought it necessary to mention my name as one of those assembled in your room, when it was wish'd some questions might be put to the Duke of Bedford.[2]

The comprehensive Administration died hard.

### (vii)

From the end of July circumstances had been shaping for the Bedfords' return to Court. The comprehensive Administration had been tried and failed ; the Rockinghams would not come in except to form a new Administration ; Grenville was unacceptable to the King ; only the Bedfords remained. They now found there were no hopes of a vigorous and united opposition. Who shall blame them for tendering their services to the Court ? And who shall blame Grafton for accepting ?

Yet it seems that Bedford was prepared to continue in opposition until the flare-up between Rockingham and

---

[1] 'Substance of what passed with the Duke of Bedford this day', November 27, 1767 ; Add. MS. 32931, f. 303.
[2] Add. MS. 32987, ff. 135-6.

Grenville finally convinced him of its futility. His decision was quickly taken : on November 27 Weymouth moved in the Lords to consider the state of the nation (which hardly suggested the Bedfords were tired of opposition), and on November 29 Conway told Walpole that they had made an offer to the Court.[1] It was conveyed indirectly, by Lord Upper Ossory to Hugo Meynell.[2] Perhaps the Bedfords knew that it would be favourably received.

The story of these negotiations is obscure. They were conducted orally, and there are few documents to indicate the course they took. Grafton's account[3] was written from memory forty years after the event, and is (like other parts of his *Autobiography* not based on correspondence or memoranda) vague and general. The best source is the account given by Walpole in his *Memoirs*.[4] Yet though the details are obscure, the main issues are clear.

The Bedfords asked for Cabinet offices for Gower and Weymouth, and a place for Rigby ; the claims of other followers were to be the subject of negotiations. Grafton had no difficulty in meeting these demands : Northington was anxious to retire, and only remained in office at Grafton's request ; while Conway, equally anxious to retire, could not well object to the admission of the Bedfords after Rockingham had refused the most pressing offers. Nor did Grafton haggle about the other terms : he was not the man to drive a hard bargain, and the Bedfords were not more eager to come in than he was to welcome them.

By December 4 the negotiations had reached the point where Bedford felt he must prepare Grenville for the parting. He seemed ill at ease : he began by complimenting Grenville, and then gave a disarming and deceptive account of the state of the negotiations.[5] Bedford said

that as to himself he would never come into office again, but that possibly some of his friends might wish to take

---

[1] Walpole, *Memoirs*, iii. 84.
[2] Walpole says that Bedford asked 'that it should never be known if no treaty was concluded'. (*Ibid.* 87.)
[3] *Autobiography*, pp. 171-3.　　　　　　　　[4] iii. 84-101.
[5] Grenville's Diary, December 4, 1767 ; *Grenville Papers*, iv. 236-8.

offices with the present set of Ministers, for that he did
verily believe the interior of the Court and the general
distress must necessarily bring on some proposition either
to the Rockingham party, Mr. Grenville and Lord Temple's,
or his own ; that he thought it a fair proceeding towards
Mr. Grenville to apprize him (and, through him, Lord
Temple, with whose behaviour towards him and his friends
he had much reason to be satisfied) that in the latter case
his friends should think themselves at liberty to take offices,
as, on the other hand, should the proposition come to Mr.
Grenville, he would likewise be free to act in that case as he
should think best.

Grenville received the news calmly and with dignity ; said

he never would in any shape whatever be forced upon the
King ; that he should ever make measures his point, more
than men ; that he wished no men to make any sacrifice of
their wishes or pretensions to him ; that he left his Grace
and his friends entirely at liberty to take what part they
pleased, as he and his were likewise.

'They parted with great civility. . . .'

Grenville had no reason to consider this communication
as confidential ; he told Whately about it the same day ;[1]
and soon the news spread around the town.  West had got a
hint of it by December 7 ;[2] and on December 9 Onslow was
boasting to Newcastle 'that all opposition seems at present to
be broke to pieces'.[3]  Newcastle had not been in good health,
and had gone to Bath.  Rockingham did not find it easy to
break the news to him : perhaps he feared Newcastle's
recriminations at his own errors of judgment.[4]  On December
10 he wrote to Newcastle.[5]  The first part of his letter dealt
with election affairs ; then in the middle occurs this passage :

Thus far my letter is not unpleasant to me to write or will
I hope be unpleasant to your Grace to receive.

[1] Whately to Grenville, December 4, 1767 ;  Grenville (J. M.) MSS.
[2] West to Newcastle, December 7, 1767 ;  Add. MS. 32987, ff. 192-3.
[3] *Ibid.* ff. 218-19.
[4] Albemarle, who was abroad and had not received the news, wrote to
Newcastle on December 13 : 'I am afraid the Bedfords are too strongly
attached and connected with G. Grenville to entertain any hopes of dividing
them'.  (*Ibid.* f. 254.)                    [5] *Ibid.* ff. 222-5.

I must now open to your Grace an information on the subject of politicks, and I do beg of your Grace not to torment yourself about it. What I send you is not *absolutely* certain but from various circumstances highly probable.

After giving the news that the Bedfords were negotiating with the Court, he concluded :

Think only upon subjects that please you and don't let any awkward circumstances dwell upon your mind — I am sure in health it is a good rule and in sickness a very necessary one.

Your Grace sees I am not in low spirits and would not have you to be so.

Was this only concern for Newcastle's health ? Or did Rockingham feel uneasy about his own miscalculations ?

(viii)

The negotiations were protracted by the difficulty of accommodating Lord Weymouth, and by Grafton seizing the occasion to make changes in the Secretary of State's office.

Weymouth wished to become Secretary of State for the Northern Department,[1] but did not press this too closely since it would involve dropping Conway. He proposed instead to 'divide the Secretary's place with Lord Shelburne, taking either the European or the American department'.[2] This produced reactions from Conway and Grafton of a kind the Bedfords may not have anticipated, but which they quickly tried to turn to their own advantage.

Conway saw the accession of the Bedfords as an opportunity to retire with honour from a place which had long disgusted him. Six months ago this would have been countered by Grafton threatening his own resignation. But times had changed : Townshend was dead, and it was the unambitious and phlegmatic North who would now step into Conway's

[1] On September 6, 1768, Weymouth applied to Grafton for the Southern Department, in case Shelburne were dismissed. In his letter he writes of a proposal Shelburne had made to change departments when Weymouth took the Northern Department, which he then declined for reasons which no longer existed. (Grafton MS. 799.) [2] Walpole, *Memoirs*, iii. 84.

shoes as Minister in the House of Commons — a much more pleasing prospect. Moreover, Grafton was tiring of Conway's conscientious scruples. Did the Bedfords divine this? It would seem so, since they now began to press for Conway's resignation, which would leave the Northern Department free for Weymouth.

On December 4 Grafton informed Walpole of the state of the negotiations. Walpole was indignant that Conway should appear to retire at the insistence of the Bedfords, 'treated the proposal as an unheard-of impertinence in a fragment of a minority', and told Grafton that he 'could not in honour give up Mr. Conway'.[1] He made some impression, but saw plainly that Conway could not be prevented from resigning, and that Grafton would not make much effort to dissuade him. His schemes were subtle and tortuous, but the utmost he could do was to persuade Conway to hold the seals *pro tempore* and then resign them to Weymouth. When Parliament met after the Christmas recess North took over from Conway as Minister in the House of Commons,[2] and on January 20 Weymouth kissed hands for the Northern Department. Conway remained in the Cabinet.

Grafton in his turn had responded to the Bedfords' original proposal that the Southern Department should be divided and the colonies become the concern of a third Secretary of State. It was not a new idea: it had been under consideration during Rockingham's Ministry, and as recently as August 1767 it had been suggested that Conway should become Secretary of State for the Colonies. It appealed to Grafton not as an administrative reform, but as a means of driving Shelburne to resign.

It is difficult to account for the feeling Shelburne roused in his contemporaries: no public man of this period was so disliked or distrusted. The charges brought against him by Grafton and the King — that he was 'cold', 'not confidential', and 'a secret enemy' — seem to betray fear and envy as well

---

[1] *Memoirs*, iii. 89.
[2] Walpole (*ibid.* p. 106) says that the King 'insisted' on Conway remaining Minister in the House of Commons, but it is clear from reports of debates that North had become the Minister.

as distrust. Though able, intelligent, and concerned for the public welfare, he was not an easy man to work with : he was impatient of triflers, and took little pains to conceal his contempt. The King told Newcastle in July 1766 that Shelburne would make a very good Secretary of State,[1] but by December 1767 had long been anxious to see him go. Grafton fully shared this feeling.

On December 11 Weymouth informed Grafton that 'there was the greatest desire in his friends to make no difficulties', but that Shelburne must be asked 'what part the division of his Lordship's office would cause him to take'.[2] The King, 'thoroughly convinced' that Shelburne's reply would be to resign, authorized Grafton to sound him that evening.[3]

Grafton was plainly ill at ease at this interview, and uncertain how to put his proposal before Shelburne.[4] He talked first of the need to take in 'any great body of men', of the 'openings from different parties' he had received (who, besides the Bedfords, had made such an 'opening'?), though they were but 'faint glimmerings'. Next, he changed his ground : Shelburne's department was too big for one man, he had always thought that 'it ought to be separated', 'a Solomon in the situation' of Shelburne could not 'go through it'. Shelburne protested he had 'not heard the least of what has been carrying on or projected' since Chatham's illness. He continued :

Your Grace will only give me leave to ask you for curiosity whether any American event has given rise to this new opinion of your Grace's, for I presume it is so far new as to have been conceived since the forming of the present Administration, else if your Grace had possessed it then so

[1] Newcastle to Rockingham, July 26, 1766 ; Add. MS. 32976, ff. 255-6. But this did not signify much : the King was usually effusive to anyone entering his service. He told Bristol in August 1766 that he had long wished to make him Lord Lieutenant of Ireland (see above, p. 271), and (according to Walpole) said to Gower in December 1767 that 'he had never been happy since they parted'. (*Memoirs*, iii. 101.)

[2] Grafton to the King, December 11, 1767 ; Fortescue, I, no. 567.

[3] The King to Grafton, December 11, 1767 ; *ibid.* no. 568.

[4] Shelburne's memorandum ; Fitzmaurice, *Life of Shelburne*, i. 327-9.

strongly, you would certainly have urged it at that time as by far the properest.

Grafton denied that he meant anything personal, nor was he dissatisfied with Shelburne's conduct of American affairs : indeed, he wished Shelburne to remain responsible for America. It was simply that the Southern Department was too much for one man ; 'a horse . . . could not go through the business . . . properly'. So decided was his opinion, Grafton said,

that no consideration whatever should make me continue at the head of the Treasury, and any person whatever in the Kingdom, be it who it will, in possession of that department in its present extent. There is no saying what I might do, engaged in the present general election as I am, till that was over, but the first convenient opportunity either he or I should leave the King's service.

Shelburne agreed to consider the proposal, and Grafton asked for a further talk the next day.

On December 12 Shelburne, after regretting that 'this thing had not been thought of at first, when Lord Chatham's sentiments upon so important a subject might have been known, submitted with 'a most cheerful acquiescence'. Though Grafton pressed him to take the American department, 'as the Bedfords cannot be trusted with it on account of different principles', he refused to take upon himself 'the framing and modelling of this new office'. But, as he wrote to Lady Chatham on December 22, he desired Grafton to 'understand the word *acquiescence* in its strict sense, and that solely on account of Lord Chatham'.[1]

Were the Bedfords solely concerned to force Shelburne's resignation or to divide the Southern Department ? Had they some other object in view ? The King had stipulated that they should receive only two Cabinet offices ; [2] since Bedford

---

[1] *Chatham Correspondence*, iii. 300-2.
[2] The King wrote to Grafton on January 26, 1770 : 'When a certain party came two years ago into office you in the most solemn manner promised me that they should have but two Cabinet offices, and that though their friends might in futurity expect an addition of lucrative employments, it must not be of Ministerial ones'. (Grafton MS. 545.)

did not wish for office, Gower and Sandwich had better claims to the Cabinet than others of the Bedfords. But Sandwich, who had already been Secretary of State, was passed over for Weymouth, and had to be satisfied with the office of joint Postmaster-General. Although (West wrote to Newcastle on December 21) he 'would even have taken any thing less, provided Huntingdonshire could have seen he had the Court favor, the regnant principle of his soul',[1] did he resent the preference shown to a younger, less experienced, and less able man ? And did the Bedfords try to take the opportunity of the division of Shelburne's office to force another Cabinet post from Grafton ? If so, they failed : Grafton 'thought it necessary to bring Lord Weymouth . . . to the most plain declaration' that the Post Office was to satisfy Sandwich.[2]

On December 13 Shelburne sent Lady Chatham a full account of his conversations with Grafton.[3] 'My sincere and only wish', he wrote, 'is to do what is agreeable to Lord Chatham. . . .'

> My reason for not choosing the new department proposed [he continued] is no dislike to the office, but that I think the general system affected by it : but if Lord Chatham desires I should do it, I am very ready to take the part he wishes, notwithstanding my own earnest inclinations.

Chatham, his illness 'disabling him from business', refused to advise ;[4] and Shelburne adhered to his original preference.

On December 17 Weymouth notified to Grafton the Bedfords' acceptance.[5] Grafton in his *Autobiography* writes that the terms were 'short of those which Lord Chatham would have agreed to'.[6] In 1766 Chatham had offered places to Gower, Weymouth, and Rigby, and had only held out expectations to others. Grafton in 1767 provided for Gower, Weymouth, and Sandwich ; gave Rigby the place of joint Vice-Treasurer of Ireland, with a promise of the Pay Office

---

[1] Add. MS. 32987, ff. 370-1.
[2] Grafton to the King, December 12, 1767 ; Fortescue, I, no. 570.
[3] *Chatham Correspondence*, iii. 292-8.
[4] Lady Chatham to Shelburne, December 14, 1767 ; Lansdowne MSS.
[5] Grafton, *Autobiography*, pp. 173-4, dated 'Thursday night, eleven o'clock'.                                                  [6] *Ibid.* p. 173.

upon a vacancy ; obtained in 1768 the Garter for Marlborough, the Bedchamber for Bolingbroke, and a diplomatic post for Lynch ; and did not neglect the claims of Bedford's other followers. The Bedfords made opposition pay.

Camden is reported to have said that 'the difference of the opposition was clear, as it was impossible for *Stamp Men* and *No Stamp Men* ever to agree'.[1]  In opposition only ? Hillsborough was appointed to the American department which Shelburne had refused, and the balance in the Cabinet was tilted in favour of 'Stamp Men'. It was an event big with foreboding. When the repercussions of Townshend's American duties began to be felt in England, the 'Stamp Men' had gained control in the Cabinet. Yet Grafton could plead that in admitting North, Hillsborough, and the Bedfords into the Cabinet he had only followed the line marked out for him by Chatham. And he had done so only after the Rockinghams had refused his offers. How difficult to distinguish between what matters and what seems to matter ! None of the politicians in 1767 were thinking of America ; while those who prided themselves on their friendship for the colonies did not realize that their faction fights would place 'Stamp Men' firmly in power.

When it had become clear that the negotiations were to be successful, and Conway saw himself almost relieved of a burden he had so unwillingly borne, he seems to have made an attempt at reconciliation with Rockingham.  On December 13 Richmond wrote to Rockingham :

I have but a moment's time to save the post and yett must write to scold you heartily for not returning Conway his visit, when you had told me you would go to see him even before you expected he would call upon you.  Surely whatever either of you may feel, 'tis wisest to keep [up] forms at least, that your coming together may not be render'd impracticable.  That you may is my only wish, as I think it the only sensible plan, exclusive of my real friendship for you both ;  and who knows but the time may be near at hand.  I may be mistaken, but I think I see a glimmering

---

[1] West to Newcastle, December 3, 1767 ;  Add. MS. 32987, ff. 149-50.

of light. Pray therefore be friendly at least in appearances to the world.[1]

Rockingham replied on December 14 :

> Alas, that that person should attend more to such trifling outward appearances than to all the former proofs I had given of regard and friendship. Time was when as a friend I advised as a friend ought, and recommended the conduct which on the line of character was undoubtedly the most direct and being so contrary to immediate interest would not have committed the person in the eye of the world to any ambiguity. . . . I have some idea that General Conway was not early acquainted with the steps taken in this matter, possibly on a supposition that he would readily go back to the army line entirely. . . . *We* wait with all patience for the denouement of all these political meanderings and tho' they don't afford matter of *prospect* to us as a party yet they please as they seem to throw an honorary lustre on our own proceedings when our conduct and that of others are compared. What wonderful satisfaction it must be to be in Administration where scarce any *two* can justify in reason their having the slightest mutual confidence.[2]

The Bedfords had got their places and the Rockinghams their 'honorary lustre', so everybody was happy.

[1] Rockingham Papers, R1-565.
[2] *Ibid.* R9-8. Copy in Lady Rockingham's hand. It is not marked to whom it was addressed, but it was obviously to Richmond.

# CHAPTER IX

# THE GENERAL ELECTION OF 1768

'THE Court are sanguine', wrote West to Newcastle on December 21, 1767,

> applauding the Duke of Grafton's abilities in dividing the opposition and getting this vast acquisition, and declaring nothing can be done now but Lord Rockingham's shaking hands with Mr. Grenville and shewing their joint feeble efforts for another two or three years.[1]

The Court was too sanguine. Still, allowing for that, this was a rough forecast of what was to happen. How did the Rockinghams receive the news of the Bedfords' return to Court? And what were their tactics now that the comprehensive opposition was dead?

Hardwicke, at least, agreed with the general opinion at Court. He wrote to Newcastle on December 22 :

> These very important changes in the Administration make a very material difference in the state, strength and abilitys of opposition. Indeed I think the breaching of that *corps* which gave the Court a great deal of trouble last *Session*, and made them apprehend more in *future*, had they stuck together, is a master stroke in the policy of the Cabinet.[2]

Bessborough thought the same, and could not refrain from saying, 'I told you so'.

> I was laughed at by some of our young friends [he wrote to Newcastle on December 26] when I told them that the

[1] Add. MS. 32987, ff. 370-1.
[2] *Ibid.* f. 402. 'The principle of party is extinct', Hardwicke wrote to Charles Yorke on December 30, 'at least so divided and frittered out that it forms no band of union which has either consistence or stability, and interest carries every body *to the shop* which distributes the loaves and the fishes.' (Add. MS. 35362, f. 172.) The Yorkes' complaint with party was that it had denied them their share of the loaves and fishes.

very thing would happen which has now happened, and
indeed I saw they would be tired of holding out because I
knew their circumstances.  Our young friends' language was,
*let us but keep off*, and they will come to us.  Had your
Grace's opinion been taken I know this would not have happened.  But as to looking forward, for my part I see no
light.  I think they have a prospect of permanency that is
as much as any Ministry can have.[1]

Rockingham professed to think differently : he could not,
of course, admit that the only result of his policy had been
to strengthen the Administration.

The want of the probability of permanency [he wrote to
Newcastle on December 22] may be matter of regret to
those who embark in this venture, and indeed I can not
join in their lamentations on that head and am not much
moved by them.  If any amongst those who enter had expressed a reluctance for the consideration how *doubtful* the
conduct would be on points of honour — principle — system
— etc. it might have been worth some attention.[2]

The way back to Court, so long open to him, had now been
closed ;  Conway and Grafton had been finally written off ;
there was nothing to gainsay vigorous opposition.  Nothing,
that is, except the complete lack of enthusiasm for it among
his followers.  It was one thing to oppose in the spring of
1767, with the Bedfords and Grenvilles as auxiliaries, and the
Cabinet timid and divided ;  it was quite another matter in
December, when the Bedfords had deserted, the Grenvilles
were weary of unprofitable and meaningless strife, and the
Court heartened by their accession of strength.  Besides,
what points were there for opposition ?  And to what purpose ?

I do not see [wrote Charles Yorke to Hardwicke on January
19, 1768] why your Lordship should affect a very busy lead
in an *opposition* so narrowed, so reduced as it has been by
late events, and pointed at no object ; especially in the last
short session of an expiring Parliament.  Our friend's conduct means nothing but a *visionary* point for himself.[3]

[1] Add. MS. 32987, f. 432.          *Ibid.* ff. 393-5.
[3] Add. MS. 35362, f. 175.

But Rockingham persevered, even though he did not know whither he was going — it is easier to keep to a system, even after the conditions in which it was framed have changed, than to think out a new one. At least it might prevent an embarrassing post-mortem. Besides, the Dividend Bill had to be renewed before Parliament was dissolved, and 'consistency' required that the Rockinghams should oppose it. On December 16, 1767, they divided in the Commons on the second reading, but were beaten by 128 to 41. On January 22, 1768, the voting on the report was 120 to 25 ; on the third reading (January 25), 131 to 41.[1] These divisions only revealed opposition's weakness to the world, and underlined the Court's triumph in detaching the Bedfords.

Rockingham had little hope of doing better in the Lords : Mansfield was 'rather cold in this matter' ; the Grenvilles had no zest for the work ; so many peers were out of town that Rockingham did not expect to muster more than twenty.[2] On February 4 the Court carried the commitment of the bill by 73 to 35.[3] Temple spoke against the bill, but his speech did not please the Rockinghams. He declared 'he should continue to abide by those friends out of office who were not inclined to despondency, but determined to support the superiority of Great Britain over all the colonies and dependencies'.[4] Shelburne's speech 'contained some curious matter for speculations'.[5]

He declared his only hopes of any good arising to this country in ultimately settling the great affair with the India Co. was fixed upon the *flattering prospect* of a great and noble *Earl's* recovery, and being able to take Administration upon him. He seemed to address his speech entirely to the Duke

---

[1] Conway and his nephews, Lord Beauchamp and Henry Seymour Conway, voted against the Court on this division.
[2] Rockingham to Newcastle, January 27, 1768 ; Add. MS. 32988, ff. 81-2.
[3] There is a list of the minority in Add. MS. 33036, ff. 285-6.
[4] West to Newcastle [February 4, 1768] ; Add. MS. 32988, ff. 174-5. There is nothing about this in Rockingham's report of the debate (Rockingham to Newcastle, February 5, 1768 ; *ibid.* ff. 170-3). Instead, he makes Temple say 'that he was now and would always be ready to support right measures and right propositions and whatsoever set they came from — it would make no difference'.                                     [5] *Ibid.*

of Grafton, and both in gesture and in matter shewed plainly
that he and the noble Duke are not on the best terms.

Bedford and five of his followers voted with the opposition,[1]
Weymouth declaring 'he hoped it would be the last time he
should differ from the supporter of this bill'.[2] 'Consistency'
was not a virtue peculiar to the Rockinghams.

Apart from the Nullum Tempus Bill,[3] and an attempt by
Beckford to pass a bribery bill,[4] the remainder of the session
contained little of interest and passed easily for the Court.

### (ii)

There is a passage in a letter from Richmond to Burke, dated
September 26, 1774, which deserves careful study by all who
write on eighteenth-century elections.  Burke had asked
Richmond to exert his influence in favour of Lord Verney who

[1] Gower, Weymouth, Waldegrave, Sandwich, and Essex.
[2] *Ibid.* ff. 174-5.                              [3] See above, p. 243.
[4] Beckford's bill was introduced on January 26, 1768 : it would have
obliged members to take an oath that they had not used bribery in their
elections.  On February 19 the House went into committee on the bill but
was unable to provide a quorum, and the bill was dropped.  It was taken
seriously only by old Tories and new Whigs — the Tories looking to the
past, the Whigs to the future.  Their aims did not greatly differ.  On
February 17 Dowdeswell moved a clause 'for the better securing the freedom
and independency of Parliament, in order to prevent the officers of Excise,
Customs and Salt from voting in elections'.  (West to Newcastle, February
17, 1768 ; Add. MS. 32988, f. 355.)  This became law in 1782.  And here
is part of some notes Newdigate made for a speech on Beckford's bill :

'Not sufficient of itself to restore
you must unravel by degrees
the strong lines of the *web*
Remount to the first *principles* of the cons[titution]
repeal *Sept*[ennial] Act
not to introduce *Trien*[nial] Parl[iament]s
but *annual*
to restore the ancient *weight* and *dignity* of families honors and great
estates w[oul]d ease the noble and great of their anxieties
who now sit brooding over their borough[s] eying with the utmost
sollicitude the birds of prey from the East and W[est] who are hover-
ing over them
c[oul]d wish even to see restord the pay to the Members the weekly
pay, for then men w[oul]d take care to see they earn'd it'.
(Newdigate MS. B2548.)

There was much in this which the City Radicals and even the Rockinghams
of the 'seventies would have approved.

was a candidate for Buckinghamshire at the General Election. Richmond replied :

> Although I have no political connexion, I have some remains of old family acquaintance with Lord Temple, and should not choose to offend him so much as I myself should feel at any other person for an endeavour to oppose a family interest. There are few things I would not do to oblige you ; but I confess that, not knowing Lord Verney, and having no other reason to wish him better than Lord Temple, except for his friendship for you, I do not think it would be right for me to interfere, where I have so literally nothing to say.[1]

Here is one of the magnates of the Rockingham party refusing to support one of Rockingham's followers because he does not wish to oppose a family interest. In 1768 elections had little to do with politics, and almost nothing with party. Electoral interest was akin to property, and election contests had a local, but rarely a national significance. Candidates did not stand as party men ; and electoral alliances cut across party connections.[2] Party was rarely a factor in victory or defeat.

Parliament was dissolved on March 11, 1768. But for months candidates and agents had been preparing for this day, and bewailing the expense and confusion of a General Election. The old cry that the landed interest was driven out by stock-jobbers and East India speculators was raised again, as in 1761, with hardly any more justification. On December 19, 1767, Chesterfield wrote to his son about his efforts to find him a seat in Parliament. He had applied to Chatham over a year ago, but nothing had happened : now he was looking for a 'venal borough'.

> I spoke to a borough-jobber [Chesterfield wrote] and offered five and twenty hundred pounds for a secure seat in Parlia-

---

[1] *Burke Correspondence*, i. 484-5.

[2] The Norfolk election of 1768 was a good example. Whately wrote to Grenville on October 23, 1767 : 'I am very sorry to find that Lord Buckingham and Sir A. Woodhouse are of different parties in Norfolk, when they agree so well in their political conduct elsewhere'. (Grenville (J. M.) MSS.) Charles Yorke gave his interest to the sitting members, Wodehouse and Thomas de Grey ; Newcastle and Rockingham supported Wenman Coke and Sir Edward Astley.

ment ; but he laughed at my offer, and said, that there was no such thing as a borough to be had now ; for that the rich East and West Indians had secured them all at the rate of three thousand pounds at least ; but many at four thousand ; and two or three, that he knew, at five thousand.[1]

Rockingham told the same story.

The great expences of elections [he wrote to Newcastle on November 10, 1767] have indeed too much in general deterr'd the prudent and proper persons from attempting to come into Parliament.

Gentlemen possessed of 2 or 3000£ per annum estates feel that their fortunes will not bear an extraordinary out-going of 3 or 4000£ for a seat in Parliament, and the additional expences incurring by a long residence in London.[2]

There was no lack of candidates, in spite of the alleged higher price of seats : the difficulty was to find 'prudent and proper persons'. 'It is from the next Parliament', wrote Newcastle to Keppel on November 12, 1767, 'that this country must be saved, and the cause of those who wish it best be supported.'[3] The Parliament of 1768 was to be responsible for some of the most fateful measures in British history, but history is usually made by men who are ignorant of what they are about. How did the Court and opposition fare at the General Election, and what effect did the new members have on the party composition of the House ?

There is little material for a study of the Treasury's activities at this election. There is nothing in the Grafton Papers to match Newcastle's voluminous correspondence, or Robinson's carefully compiled lists. Grafton disliked and neglected election business, and no one who has read eight-eenth-century election correspondence will censure him for that. He made 'many irreconcileable enemies', Walpole wrote, 'by imperiousness, and refusing himself to all access'.[4] He did not interfere at Rye or Seaford, where Newcastle's influence was dependent upon the Treasury's favour. He

---

[1] *The Letters of Lord Chesterfield*, ed. by Bonamy Dobrée, vi. 2832.
[2] Add. MS. 32986, ff. 329-32.
[3] *Ibid.* ff. 391-2.                          [4] *Memoirs*, iii. 88.

Z

seems, indeed, to have been unwilling to interfere in any election where his 'old friends' were concerned. So early as October 20, 1767, Bradshaw suggested finding a candidate to oppose Admiral Keppel at Windsor,[1] but nothing was done about it. When Newcastle was faced with a contest at Lewes, Grafton allowed Barrington to assure him that the Treasury would be neutral.[2]

Here is the story of a small government servant, with no electoral influence of his own, who looked to the Treasury for assistance and did not receive it.

John Bindley had been Grenville's first choice for the seat at West Looe, in 1764, where John Sargent was eventually chosen.[3] He was then a Commissioner of Excise, but ambitious of coming into Parliament.[4] However, Bindley was not acceptable at West Looe, from 'the report which had been spread that he was the first proposer of the tax upon cider'.[5] He entered Parliament in December 1766 as M.P. for Dover, probably through the influence of Townshend, who employed his services at the Exchequer.[6] After Townshend's death he was neglected : he contested Reading in 1768, but was defeated. He set up in business as a wine-merchant, but failed. He appears in a list of pension holders drawn up for Shelburne in August 1782 as receiving a pension of £1000 per annum.[7] Under the heading 'On what cause' is the note :

Annually employed in forming the taxes.

N.B.   Said to have been promised to be Commissioner of Excise.

---

[1] Grafton MS. 301, part printed in *Autobiography*, p. 181.
[2] Barrington to Newcastle, March 7, 1768 ; Add. MS. 32989, f. 69.
[3] See above, p. 262.
[4] Grenville to James Buller, November 17, 1764 ; Grenville's letter book (Huntington Library).
[5] Grenville to Buller, December 11, 1764 ; *ibid.*
[6] Townshend to Grafton, March 29, 1767 ; Grafton MS. 451. Bindley was consulted on matters relating to customs and excise ; Townshend's financial adviser was Samuel Touchet, M.P. for Shaftesbury. 'He and he alone', wrote Townshend to Grafton in June 1767, 'has the merit of whatever has been honourably done in this winter for the public and the Treasury in the choice of Taxes' (*ibid.* 454). Touchet was also neglected by Grafton : he contested Shaftesbury in 1768, but was defeated.
[7] Chatham Papers, 229.

Recommended much by Sir G. Cooper, who reports also Lord North's high opinion of his services.

In short, Bindley was the type of man whom it was the business of the Treasury to bring into Parliament, had Grafton done his job properly.

(iii)

Portland, Newcastle, and Rockingham each had their election difficulties, but the problems which faced them were quite different.

Portland had four contests on his hands, and emerged victorious in three. Most important was his struggle with Sir James Lowther in Cumberland and Carlisle. Lowther was Bute's son-in-law ; he had also recently obtained from the Treasury a grant of part of Portland's Cumberland property, the better to cripple his rival.[1] Portland, therefore, was depicted by the Rockinghams as fighting for 'the cause'. But for what cause ? 'I . . . am extremely sorry', wrote Lord Ravensworth to Portland on August 31, 1767,

for the contest I find is going on for the county of Cumberland and Carlisle ; and particularly so as your Grace and Sir James Lowther, the principals on each side, are at the head of two old Whig familys for which I have ever had a great regard and have always wish'd united in publick as well as county matters.[2]

Though Lowther was in 1768 a follower of the Court, he went over to the opposition in 1775 ; and though the grant of Portland's property was hardly just, it was legally correct.[3]

However, Portland won his fight : Lord Edward Bentinck and George Musgrave were elected at Carlisle, and Henry Curwen for Cumberland ; and though Lowther got himself returned as the other member for Cumberland he was unseated on petition in favour of Portland's second candidate, Henry Fletcher.[4] In addition, Portland had the pleasure of seeing

[1] See above, p. 243.    [2] Portland MS. 352.
[3] It was annulled in the courts, but on a legal technicality.
[4] When Fletcher showed a disposition to compromise the Cumberland election, Rudolph Bentinck wrote of him to Portland (August 11, 1768) : 'Generally in publick his conversation is right enough, but in private he is a Tory to all intents and purposes'. (Portland MS. 59.)

his rival lose one seat in Westmorland to Thomas Fenwick.[1]

Portland had to face an opposition at Wigan from a local man,[2] and he tried to carry Callington by a *coup de main.* This was his only defeat. His members all became loyal supporters of Rockingham, George Byng (returned for Wigan) being one of the most active and enterprising of the party during the American war. Two of Portland's brothers-in-law were also returned in 1768 : Lord Grey for Staffordshire, and Booth Grey for Leicester.[3] In all, Portland increased the Rockinghams' strength in the Commons by four.

Poor Newcastle suffered badly at the General Election of 1768. He had begun preparing for it long before anyone else — he told Rockingham on December 9, 1766, that it was 'high time to be thinking' of 'the securing a good Parliament at the next General Election'[4] — yet when the dissolution came he was unprepared. His difficulties were not with the boroughs where his hold was weakest, and where he could have been challenged by the Treasury — Rye and Seaford ; but where he had had influence for over fifty years — East Retford and Lewes.

At East Retford he had an easier passage than there was reason to expect. The trouble was that one of the sitting

---

[1] He voted with the opposition, 1768–74, when he was defeated for Westmorland.

[2] Here is an amusing sidelight on the election at Wigan. 'Don't you think', wrote Beaumont Hotham, one of the candidates, to Portland on February 26, 1768, 'that it might be of service to the good cause in all the distant elections, if a paragraph or two appeared immediately after the dissolution in all the news papers, asserting confidently a change of his Majesty's Administration, and specifying the persons who are to compose it. This repeated once or twice, with an air of authority, after a preparatory paragraph of "We hear a great change in the Administration is to take place before the meeting of the new Parliament", would surely influence many wavering people, and might stagger some who would otherwise be determined. If you are of this opinion pray put it into proper hands, but let the intelligence by [sic] communicated by *every* paper, and particularly by the evening papers, which are the only kind that are read in the country. George Byng burns to compose this Administration, but I will not gratify him so much as to let him inclose it to you.' (Portland MS. 312.)

On the other hand, David Hartley at Callington 'had but one object in view, viz. to consent to nothing that is unbecoming or wrong . . . or . . . have any proceedings to be ashamed of'. (Hartley to Portland, March 14, 1768 ; *ibid.* 295.)    [3] Both voted with the Rockinghams.

[4] Add. MS. 32978, ff. 235–41.

members was 'that chit Jack Shelley' — the man Newcastle loathed most. The other member was John White. It had gone against the grain for Newcastle to re-elect Shelley in December 1766 ; to do so at the General Election was more than he could bear. But if Shelley, supported by Lincoln, insisted upon standing, the quarrel between Newcastle and Lincoln would be paraded in public, and Shelley would probably be returned. Grievous were the Duke's complaints ; loud were his calls to his friends for advice and assistance.

I did not indeed think [he wrote to Rockingham on October 13, 1767] fifty years ago, or indeed any one year since, that I should have wanted any assistance to oppose such cruel attempts as these. It would be of service to the cause to keep out of Parliament such a tool to power as the present Treasurer of the Household is, or any relation or dependent upon my Lord Lincoln must be.

I am ready to be for any body that these gentlemen (our friends) shall advise, but I adhere to what I declared to them all from the beginning — somebody I must have.[1]

In the end all turned out right — or nearly so. Mansfield and Rockingham arranged a compromise acceptable to both uncle and nephews. Shelley was to be returned for Newark, while White's colleague at Retford was to be John Offley, a candidate approved of by both Newcastle and Lincoln. Newcastle was well satisfied with this arrangement ; 'honest Offley' rose high in his favour ; and the sun of his approval and gratitude shone alike on Mansfield and Rockingham.[2]

Everything possible had been done to ensure Newcastle's peace of mind, but nobody had bothered to ask if the electors of East Retford would accept the arrangement. White, who managed the borough for Newcastle, was grown old and indifferent about Parliament. He had neglected the borough, and at the General Election was opposed by a local man, Sir Cecil Wray. Offley and Wray were elected.

[1] Add. MS. 32985, ff. 453-4.
[2] See Newcastle's letters to Rockingham of December 8 and 13, 1767. Add. MS. 32987, ff. 202-3 and 256-9.

Our friend White [wrote Rockingham to Newcastle on March 16, 1768] was a little too reluctant to take trouble. I really believe he always saw his difficulties at Retford which instead of trying to remedy by a little activity he fairly avoided even the appearance of being in earnest till it was too late, and was not perhaps in truth sorry to find his success impossible.[1]

'I don't call Retford lost', wrote Newcastle to George Cavendish on March 20, 1768, 'for if my friend Jack White did not care to come into Parliament, it was mighty easy for him to lose the election.'[2]   From the point of view of the House of Commons he was correct : Wray was in opposition from 1768 to 1782.   The Retford election of 1768 had no political significance.

Newcastle was not greatly concerned at White's defeat, but the loss of a seat at Lewes really upset him.   Yet he had no one to blame for it but himself.

On August 21, 1767, Newcastle wrote from Lewes to the Duke of Bedford :

I flatter myself that you will forgive me the liberty I take in assuring your Grace, that during the space of fifty five years that I have been closely connected with this county and burroughs I never was so well received amongst them as I have been this time ; and never found them more unanimous than they are at present in doing what I wish.[3]

Probably they were, but what did Newcastle wish ?   He did not know himself.

The sitting members at Lewes were Lord Edward Bentinck and William Plumer.   Bentinck was to stand for Carlisle at the General Election, and in his place Newcastle had selected Thomas Hampden, of an old Sussex family and acceptable to the town.[4]   After Newcastle's illness in December 1767 his

---

[1] Add. MS. 32989, ff. 187-90.            [2] *Ibid.* ff. 226-7.
[3] Woburn MS., lvi. f. 52.
[4] Thomas Hampden was the son of Robert Trevor, who took the name of Hampden in 1754 on inheriting the estates of his second cousin, John Hampden, of Great Hampden, Bucks.   In 1764 Robert Hampden succeeded his brother as fourth Lord Trevor.   He was a close friend and follower of Grenville.

mind was more confused than ever, and he was even more prone than usual to torment himself with legions of bogies of his own creation. First, Shelley and Grafton were attacking him at Lewes ; [1] next, it was trouble at Seaford, which gave him 'more uneasiness than any which could have happened in any other place' ; [2] then back again to Lewes, when Plumer was invited to stand for Hertfordshire and Newcastle had to find another candidate.

He complained of Plumer's 'desertion',[3] but by February 6, 1768, felt able to tell Rockingham that he was 'perfectly easy about the town of Lewes'.[4] The next day he had swung back, and was now 'very uneasy . . . not having . . . a proper person to recommend' ; [5] on February 8 he had descended to the depths of 'the greatest uneasiness about Lewes election'.[6] What was the reason for this oscillation ?

On February 8 Sir Ferdinando Poole wrote to Hurdis suggesting Thomas Hay as a candidate for Lewes ; [7] he was supported by Henry Humphrey, one of Newcastle's agents there, who warned him that the town wanted Hay and that an opposition would probably arise to any other candidate.[8] On February 9 Newcastle desired West to acquaint Poole,

> that the Duke of Newcastle has been so ill used by those he has brought into Parliament that he is fully determined to bring no man in for any one place who shall not give assurance and security to Mr. West which shall satisfy Mr. West that in all parliamentary questions whatever they will follow and do whatever the Duke of Newcastle shall advise and go with him.[9]

[1] Newcastle to Rockingham, January 27, 1768 ; Add. MS. 32988, ff. 83-4.
[2] Newcastle to Rockingham, February 3, 1768 ; *ibid.* ff. 153-6. The trouble at Seaford was that Newcastle, expecting that Lord Gage would be given a British peerage at the dissolution, wished to choose his brother, General Thomas Gage, then commanding in America. Gage preferred his brother-in-law, Sir Sampson Gideon, 'who he owned . . . was disposed to be with the Administration'. But Gage did not receive his peerage until 1780.     [3] Newcastle to Plumer, January 30, 1768 ; *ibid.* ff. 115-16.
[4] *Ibid.* f. 196.
[5] Newcastle to Rockingham, February 7, 1768 ; *ibid.* f. 208.
[6] Newcastle to Rockingham, February 8, 1768 ; *ibid.* f. 234.
[7] *Ibid.* f. 240.
[8] Humphrey to Newcastle, February 9, 1768 ; *ibid.* ff. 250-1.
[9] *Ibid.* f. 244.

West saw Poole : 'He could not answer anything for Colonel Hay, but he should not have recommended him if he had not apprehended him a true friend to the Duke of Newcastle'.[1] On this, Newcastle accepted Hay.

Then he changed his mind, and began looking for another candidate.

> The Bishop of Durham [2] and Mr. West [wrote Newcastle to Rockingham on February 15] seem to think I should recommend Colonel Hay ; but I am determined not to do it : for he may be a very honest man, and is my near relation, but he is an officer in the Army and a great favorite of my Lord Granby's, who is opposing me every where.[3]

But it was difficult to find a 'prudent and proper person' : Thomas Pelham suggested Thomas Miller, who had 'no particular attachment to the Duke of Richmond more than any other man', and whom he thought would 'attach himself solely' to Newcastle.[4] However, on February 19 West forwarded Hay's declaration, with which Newcastle was 'so well satisfied' that he reinstated him as candidate for Lewes.[5] All was well : Newcastle had succeeded in finding a candidate who would vote with the Rockinghams in Parliament.

But was that all he wanted ? The machinery had hardly been set in motion when it was halted by a spanner thrown by Pelham. He wrote to Newcastle on February 20 :

> Your Grace knows the consequence Jack Pelham [6] is of in the town of Lewes. . . . You likewise know how very ill Colonel Hay and his family have use [sic] both Jack Pelham and his brother ; [7] I fear therefore I shall have the greatest difficulty to satisfy him, as he has not been appris'd in the least of your Grace's intentions towards Hay. I wish there-

---

[1] West to Newcastle, February 11, 1768 ; Add. MS. 32988, f. 288.

[2] The Rt. Rev. Richard Trevor, uncle of Thomas Hampden.

[3] *Ibid.* f. 323.

[4] Pelham to Newcastle, February 18, 1768 ; *ibid.* ff. 379-80. The Miller family was seated at Lavant, about two miles from Goodwood. Newcastle was always jealous of Richmond's influence in Sussex.

[5] West to Newcastle, February 19, 1768 ; *ibid.* ff. 381-3. Newcastle to West, February 20, 1768 ; *ibid.* f. 389.

[6] John Pelham, of Catsfield, second cousin to Newcastle.

[7] Henry Pelham.

fore your Grace wou'd insist on Hay's writing to Jack and Harry Pelham, declaring his concern for the differences that have subsisted between them, and his desire of making it up, and to ask their interest for Lewes.[1]

Newcastle's concern for his party was now forgotten in his concern for his family. He withdrew his recommendation of Hay, which (he wrote to Hay on March 1) would be 'a perpetual exclusion of all of the name of Pelham for the future',[2] and adopted Miller. Poole warned him that Hay had canvassed the town under the impression that he had Newcastle's 'absolute promise of support and recommendation', and that he was 'resolved to pursue the point to the uttermost'.[3] The election was on March 15 : Hampden received 115 votes, Hay 110, and Miller 92. It was another triumph for 'ungrateful young men'.

The Pelham family may have suffered a defeat, but not the opposition. Hay, in spite of being an Army officer, voted consistently with the opposition until he left Parliament in 1780.

(iv)

Rockingham had the same problem as Newcastle — to find a 'prudent and proper person' on whose parliamentary conduct he could depend. But Rockingham was more fortunate : instead of losing a seat he gained one which he did not expect.

Rockingham had influence over the election of one member at York ; the other member sat on the Corporation interest. In the autumn of 1767 Rockingham's member, Sir George Armytage, pleading ill health, announced that he would not stand at the General Election.[4] Rockingham hoped Armytage might be persuaded to change his mind, but, unable to depend upon it, began to look round for another candidate. His choice of Charles Turner was rather surprising, for he had already experienced Turner's obstinacy and independence. In 1760,

---

[1] *Ibid.* ff. 393-4.                         [2] Add. MS. 32989, f. 1.
[3] Poole to Newcastle [March 1, 1768] ; *ibid.* ff. 9-10.
[4] 'Sir George Armytage', wrote Rockingham to Newcastle on March 16, 1768, 'could not be persuaded to stand on, the secret of that was Mr. Wentworth his father-in-law anxiously wished him not to stand.' (*Ibid.* ff. 187-90.)

on the death of Lord Downe, Turner had offered himself as a candidate for Yorkshire in opposition to Edwin Lascelles, who was supported by Rockingham. 'I find', wrote Rockingham on January 13, 1761, 'his agents are most industriously attempting to raise a clamour against *me*, as aiming at dictating to the county of York, in the choice of their two representatives.'[1] Turner had finally withdrawn, and did not oppose Lascelles and Savile at the General Election of 1761.

The Whig interest (as it was called) at York was centred in the Rockingham Club, and to be accepted by Rockingham's friends as a candidate Turner must become a member of the Club. This he objected to, arguing that the Club was unconstitutional since it sanctioned the use of a peer's name in parliamentary elections. He also objected to Rockingham's proposal to contribute towards the expense in case of a contest :[2] he did not wish to appear as Rockingham's candidate. His main argument, he told Rockingham on March 1, was not a quibble over the name of the Club.

> Surely, my Lord, there is a very material difference as well in argument as fact between a club retaining its general name let who will be its president, and a club adopting the name of its president. In the first case the principles of the club determine the choice of its president, in the last the partiality to the president influences the principles of the club.[3]

He asked to be excused becoming a member. Rockingham left London for Yorkshire on March 4 uncertain whether he could still persuade Armytage to stand, whether his friends would accept Turner if he did not join their club, or whether Turner would stand against Rockingham's interest.

On March 14 the Rockingham Club accepted Turner as a candidate 'upon Whig principles', Rockingham having 'indulged his punctilio of not being an absolute member of the Club'.[4] Rockingham returned to Wentworth that evening, 'in

---

[1] To an unnamed correspondent ; Rockingham Papers, R1-134.
[2] Rockingham to Turner, February 21, 1768 ; *ibid*. R1-587.
[3] *Ibid*. R1-588.
[4] Lady Rockingham to Portland [March 22, 1768] ; *ibid*. R158-123.

high good humour . . . his consenting to the admission of Charles Turner as he had no proper friend of his own to propose, having put those who were not quite his friends into mighty good temper'.[1] At Wentworth he found Lord John Cavendish who had been defeated at Lancaster ; there he had stood 'almost against his . . . consent' on the invitation of 'a great number of the principal merchants and of the gentlemen of the greatest weight'.[2] Together they received the news that Robert Fox Lane,[3] the other member for York, had declined to stand, owing to ill health, and that the Corporation had sounded several gentlemen but had not yet found a candidate. Rockingham pressed Cavendish to return with him to York ; Cavendish demurred, 'having so lately got out of one scrape',[4] but promised to consult his brothers at Chatsworth. Rockingham was to go to York, and, if he found the prospect favourable, send for Cavendish to join him.

Rockingham was in York that night (March 14) ; on March 16 Cavendish was accepted as the Corporation candidate ; and on March 21 he and Turner were elected without opposition. 'In truth, my dear Lord,' wrote Rockingham to Newcastle, 'I have never been luckier in any matter, than I have been in this election matter at York.'[5]

'Charles Turner must be delighted with being at last in Parliament', wrote Lord Fitzwilliam to his mother when he heard the news; 'it has long been the object of all his wishes, and he esteems it a greater honor to be a member of a British Parliament than to be the Grand Monarque.'[6]

I never saw Charles Turner [wrote Dowdeswell to Lady Rockingham on March 20] but from what I have heard of him, I take him to be a very honest man, of that kind of

---

[1] Lord John Cavendish to Newcastle, March 16, 1768; Add. MS. 32989, ff. 191-2.
[2] Lord George Cavendish to Newcastle, November 11, 1767 ; Add. MS. 32986, f. 355.
[3] Robert Fox Lane was classified by Rockingham as 'Bute', and by Newcastle as 'Administration'. He supported Chatham's Ministry.
[4] Cavendish to Newcastle, March 16, 1768 ; Add. MS. 32989, ff. 191-2.
[5] Rockingham to Newcastle, March 16, 1768 ; *ibid.* ff. 187-90.
[6] April 9, 1768. Fitzwilliam was then at Rome on his Grand Tour. (Fitzwilliam MSS. ; Northamptonshire Record Office.)

honour which is very nice and punctilious, but at the same time of that good humour and temper which leave him open to persuasion, and permit him to go to a Rockingham Club when it is right that he should go there. It is true what you say, you will certainly *grow to like him*, and you are so good a politician that I do not despair of reconciling you to many others *in time* whose names you can not bear at present with any degree of patience.[1]

Turner may not have been a 'prudent and proper person' in Rockingham's eyes, but no one could question the purity of his Whiggism. He spoke frequently in Parliament and voted constantly with the opposition : he was known for his violent dislike of the American war, his independence and integrity, and his distrust of aristocratic influence. Perhaps that was why he was not a 'prudent and proper person'.

## (v)

'The appearances hitherto of the new Parliament', wrote Newcastle to Portland on March 30,

> please me extremely. There are now above a hundred new Members ; and, I think, by the best judgment I can form at present, we shall have a good chance of having a great, if not the greatest part of them.[2]

On May 19 Sir Mathew Fetherstonhaugh wrote to Newcastle :

> If I can give any guess at parliamentary connections, I do not think the majority (by far) of the new Members stand well dispos'd towards the present people in power. I hear a great many free censures thrown out ; which makes me think (if our friends play their cards right) they may make us happy in a better system.[3]

The first year of the new Parliament witnessed the long-drawn-out battle over Wilkes, which accentuated and deepened party differences. What were the politics of the members who entered in 1768, and what difference did the General Election have on the balance of parties in the House ?

---

[1] Dowdeswell Papers ; printed in *Cavendish's Debates*, i. 582, as addressed to Rockingham.
[2] Add. MS. 32989, ff. 276-7.       [3] Add. MS. 32990, ff. 107-8.

On May 8, 1769, the House of Commons heard the petition of the freeholders of Middlesex against its decision of April 15, which had declared Henry Lawes Luttrell the duly elected candidate instead of Wilkes. 221 members voted for the motion confirming Luttrell's election, 152 against — the biggest minority of the session. How did the new members vote on this important question?

167 members were returned at the General Election who had not sat at the dissolution. By May 8, 1769, twelve were no longer in the House,[1] and twenty-one more had entered since the General Election [2] — a total of 176 members who had not sat at the dissolution. They composed 31·5 per cent of the House.

A list of members who voted in this division, together with a further list of 'Some additional friends', was published in the North Briton for May 27, 1769. Like all division lists for this period, it is neither complete nor accurate. 221 members (including the tellers) are given for the majority; two names are missing. Besides, among the names given is Sir E. Bayhem — an obvious mistake for Sir Edward Bayntun who appears later in the list; while Peter Legh (M.P. for Newton, Lancs) also appears among the 'additional friends'. There were two members named Peter Legh in Parliament at this time : one (M.P. for Ilchester), a government contractor who regularly voted with the Court, also appears among the majority ; the other (M.P. for Newton), a country gentleman, had already voted twice with the opposition on Wilkes's case.[3] Removing from the list the mythical Bayhem and Legh of Newton, 219 names are left, four short of the total.[4] The list

[1] They were : Jervoise Clarke Jervoise, John Lewis, Charles Lowndes, Thomas Lyttelton, Sir Frank Standish, William Strode, and Sir Rowland Winn (unseated) ; Lord George Beauclerk and Ralph Burton (dead) ; John Frederick Sackville (succeeded to a peerage) ; Sir George Macartney (vacated) ; and John Wilkes (expelled).

[2] Among these I include members returned on petition as well as those returned at by-elections, and who had not sat at the dissolution.

[3] On February 2 and 3, 1769.

[4] I here insert a warning against over-reliance on the accuracy and completeness of eighteenth-century division lists. They are rarely complete, while I have yet to find two from different sources which are identical. Some mistakes are of small account (e.g. mis-spelling of names, constituencies

of the minority contains 153 names (including the tellers) —
one short of the total.

121 new members voted in this division : 63 (52·1 per cent)
with the Court, 58 (47·9 per cent) with the opposition.  251
old members voted :  156 (62·1 per cent) with the Court,
95 (37·9 per cent) with the opposition.  The new members
divided roughly half and half between Court and opposition ;
but less than two-fifths of the old members voted with the
opposition.  The new members composed 37·9 per cent of the
opposition's vote, but only 24·8 per cent of the Court's vote.

For a time the new members continued to favour the
opposition more than the old members.  On the division of
January 25, 1770 (also on Wilkes's case), 67 out of the 180
who are known to have voted in the opposition were new
members — 37·2 per cent as against 37·9 per cent for the
division of May 8, 1769.[1]  But during the next four years the
heat engendered by Wilkes's case subsided — perhaps opposition made the mistake of bringing it up too often, and tired
out the patience of the House.  Opposition was reduced
when the Grenvilles returned to Court in 1771 ; it also lost
the support of many independents and of some ambitious
politicians.  At least fifteen of the new members who had
been in opposition over Wilkes had gone over to the Court by
the beginning of 1774.[2]

On February 25, 1774, Sir Edward Astley's motion for
leave to bring in a bill to make Grenville's Act for trying

---

wrongly attributed) ; others can easily be checked (e.g. members included
who were not in Parliament at the date of the division).  But it is rarely
possible to check whether the members did vote according to the list.  A
single division list can be used for statistical analysis where the margin of
error is not critical ; a number over a short period can be used to ascertain
a member's politics ; but the evidence of one division list is not conclusive
for this purpose.  The subject of eighteenth-century division lists, so
important for party history, deserves careful study : one would like to
know, for example, how the printers received their lists.

[1] I have used the list of the minority in Almon, viii. 190-2.  It includes
the tellers.  The correct figure is 182, excluding the tellers.

[2] They were : Lord Belasyse, Mathew Brickdale, John Buller junior,
Sir Thomas Clavering, Charles Wolfran Cornewall, Lord Donegal, William
Drake junior, Sir Robert Fletcher, George Johnstone, Francis Page, Con-
stantine Phipps, Henry Strachey, Richard Sutton, Richard Symons, and
Richard Whitworth.

disputed elections perpetual was carried by 250 to 122.  There
was a great deal of cross-voting, but the King marked on his
copy of the division list the names of the friends to the Court
who voted for the motion.[1]  Of the 176 new members in
Parliament on May 8, 1769, 152 remained ; 39 did not vote
on Astley's motion.  64 of the 113 who voted were against the
motion or are marked as friends to the Court ; 49 were still
in opposition.  The percentage of new members in opposition
had fallen from 47·9 per cent on May 8, 1769, to 43·4 per cent
on February 25, 1774.  Yet these figures do not give a correct
estimate of the decline of opposition among the new members :
many who had gone over to the Court did not vote, concerned
neither to oppose a popular measure, nor — with the zeal of
converts — to displease the Court.

To sum up :  the new members returned at the General
Election of 1768 tended to favour the opposition to a greater
degree than the old members, but by 1774 this tendency was
wearing off.  This suggests that Grafton mishandled the
General Election, and that opposition lost some followers as
interest in Wilkes's case died away.  In normal circumstances
the Court had little to fear from opposition :  in the years 1766
to 1770 it was weakness, indolence, and pusillanimity in the
leaders of the Court party which made opposition appear
formidable.

[1] Fortescue, III, no. 1403.  It is a complete list of both majority and
minority.  There is another list in Almon, xi. 66-71, which differs a good
deal from the one printed by Fortescue.  But *prima facie* the King's list
should be the more reliable.

# CHAPTER X

# THE RESIGNATION OF CHATHAM

THE summer and autumn of 1768 was a critical time in colonial and foreign affairs : issues were raised fraught with consequences for the future. Yet it was not to these that Grafton primarily gave his attention : minor but more pressing problems occupied what time he could spare for public affairs.

The first problem was raised by Wilkes's election for Middlesex. Legally he was an outlaw, but everyone knew that his outlawry would be reversed. He would then be sentenced for libel and blasphemy, with which he had been charged in 1763. Could he be permitted to remain a member of Parliament while undergoing punishment for such crimes ? Could he be expelled the House twice for the same offence ? Could Parliament proceed against him before his outlawry was reversed and sentence pronounced ? These were the questions, part legal, part political, which Administration had to answer. It was intended to summon Parliament for a short session in May, and then prorogue it until winter. What action, if any, should be taken against Wilkes this session ? This was the immediate problem facing the Court.

By April 20 the Cabinet had determined on Wilkes's expulsion : [1] no one seems to have offered any objections on principle, and Camden's suggestion that 'it would be well to consider what may be the consequence if Wilkes should be re-elected' was not pursued.[2] On April 22 the Cabinet authorized Conway and North to consult 'the Privy Coun-

---

[1] Camden to Grafton, April 20, 1768 ; Grafton, *Autobiography*, pp. 200-201. The same day the King requested Grafton to summon Conway (who had gone out of town) to a Cabinet meeting, 'to concur in the proposal of expulsion'. (Grafton MS. 513.) This was the Cabinet of April 22.

[2] Camden to Grafton, April 3, 1768 ; Grafton, *Autobiography*, pp. 199-200.

sellors and Men of Business in the House of Commons'. 'There were doubts on the expulsion', wrote Grafton to the King, 'in case the verdict was likely to be reversed ; but no difficulty to proceed to it, if to be defended by the rules of the House.'[1]

On April 25 the King wrote to North :

Tho' entirely confiding in your attachment to my person, as well as in your hatred of every lawless proceeding yet I think it highly proper to apprize you that the expulsion of Mr. Wilkes appears to be very essential and must be effected ; and that I make no doubt when you lay this affair with your usual precision before the meeting of the gentlemen of the House of Commons this evening, it will meet with the required unanimity and vigour.[2]

That night Bradshaw, Secretary to the Treasury, sent Grafton an account of the meeting.

Lord North intended to have had a general meeting this evening of those Members of Parliament to whom communications are usually made, and they had notes of invitation sent them ; but his Lordship afterwards thought it would be better, previously, to take the sense of the Members who were of the Cabinet and of the lawyers ; and notes were sent postponing the attendance of the other persons who had been summon'd — the meeting then consisted of Mr. Conway, Lord Granby, Sir Edward Hawke, Master of the Rolls, Attorney and Solicitor General, Hussey, Thurlow, Morton, Dyson, Mr. Cooper, and myself ; and of Mr. Rigby, Mr. Townshend, and Mr. James Grenville, who did not receive the second notes, and attended in consequence of the first.

Lord North very ably open'd the purpose of the meeting : Mr. Dyson stated the precedents of expulsion ; and the Attorney General informed the Company what had passed in the Courts and in what particular situations Mr. Wilkes might stand at the meeting of Parliament, as an outlaw, or as suffering an infamous punishment in consequence

[1] Grafton to the King, April 22, 1768 ; Fortescue, II, no. 612. The sentence quoted above is taken from the original in the Windsor Archives. As printed by Fortescue it reads, 'since the verdict was likely to be reversed'.
[2] *Ibid*. no. 613.

2 A

of his conviction.  Mr. Hussey [1] was strongly against a second expulsion for the same offence, *in being the author of a political libel* ; for he said his conviction for the poem could not be thought of in the House of Commons without coupling it with the means used to obtain evidence against him — in a word, the greater part of the company seem'd struck with Mr. Hussey's objections, but I think it might be collected that all, except himself, will be for expelling Wilkes upon the double ground of outlawry and conviction, and Mr. Conway declared as much before he went away. As Lord North intends sending a messenger to your Grace in the morning I take the liberty of conveying this, as my sense of the sentiments of a meeting which were not called upon to declare the part they respectively meant to take, nor informed that government had come to any resolution upon the subject of Mr. Wilkes.

Lord North will send circular letters requesting a full attendance at the opening of the session ; and it is necessary whatever may be determined in regard to W—— for there is great reason to believe that an attempt will be made to place Mr. Dowdeswell in the Chair as Speaker, and such an attempt should be defeated by a great majority.[2]

'It turn'd out pretty well', wrote North to Grafton on April 26, and added :

Mr. Hussey will certainly be against expelling Wilkes, tho' he declared he had not form'd his opinion entirely, and I dare say had not at that time.  But the bias of his mind appear'd against it ; I am sorry for it.  He is a most amiable estimable man, and gives a credit to every question he supports.  The rest of the company I think will be with us, tho' many of them prefer'd the ground of outlawry to that of the conviction, and most of them disliked expelling Wilkes twice for the same crime.  We shall have them however with us ; Dyson, who was present and heard what past, will endeavour

---

[1] Richard Hussey, M.P. for East Looe.  He was Attorney-General to the Queen.

[2] Grafton MS. 309.  Dated 'Monday night, 12 o'clock' ; docketed 'April 1768'.  There appears to have been no foundation for the rumour that the Rockinghams intended to run Dowdeswell for Speaker.  (See Rockingham to Newcastle, May 1, 1768 ; Add. MS. 32990, ff. 1-4.)

to settle the mode that will best take in all the different opinions.[1]

On April 27 Wilkes was committed to the King's Bench prison to await the reversal of his outlawry next legal term. He was fast becoming the idol of the London mob : they intercepted the Marshall's coach, took off the horses, and drew Wilkes in triumph to Spitalfields. He eventually escaped from his admirers and surrendered himself to the King's Bench prison that evening. While the legal proceedings were still undecided Administration had no strong case for expelling Wilkes, and did not want to run the risk of doing so without an overwhelming majority. It was better to wait until Wilkes had been sentenced, even though 'the law's delay' gave the opposition time to prepare their ground.

What was the attitude of the Rockinghams to these events ? The Burkes (so Charles Lloyd reported to Grenville on April 30) went to see Wilkes in prison.[2] Yet Rockingham was wary of committing himself. Though he thought it 'very probable' that the Court intended to deal with Wilkes when Parliament met, he did not press his friends to attend. He wrote to Newcastle on May 1 :

I have not nor shall not in the present moment write to press our friends at a distance to come up. Your Grace well knows that it is much to ask or desire gentlemen to come in summer to attend Parliament even if there was *known* actual business but upon the chance of there not being any it would be still more difficult.[3]

Wilkes's case, in fact, so far had excited little interest among the Rockinghams : they disliked and distrusted him, and had not yet discovered any legal or constitutional issues in his expulsion. Not until it became a measure of the Court was opposition interested.

Parliament met on May 10. A mob assembled outside the House of Lords, some crying 'Wilkes and liberty', others 'that bread and beer were too dear and that it was as well to

---

[1] Grafton MS. 472. Dated 'Tuesday morn.' ; docketed 'Ap. 28th 1768'. April 28 was a Thursday ; the correct date should be April 26.
[2] Grenville (J. M.) MSS.          [3] Add. MS. 32990, ff. 1-4.

be hanged as starved'.[1] Another mob attempted to rescue
Wilkes from prison ; troops were called out ; and a number
of people were killed in St. George's Fields. During the next
few weeks London was the scene of constant rioting, and the
government, with insufficient troops, only kept order with
difficulty. There was real discontent and hardship among the
labouring classes — the sailors went on strike for higher
wages and attempted to picket all ships in the port of London
— and hungry men with nothing to do are easily exploited.
Wilkes identified his cause with theirs, and it became formidable
from economic distress.

Neither government nor opposition had any policy but
speedy repression of these disorders. Grafton and the King
would have agreed with Newcastle's opinion of what should
be done.

> It is certainly necessary to encourage the civil magistrate
> to support his authority ; for if that is not done, we must
> be either governed by a mad lawless mob, or the peace be
> preserved only by a military force ; both of which are
> unknown to our constitution : and therefore every honest
> man who wishes well to it ought to exert himself in the
> support of the civil magistrate.[2]

It was the fundamental task of government to preserve order,
if necessary by using soldiers ; the opposition's only criticism
was that Ministers had been lacking in vigour and energy.
But on one point they were sensitive : when Barrington
introduced a bill permitting the militia to be called out in
cases of riots, it was opposed from all quarters of the House.
'Lord Barrington declared he presented the bill on his own
opinion, not by order or even with the knowledge of Administration . . .',[3] and the bill was dropped. This was the background to the first session of the 1768 Parliament.

---

[1] Rockingham to Newcastle, May 10, 1768 ; Add. MS. 32990, ff. 35-6.
[2] Newcastle to Rockingham, May 13, 1768 ; *ibid.* f. 53.
[3] West to Newcastle, May 17, 1768 ; *ibid.* ff. 89-90. James Townsend
spoke against the bill. Rockingham, in the report of the debate which he
sent to Newcastle (*ibid.* ff. 87-8), wrote : 'Chauncy Townshend opposed
the measure, which caused some speculation'. Chauncy Townsend had been
defeated at Aldeburgh at the General Election, and was not in the House
at this date.

On May 12 North held a meeting 'of the principal parts of the Administration, except the Ministers themselves', to consider whether any action should be taken against Wilkes that session. On May 16 Newcastle sent an account of this meeting (which he had got from Onslow) to Rockingham.[1]

Sir Gilbert Elliot proposed that it should be brought on immediately, and that he would make the motion that Mr. Wilkes should be expell'd the House. And this he insisted upon doing very strongly. Lord Barrington, Mr. Dyson, and all my Lord Bute's friends ; Mr. Rigby, Mr. Thurloe, and all the Bedfords were violently for it. Lord Granby, young Tommy Townshend, Pryse Campbel, and Mr. Onslow . . . were as violently against it. Lord Granby said that such a step as was proposed to be taken at this time, when people's minds were so much inflamed, might produce the worst consequences, and might very probably cause a rebellion, and therefore he was strongly against this motion and would oppose it to the utmost of his power.

Sir Gilbert still persisted in his opinion, and that he would make the motion, but before they parted he was somewhat soften'd, and it was thought less inclined to pursue what he seem'd at first to be so resolutely determined to do.

And on May 14 Bedford told West

that the Parliament ought not to rise without concluding Mr. Wilkes [sic] affair, and if other means were thought too strong they should sit ten [days] or a fortnight to hear the petition against him and turn him out for incapacity, as his Grace said he was clear after reading the laws of outlawry that no person under such a judgment though it should be afterwards judged erroneous was capable of being elected.[2]

When Henry Lawes Luttrell [3] moved in the Commons on May 18 to ask why legal action had not been taken against Wilkes when he returned to England, Administration were clearly embarrassed. North argued that 'it was not possible for any body to tell who was the proper officer of the Crown'; while de Grey, Attorney-General, said that 'he did not look

[1] *Ibid.* f. 71.     [2] West to Newcastle, May 14, 1768 ; *ibid.* f. 63.
[3] M.P. for Bossiney, later Wilkes's opponent in Middlesex.

upon himself as the proper officer'.[1]  The Court had now
decided to do nothing about Wilkes until next session : their
immediate concern was with the riots, and for this reason they
decided only to adjourn Parliament and not prorogue it until
the disturbances were over.

'Members are leaving town in droves,' wrote West to
Newcastle on May 19, 'every thing appears quiet . . . but
all sides agree the meeting in the winter will probably be as
discordant and violent as has been known.'[2]  On June 8
Wilkes's outlawry was reversed ;  and on June 18 he was
sentenced to twenty-two months' imprisonment, fined £1000,
and ordered to find securities for good behaviour.  It seemed
that his measure had at last been taken, yet he was to prove a
greater source of unrest in prison than when free.  He had
now added the martyr's crown to the cap of liberty, and was
in a fair way to becoming the scourge of the Court.

(ii)

The terms upon which the Bedfords returned to Court in
December 1767 had been a minimum — designed to satisfy
the big fish, and to give an earnest of the Court's good intentions
towards the smaller.  The time had now come to put those
intentions into effect, and the Bedfords did not find Grafton
grudging or ungenerous.

Rigby had been promised the place of Paymaster-General
as soon as it became vacant :  it was at this time shared by
George Cooke, a Chathamite, and Thomas Townshend, one
of Rockingham's 'old friends' who had remained in office in
1766.  In June 1768 Cooke died, and Rigby hastened to claim
the fulfilment of Grafton's promise.  Grafton behaved 'in the
most open, friendly, and obliging manner possible', and
appointed a day for kissing hands.[3]

---

[1] West to Newcastle, May 18, 1768 ;  Add. MS. 32990, f. 95.
[2] *Ibid.* f. 103.
[3] Rigby to Bedford, June 8, 1768 ;  Woburn MS., lvii. f. 74, part printed
in *Bedford Correspondence*, iii. 400-1.  'The rest of his discourse', Rigby
added, 'upon the present distracted times is as manly, right-headed, and
sensible as possible.  I only wish he would stay upon the spot and execute
as well as he discourses.'

Grafton proposed that Townshend should take over Rigby's place of joint Vice-Treasurer of Ireland ; and since he would lose neither in income nor rank by the exchange, seems to have anticipated no difficulty. Perhaps he took Townshend's consent too much for granted. According to the story Townshend told Rockingham, Grafton neglected to communicate

> any thing of the intended arrangement before he wrote to him to go to Court to kiss hands for the Vice-Treasurership of Ireland — notwithstanding Townshend had tried for some days to see his Grace and had wrote to his Grace to that purpose without receiving answers.[1]

Camden was sent to try to bring Townshend round, but failed to get him to consent to the exchange.

> The motives of his resolution [wrote Camden to Grafton on June 9] as far as I could collect them were these, that in the first place that the measure was denounced to him on Wednesday in an abrupt manner without any previous communication. This complaint was branched out into a variety of particulars, which I cannot well crowd into the compass of a letter, declaring at the same time that if your Grace had represented to him before the vacancy happened or indeed after, the necessity you lay under of making this arrangement, he should have yeilded to it with facility. The second objection was that he could not bring himself to yeild place to Mr. Rigby and in this part of his complaint, which was purely political, I drew him into a declaration that the Bedford party was preferred, and so far as he could judge meant to take the lead again and give law to the whole Administration.[2]

Camden professed to believe that Townshend's suspicions of the Bedfords were not well founded : he was soon to think differently. 'I am heartily grieved at this event', he concluded, 'but your Grace is engaged and can not recede.'

Nor was Grafton in the mood to recede : he intended to prove himself a true disciple of Chatham, by combating

[1] Rockingham to Dowdeswell, August 11, 1768 ; Rockingham Papers, R1-617.  [2] Grafton MS. 29.

faction with 'firmness'. On June 10 he submitted for the King's consideration

> whether the different reports spread in the world on this subject to shew that the Administration can be made to deviate on Mr. Townshend's account from their plan formed, can be so effectualey stopped as by Mr. Rigby's having the honor of kissing the King's hand to day.[1]

Rigby kissed hands the same day ; Townshend refused to accept Rigby's place ; Grafton began looking round for someone else. 'The Duke of Grafton seems no otherwise hurt at this', wrote Rigby to Bedford on June 10, 'than that he is sorry to see an old acquaintance so wrong-headed ; indeed for any publick reasons, it is a measure not much to be repined at.'[2]

This, of course, was grist to the opposition mill.

> Your Grace knows [wrote Rockingham to Newcastle on June 13] I have always had a partiality towards Tommy Townshend, and do believe that the present warmth arises from his never having been quite so satisfied in his own mind since he separated from us. . . . If he continues firm he will do himself much honour and notably distress some of our old acquaintances and indeed it may have good consequences if the example operates.[3]

It was 'a further proof of the good understanding . . . between the Bedfordians and the Butes'.

Townshend tried to adorn his refusal with a glitter of principle : he told Rockingham, 'that he hoped no one would think that his quitting had arose from any bickering about this or that office, or that he had wished or desired an office, which he had not'.[4] But the return of the prodigal is seldom welcomed by those who have toiled and sweated during his absence, and have not yet had their reward.

> As to our friend Townshend [wrote Meredith to Portland on July 20] I love him the best of all the adherents to office.

---

[1] Fortescue, II, no. 626.

[2] Woburn MS., lvii. f. 78 ; part printed in *Bedford Correspondence*, iii. 401.    [3] Add. MS. 32990, ff. 206-7.

[4] Rockingham to Newcastle, June 17, 1768 ; *ibid.* ff. 216-18.

But I think he had better have assumed a little philosophy than lost £3300 a year for a slight inattention to himself ; as he had endured with so perfect a resignation the insults and injurys done to the public, and wantonly exercised on those friends, whom he, of all men, should never have forsaken. He seems in an awkward situation ; for it will hardly become a *measure* to put him high again in office ; and, I am afraid, he has lost that ground of affection on which he was first advanced.[1]

Townshend went into opposition over Wilkes in 1769 (yet he had not opposed Wilkes's expulsion when consulted in 1768 [2]), and became one of the most active opponents of the American war. He returned to office under Rockingham ; became Secretary of State and a peer under Shelburne ; and continued in office under Pitt. But one wonders what his career might have been had Grafton been more temperate in 1768 and had not tried to imitate Chatham.

Grafton was also trying to satisfy another of Bedford's followers, and was equally indifferent about the resistance he might encounter. On June 8 he asked the King to appoint William Lynch (M.P. for Weobley) Envoy Extraordinary to Naples, without having consulted Shelburne in whose department the post fell. 'How his Lordship will like this rap', wrote Rigby to Bedford on June 8, 'I can't tell, but nobody seems to care.' [3] It was clear that this discourteous behaviour was meant to force Shelburne into resigning, upon a trivial matter for which he could not expect Chatham's support. But Shelburne, though snubbed, would not go ; he proposed Lord Tankerville for the post ; Grafton objected that Tankerville was too young (he was only twenty-four) ; the King referred the dispute to 'those usualy consulted on state affairs' ; [4] Conway suggested transferring Sir Horace Mann from Florence.[5] But neither side wanted a compromise, and so this miserable dispute dragged on. 'I am for decisive measures', wrote Rigby to Bedford on July 4, 'and either for

[1] Portland MS. 416.  [2] See above, p. 355.
[3] Woburn MS., lvii. f. 70.
[4] The King to Shelburne, June 17, 1768 ; Fortescue, II, no. 628.
[5] The King to Grafton, June 20, 1768 ; Grafton MS. 516.

removing that Secretary or shaking hands with him, and I took the liberty to tell the Duke of Grafton so yesterday, when I din'd with him.' [1]

This was sound advice, but Grafton could not take it. Both he and Shelburne were living under the shadow of Chatham : though denied his assistance, they knew that he might one day recover and demand a reckoning. The changes Grafton had made in the Administration had been adumbrated by Chatham, and Grafton could claim that he was merely following the line traced out for him by his leader. Yet it was one thing for the Bedfords to enter a Cabinet dominated by Chatham ; quite otherwise when Grafton was the *de facto* Minister. He was afraid to exercise his power in any way that might involve Chatham's disapproval. He tried to force out Shelburne by snubs and insults, but Shelburne, equally concerned to retain Chatham's approval, would not resign without his sanction. So he remained : disliked and feared by the King and Grafton ; at odds with his colleagues ; in a Cabinet no longer of Chatham's making, and drifting towards a policy he had rejected.

Camden, believing 'that most of the difficulties among great men arise from misapprehension or mistakes of each other's intentions', now intervened in the dispute between Grafton and Shelburne.[2]

I can't help making this observation [he wrote to Shelburne on June 24, 1768] because the Duke has assured me with such solemnity as persuades me of his sincerity that he has not proceeded in this business out of any personal respect [*sic*] [3] whatever towards your Lordship, but the real conviction that Lord T.'s youth and inexperience make him unfit to support the important charge of this embassy. . . . If your Lordship can be brought to believe as I do sincerely, that the Duke's motives have been no other than I have represented, I should think the offence was removed and nothing left for consideration upon this affair but the fitness of the person.

---

[1] Woburn MS., lvii. f. 86.     [2] Lansdowne MSS.
[3] Camden, by this slip of the pen, gives the real state of the case, and perhaps reveals his own opinion.

Shelburne was not to be moved : he declared himself satisfied that Tankerville was 'the most unexceptionable as well as the fittest person' for the appointment.[1]   There, for the time being, the matter rested.

Grafton, apparently manly and imperious, was basically immature, uncertain, frightened, and lonely.   In 1767 he had looked to Conway for support, and had declared he would not continue without him.   Now his relations with Conway had cooled and he turned to Camden.   But Camden was a weak, timid man, who also required someone to lean upon. 'You are my Pole Star,' he wrote to Grafton on October 4, 'Lord Chatham being eclipsed.'[2]   They hung together like drunken men, each trying to convince himself the other was sober.   Professing no political allegiance but to Chatham, they had imbibed his principles without the conviction and authority which alone could enforce them.   They bear a heavy share of the responsibility for the follies and blunders of 1769, yet it may be questioned whether the responsibility does not go deeper.   If the flock wanders and gets lost, is not the shepherd to blame ?   And if the shepherd fails them how can the poor sheep find their way home ?

### (iii)

On July 19 news reached London of riots at Boston ; three days later came despatches from Virginia, 'still more alarming than those from Massachusetts Bay'.[3]   Charles Townshend's duties and customs regulations had passed with very little comment in Britain ; in America they were received with protests and disturbances similar to those which had followed the Stamp Act.   The American problem was again coming to the fore, in circumstances unfavourable to pro-American feeling in Britain.

Hillsborough, a weak man, totally unfitted by convictions or character to be in charge of American affairs, was panic-stricken on receiving this news.   A military force, he declared,

[1] Shelburne's undated draft of his reply ; *ibid.*
[2] Grafton, *Autobiography*, pp. 215-17.
[3] Hillsborough to the King, July 22, 1768 ; Fortescue, II, no. 638.

must be sent to America at the shortest possible notice ;
Grafton was summoned to town and the Cabinet hastily called
together ; Hillsborough wished Parliament to be summoned
as soon as possible.[1] 'His Lordship seemed really alarmed',
wrote Bradshaw to Grafton on July 22, 'and he is not apt to
start at trifles. General Gage cannot send a great force to any
part of America, and if that force should meet with a check
it is but too likely that the whole continent would join in actual
opposition to Government.'

A comprehensive examination of American affairs could
only be undertaken when Parliament was sitting : all the
Cabinet could do now was to attempt to stiffen governmental
authority in America. This was done in two ways : reinforce-
ments were sent to Boston, and a resident Governor was
appointed for Virginia.

The Governor of Virginia was Sir Jeffrey Amherst, who
had commanded in North America during the Seven Years'
War. He had been appointed to Virginia in 1759, but had not
resided there since 1764. His appointment was regarded as a
reward for his services during the war, and in quiet times his
non-residence would have passed unnoticed and done little
harm. But when the Council of Virginia as well as the
Assembly joined to protest against the authority of the mother
country, there seemed an obvious need for a resident Governor.
So Hillsborough thought, and the Cabinet supported him.

But would Amherst wish to go now that his office had
lost the character of a sinecure ? Hillsborough thought not,
and that Amherst would not object to relinquishing his government if suitably compensated. Here is the account Lord
Albemarle (a close friend of Amherst) sent to Rockingham
on August 2 of Hillsborough's proposal and Amherst's reception
of it :

I will now give you an account of the transaction, and
tho' I have not seen my freind Amherst beleive you may
depend upon my information. On Wednesday [July 27] the
new Secretary of State for the Colonys sent to him, and he
thought it was to propose to him to take the command in

[1] Bradshaw to Grafton, July 22, 1768 ; Grafton MS. 305.

North America, which he was ready to accept of, but was very much surprised to hear his Lordship say that he supposed it would be disagreable to him at this time to go to his government and as the people of Virginia were in a very unquiet state at present that his Majesty had thought of sending Lord Botetot [sic] Governor there, to reconcile the minds of the Virginians, that the King had the greatest regard for and opinion of Sir Jeffery and that his Majesty would make it up amply to him in some other shape.    Sir Jeffery answered that he had received the government as a mark of his late Majesties approbation of his services, that if his present Majesty thought him improper for that trust, or unequal to it, that he must submit to his Majesty's pleasure, but at the same time declined a pension of any sort, that thank God he was able to serve, and when worn out in the service if his private fortune would not support him he would ask assistance from the Crown.    All this the Secretary of State promised to report, and Sir Jeffery returned into the country.    That very evening the government was given to Lord Bottetot and he kissed hands on Friday [July 29].[1]

Instantly a first-rate political crisis arose — not about American policy, but about compensation to Amherst.    On July 31 Amherst sent Grafton what he considered to be due to him as compensation for his government.[2]    He asked for 'a distinguished mark of honour for his services in North America' — a British peerage with remainder to his brother, and one of the first American peerages if any were created ; 'an equivalent to the income as Governor of Virginia' ; and a grant of the coal-mines in Cape Breton or an equivalent grant of lands in America.    He requested Grafton to submit his letter to the King.

These exorbitant terms were rejected by the King, who boggled (as he always did) at the request for a peerage. Grafton informed Amherst, who replied on August 10 :

No one can be more truly sensible than I am of the gracious favour his Majesty is pleased to honour me with in thinking me worthy of a grant of lands in America, and that my pretensions would stand foremost if ever a measure for peers in

[1] Rockingham Papers, R1-615.                    [2] Grafton MS. 696.

America should come under consideration, but I beg with the most humble submission to say that my present situation, in my poor opinion, calls for the distinguished mark of honour which I therefore took the liberty of presuming to request of his Majesty, and as I am so unhappy as not to appear deserving of it I most humbly hope the King will pardon my taking the step (very contrary to my inclinations) which seems to be the least dishonourable to me on this occasion.[1]

This step was the resignation of his regiment. But the King was not prepared to give in to sulks and threats. 'Nothing can exceed the obstinacy of Sir Jeffery Amherst on this occasion', he wrote to Grafton on August 11, 'and shall hourly expect to hear of his resignation ; as nothing that the most capcious man could catch at has been done, I shall undisturbed hear any abuse that may be thrown.'[2]

Amherst did resign, but was eventually pacified through Conway's good offices with the promise of a peerage at the next creation.

Lord Botetourt, the new Governor of Virginia, had given Grafton a good deal of trouble in January 1768 when he had threatened to move a vote of censure on Chatham in the Lords. Botetourt had engaged in a copper works which had failed ; he had applied for a charter of incorporation to prevent his estates from being liable for the debts ; but Chatham had refused to put the Privy Seal to the charter.[3] The affair had been smoothed over by placing the Privy Seal in commission for a few days, but it had given Grafton and the King some anxious moments. His appointment to Virginia arose from his impecuniosity ; yet Walpole (no flatterer to Botetourt) admits that he proved a popular Governor.[4]

One aspect of this affair struck the Rockinghams forcibly. Botetourt was a former follower of Bute, and they saw his appointment as proof of Bute's influence. 'I cannot learn', wrote Albemarle to Rockingham on August 2, 'that there are any objections to Sir Jeffery, tho' I suspect there must be

---

[1] Grafton MS. 689.                                    [2] *Ibid.* 123.
[3] Walpole (*Memoirs*, iii. 108) suggests that Chatham regarded it as a fraud on Botetourt's creditors.                          [4] *Ibid.* p. 156.

some old grudge from the Bute corner, from whence this transaction must certainly have its source.'[1] 'I can not account for Lord Botetot being made Governor', wrote Rockingham to Newcastle on August 11, 'but by the desire of Lord Bute.'[2]

Yet there were some of Rockingham's followers who looked beyond this petty squabble, and were seriously concerned at the news from America. To those who recommended moderation towards the colonies it was a hard blow and boded trouble for the future.

I am afraid these same colonists are above our hands [wrote Savile to Rockingham on July 31] and I am almost ready to think that G. G.'s Act only brought on a crisis twenty or possibly fifty years sooner than was necessary. This indeed is regarding colonies almost all the ill that can be done, for in my opinion (which may be in this a little singular) it is in the nature of things that some time or other colonies so situated must assume to themselves the rights of nature and resist those of law ; which is rebellion.[3]

On August 14 Dowdeswell wrote a long letter to Rockingham in which he discussed the news from America.[4] Though he described his ideas as 'very little digested', this letter contains the fullest statement of the attitude of the better element of the Rockingham party towards the American problem.

If the example of Boston is not followed at New York and other places [wrote Dowdeswell] so as to make it a general concern of the colonies on the continent, there is no difficulty in the case. But if it is, as it probably will be, then the question becomes very serious.

On the one hand, the mother country gives way on prudential considerations, and through fear of consequence. Charles Townshend's duties are I believe not so heavy as to justify one in saying that they are grievous burdens on the colonies. The people there did not appear to make their stand against *these duties* on account of their pressure, but against the general principle of raising *any* revenue in

---

[1] Rockingham Papers, R1-615.     [2] Add. MS. 32990, ff. 405-7.
    Albemarle, ii. 75-6.            [4] Dowdeswell Papers.

America. . . . One might argue for the repeal of Charles Townshend's duties as injudiciously laid, being injurious to the manufactures of this country, and operating as bounties upon the like manufactures of America. But this would be avoiding the real question : it would hardly be patching up the sore, healing it at top to break out again hereafter. A repeated opposition from that side of the water, upon a principle directed against all duties for revenue must be met. It must either be admitted which is timidity, weakness, irresolution, and inconsistency : or it must be resisted, and the arms of this country must be exerted against her colonies.

Savile and Dowdeswell both saw the American problem in terms of sovereignty (which Chatham professed to believe was not the case) : neither had any solution.

If the Americans [Dowdeswell continued] found their petition upon that principle of right which goes against raising any revenue at all in America, they ought to pray not only against Charles Townshend's duties but against all duties *laid for revenue*, against those very duties which a few years ago we were told they were so willing to pay. If they succeed in such a petition they obtain a great charter, depriving this country in all future times and in all future circumstances of the power of raising any revenue there for the general support of its own authority, a power which the experience of these times will render this country extremely cautious of making use of, but which no human wisdom can foresee it may not, some time or other and in some change of circumstances on both sides of the water, be equitable as well as necessary to exert. But they do more : their charter will be much more extensive. The distinction between external and internal taxes has been found frivolous, as indeed I always thought it. And your Lordship knows that I have never been able to distinguish between the right of passing one law and the right of passing another. Their claim of right admitted will give them in my opinion a charter against being bound to any laws passed without their consent. I am afraid therefore such a petition is not to be supported.

I have said before that we have no reason to hope they will act in a temperate and wise manner. But if their petition went not upon the general principle of right, but upon the peculiar circumstances of their case, and expressed their hopes that after the repeal of the Stamp Act no further proposal for raising revenue upon the colonies, confined as they are in their trade and distressed in their circumstances, would have been received and entertained, and their apprehensions that the duties laid in 1767 are a renewal of the same system, alarming therefore in a great degree to the colonists and hurtful to the manufactures of this country, I should think notwithstanding anything already passed there would be no difficulty in supporting a petition so decent and at the same time so reasonable.

If the Ministry bring the matter before us, it must be either for our approbation or our advice. The first must wait their conduct. We know little at present of what they have done, nothing of what further they will do. Their sending two ships of the line and two regiments is not I think a reprehensible measure in a Ministry which at present at least does not intend to propose a repeal. . . .

If they come for advice, it will depend much on future events. If the ships and troops restore peace at Boston and other places, and procure an execution of the laws, the point is then carried, the sovereignty of this country is then exerted, and if the repeal of Charles Townshend's duties will add good humour to submission there can not I think be an objection to it. I am sure I see no danger in relaxing after submission is once obtained. But if the ships and troops are resisted, and you have in fact what some men seem to have wished, civil war in America, there are but two things left, either to fight to the last in which case this country will be undone, or to treat with the contending party, depart from your own dignity, weaken your authority, and by giving up in time a part of your rights preserve the rest.

When I sat down to write, I did not foresee what conclusion I should come to : but I think at last it is this.

It is the duty of the Administration to support the government of this country, and obtain an execution of the laws. They are not to suppose resistance. Their case differs from ours in this. We had a real grievance, a very heavy tax from which we meant to relieve the colonists. The tax now in question is no heavy burden upon them : and the objections to it should rather come from this side of the water than from them. The Ministers have therefore a principle to meet, but no grievance, unless the principle of the colonists is right and ours is wrong, a thing not to be admitted by the Administration or by us. As to the Americans, they have no pretence to relief if they combine their grievance with their principle : but I am afraid they will never separate them. The establishment of the commission is to them a greater grievance than all Charles Townshend's duties, because the object of it is a collection of revenue upon system. Had it been proposed in our time I should have liked the thing well enough, but I should have advised the sending it out under some other name, made commerce its first object, and the revenue a secondary object only for defraying the expences of that commission and of the civil government. I think therefore that they never will apply in any moderation, nor confine their prayer for relief so as not at the same time to lay in their claim of right. If anything is done therefore it will not be of their own application, but the act of Great Britain upon the commission of Administration or ours after submission or pending the struggle and in order to end it. If they submit and make no resistance I should like very well the repeal of C. T.'s duties, but they are really too insignificant to be an object either to them or to us, and to go further would be in favour of their principle and tend to revive their claim some other day. But if the struggle comes on, I should be sorry to have it known as my opinion, I must however confess to you that I think we shall be soon trying who shall stand most forward in proposing terms of accommodation to end a struggle by which this country, possessed of everything has everything to lose and nothing to get. For a contest with the colonists, supported as they will be by the enemies of this country, must be destructive to us in the first place. . . .

This leads me to my decision for much moderation. I could find much to say against any dissent that any man could offer : but upon the whole moderate measures are less dangerous, and if we come off at last with a loss those must answer for it who have wantonly and unnecessarily revived the question, and I believe now profess that these duties were laid merely as a test to the Americans. . . .

Your Lordship will observe that I write this on a sudden, and that my thoughts on the most difficult subject I ever knew are very little digested.  I foresee that we shall be driven to decide on the American question whether it is best to adhere and risk everything, or to relax and give up a great deal.  If I incline one way more than the other it is to the choice of the less evil.  Port duties laid for revenue only are in their nature the same as qualified stamp acts.  We may with great consistency give up the one, as we rejected the other.  However, don't be hasty in showing this letter. I send it you crude and undigested, without reserving any copy of it.  I would not offer or give my opinion upon much longer preparation to any other man :  and I am not so confident in this opinion as not to think I may find cause to change it.

A clear and honest analysis, leading to the conclusion that the American problem was insoluble in terms admissible to the British Parliament.  Stripped of rhetoric and divorced from party the American problem is seen in much the same light by both Dowdeswell and North.  Yet statesmen are not judged by principles, but by their day-to-day treatment of concrete and unforeseen situations.  Some political questions are best shelved until conditions are more propitious for their solution :  tolerance, moderation, and refusal to fight out an issue may not solve a problem in the present, but may make its solution possible in the next generation.  Newcastle saw the danger of forcing matters, and pleaded for moderation.  He wrote to Rockingham on September 12 :

I hope our friends will adhere to the principles which they acted upon when we repealed the Stamp Act.  It is the same question, and my Lord Hillsborough's view plainly is to set up and support the contrary doctrine there.  I hope we shall disappoint him.  For I think when it comes to that the Parliament will never join in a measure that must totally destroy all connection with the colonies, and is directly contrary to their proceeding in the repeal of the Stamp Act and the principles upon which that repeal was founded.

I doubt by great mismanagement the measure of con-quering the colonies and obliging them to submit is become

now more popular than it was. It is certainly the measure
of the Administration and I am afraid some of our own
friends are a little tender in that point. But it must not be
submitted to, and for my own part, whoever is for it, I must
in conscience enter my protest against it ; and I hope our
friends will well consider before they give in to so destructive
a measure.[1]

The old man hobbled down to the House of Lords to enter
his proxy for the next session, which he did not live to see,
and there met Camden.

He was extremely civil and gracious [Newcastle wrote to
Rockingham on September 15] and if I had not been so much
fatigued I should have talked plainly to him upon the present
design of the Administration to force the colonies to submit
to the very measure (for the question is the same, as it is to
force the colonies to submit to their being taxed by the
Parliament here) which he, my Lord Chancellor, had so
strenuously opposed, and was one of five only who protested against it. He let drop something which shew'd
*he was not pleased*, and implied as if he had not much
to do.[2]

Camden saw as clearly as Newcastle that the Cabinet
would be under pressure from Hillsborough and the Bedfords
for 'strong measures' in America, and that Parliament would
never admit the American principle denying the right of
taxation.

I submit to the Declaratory Law [he wrote to Grafton
on October 4] and have thought it my duty upon that
ground, as a Minister, to exert every constitutional power
to carry the Duty Act into execution. But, as a member of
the legislature, I cannot bring myself to advise violent
measures to support a plan so inexpedient and so impolitic.
And I am very much afraid (I speak this confidentially to
your Grace) that if a motion should be made to repeal the
Act, I should be under a necessity to vote for it. But there

---

[1] Add. MS. 32991A, ff. 94-6. There is a similar letter to Dowdeswell,
dated September 17, 1768 ; *ibid*. ff. 111-12.
[2] *Ibid*. ff. 101-2.

are so few in my way of thinking, that such a motion is not to be expected.

I am very sensible that a difference of opinion on a subject so serious and important may be prejudicial to the Administration ; and I lament the occasion, being persuaded that a most perfect union amongst us is essential, and I will labour to effect it with my best endeavours : but I do fear most exceedingly that upon the American question the Bedfords and myself will be too far assunder to meet. I must maintain my own ground : the public knows my opinion, and knows theirs. Neither of us can be inconsistent with ourselves.[1]

Moderation and tolerance require the aid of moral courage and conviction to be able to do their work. Camden, after stating his opinion, was prepared to acquiesce in the Cabinet's decision : such had not been Pitt's conduct in 1761. Had Camden resigned in 1768 or 1769 he would have incurred the charge of throwing the Ministry into confusion in order to preserve his own conduct spotless ; and opposition would have taken advantage of his resignation for party ends. Yet he did resign in 1770 in circumstances less favourable to his reputation, and the fall of an empire creates more confusion than the fall of a Ministry.

(iv)

At the beginning of September Grafton began once more to turn his energies to the task of ousting Shelburne. The King backed him ; the rest of the Cabinet were either favourable or indifferent ; yet it took him six weeks, and at the end he found he had lost Chatham as well.

On September 6 Weymouth wrote to Grafton to ask for the Southern Department, 'in case any alteration takes place', since 'the most material business to this country must go thro' the hands of him who has the Southern correspondence'.[2] 'Lord Rochford is come over', wrote Mansfield to Newcastle the same day, 'I guess to be Secretary of State. Those here,

---

[1] Grafton, *Autobiography*, pp. 215-17.  [2] Grafton MS. 799.

to whom it was offered, it seems declined.'[1] The fox was in sight ; the hounds were baying ; and Grafton, master of the hunt, directed them on.

Yet Grafton was uneasy. What would be Chatham's reaction ? And, if Chatham disapproved, what would Camden do ? Suppose Chatham resigned and was followed by Camden : was it worth turning everything upside down in order to be rid of Shelburne ? Grafton was prepared to run the risk, but wished to cut down the chances of such an outcome to a minimum. He tried to win Camden's support, the better to face Chatham's disapproval and in the hope of being able to save the Great Seal if Chatham resigned.

On September 14 the King had a conversation with Camden about Shelburne.

He said [the King wrote to Grafton on September 15] he had long looked upon that measure as inevitable but that as the Lord who held that employment had been recommended by Lord Chatham, he thought it best for himself to take a neuter part on this occasion, tho' privately he could not conceal his thoughts to me ; and that he must add, that Lord Shelburne had not only lost your good opinion but that of every one of the other active members of the Cabinet ; and was even shy with him, because he had not succeeded in raising doubts in his mind. I dropped the idea of Lord Rochford which seemed to please him, as he could neither be called of the Bedford connection nor adverse to the Earl of Chatham. He then concluded with telling me that the news from Hayes does not mend, and that he himself entirely despairs of seeing that able man ever in a state of health to be of any farther use in publick affairs.[2]

Grafton proposed to write to Camden, but delayed : was it mere indolence, or did he hesitate to take the irrevocable step ? But on September 23, probably irritated by Shelburne's refusal to yield on the nomination to Turin,[3] he at last informed Camden that Shelburne's dismissal was decided. Camden replied on September 24 :

[1] Add. MS. 32991A, f. 69.    [2] Fortescue, II, no. 651.
[3] The King to Grafton, September 22, 1768 ; *ibid.* no. 658.

I understand your Grace's plan is fixt ; and I saw plainly, the last time I was in town, that Lord S——s removal was determined. What can I say to it my dear Lord ? It is unlucky.

The Administration, since Lord Chatham's illness, is almost entirely altered, without being changed ; and I find myself surrounded with persons, to whom I am scarce known, and with whom I have no connection. Lord Chatham is at Hayes, brooding over his own suspicions and discontents. His return to business almost desperate ; inaccessible to every body, but under a persuasion (as I have some reason to conjecture) that he is given up and abandoned. This measure for aught I know, may fix his opinion, and bring him to a resolution of resigning. If that should happen I should be under the greatest difficulty.

I am truly my dear Lord, distressed : I have seen so much of Courts, that I am heartily tired of my employment ; and should be happy to retire upon a scanty income, if an honorable opportunity offered to justify my retreat to the King, and your Grace : but that step I will never take without your consent ; till I find I have lost the King's favor and your confidence : unless I should be forced by something more compelling than the Earl of S——'s removal.

After all, though your Grace is so good as to relieve me from any opinion on this subject, yet the case being stated as it is that either your Grace or the Earl must quit, my opinion is clear in a moment that your Grace must remain.[1]

Although Grafton had now taken his decision he was reluctant to put it into action, and had to be prompted by his Sovereign, by one of his colleagues, and by a subordinate. On September 30 Weymouth saw the King, and wrote an account of his conversation to Grafton.

The first word he said to me was to ask if it was decided and added that he hoped it was. I explained to him as cautiously as possible the present difficulty without communicating the letter which your Grace shew'd me in confidence,[2] and which I consider as of too private a nature to

---

[1] Grafton, *Autobiography*, p. 214, misdated September 29. Instead of 'a scanty income' Camden originally wrote 'the first opportunity'.
[2] Camden's letter of September 24.

be mentioned by me. I stated the suspicion and danger of its disgusting Lord C. and the bad consequence that wou'd attend such an event (which I can assure your Grace I shou'd be as sorry to see as any man), the difficulties into which it wou'd throw the Chancellor, and the *éclat* that it wou'd give to the person removed. The K. did not seem to think that such an event wou'd happen, but said that he was *dipp'd* and that he had done his part in it. In short 'tho' I knew that the K. wish'd this measure very much, I did not expect to find him so warm in his expressions upon it. I hope I did not go farther on my side than I ought, and I don't see how I cou'd avoid telling in some degree the difficulties that delay it. I only mean this for your Grace's information, and shall only add not singly in my own name but in Lord Gower's and Mr. Rigby's, who have just been with me, that the only wish we have on the subject is, that your Grace shou'd do whatever you shall think most proper ; and that let it end in any manner that it may, we shall on all occasions be ready to shew the most cordial confidence in the Chancellor.[1]

The same day Bradshaw wrote to Grafton.[2] Camden's letter, 'of too private a nature' to be mentioned to the King, had been communicated to Rigby and by him to Bradshaw. 'I will not presume to say any thing upon so important a subject', wrote Bradshaw, but then went on to say :

If the state of Lord Chatham's health is such as it has been represented from every quarter for the last two months, he may live many years without a chance of returning to the King's councils. Your Grace is no stranger to his circumstances, and as I must consider him at this time in the absolute power of Lady Chatham I cannot think she would throw away so great a part of her present income as arises from the Privy Seal from any considerations respecting Lord Shelburne. I have ventured to make this observation because Mr. Rigby told me Lord Chancellor's letter stated such a resignation rather as a possible than probable event ; the anxiety which has induced me to trouble your Grace with this letter does not now arise from an opinion of the necessity of removing Lord Shelburne, but from my fears that you

[1] Grafton MS. 798.          [2] *Ibid.* 306.

have already gone so far that it will be more dangerous to stop than to go on — but this your Grace's judgement can best decide ; I would however humbly submit to you whether, as your Grace will not be in town for many days, you will not acquaint his Majesty by letter of your opinion upon this matter which, by what he said to Lord Weymouth, he seems impatient to receive.

Grafton did not inform the King of the contents of Camden's letter until October 2. Even now he tried to throw the responsibility for Shelburne's dismissal on to the King.[1] His letter of October 2 is one of the longest he ever wrote to the King — it reads as if he was afraid of coming to an end. After summarizing Camden's letter, Grafton goes on :

The Duke of Grafton will not trouble the King with observations on a letter which his Majesty's own penetration will furnish so fully on these expressions from an honest and wellmeaning servant of the King's stating his distresses on an occasion wherein he may foresee the aspersions that malice will throw out against the Lord Chancellor, as if he was concerned in undermining the patron under whom he was first known to his Majesty. The Duke of Grafton may perhaps from a similitude of situation feel this more strongly than an other ; and therefore will only presume to dwell on that part which concerns the King's affairs and the ill effect that the apprehended resignation would bring to them at the opening of a new Parliament, and which could be the only means of giving any eclat to the Earl of Shelburne, if he was no longer in the King's services. The decision of the business is too delicate from these circumstances for the Duke of Grafton to venture to lay his humble opinion before his Majesty : he has presumed only to state consequences which the King nor he himself had not foreseen as possible before the receipt of the Lord Chancellor's letter, and he humbly entreats his Majesty to give them that consideration which the importance of them to his service make them deserve ; and humbly to assure his Majesty that, whenever the King shall be graciously pleased to express to the Duke of Grafton on which side his Majesty sees the greatest

---

[1] Fortescue, II, no. 660.

prejudice likely to fall on the affair of [*sic*] government, it
shall then be the Duke of Grafton's study to forward it with
that zeal and duty with which he shall pursue every thing
for the King's service, dignity, and honor.

Thus Grafton tried to hide his uneasiness and put on a
bold face. How easy it had been to drop Tommy Townshend !
If only Shelburne had resigned over the appointment to Turin
what a lot of trouble would have been saved, and how much
lighter would Grafton's correspondence have been. The
King had now to take him in hand, and show him exactly what
to do. He was to go to Lady Chatham (the King wrote on
October 5), and 'explain in a concise manner' the reasons why
Shelburne must be removed.[1] She would convey them to
Chatham and (concluded the King), 'I cannot then see any
reason to fear Lord Chatham will act improperly, nor indeed
. . . has he any right to do it'. Little children afraid of the
dark have to be assured that there is nothing to be frightened
of, and that daddy and mummy will protect them.

On October 5 Grafton wrote to Lady Chatham (from
Newmarket), requesting a conversation with her 'for one
quarter of an hour'.[2] That unfortunate lady had not merely
to bear her husband's whimsical moods and ill health, but also
its consequences on his political friends : whenever they
needed guidance, since they could not get it from Chatham,
they applied to his wife. She, the inferior priestess who
guarded the oracle, had already been applied to by Shelburne ;[3]
now it was Grafton's turn to try to penetrate beyond the
veil.

He saw Lady Chatham on October 9. Instead of 'one
quarter of an hour' he had 'a very long conversation with her',
but

he left her Ladyship without being able to draw from her
discourse any thing strong enough to decide clearly how
far the circumstance of the Earl of Shelburne's removal will
affect the Earl of Chatham's situation in his Majesty's
service. The Duke of Grafton begged of her Ladyship to

---

[1] Fortescue, II, no. 661.  [2] *Chatham Correspondence*, iii. 334-6.
[3] See above, p. 331.

take the opportunity she should judge the most proper to assure his Lordship that as long as his Lordship's conduct in the Ministry affected the Duke of Grafton only, he should go on as he had done to bear it with the utmost temper and without complaint, remembering that it was Lord Chatham who placed him there, but if his duty to his country as well as to his Majesty called him to advise his removal, as he thought it did at this time, that he did rely on the Earl of Chatham's assurance to ascribe it to a necessity which the welfare of the King's affairs made indispensible. Her Ladyship said that on this head she knew Lord Chatham's sentiments, as he had often said on hearing the report spread about, that if it took place he saw that his Majesty's affairs would be most truly prejudiced by the loss of the Earl of Shelburne's abilities. To which the Duke of Grafton could only reply that he sincerely lamented with her Ladyship the unlucky circumstance ; and that he should and would join in the same opinion with the Earl of Chatham, provided those abilities were not on every occasion turned to thwart and not to assist his Majesty's government ; the truth of which, if known to the Earl of Chatham, would undoubtedly cause his Lordship to judge differently on this event.[1]

Did Grafton really doubt what the result of Shelburne's dismissal would be ? Did he go expecting a categorical answer from Lady Chatham — that Chatham would or would not resign ? Did he not realize that Lady Chatham would never commit herself without Chatham's authority ; and that the phrase, 'his Majesty's affairs would be most truly prejudiced by the loss of the Earl of Shelburne's abilities', was a clear warning of what would follow ? Or was he even now trying to push away unpleasant reality ? But he had gone too far. The King wrote that on Wednesday [October 12] 'we will fix on the most eligible means of putting it into execution'.[2]

They never did. On October 12 Chatham wrote to Grafton to ask the King's permission to resign.[3] He gave his 'weak and broken state of health' as the reason, but lamented

---

[1] Grafton to the King, October 10, 1768 ; Fortescue, II, no. 663.
[2] The King to Grafton, October 10, 1768 ; *ibid.* no. 664.
[3] Grafton, *Autobiography*, p. 221.

'the removal of Sir Jeffery Amherst [1] and that of Lord Shelburne'.   Grafton attempted to excuse himself and begged Chatham to reconsider his decision.[2]

> But my Lord [he wrote on October 12] having myself given way some time ago to your entreaties to me to remain in my present post when your health was at least as bad as it now is, I have some right to claim from you a return of the same conduct when I see, as your Lordship was pleased then to say, that nothing could be so truly serviceable to his Majesty's affairs.   Give me leave to recall this conversation and assurance from your Lordship to your recollection, and on the ground of it to entreat your Lordship not to deprive his Majesty of that support which even the hope of your recovery gives to his government.

On October 13 Grafton sent the King copies of Chatham's letter and his reply.

> The Duke of Grafton presumes to add his humble opinion [he wrote] that if the Earl of Chatham should unfortunately persist in his intention of resigning, it is well that no step has been taken towards the removal of the Earl of Shelburne, and that what has passed upon it is conversation only and even that confined to the very principal of his Majesty's servants : [3] as the Duke of Grafton can not but think the difference to his Majesty's affairs to be very wide, whether the Earl of Chatham resigns on the removal of the Earl of Shelburne, or by the last Lord following the resignation of the first.[4]

The King professed surprise at Chatham's wish to resign, and considered it an 'unfriendly part'.[5]   On October 13 Chatham repeated his request,[6] nor could he be dissuaded by the King.[7]   The King drew comfort from Chatham's 'open avowal that his illness is alone the cause of his retiring',[8] and

---

[1] Chatham was always careful of the interests of naval and military officers who had served in the Seven Years' War.

[2] Grafton, *Autobiography*, pp. 222-3.

[3] Rigby and Bradshaw ?                    [4] Fortescue, II, no. 666.

[5] The King to Grafton, October 13, 1768 ;  *ibid*. no. 667.

[6] Grafton, *Autobiography*, p. 223.

[7] The King to Chatham and Chatham to the King, October 14, 1768 ; Fortescue, II, nos. 669 and 670.

[8] The King to Grafton, October 14, 1768 ;  *ibid*. no. 671.

that Camden would have no difficulty in remaining.  But Camden feared otherwise.  He wrote to Grafton on October 14 :

Your Grace and I feel for each other.  To me I fear the blow is fatal, yet I shall come to no determination. If I can find out what is fit for me to do in this most distressed situation, that I must do, but the difficulty lies in forming a true judgment.  Whatever my decision may be, I will never resign my active endeavors to support the King's service, or my unchangeable attachment to your Grace.[1]

And again on October 16 :

Nothing could give me so much satisfaction as to join with your Grace in one line of conduct ;  and yet I see plainly that our situations are different, and the same honour, duty to the King, and regard to the public, operating upon two minds equally aiming at the same end, may possibly draw us different ways.[2]

Camden remained undecided until he went to fetch the Privy Seal from Hayes, when Chatham (according to Rigby) 'intreated the Chancellor not to think of quitting the King's service and declared his strongest wishes for the support of the present Ministry'.[3]  Thus Camden remained in a Cabinet whose measures he afterwards claimed were thoroughly repugnant to him.

Shelburne and Barré resigned, but Dunning remained in office at Camden's request.[4]  The King advised Grafton to speak to Granby, whose dislike of the Bedfords made him

[1] Grafton, *Autobiography*, p. 224.
[2] *Ibid.* p. 225.  Instead of 'our situations are different' Camden originally wrote 'are the same'.
[3] Rigby to Bedford, October 31, 1768 ; Woburn MS., lvii. f. 206.
[4] Camden to Grafton, [November 4, 1768] ; Grafton, *Autobiography*, p. 225.  There is a letter from Barré to Shelburne in the Lansdowne MSS., dated 'Friday night' (probably October 28, 1768), in which Barré gives an account of a conversation with 'our friend' (almost certainly Dunning).  'He seems very unhappy,' wrote Barré, 'we discoursed very openly, he express'd a great deal of satisfaction at my taking upon me to advise him in his present situation ; retiring he swears would be happiness to him, he only wishes to know how and when, and above all would do anything that he thought would add to your consideration.'

'open to what ill intentioned persons may suggest'.[1]    No one else showed any inclination to resign.

The Privy Seal was first offered to Northington, but declined ;[2] next Egmont was considered, but 'though esteemed the most proper person' it was thought that his appointment might offend Chatham.[3]    At Grafton's suggestion it was then decided that the Lord Privy Seal should not be of the Effective Cabinet.[4]    Even so, North applied on behalf of Halifax,[5] and Sandwich ('not . . . thoroughly easy in his present situation') applied direct to Grafton.[6]    It was, however, given to Bristol, hitherto a follower of Chatham.[7]

[1] The King to Grafton, October 17, 1768 ;  Grafton MS. 526.
[2] The King to Grafton, October 22, 1768 ;  ibid. 528.
[3] The King to Grafton, January 26, 1770 ;  ibid. 545.
[4] The King to Grafton, October 22, 1768 ;  ibid. 528.
[5] North to Grafton, October 24, 1768 ;  ibid. 473.
[6] Copy of Sandwich's letter to Grafton, October 24, 1768 ;  Woburn MS., lvii. f. 194.
[7] See above, p. 275.

# EPILOGUE

WHEN Chatham resigned in October 1768 ten more years of life remained to him. They were years of disappointment, frustration, and tragedy. His advice was not asked, his warnings were ignored, his co-operation was rejected. He stood by helpless to avert the evil which was descending upon his country, while mediocrities grappled with problems to which they were unequal. Like Churchill in the bitter years before 1939, he saw the approach of a war which might have been averted had his counsel been followed ; but, unlike Churchill, he was not permitted to make Britain's darkest hour her finest. For by 1776, even had the King recalled Chatham, it would have been too late to prevent the disruption of the British Empire.

Chatham was incomparably the greatest British statesman of the eighteenth century : none could match him in boldness of purpose or extent of achievement. Almost alone among his contemporaries he saw the vision of Britain expanded across the world, and set her feet firmly on the path of imperial greatness. The loss of Britain's fairest provinces did not destroy her empire or quench the fire Chatham had kindled. Though his last years were sad, much of his work endured : North America remained the home of English-speaking peoples, Britain enlarged her foothold in India to comprehend almost the entire continent, and her sense of power and purpose developed in spite of her defeats in the American war.

Creation in affairs of State seems necessarily to involve destruction, and the monuments of statesmanship are usually erected at the cost of lesser edifices. The politician accepts the institutions of his age and nation, and is bound by their limitations ; the statesman with vision or purpose tends to disregard the opinions of lesser men, and ignores or circumvents the interests of parties. Gladstone, convinced of the

385

justice of Home Rule for Ireland, split the Liberal party ; and Lloyd George, absorbed in the struggle against Germany, ruined the party which Gladstone had weakened. Chatham gave Britain supremacy over the North American continent : yet he was the principal obstacle to the union of those most inclined to sympathize with the colonists, and destroyed any possibility of a united opposition when war came.

His aggressive temperament could not adjust itself to the normal tasks of an eighteenth-century Minister — the disposal of patronage and the safeguarding the Court's majority in the House of Commons. More than any other Minister of his age he placed the public welfare in the forefront of politics. He was a fighter, and he fought best when alone. Compromise and conciliation are required of the politician, and he cannot afford to flout organized opinion. His values are relative not absolute : he must shape his policy to secure general agreement. Chatham could inspire men but could not work with them, and refused to encumber himself with a following in Parliament. In times of crisis, when other men flinched or panicked, Chatham stepped forth confident and fearless ; but he was unfitted for the day-to-day business of opposition or office.

Moreover, he looked with contempt upon the work of cultivating a majority in the House of Commons. He had little respect for Newcastle who, from 1757 to 1761, had the thankless task of preserving that majority which enabled Pitt to triumph in 1759 but never stirred a finger when he resigned in 1761. He cared neither for the friendship nor the enmity of politicians who thought in terms of places and patronage. His only regret when the Rockinghams resigned in November 1766 was that they included two Admirals who had served in the Seven Years' War ; a fortnight later he saw the Bedfords go into opposition without a qualm. Hardly a quarter of the House of Commons in 1766 could be described as party men, yet their influence in the House was out of all proportion to their numbers. Chatham never realized until it was too late the significance of rudimentary political groups. In 1766 he treated them as of little account, yet in July 1767 Rockingham, with less than fifty followers in the Commons, was a formidable figure, and in December it was worth making sacrifices to secure Bedford and his twenty votes.

Few Ministers would have dared to flout the reality of political connection as Chatham did in 1766 : he was the last who was able to do so. Henceforth party became a permanent element in the House of Commons, though it was long before its influence was all-pervasive. Chatham was the last English statesman to attempt to rule without the aid of party. Even had he maintained his health in 1767 he would have been compelled to seek the support of some political group to strengthen his position. It was not his illness alone that wrecked his Administration : it was the mixture of grandeur and aloofness which made so great a statesman so poor a politician.

# INDEX

THE END

PRINTED BY R. & R. CLARK, LTD., EDINBURGH

# Date Due

| | | | |
|---|---|---|---|
| | | | |
| | | | |
| | | | |
| | | | |
| | | | |
| | | | |
| | | | |
| | | | |
| | | | |
| | | | |
| | | | |
| | | | |
| | | | |
| | | | |
| | | | |
| | | | |

Demco 293-5